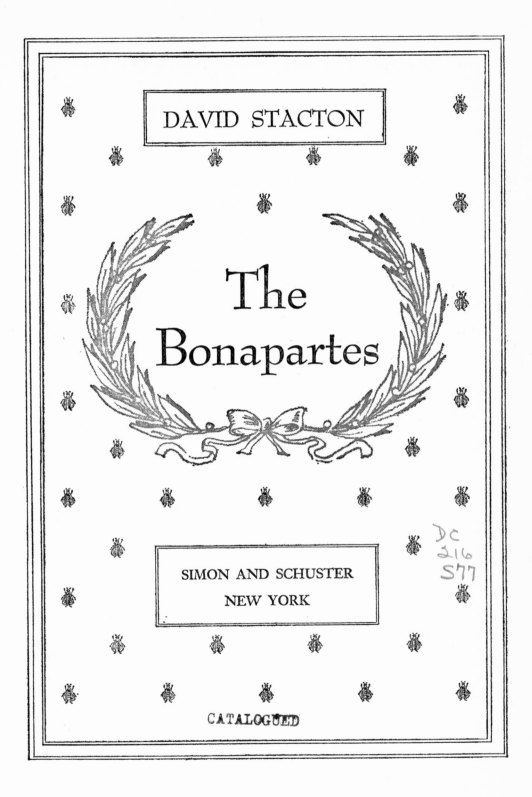

DAVID STACTON

The
Bonapartes

SIMON AND SCHUSTER
NEW YORK

LIBRARY OF CONGRESS CATALOG CARD NUMBER: 66-13847
MANUFACTURED IN THE UNITED STATES OF AMERICA
DESIGNED BY EDITH FOWLER

NOTE: *During the nineteenth century, the French franc was a relatively stable currency. During the period under discussion, 1814 to 1870, there were five francs to the dollar and five dollars to the pound. Both dollar and pound were worth between four and five times what they are today, as far as purchasing power goes.*

I fear nor goad nor stone nor sling,
　　Nor anything that lives.
I do not fear a single thing,
　　Except my relatives.

> —Ryder's translation of the
> Elephant's song from the *Ramayana*

Of all birds, only the eagle has seemed to wise men typical of royalty—neither beautiful nor musical, unfit for food, but carnivorous, insatiable, hateful to everyone, the curse of everyone, and not only superior to all in its capacity to do harm, but stronger than all in its desire to do it.

> —ERASMUS

THIS is a book not about Napoléon, but about his family and what became of it, after 1814. Today, counting Swedish, Austrian, Italian, French, Polish, Danish, German, Spanish, English, and Dutch descendants, there are over 280 members of the family extant, but of the lot there are only two Bonaparte males, Prince Louis Napoléon Jérôme Victor, and his son, the first Bonaparte to be born on French soil in ninety-four years. For the family bred itself out, by producing a predominance of daughters.

In Napoléon's day he had a mother, a half uncle, four brothers, three sisters, two wives, a son, two illegitimate sons, an adopted son, an adopted daughter, an adopted niece in the second degree, and thirty-two blood nephews and nieces to worry about. This does not include the children of his adopted son Eugène.

The Beauharnais—the ex-Empress Joséphine and her children and niece Hortense, Eugène, and Stéphanie—were French. But though Napoléon ordered his family to consider itself so, the Bonapartes were not. Indeed Mme Mère made herself laconic, chiefly to conceal her Corsican accent, and never managed to master the language. Many things about the Bonapartes become clearer when we remember the one thing the Emperor wished to have forgotten, that Joseph, Napoléon, Lucien, Elisa, Louis, Pauline, Caroline and Jérôme were in actuality Giuseppe, Napoleone, Lucciano, Maria-Anna, Luigi, Maria-Paola, Maria-Annunziata, and Girolamo. Moreover they were Corsicans, a histrionic, vehement, and independent lot. Corsica had become a French possession only in 1768, the year before Napoléon was born. And even then it had to be fought for, since the local patriot Paoli had raised an army to make it independent and was difficult to put down.

The Buonapartes (Napoléon did not change the spelling until his Italian campaign) belonged to what the French call the nobility of the robe, which is to say they had been lawyers, not large landholders or courtiers. Originally they can be traced back to fifteenth-century Tuscany, with a little juggling here and there in the female line. The maternal strain, the Ramolino, was equally ancient, equally obscure, better bred, both physically and otherwise, and came from Genoa. The father, Carlo Buonaparte, was a glittering wastrel. It was the mother, Mme Mère, who kept the family going, until such time as Napoleone, the second son, could take over its direction.

All the Bonapartes except Elisa were a handsome lot, and Napoléon, of course, was a genius. They were also intensely dramatic. Their good inheritance stopped there. They had short stubby legs; they were quarrelsome and avaricious; cancer of the stomach was endemic for males, cancer of the womb for women; they had very poor circulation, bad digestion, suffered horribly from cold and nausea, and were decidedly neurasthenic. They were highly sexed, and their sex habits were in most of the family distinctly odd. And with the exception of Lucien, they had trouble producing male heirs, and very bad luck with those they did produce, who tended to die either youthful or young. The Beauharnais, on the other hand, had no such difficulty. Which was one reason the Bonapartes hated them so. They also incessantly plotted against each other.

"Must I then isolate myself from everyone? Must I rely upon myself alone?" Napoléon asked in 1804, after one of these family spats. By 1810 he had had occasion the better to order his thoughts. "I do not believe that any man in the world is more unfortunate in his family than I am" had by then become one of his many final statements on the matter.

To be accurate, he had not one family, but three, as well as two illegitimate children. And he greatly hampered his own movements by a Corsican loyalty to all of them.

To begin with those who caused him least trouble, there was the ex-Empress Joséphine and her children, Hortense, Queen of Holland, and Eugène, Viceroy of Italy, whom he had adopted. There were also two nieces or cousins by marriage, Stéphanie, Grand Duchess of Baden, and Émilie, Mme Lavalette.

His second family consisted of the Empress Marie Louise and his son by her, the King of Rome. In 1814 the King of Rome was only three going on four, and the Empress did nothing to vex Napoléon until after his fall.

It was his own family which caused the trouble. It was as clamorous as it was numerous.

At the head of it stood Mme Mère, a formidable woman, perhaps the only person he was afraid of. She recognized Napoléon as head of the family, but took sides against him whenever she chose. She also gave him good advice, which he seldom took. Though not greedy, she was an accomplished miser. She refused either to take part in, or to keep up, the pomps of Empire.

Her closest crony was her half brother and junior by twelve years, Cardinal Fesch, Cardinal Archbishop of Lyons. He was half Swiss and a canny businessman. At first, as an abbé with some hope of modest preferment, he was the most successful of the family. Abbés may, with some trouble, for they are only in lay orders, wrangle themselves out of the Church. His acumen getting the better of their lukewarm piety, Fesch had had himself secularized long enough and soon enough to make a fortune as a sutler, during Napoléon's Italian campaigns, by purveying spoiled stores and inferior equipment to the armies. His subsequent investments had made him rich. When Napoléon signed a concordat with the Pope, restoring Catholicism to France, Fesch was made Cardinal Archbishop of Lyons, so he might act as the First Consul's personal diplomatic emissary to the Vatican. Unfortunately, he did not approve of Napoléon, because as Emperor the First Consul soon had the Pope a prisoner at Fontainebleau. He was a loyal friend, but only to Pius VII and Mme Mère. He was a bonviveur, a glutton, and an accomplished diner out. His passion was the collection of Italian, Dutch, and Flemish primitives, of which he had somewhere between thirty and forty thousand, a haul he had begun to amass during his secular days in Italy, the cornerstone being a few things he had stolen from the Pitti Palace. In old age he developed a mystical streak which, among other things, undoubtedly if indirectly helped to kill his nephew. In 1814 he was fifty-three.

Napoléon's brothers and sisters were Joseph, ex-King of Spain, Jérôme, ex-King of Westphalia, Louis, ex-King of Holland, Pauline, Princess Borghese and Duchess of Guastalla, Elisa, Grand Duchess of Tuscany, Lucien, who had no title and was in contumacious but equanimous exile in England, and Caroline, Queen of Naples, the worst of the lot. The sins of the others were venial. She was a traitor. Of the whole family, only Pauline, a flighty woman, helped make Napoléon's fall easier.

On the outer fringe of the circle stood Miss Elizabeth Patterson of Baltimore, otherwise Mme Bonaparte, or Mme Bonaparte-Patterson, Jérôme's unfortunately legal but disavowed American first wife, and her son, Bo. She had a pension from Napoléon and, as a wronged woman, the approbation of a continent. She began life as a society belle and ended as a gorgon. She was to pester the Bonapartes for the next fifty years.

It is interesting to speculate upon what would have happened to these people, had not the backwash of a revolution cast their brother upon a throne. They would have been eccentrics anywhere, but village eccentrics on a backward island, not princes and princesses on a world stage. Their father, Carlo, was a foppish ne'er-do-well who attitudinized all day and fornicated all night. But he had some skill at place seeking and lawsuits, and was able to have his children educated at public expense. Their mother's contribution had been some money soon spent, a vineyard or two, a summer cottage, a firm will, and an extensive connection. She once calculated that in time of trouble she could count on the assistance of about 200 armed men. "Corsica is merely a barren rock, an imperceptible corner of the earth. France, on the contrary, is large, rich, and densely populated. Now France is ablaze—it is a noble bonfire, my son, and worth taking the risk of being burnt!" This was her advice to her most able son. The Bonapartes were nothing if not theatrical, and they were never off stage for any longer than they could help. Louis and Lucien wrote very bad plays, Napoléon knew Corneille by heart, and even on Elba had his own theater (in a converted warehouse). Pauline and Caroline liked to act in comedies. Elisa preferred tragedy (so did Napoléon); Jérôme, actresses. They ranted. They raved. They wore buskins. Everything and every public event was produced, usually by the painter David, a stage designer of enormous skill but somewhat fantastic taste. Napoléon always planned the uniforms of his troops before a campaign. Jérôme, the most expensively dressed man in Europe, went so far as to put off his campaigns if the uniforms weren't ready. Caroline's husband, Joachim Murat, thought nothing of leading a cavalry charge in a blaze of diamond-studded osprey plumes.

Under any conditions, they would have been the chief spectacle of their village. Joseph, who feeling the temper of the times had given up the priesthood in order to become a businessman, would have been at fifty the prosperous owner of a few small fields and a fallen-down house or two, not the ex-king of two kingdoms. Louis would have been the town crank, or somebody's uncle who had never married. Lucien, after a few years' spouting at the local liberal clubs, would have been an obscure lawyer with a Phoenician pot or two to show his love of archaeology. Jérôme would have been a black sheep anywhere, but in Corsica there are no greener pastures, indeed there are few pastures at all. Some years as an impoverished fop, and that would have been the end of him. Instead, in the course of an undeservedly long life, he spent more of other people's money than any other living man. Cardinal Fesch would have been the seedy canon of Ajaccio cathedral, his original fate. Elisa would have been an embittered spinster bluestocking, Caroline a provincial social climber, Pauline the village beauty and the village flirt; Napoléon himself would have been the local commander of a disused artillery battery. Mme Mère would have continued to put up olives in *eau de vie* and to save a little, but only a very little, money.

Instead, Pauline (Paoletta), then a child, had danced into the deathroom of her uncle, Canon Lucciano, and mischievously pulled the string which revealed that his mattress was stuffed with 2,000 gold louis, his lifetime savings, the foundation of everything that was to happen to them afterward.

T HE first of the three crownèd brothers to lose his throne had been Louis, King of Holland. He was also the last to give up his pretensions to it.

"A man must live in accordance with his position," warned Napoléon. "If he has ceased to be king, it is ridiculous to pose as one. Rings adorn fingers, but they fall off, and the fingers remain."

This was not the attitude of Louis, who had lost the use of his fingers and could write a letter only by means of a special rigid glove to which a pen had been riveted. In 1814 he was only thirty-six, yet he behaved like a querulous invalid. It was his singular notion that the Dutch, on whom he had been imposed, were eager to have him back.

Napoléon explained his conduct by saying he was mentally deranged. This was untrue. He was physically deranged. He seems to have had locomotor ataxia, the result of syphilis contracted in youth and never properly treated or cured. He had always been paranoid, and the progress of the disease did nothing to improve his disposition.

Despite partial paralysis, he was an indefatigable scribbler, having written plays, a novel called *Marie, ou Les Peines d'Amour* (in which his wife Hortense was one of the villainesses), and a history of Holland chiefly devoted to blaming Napoléon for everything and exonerating himself of the same charges. He also wrote verse, of which the following is a sufficient sample:

> *Victime de ma confiance,*
> *Sous d'injuste noeuds gémissant,*
> *Loin des amis de mon enfance,*
> *Je souffre et meurs à chaque instant.*

Jeté sur la rive étrangère
Par un sort que je dois haïr,
Hélas! Pour comble de misère
Je ne dois ni ne puis mourir.

This not only sums up his poetry. It sums up Louis. And true enough, he neither could nor would die, but continued to harass his family and everyone else within reach until 1846, thus outliving every sibling but Jérôme. In his own view, this merely added up to sixty-eight years of prolonged anguish.

Yet he had begun well enough. In youth he had his full share of the Bonaparte looks, but he was heavier-lidded than the rest of them. He had always the air of holding something back. What he held back, from any encounter, was himself. He remains an enigma without a secret, one of those anonymous, neatly turned-out young men to be found on the outer fringes of large parties who manage to suggest by their manner that though nobody here is in a position to know them, nevertheless they have condescended to come. By these and other innate skills, he early managed to vex many. Above all, his manner suggested that, whatever the facts of the matter, he was right. It has been suggested, most intensively by the English Freudian Ernest Jones, that he was homosexual. It would be more accurate to say that he preferred men to women, and himself to either.

For some incomprehensible reason, it was Napoléon's whim to believe that Louis was an incipient military genius. So in 1786, when Louis was nine, he decided to take the boy into barracks with him and teach him mathematics and drill. In 1791 he actually did so. "I can easily see that he will turn out a better fellow than any of the four of us. But then none of us had so fine an education."

He did not turn out the best of the four of them. He did not like mathematics, he did not like taking orders, and he loathed French irregular verbs. What he liked was reading *Paul et Virginie* and other sentimental novels. He even wrote to the author, to ask if that sugary work was based on truth, in order "to console his sympathetic sorrow by being able to say what was founded on fact and what on imagination."

His brother took him to Italy, where he behaved well, by saving Napoléon's life at Arcola. As a reward he was taken on to Egypt. Not one but several veils have been drawn over his behavior there, but it appears to have been both indolent and lewd. The sound of Nelson destroying the French fleet at Aboukir annoyed him. He did not take part in the capture of Cairo. His character was beginning to emerge.

On October 9, 1798, he was packed off to Europe, on a ship inappropriately named the *Vif*. He spent five months on a voyage that should have taken as many weeks, and then took two months' leave of absence, during which he helped his brother Joseph with *his* novel, which was about a shepherd and shepherdess undergoing the horrors of war in an Alpine peasant's hut. (Lucien's novel, on the other hand, *La Tribu Indienne,* was set in Ceylon. It was about a beautiful huntress who lay about on an elephant skin.) By 1800 Louis was so worn out that he adamantly refused to campaign and went off to take the waters at Aix. There he began work on a novel of his own.

Napoléon obstinately persisted in regarding him as a military genius *manqué* but had found a new use for him. "There is no longer any need of our worrying our minds about looking for my successor. I have found one. It is Louis. He has none of the defects of my other brothers, and he has all their good qualities."

An heir was imperative, and Joséphine, who seems to have had an early menopause and was seven years older than her husband, in order to consolidate her own position decided to marry her daughter Hortense, whom Napoléon had adopted, off to Louis. It was a disastrous marriage. Louis was totally unsuited to be anybody's husband. Hortense, who was shy and dependent on her mother, was suited for marriage, but not to Louis.

Hortense was eighteen, gracious, agreeable, rather attractive, though not pretty, good at her studies, by nature romantic, and an amateur both of the piano and of the paintbrush. She was as proper as she was accomplished. But what she needed by way of a husband was someone to lean on, and when used for these purposes, Louis had a tendency to give way. Also, she could not stand him.

For his part, Louis, who had been vacationing with the King of Prussia, liked the idea no better, and when he returned, he avoided court and took refuge at his country house at Baillon, a damp, lugubrious place surrounded by marshes, not far from Joseph's estate at Mortefontaine. Not feeling safe even there, he next fled to his regiment, the 5th Dragoons, at Bordeaux. He did not return until September of 1801.

The marriage was announced in October. Louis began to ingratiate himself at once. "If your popularity has not spoiled you," he told Hortense, "you must be an angel. There can be no in between. Either you are all good or all bad." He then presented her with a twenty-page letter outlining the highlights (apparently mostly imaginary) of his erotic adventures to date, and requested a similar register from Hortense, who said, perhaps not in an altogether tactful tone, that so far she had nothing to confess. Nor, as it happens, had she.

The marriage took place January 4, 1802. Joséphine once said that Louis loved Napoléon "as a lover his mistress." Hortense was not Napoléon. Louis soon took to searching her rooms at night with a candle, to see if anyone else was there. Somehow or other he got her with child, but did not believe it. He became convinced (Caroline, who hated the Beauharnais, did much to persuade him) that the father was Napoléon, largely because Hortense sometimes played chess with the First Consul in the evenings.

When the child, a few days premature, was born, Napoléon did not help matters by saying, "Here is our Dauphin." Louis paused to inspect the child, and then went off to Montpellier, apparently on good terms with his wife again, except for one curious stipulation. Lucien had abetted his sister Caroline in spreading rumors of incest, so Hortense was forbidden to stay overnight in the same building with Napoléon. She did stay overnight, and told Joséphine and Napoléon why she had been ordered not to. Louis promptly proposed a separation. When Hortense agreed, he became even more annoyed, and went away again. All told, of his three children (Hortense had four, but did not mention the anomaly to anyone) he accepted only the second, Napoléon Louis, as his own.

In May of 1804 Napoléon had himself created Emperor. The family nagged its way up the ladder right behind him, and Louis was made Constable of France, an ancient office revived in order to augment his income. Since Napoléon wished to adopt his first child, Napoléon Charles, Louis forbade Hortense to see any of her relatives, and in particular, "your unprincipled mother." Joséphine was by birth a Tascher de la Pagerie. When a Tascher cousin arrived from Martinique to see Hortense, Louis threatened to run him through with a sword. What irritated him most, it seems, was Hortense's popularity.

It was at this time that Hortense encountered Charles de Flahaut, a pink-faced, gangly sublieutenant who had been, up until then one of Louis's favorites. If not of good family, he was at least of splendid descent, being, as it happened, the illegitimate son of Talleyrand and the adopted son both of Flahaut, his nominal father, and of de Souza, his mother's second husband and at that time Portuguese Ambassador to France. Louis promptly had him denied admittance to the house, so Hortense saw him elsewhere. "He continues to show me kindness," wrote Flahaut to his mother. "I am dining with him today. He occasionally puts me under arrest, but it is all done in a very friendly way."

And so it was, but not all the paths to self-advancement are without oddity. Nonetheless, there were problems. "I was not offended by your silence," wrote Louis to Flahaut. ". . . What really hurt me was your writing that you couldn't think of what to say to me, or how to begin." Louis never seemed to know how to begin either, so Hortense inherited Flahaut.

In 1804 Louis bought his estate at St. Leu, from which both he and his wife were later to take their (separate) titles in exile. When she returned from St. Leu to Paris, it was to discover that Louis had raised the walls around the house by several feet and had put a sentry box under her bedroom window. He had also walled up all doors but one leading into her quarters and moved his bed into her bedroom, the better to supervise her second pregnancy. After Napoléon Louis was born, the couple returned to St. Leu, where Louis had the gate in the park wall bricked in, forbade the ladies in waiting to walk in the grounds, and hired spies to read their correspondence.

He found nothing.

On June 3, 1805, Louis was made King of Holland. His first act on arriving in his kingdom was to forbid all references to Hortense in public prayers. Only the King, he said, was worthy of being recommended to the Deity.

Dutch damps disagreed with Louis, so he went off on a round of the spas. All told, he spent more time in hot water than he did in Holland. Nonetheless he set himself to learn Dutch and took his duties seriously. This brought him into immediate conflict with the Emperor, who wished Holland run for France's benefit, not its own. Napoléon had also hoped that Louis would be popular and that Hortense would charm the Dutch. Instead, Louis spent most of his time

17

shut up in an obscure country house with his usual second-rate cronies and not only refused to permit Hortense to appear in public, but demanded that her name be omitted from the patronage lists of all Dutch charities to which she subscribed. Hortense was left in Amsterdam, in the Royal Palace. It had been the town hall and law courts, and her salon was therefore tastefully embellished with black and white skulls in stonework, since it had previously been set aside for the detainment of the condemned.

Napoléon's system of putting an embargo on all British goods to the continent ruined Dutch trade. Louis connived at smuggling. Napoléon retaliated by having guards put on the canals. But Holland has a great many canals. He therefore took the southern provinces into the French departmental system. When Louis turned hostile, the Emperor threatened to occupy the country. At the same time the marriage degenerated to the point where its collapse became a public spectacle. Napoléon rebuked Louis. Since Hortense denied having complained to the Emperor, Louis blamed the French Ambassador and banned him from court. He also took to waking Hortense in the middle of the night to tell her she was killing him. Then unable to die, he presented her with a document in eight articles designed to restore their marriage to an ideal state.

When her son Napoléon Charles, the eldest, died, she went south to the Pyrenees. Louis for once behaved well. Ultimately, on April 21, 1808, their last child, Louis Napoléon, the future Napoléon III, was born. It was to be the one of his children Louis was to dislike most, and he never ceased to claim it was not his own. (Though it was. Hortense did not become Charles de Flahaut's mistress until somewhat later.) "It is a consolation to live so far from you, to have nothing to discuss with you, nothing to do with you, nothing to expect from you. If I have anything to fear, at least it is not from you," Louis wrote his wife, by way of congratulation.

Napoléon suggested they live together again, but let the matter drop. "Louis is a good man," he said, "though nobody seems able to live with him." Then he changed his mind and forced Hortense to return to Amsterdam. In March of 1809 he occupied the country as far as the Meuse. Hortense did not stay long. Louis now made it his habit not to speak to her at court. On May 16 she left him for good.

Though leaving Louis his title of King, Napoléon decided to occupy all of Holland. Louis decided to cause maximum embarrass-

ment in the only way open to him. He would become a self-adver-
tised fugitive from his brother's tyranny. This form of revenge had
been planned for some time, and with prudence and secrecy. He had
his diamonds sent out of the country. He sold, very privately, his
real estate. He drew ten thousand gold francs out of the State Bank.
On July 3, 1809, he sent out three documents, the first his abdication
in favor of his son, Napoléon Louis, or, failing him, Louis Napoléon;
the second, a protest against his brother's acts as Emperor; the third,
a proclamation to the people of Holland. Then he had dinner.

At eleven that night a carriage drew up in the lane outside his
retreat at Haarlem, and leaving behind him his favorite son, but taking with him his favorite dog, a mongrel, Louis made his escape.
Characteristically, on the way to the carriage he fell into a ditch.
Nonetheless he went on. He was enjoying himself. The dog was run
over and killed at one of the posting stops. By dawn he was approaching the German border. This was the last anyone on the Imperial side was able to learn of his movements for the next two
weeks. It was then discovered that he had, as usual in any emergency, gone to take the waters, this time at Töplitz, in Bohemia, in
Austrian territory.

To his displeasure, his abdication meant that Hortense would be
Regent of Holland, until Napoleon seized it. This was not, however,
to be for more than a week, nor was she there. At last, at the age of
twenty-seven, Hortense, to whom Napoleon gave the estate at St.
Leu (Louis wrote to forbid her to accept it, a letter she sensibly
ignored), was free to live as she wished. And what she wished was
Flahaut.

Louis continued, from a discreet distance, to annoy everyone else
and to embarrass the Emperor as much as possible. Taking the title
of Comte de St. Leu, he begged refuge of his brother's worst enemy,
the Emperor of Austria. This was granted. Then he proposed to
Cardinal Fesch that he take over Fesch's property at Corsica and live
there. Fesch, however, accumulated property, he did not relinquish
it. In addition, he and Mme Mère virtually ruled Corsica through the
Prefect of that department, who was their creature, and they had no
wish to share their rule.

Louis sent protests against the annexation of Holland to the Em-
perors of Austria and Russia, and removed himself to Gratz, in

Styria, a hundred miles south of Vienna. It was a small provincial capital where he could pose as he would before and with the local dignitaries. Napoleon allowed him to keep his title and gave him a revenue of 2,000,000 francs. Louis refused the money, but kept the title.

Most of his time was spent in playing his numerous doctors off against each other. He also maintained a large correspondence, most of it for the benefit of the secret police who intercepted it. He stayed in Gratz for two years. The birth of the King of Rome was a severe blow to him, since it meant his own son was cut out of the succession. In 1812 he translated some odes of Horace and took the news of the disasters in Russia well. Neither did the events of 1813 in any way disturb him. They did arouse his patriotism, both French and Dutch. When Napoleon reached Mayence, on his flight back to Paris, he found a letter waiting for him from Louis, warmly suggesting his own immediate restoration to the Dutch throne. This would help the Emperor, Louis thought, by assuring the loyal support of the Dutch people.

On August 2, 1813, since the Emperor of Austria was about to join the Allies against Napoléon, Louis felt it only loyal to remove to Switzerland. From Switzerland he offered to return to France, on the condition that he might be restored to his throne once peace was reestablished. At the same time he refused to do anything in violation of his oath to the Dutch Estates. The Emperor ignored this tempting offer. Louis could not understand why, and complained to Mme Mère that he had left Austria, at some inconvenience to himself, only in order to make things easier for Napoléon.

At Basel, Murat came through, fleeing back to Naples from the Battle of Leipzig, and suggested treason. Louis was not a traitor. On the other hand, it does not seem to have occurred to him to tell Napoléon that Murat was. Instead, he wrote to demand surrender of the Netherlands to himself, and was so certain of the response that on November 3, 1813, having crossed the frontier, he arrived at Mme Mère's chateau at Pont sur Seine. Napoléon announced that if he persisted in claiming to be King of Holland he would be arrested.

Louis returned to Switzerland, then fled from it again and went to Lyons, where he arrived on Christmas Eve and stayed with Cardinal Fesch. By New Year's Day, 1814, he was at his mother's town house in Paris. It was the day Blücher crossed the Rhine. "I have come,"

20

wrote Louis to Caulaincourt, the Minister for Foreign Affairs, "only as a Frenchman, to share the dangers of the moment, and to make myself useful insofar as I can."

But his means were unaccountably limited, and assistance took the form of lurking in his mother's house exclusively. Nobody paid much attention. Napoléon's faith in Louis's military genius seems finally to have abated. Toward the end, the ex-King of Holland had a brief scare when it was proposed to leave him in Paris as president of a commission to control the city, but fortunately his conscience did not allow him to accept the office, unless the crown of Holland (again) was assured him. Most of his time was spent supervising Hortense's conduct from an irascible distance.

If Napoléon found Louis's arrival as annoying as it was unexpected, the behavior of Joseph and Jérôme drove him to fury. In the case of Joseph he had perhaps some cause for surprise, but Jérôme had always been the wastrel of the family.

Of the three kings, Joseph was the first to arrive a fugitive in France. Napoléon's relations with him were more complex than those he maintained with his other brothers. For one thing, he was the most prudent and dependable of the lot. For another, he was the oldest. And then, it was Joseph who had really founded the family fortunes, by his marriage to Julie Clary in 1794. The Clarys were merchants and bankers, and her dowry had financed the beginnings of the regime. Nor had she minded the uses to which it had been put, for though she and Joseph seldom lived together, they got on extremely well.

Joseph was forty-six in 1814. Efforts had been made to convert him into a diplomat, but he remained to the end exactly what he was to begin with, a businessman. His manner was judicious even when he was not. He was nobody's favorite, and yet he was respected. He liked to dabble in real estate. He kept a mistress or two, usually discreetly. He would have preferred a quiet existence at Mortefontaine, his chateau in the country, to an Imperial career.

He had long felt the resentment natural to a titular head of a family overshadowed by a more brilliant younger brother, but it was not a deep resentment. Unfortunately it bobbed up on the surface at unlikely and ill-chosen times. He was an excellent bureaucrat. What he was not, was a king or a military commander. As for his wife, though pleasant enough, she absolutely refused to be a queen. Her usual plea was ill health. But he and Napoléon worked in tandem tolerably well to improve the family fortune, if only because Joseph was of too placid a temperament to quarrel for long.

In appearance he was the Bonaparte who most took after their father, but without the panache. He was competent but not colorful. One always felt that one had to lower one's voice when talking to him, or at any rate to take the sparkle out. This did not prevent him from shouting himself. He felt himself born to be a worthy. As a result, for he made no secret of this, many people found him somewhat irritating, among them his wife. She was, however, devoted to their daughters, and was always ready to welcome him on those rare occasions when he returned home. She also, years later, loyally assisted him on his deathbed, which she did not long survive. She was what is known as *jolie laide*, and like most such women, she was an agreeable person, though a little dull. She was devoted to her brother Nicolas, a banker, who managed Joseph's investments and managed them extremely well, being prudent enough to maintain capital abroad, where it could not be gotten at, no matter what happened in France.

The trouble with Joseph was that in a scintillating family (even Louis was a brilliant hypochondriac and a paranoiac of no little skill), he had no special abilities whatsoever, only the craft and sullen art of saving well. Physically he had early tended toward corpulence. He was domestically lubricious, restricting himself to one mistress at a time, usually the same one for years. He saw to it that they were not an undue expense.

Apart from his marriage and his other investments, Joseph had the reputation of being a bungler. It was a reputation quietly earned. In youth both he and Lucien had been suspicious of Napoléon.

"I say to you in the fullest confidence," wrote Lucien to Joseph, "that I have always seen in Napoleone an ambition that is not indeed altogether selfish, but which influences him more powerfully than any love for the public welfare. I think that in a free state he is a dangerous man. He seems to me greatly inclined to be a tyrant, and I think that if he were a king he would be quite capable of playing that part, and that his name would be an object of detestation to posterity and to every thoughtful patriot. . . . I think he is quite capable of turning his coat to protect his own interests."

Joseph married Julie Clary and 150,000 francs when Napoléon had merely begun to rise, a fortune for the family in those days. In return, Napoléon found him perquisites. Joseph rose from Assistant Commissary Agent to the Republic, at 6,000 francs a year, to Ambassador to Rome, at 60,000, in four years. He was a total failure as an ambassador. Napoléon left him in Paris to manage the family fortunes. At this he did better. For one thing he short-changed Joséphine in her allowance and refused to give her half the purchase price of Malmaison as Napoléon had promised her. Malmaison cost nearly 300,000 francs. Joseph's own country estate, Mortefontaine, which he bought at about this time, cost 258,000, not counting repairs; and for good measure he acquired a town house at the same time, for 66,000, plus 28,000 for alterations.

Mortefontaine, nineteen miles out of Paris, north on the Chantilly road, included forests, two lakes, its own river, pasturelands, a château and farms. He was to prefer it to either of his kingdoms. And in the beginning Joseph was astute at avoiding a variety of booby traps lovingly presented to him by the First Consul in the form of gifts. These included the presidency of a projected Cisalpine Republic and the chieftainship of the Military Department of the Swiss Confederation. Nonetheless, when the Empire was inaugurated, he was made Grand Elector, with an allowance of a third of a million francs, and Prince of the Empire, which gave him a civil list of a million. On January 19, 1806, he was created King of Naples. By this time his name had been changed to Joseph Napoléon, for official purposes and on Napoléon's orders. The Emperor was insistent on perpetuating not so much his family as himself. It was also his intention that his regnant brothers should be surrogate Napoléons, without volition of their own, there only because he could not be everywhere at once. One way or another, everyone in the family, except Cardinal Fesch and Mme Mère, was forced to call himself or herself and his or her children Napoléon. There was even a female Napoléone (Elisa's daughter).

The result, of course, was trouble. It infuriated the Emperor when his brothers disobeyed him, and of course they always did. Joseph had ever been sober as an owl. To be royal made him plummy. Napoléon kept his armies loyal and solvent out of the loot of those countries they could conquer. Joseph, who felt he had a duty to his new subjects, forbade looting and contracted for supplies in the Papal States. He then moved into the palaces at Naples. Napoléon said he was living in a fool's paradise and did not know how to govern. This was only half true. Joseph did know how to govern; what he did not know how to do was to impose his government. The Abruzzi was never subdued during his reign (1806-1808). He remained King not of Naples but in it. His wife refused to join him, until Napoléon ordered her to visit what was, after all, her own kingdom.

Joseph's administration, if ineffectual, was admirable in plan, and he was popular at least in the capital. But the regime had to be paid for from Paris, so Napoléon removed him and made him King of Spain instead. The offer was made because there was no one else to whom the Emperor dared make it, and it was accepted because Joseph was ignorant of Spanish affairs and had no way of knowing that his new kingdom was on the eve of a national insurrection. Caroline Murat and her husband were moved into Naples in his stead.

Napoléon's Spanish policy was first among his mortal errors. So far he had conquered countries too weak to defend themselves and had overturned not peoples, but merely their rulers. In Spain he was up against a house-to-house resistance. The Spanish Royal Family was Napoléon's prisoner, in France. The Spanish fleet had been sunk at Trafalgar. To maintain the Continental Blockade, Napoléon marched armies across Spain to Portugal. They could not, however, hold it, for Napoléon had never before been up against guerrilla warfare or a united populace, or indeed any country so vast, empty, and disorganized as was Spain.

Joseph had had to be offered the Spanish crown twice before he could bring himself to accept, but from the relative safety of Bayonne (Goya had paused there, but had preferred the more prudent distance of Bordeaux), Spain seemed an excellent country to rule. He seems not to have heard the popular Spanish remark, that though he might have put the Spanish crown in his pocket, he would never put it on his head.

Pausing only to empty the Naples treasury, or what was left of it, into the lap of his mistress, the Duchess of Atri, Joseph set himself to approving a liberal constitution, which Spain did not want, and abolished the Inquisition and the provincial customs houses, which it did. The Catholic Church was left otherwise untouched, and only Spaniards were to be given public offices and employments.

It did no good. He was up against a state of mind. The Spaniards might be poor and defenseless, but they had one immense power: they were religious bigots. Joseph might be a (very) nominal Catholic, but since Napoléon held the Pope a prisoner, that made all Frenchmen atheists, which in turn made them fair game. They did not want the Inquisition abolished. They were fond of it; it was one of their blood sports. They did not want a liberal King who would better their condition; they wanted their own King, who would leave them as they were. The intellectuals were a tiny class and counted for nothing; as for the more powerful of the nobility, they had battened on the provincial customs dues for years, and did not wish them done away with.

Joseph was proclaimed King in Madrid, on July 24, 1808, but the French armies could not hold the capital, and he could not hold it either. He distributed largesse to the people. The people merely left the money lying in the streets. By the beginning of August he had been forced to take refuge in Burgos, a muddy, gloomy town. Joseph had second thoughts and asked to have Naples back.

Napoléon's reaction was to send his most experienced generals across the Pyrenees, well aware that Wellington had already landed at Lisbon. If Wellington (then Sir Arthur Wellesley) had not carried prudence to the point of immobility, the Spanish campaign might have been over far sooner.

As it was, an increasingly reluctant and very angry Joseph was forced to pretend to rule Spain until 1813. Napoléon made matters worse by directing the Spanish campaigns himself and not telling Joseph what he had done. They were somewhat difficult to direct from Paris. Spain was divided into autonomous sections, under Marshals Soult, Masséna, Suchet, Marmont, and Dorsenne, each with his own army. They sacked the country for what they could get. When bullion convoys were sent to Joseph, the Marshals helped themselves to what they needed as the wagons passed through their territories. When the war with Russia came, Napoléon further weakened defenses by drawing off troops for that campaign. In the south, Soult regarded himself as King of Andalusia and refused to accept or obey orders from Joseph. Instead he communicated directly with the War Department in Paris.

The final disaster came in 1813. Soult was recalled and withdrew through Madrid with a lengthy baggage train of personal plunder, the sack of Andalusia. Masséna behaved in the same manner. Wellington was made commander not only of the British, but of the Spanish insurrectionist forces as well. Though he did not begin his final advance until May 13, 1813, Joseph fell back on Valladolid on March 23. He was told by Clark, the French Minister of War, that he was to act as a French commander in chief, not as King of Spain. Unfortunately his subordinates and his Marshals disregarded his orders and usually refused to consult him.

The road from Madrid ran through Valladolid and was clogged with refugees, officials, and carts and carriages impressed to carry the boodle. These convoys were miles long and took days to get over the Guadarrama range. Joseph fell back on Burgos. There was no food. From Burgos the royal refugees went on to Vittoria. From Vittoria the 2,000 Spanish families who had accepted Joseph's sovereignty thought it prudent to flee into France over the Pyrenees. They were contemptuously referred to as *Josephinos*. Joseph decided to make a stand at Vittoria, though his position was indefensible.

From Mortefontaine, Julie, as reluctant to enter Spain as she had been to visit Naples, from time to time allowed herself to express a distant concern. She need not have worried. Instead of putting his remaining troops to rights, Joseph spent most of his time with his Spanish mistress, the Marqueza de Monte Hermoso. He put his faith in his heavy guns. Unfortunately they were useless, since his generals had commandeered the gun horses to help pull their loot to France.

The battle of Vittoria took place on the 21st of June, 1813, beginning at four A.M. and lasting all day. By six in the evening the British had won it. Joseph fled, greatly impeded by his own followers, and was forced to leave most of his own loot behind. "You've had your battle, and it seems to be a lost one," said his chief military adviser. It was also his last one.

Joseph lost his carriage, the pick of the Spanish picture collections (Wellington was later given the best of it by a grateful if aesthetically indifferent King Ferdinand VII), his private papers, his plate, 27,000,000 francs, 1,500 wagons, 150 guns, 400 artillery carriages, and, of course, most of his army. It was a rout. Drivers cut the traces rather than have their flight impeded by their loads. It was raining heavily. Joseph was forced to sneak down into France by obscure and mountainous back ways, which took him the better part of a week. To make matters worse, his treasurer had been killed, and he had not a penny. He was forced to borrow money to go on with from his brother-in-law.

On June 28 he left Spanish soil for the last time and settled in the Château de St. Pée de Nivelle, near Bayonne. He had somehow managed to get half a million francs from Valencia. The money might better have been spent on the army. Instead, he gave it to his household and personal guard and for the relief of Spanish refugees at Auch. The Marqueza de Monte Hermoso had followed him. Incredibly, he wrote to the War Department at Paris, asking for promotions for his entire staff. Instead, Soult, Duke of Dalmatia, was appointed to direct all movements along the Spanish frontier. Joseph regarded Soult as his enemy, and to still quarrels and get Joseph away where he could do no harm, Napoléon gave him permission to return to Mortefontaine incognito. Under the name General Palacios, Joseph arrived there July 30, glad to be back but followed by his exiled court. The Marqueza was established in Paris.

He was the first of the uprooted kings to return.

The second to come back was Jérôme.

Born in 1784, he was the youngest of the brothers. In his childhood he had been nicknamed Fifi, and Fifi he remained. He was the most splendidly and expensively idiotic of all the Bonapartes. Like Caroline, he was thoroughly spoiled. Unlike Caroline, he had no brains whatsoever. He was wayward, capricious, undisciplined, irresponsible, handsome, and well dressed, but not a dandy, merely an exhibitionist. He was also libidinous.

Napoléon, undeterred by proof positive that Joseph was not a diplomat and Louis not a military genius, decided that Jérôme was to be the naval member of the family. His mother frowned on this ambition, for it was her impression that maritime life combined "the horrors of fire *and* flood." In 1800 he was sent off on a Mediterranean cruise with Admiral Gantheaume, a dependable man (his notepaper bore a star, the letter *B*, and the device, *Je navigue sous son étoile*).

Napoléon instructed the Admiral, "I send you Citizen Jérôme Bonaparte, who is to serve apprenticeship to the navy under your orders. You know that he must be kept strictly in hand, and has much lost time to make up. Insist on his exactly discharging all the duties of the profession which he has adopted."

Gantheaume sensibly did nothing of the sort, for he was an excellent judge of men and knew which ladder led up and which down. Instead he lent Jérôme money and allowed him to pose as the captor of an English ship, the *Swiftsure*, which he had himself taken. The cruise lasted eight months. At the end of it Jérôme began to pose as a naval veteran and as an authority on maritime affairs. When he presumed to lecture the Emperor on these subjects, he was shipped off on a cruise to the West Indies, a girlish, insubordinate boy of eighteen. It should be added, however, that Jérôme's only sexual eccentricity was to marry off his mistresses to his close friends, in order to make sure that they would always be available.

The fleet arrived in the West Indies at the end of January 1802. Jérôme soon found an excuse to return to Paris, and Napoléon as rapidly one to send him right back again. Since Jérôme did not happen to find naval uniforms flattering, he insisted upon wearing that of a hussar instead, sky-blue jacket and scarlet waistcoat. He was very good at dining ashore, and it was on this voyage that he picked up his lifelong pimp, secretary, and crony, Lécamus.

He was ordered back to France. Instead he went to America, reaching Norfolk, Virginia, on July 20, 1802. From Norfolk he went to Washington, where Pichon, the French Consul General, lent him money and advised him to move into a hotel owned by Joshua Barney. Barney also owned a hotel in Baltimore, where he was acquainted with a businessman named William Patterson, who had among other children a daughter, Betsy, who was an extremely ambitious girl.

Thus began the hectic saga of the American Bonapartes.

Baltimore was at that time a town of 4,000 people. Jérôme met the Pattersons through Samuel Chase, the politician. William Patterson, a native of Donegal, was probably at that time the second richest man in America (the richest was John Carroll of Carrolltown). He was a shipbuilder, trader, businessman, and owner of real estate, middle-aged and well married. He knew everyone of importance in America in the worlds of business, banking, and politics. Though he went so far as to have himself painted by Thomas Sully, he had not much interest in the arts.

Elizabeth Patterson is sometimes referred to as "bewitching Betsy Bonaparte." It is extremely difficult to see why. She had been born February 6, 1785, which made her three months older than Jérôme. She had charm, intelligence, and a truly flabbergasting beauty, of the sort that does not fade. But it is hard to believe in the helpless naiveté of any woman whose favorite reading as a child was the *Maxims* of Rochefoucauld (her other favorite book was Young's *Night Thoughts,* which is not, on the whole, much more promising).

She was well educated, by American standards (though not by French: Pichon said that "like all young persons in this country her education was limited to very little"). She spoke fluent if schoolgirl French. More importantly, her pleasure as a child was to stay with her father during his working hours and so acquire a certain amount of useful information about investment banking, real estate, trade, contracts, and business law. She had brains and determination, and as she said much later she would have married the devil himself to get out of Baltimore. Like many another Southern belle, she also had an iron whim.

To Jérôme the matter was quite simple. He wanted Miss Patterson. He could not have Miss Patterson unless he married her. To Miss Patterson the matter was equally simple. She wanted him to want her. He could not have her unless he married her. The only people to be pitied were Pichon, the Consul General, whose career the marriage nearly wrecked, and perhaps Mr. Patterson, who had to pay for it. What Elizabeth wanted, Elizabeth got.

Pichon temporized and sent off warnings to France. He was deceived by a trick. Lécamus came to tell him the marriage had been canceled. This welcome news was accompanied by a demand for $10,000. Pichon found the money. Jérôme advanced to New York and demanded $2,000 more. He received $1,000. Pichon was not a rich man.

With these sums in hand, Jérôme doubled in his tracks. Pichon had written Patterson senior that under French law Jérôme could not legally marry without his surviving parent's permission, since he was underage. Jérôme had not bothered to tell his hosts that he was a minor. Patterson consulted lawyers. Elizabeth stormed, and went right on storming, until at last her father gave in.

Since neither William Patterson nor his daughter was a fool, but Jérôme was, the marriage contract contained a clause that "If the marriage is annulled, no matter by whom, Elizabeth Patterson is to have the right to a third of her future husband's fortune."

Jérôme, having no fortune, was quite willing to sign this. The marriage was held on Christmas Eve, 1803, by special license. The officiating priest was Archbishop Carroll of Baltimore. The Mayor of Baltimore was present. Jérôme was gorgeously dressed in purple satin and diamond buckles. His wife's dress, according to a witness, could have been stuffed in one of his pockets. She wore, if not nothing, at least less than had ever been seen in America before.

The marriage was not without advantages as far as her relatives were concerned. General Smith, an in-law, thought it might make him United States Ambassador to France. His brother, who was Secretary of the Navy at the time, thought it diplomatically advantageous to future treaty negotiations. Senator Nicholas, another in-law on the maternal side who had a finger in French commerce, saw much to be gained by marital influence. Jérôme himself hoped to be made French Ambassador to the United States.

The honeymoon was spent at one of William Patterson's estates, at William Patterson's expense, which he had foreseen but had been unable to prevent. Pichon received a letter from Lécamus on Christmas day, announcing the marriage and asking for another $4,000. Jérôme, he added, was "expecting it with impatience." He did not get it.

During the following week everybody wrote letters. Jérôme and Elizabeth wrote to Mme Mère and to Joseph. Pichon wrote to exonerate himself of any charges of complicity. William Patterson not only wrote to the First Consul, now his son-in-law, but sent the letter by his own son Robert.

As it happened, the news reached Napoléon not by any of these means, but through a notice in the British press, which did nothing to diminish his rage. The rest of the family seemed rather to be amused by the marriage than anything else. This also did nothing to diminish his rage.

Jérôme was told he would be forgiven only if he returned without his wife, and that if he did return with her, she would not be allowed to set foot on French soil, which, at this time, included most of the European continent. Pichon was ordered to cut off supplies.

Jérôme stayed in America for fifteen months. During that time, Napoléon had himself made Emperor. Jérôme's name was left off the roster of new Princes. Though deprived of his title, Jérôme's extravagance was on an imperial scale not even Mr. Patterson could or would long sustain. But it was difficult to get the couple out of America, because the British were patroling the coasts.

In October of 1804 an attempt was made to reach Europe. The boat ran aground on a mudbank. Elizabeth was pregnant and almost drowned. More important, Jérôme lost $3,000 and $4,200 for his passage money, and the captain threatened to sue for the cost of the brig.

On February 2, 1805, Napoléon induced Mme Mère to depose with a notary her protestation against the marriage, and a decree of March 11 pronounced it void and any children by it illegitimate. On the 3d of March Mr. Patterson, who by this time was feeling vexed all round, and who possessed among other things a small fleet of his own, got Jérôme, his wife, his brother-in-law, and the indispensable Lécamus aboard the fast clipper *Erin* and wished them godspeed to Lisbon. It was Jérôme's theory that the sight of Elizabeth Patterson would warm the Emperor's heart. The *Erin* dropped anchor in Belém roadstead April 9. It was immediately surrounded by a French guard, who came out in small boats, and the Consul General came aboard and pointedly asked what he could do for *Miss Patterson.*

"Tell your Master," said Betsy, "that Mme Bonaparte is ambitious and demands her rights as a member of the Imperial Family."

She was forbidden to land anywhere in Spain, France, Portugal, or Holland. Jérôme was ordered to come to Milan, where the Emperor was, by the most direct route. If he deviated from the route, he would be put under arrest. If Elizabeth entered France, she would be expelled. If she took back her maiden name, she would be given a pension of 60,000 francs a year, on condition she return to America. The marriage was civilly annulled in France. The Pope had refused to annul it.

Jérôme deserted. "The worst that can happen to us is only that we may have to go to some foreign country and live there quietly, and as long as we are together we are certain to be happy," he wrote Elizabeth, from somewhere along the way. He was never to see her again, except once, briefly, in passing, years later, in an Italian picture gallery, when he had the pleasure of pointing her out to his second wife.

One way or another, Elizabeth was to bother the Bonapartes for the next fifty years. For the moment she refused to return to America. She made her reasons clear. "I hated and loathed residence in Baltimore so much that when I thought I was to spend my life there I tried to screw up courage to the point of committing suicide." Nor did she come to think much better of Jérôme. When he offered her 200,000 francs a year, she said, "I prefer to be sheltered under the wing of an eagle to being suspended by the quill of a goose," and refused his offer in favor of accepting Napoléon's 60,000.

Now she sailed for Holland, where she was kept from going

ashore and guarded by a French ship of the line of sixty-four cannon. She went on to England, where she was greeted by large crowds, as a conspicuous victim of Old Boney's tyranny, which exactly suited her book. She was received in society and went everywhere. This gave her the opportunity of publicizing her sufferings, to Napoléon's fury. She and her brother took lodgings in Camberwell, then a village two miles outside London. There, on July 7, 1805, her son was born. He was not to be baptized until four years later, but his name, Jerome Napoleon Bonaparte, and the birth were registered by a notary and countersigned by the Austrian and Prussian Ambassadors to Great Britain, for Elizabeth wished later to claim his rights as an Imperial Prince. Jérôme wrote to her surreptitiously, begging her to keep some pomp in her house, specifically four horses and a large staff, and to entertain widely. He also said she was to return to America and was not to refuse any money Napoléon might send her.

"You know me, Elisa, and you know that nothing can detach me from you," he wrote from Bahía. "The object of every step I take, my one care, my constant anxiety is to see once more my dear Elisa, my dear little wife, without whom I could not live, and my little Napoleon Jerome [somehow he got the name backwards]; that is the name of our son."

In October of 1805 Elizabeth returned to America, though only provisionally. And in the fall of 1806 Jérôme quite contentedly married Catherine of Württemberg, though for a while he went on writing devoted letters to Elizabeth.

Catherine was the daughter of the fattest man in Europe and the meanest, who had been made King for cooperating with Napoléon. Though she had only three dresses and almost no money, Catherine was an accomplished and pleasant young woman, stout, with blond hair, blue eyes, and small hands. Her outstanding characteristic was loyalty, unfortunately for her to Jérôme, with whom she fatuously fell in love.

By this time Jérôme had been recognized as an Imperial Prince, made a rear admiral, and given a million francs a year. The Rear Admiral was then packed off to Prussia and a military campaign. He did not distinguish himself. Mostly he stayed in his palace at Breslau. Nonetheless, a victory was again arranged for him, this time at Glatz.

Horace Vernet, who did a battlepiece to commemorate the occasion, was forced to call it *Prince Jérôme at the Storming of Glatz*, however, since Jérôme had wisely stayed out of range of the Prussian guns. He was amply rewarded all the same. "My brother," wrote Napoléon, "I have just signed the peace with Russia and Prussia. You have been recognized as King of Westphalia. This kingdom will include all the states of which you will find the list hereto annexed."

Everybody had been forced to contribute something. Prussia, Brunswick and Hanover handed over bits and pieces, and the Prince of Orange was induced to add the Abbey of Cerney. The Duke of Brunswick-Wolfenbüttel, who had been killed at Jena, posthumously contributed his lands, which were now decreed confiscate. The Prussian fief of Stolberg went into the pile, and so did Hesse-Kassel's domain of Rietburg. The result was a bankrupt, ungovernable hodgepodge, with a capital at Kassel.

Jérôme married Catherine August 22, 1807, at Paris. War had delayed the marriage. Napoléon paid his debts, which amounted to 3,000,000 francs, and on November 18, 1807, the couple started out to take possession of their new kingdom.

As a military man, Jérôme had always some excuse. If all else failed, it was hemorrhoids, which kept him inactive for three touchy months during the campaigns of 1807. As King of Westphalia he was not much more convincing. Once, in Paris, unable to assure the manager of a restaurant of his identity, he had been forced to hand over his watch in pawn for the meal. Since it was an expensive watch, the proprietor turned it over to the police, who turned it over to Fouché, the head of Napoleon's police, who took it to the Emperor. Thus his identity was finally proved, but since it had been given to Jérôme by Joséphine, Napoléon had been angry to see it so lightly pawned. Jérômé was like that.

Westphalia was not very convincing either. It smacks of *Candide*. A Frenchman who was called to court because the pickings were said to be good there could not even find it and spent months searching for it toward Turkey and Austria. When he did find it, he was named Director of Customs.

This was the first state Napoléon had invented, and he wanted it to have the advantages offered by the Napoleonic Code. When it came time for the first courts to sit, it was discovered that there was not a copy of the Napoleonic Code in all Westphalia, and justice had to be suspended until one could be sent from Paris. And so went most of the affairs of the new country, for everything had to be sent from Paris, including the King. It was difficult to rule, and to his credit, Jérôme did not try.

Instead he spent money.

The country was crippled by Napoléon's financial exactions and by levies of manpower. Jérôme did not help matters by giving his cronies from naval days estates, titles and allowances. He even invited Elizabeth to come. "I have no doubt Westphalia is a large kingdom, but it is not large enough for two Queens," replied Elizabeth. Napoléon, when he heard of this, decided she was worth her pension.

"You have allowed bills to be dishonored," snarled the Emperor. "And that is not the act of a man of honor. I never allow anyone to fail me. Sell your plate and diamonds. . . . Sell your furniture, your horses, and your jewels to pay your debts. Honor comes first of all!"

Jérôme's response was to buy more diamonds. He had some odd ways of raising money. One was firework displays, which were illegal in Westphalia. They were paid for out of the fines levied for having fired them. In six years he built up a national deficit of over 14,000,000 francs; out of a population of 2,000,000 he had supplied Napoléon with half a million recruits.

His civil list was set at 5,000,000 francs a year, drawn against his dotations.* Jérôme gave the dotations away to favorites. His own attention to the problem of ruling was confined to the compilation of an enormous folio entitled *Etiquette de la cour royale de Westphalie*. His pimp, Lécamus, was given a German title (Fürstenstein) which he could not pronounce. For some reason it always came out Furchetintin. He also received 40,000 francs a year and was made Minister of Foreign Affairs. Norvins, another time server, said, on the contrary, that he was minister of affairs that were foreign to him. This is perhaps the only surviving example of Westphalian wit.

---

* Dotations were the revenues, but almost invariably not the source from which such sums were drawn, settled by a ruling monarch upon those delegated to represent his authority, in order that they might maintain both their clerical staff, if they had one, and the proper splendor of their office. They took the form of such things as one-tenth the profits from farming the tobacco tax, a lien against postal charges, the privilege of selling certain offices, or hearth money. They were an inevitable source of personal and administrative corruption.

One of the councilors of state opened a bawdy house out of money made from the conscription he was supposed to direct. The money came from the sale of human substitutes. One of the military governors of the country was Rewbell, a potmate who had married a cousin of Miss Patterson.

The treasury was in good hands, too. One of Jérôme's mistresses had turned it over to Baron von Bülow, a man so lazy he had to be waked to sign documents. The treasury opened with a deficit of 6,000,000 francs and a debt to France of 26,000,000. Jérôme borrowed 2,000,000 from the Jews of Hesse (Jacobsohn was his chief creditor), but spent 850,000 of that sum on coronation robes. And so it went, most of it on his mistresses, of whom he had a great many.

Another expense was the private theater. It cost 500,000 francs a year, or one-fifth the national revenues. Its director, Blangini, once pleased Jérôme by putting on a stark naked operetta. It was called *The Comic Shipwreck*. He did not go unrewarded. Life in Westphalia was so irregular that one night Jérôme was arrested for drunkenness by his own police.

Catherine, like the rest of the family, called her husband Fifi. Fifi called her Trinette. Sometimes Trinette liked to appear at court balls disguised as an American Indian squaw. She also began to spend money as freely as her husband did. She ordered gowns by the dozen from LeRoy, the first of the great men milliners, statues from Elisa's workshops at Carrara (these *had* to be paid for), furniture by Jacob, and some special merino sheep from Rambouillet to decorate the grounds of Napoleonshöhe, the palace, which promptly caught fire and burned down. Jérôme merely requisitioned a street, blocked off both ends, threw the houses together, and took up residence there.

The Rewbells, sensing that the ship of state was about to sink, departed for America, leaving behind them very large debts. "My poor Betsy," wrote Mrs. Rewbell to Mme Bonaparte, "it would be better if your husband were dead." La Flèche, Baron von Keudelstein, absconded with what was left of the year's civil list, some 1,600,000 francs.

In 1812 came preparations for the invasion of Russia, and Jérôme was ordered along. God knows why, but he expected to be made King of Poland. So the last months of 1811 and the first of 1812 were spent squandering what remaining revenues Westphalia had. Everybody got something. Lécamus got the most (200,000 francs). On New Year's Eve there was a lottery of jewelry. Catherine bought

35

another 200,000 francs worth of dresses from LeRoy, and Jérôme gave her a pair of diamond earrings worth 100,000.

Jérôme's notions of how to march to war included a wardrobe filling seven wagons, sixty pairs of boots, 200 shirts, 318 silk handkerchiefs, bedding, toilet services, and several cases of Eau de Cologne. There were wagons of furniture, and one for the dinner service, a chef, silver-lined saucepans, a *batterie de cuisine*, a complete staff, and his own waiters. One wagon contained nothing but military and civil decorations and ornamental swords. He took deerskin drapes for his beds, dressing gowns, bathrobes, a silver chamberpot, and an auxiliary mistress, Mlle Alexander, whom he had married off to Escalon, a functionary in his Ministry of War. He took with him his secretaries, his physician, and a personal staff. Even when making a rapid inspection, he never traveled with less than six carriages.

Somehow he reached Warsaw, where he set up housekeeping in the Brühl palace. He was twenty-seven. "If he had a little more legitimate claim to royalty and a little less boyish vanity, he might have passed for a distinguished prince," said the Abbé de Pradt, Napoléon's Ambassador to the Grand Duchy of Warsaw. Napoléon was even more acid. "I said to him, if you intend to go to the army as a king you had better remain at home. Why, then, has he come? He had only to remain at home."

Catherine had been left behind as Regent, though nobody ever told her what was happening or asked her advice as to what to do next. At last she demanded to see the national accounts, and when she did see them she took to her bed, weeping, and would speak to no one.

Jérôme was not a success as a soldier. It was necessary to put Davout over him, with secret instructions to countermand anything the King of Westphalia might see fit to order done. Jérôme deserted in a huff, marching off with his personal guard, leaving behind him some 25,000 Westphalians in Russia, of whom 2,500 survived, though only as prisoners at Danzig and Küstrin. He reached Napoleonshöhe on August 11, at night. "My health," he explained to Catherine, "could not withstand the climate." And he began to plan his coronation, which had been omitted so far. He ordered a royal crown in brilliants and negotiated with Amsterdam for some diamonds, turquoises, and emeralds. At this time he had three mistresses and was planning to divorce Catherine in order to marry the Countess of Löwenstein-Wertheim, though he was temporarily saddened by the death of his illegitimate child, Elisa, to whom his wife had stood as godmother. Another of his mistresses, the Baroness von Keudelstein, ran away with Catherine's brother, Paul of Württemberg (her husband, it will be remembered, had fled with the civil list a year before).

Undeterred by these complications, Jérôme took the time to erect a statue to Napoléon on November 12, 1812. It was dedicated to The Founder.

1813 was the year of Napoléon's military and political collapse. Jérôme proposed to build an opera house, financed by the contents of the Westphalian war chest. Though convinced the Westphalians truly loved him, he had the sense to send Catherine on ahead to France. But this may only have been because his newest mistress demanded her removal. He then fled himself, with hasty pomp, toward the French border. But he did not immediately cross it. He wished to remain King as long as possible, though a traveler who saw him and his retinue at this time said the Westphalian court in exile resembled nothing so much as a bunch of broken-down actors carousing in a barn.

"Surely," said Reinhard, Napoléon's special envoy in such emergencies, "Your Majesty is not reigning here?"

"Yes, I am a sovereign here just as I was at Kassel," said Jérôme, and bade Reinhard, if he had anything to propose, to see the Westphalian Minister for Foreign Affairs (Lécamus).

Catherine and a suite of forty had arrived in France in March of 1813. She had no money. The Emperor finally agreed to support her on the understanding that all bills would be sent to Kassel. She was relegated to Meudon, but did not like it there and made a round of country-house visits. Mortefontaine pleased her best. Otherwise she stayed with Mme Mère or Cardinal Fesch.

Jérôme had acted through the banker Perregaux, and with the proceeds from Westphalia, he bought two domains in France (which he reached on November 14, 1813, followed by the tatterdemalion Westphalian court). One of these was Villandry, in Touraine, the other Stains, near St. Denis and noted for the beauty of its park. The latter Catherine pretended to have bought for herself, in order to avert Napoléon's rage. The ruse did not succeed.

"I am indignant that, when everyone must sacrifice his interests to the defense of the country, a King who has lost his throne has so little tact as to buy estates and to thus seem not to care for anything but his own interests," wrote Napoléon. In addition it was pointed out to Jérôme that *foreign* princes were not allowed to own property in France (legally, Joseph had made Mortefontaine over to Julie).

He was allowed to join Catherine at Compiègne, which pleased him so much that Catherine at last became pregnant, though of course the Löwenstein was along too.

So was the rest of the Westphalian court. Jérôme gave dinners, played tennis, went hunting, and paid state visits to Mortefontaine. Compiègne, the château and all its contents, were Napoléon's property, which is to say they belonged to the French Crown. In order to pay his expenses, Jérôme gave his court carte blanche to sell whatever they pleased. The Governor of the Château tried to intervene, but conditions in France were now so chaotic that there was not much he could do.

He was making his own preparations. As early as the previous November he had asked Catherine to suggest to her father, the King of Württemberg, that no matter what happened, he should intercede to save Jérôme, who, moreover, demanded indemnities for the occupation of Westphalia. Meanwhile he moved to Stains, where he had a gang of workmen making repairs. But looting went on as usual, and Stains was very cold. So he and Catherine moved once more, this time into Cardinal Fescsh's house in Paris (Fesch was in Lyons). Jérôme said he wished to assist Marie Louise in a regency. Napoléon forbade her even to receive him and ordered Jérôme to dismiss his Westphalian court. Jérôme consented at the most merely to diminish it. He would, however, assist Joseph to defend the capital, he said.

But somehow Jérôme did not seem the right man to be trusted to govern Paris. Napoléon snubbed him. Catherine began to pack.

The fourth brother was Lucien, always credited with being the most brilliant of the lot. If so, it was a brilliance which came to very little. He was an orator who had laid the foundations of his fortune during an embassy to Spain and enhanced it remarkably when Minister of the Interior, by the sale of land and concessions to trade in Louisiana, whose sale to America he therefore opposed and never forgave Napoléon for. His brilliance certainly does not appear in his two epic poems, his novel, his plays, or his autobiography. Perhaps his most enduring contribution was to Etruscology. This consisted chiefly of his having the ancient town of Verulonia on his Italian property and from time to time digging out a tomb. He certainly found some splendid things in this way.

Lucien's chief literary monument was an epic poem, *Charlemagne*, published in 1811 and dedicated to Pope Pius VII. Here are two samples from Canto X, stanzas xlvii and xlviii, in the version of the Reverend S. Butler, D.D., who succeeded to the Reverend Francis Hodgson, A.M., who died while trying to translate it.

> Howe'er the struggle of our valour speeds,
> Our bloody wars are not thy children's deeds.

> When conquest makes the Neustrian realm our own,
> Plain is their passage to their father's throne:
> A child of Carloman may guiltless be,
> Yet take Austrasia's diadem from me. . . .
> Still would I ne'er thy bosom's wish constrain;
> Free, though protected, in my camp remain;
> Thyself decide the tenour of thy fate,
> And let thy choice on time and conquest wait:
> I will restore thee to thy rightful land;
> In all the rest I follow thy command.

In his preface, the Reverend S. Butler informs us that he hesitated, in translating, between the styles of Dryden and Pope, and would have preferred that of Dryden, but that the Reverend Francis Hodgson had commenced in the vein of Pope, and that it seemed wiser to go on that way. The original, except for a different rhyme scheme, has no style at all but is sheer fudge all the way. And so, it is to be feared, was Lucien. In 1814 he was thirty-nine.

Jérôme was an extravagant incompetent. Louis was a contumacious invalid. Joseph was of a saving disposition and of a prudence unsuited to military life. Lucien's contribution to the family amity was an excessive uxoriousness and a complacent sense of self-congratulated virtue. He produced fourteen children by two wives and was devoted to all of them. He was also jealous and envious of the Emperor, to whom he liked to give advice and toward whom he felt superior, both in accomplishment and intellect.

One of his fancies was to give people neoclassical names. It was he who persuaded his sister Maria-Annunziata to become Caroline. For a while he was himself Brutus. While Brutus, he had married Catherine Boyer, whom he called Christine. She was the illiterate daughter of the man who kept an inn where he had been staying. Christine had a good character and an unruffled disposition, and, moreover, died on May 14, 1800, before Napoléon's Imperial ambitions had got the best of him.

In 1803, when Napoléon was already First Consul and planning to make himself Emperor, Lucien was secretly married to Marie Alexandrine Jouberthou, the widow of a speculator who, upon becoming bankrupt, had removed himself to Santo Domingo, leaving Mme Jouberthou behind. At the time of the marriage-christening (Lucien had begotten a son upon her, as was his habit), proof that M. Jouberthou was dead was still lacking. As a matter of fact it was later proved that he had died June 15, 1802, which was convenient, considering the circumstances.

Napoléon had been planning to marry Lucien to the Queen of Etruria (a Spanish Infanta). The first marriage had been religious and secret, but in October Lucien went through another and this time civil marriage to Alexandrine. This, unlike the other, could not be kept from the First Consul.

There was a family war. Nor did Lucien always express himself tactfully. When Napoléon taunted him with having married a widow, he said, "Maybe. So did you. But mine is not old and smelly." This reference to Joséphine was neither welcomed nor forgotten. Napoléon sent Lucien into exile, to Rome, though with an introduction to Pius VII, saying that he was to "devote himself to the study of antiquities and history."

"I am going away with hatred in my heart," said Lucien.

After tempers had cooled, Napoléon, who needed the one intelligent member of the family badly, was willing to do anything within reason to win his support. He offered not once but many times to allow Lucien to live morganatically with Mme Jouberthou, if only he would divorce her and make a marriage more suitable, and also more useful, to the newfound Imperial dignity.

But Lucien, a prickly as well as a huffy man, stood upon his dignity. He backed Jérôme's American marriage. He fired off ultimatums. He made himself comfortable. In 1806 he offered a large loan to Pius VII. Pius refused, but said that the money would be welcome

40

as the purchase price of the lands and fief of Canino. The money and the fief changed hands. Lucien was rich enough to have his own theater and picture gallery, and the exploitation of the ironworks and mineral springs, not to say antiquities, on his new properties made him even richer. He bought the Palazzo Nuñez in Rome. He had a villa at Frascati. He began his epic poem, of which the hero was not Charlemagne but Pope Leo III. It was a *roman à clef*, with Pius VII as Leo and Napoleon as the first Holy Roman Emperor.

When his uncle, Cardinal Fesch, proposed a reconciliation with the Emperor, Lucien asked, "Have you forgotten all honor, all religion? . . . Spare me the useless insult of your cowardly advice. In a word don't write to me again until religion and honor, which you are now trampling under foot, have dissipated your blindness. At least hide your base sentiments under your purple robes, and follow in silence your own path along the highway of ambitions."

All the Bonapartes had a vivid epistolary style.

In February of 1808 French troops occupied Rome. This made Lucien's position difficult. He borrowed 600,000 francs from his brothers and spoke of going to America.

"Let him go," said Napoléon. "Otherwise he may expect to be arrested with his wife and children and to die in prison. If I once take rigorous measures, there will be no resource left for him. It will be called tyranny, but what matters what men say?" He then allowed two sets of passports to be made out for Lucien, allowing him, his family, and his household to leave the Empire. At any rate he knew this had been done and himself did nothing to interfere.

Lucien left for Cagliari on August 7, on an American ship, the *Hercules*, accompanied by his wife, five daughters, three sons, a doctor, the Abbé Malvestito, a tutor, an artist, his secretary, and twenty-seven servants. His art collection was in the hold.

It could scarcely be called a clandestine escape. Sardinia was in the hands not of its king, but of the British navy. Neither the British nor the Americans at that time recognized the sanctity of a neutral flag (they were not officially to do so until 1856). So instead of proceeding from Cagliari to Corsica (his avowed destination) or America, Lucien was packed off to Malta instead.

This may neither have altogether surprised nor displeased him, but his quarters at the Malta lazaretto did. He was allowed to remove to the Castle of St. Anthony, where he remained until the end of the year. Then the British shipped him off to Plymouth, a voyage which in the winter months took six seasick weeks (all the Bonapartes were bad sailors).

The party arrived off Plymouth on December 12, but could not land because of the rough seas. Lucien and his family landed December 13. His reply to the state messenger authorized to grant him asylum was very much of a piece with his replies to everybody. "I have been made a prisoner illegally and I protest against everything which myself and my family have undergone since we quitted the port of Cagliari! I demand to be allowed to resume my journey, and beyond that, Sir, I refuse all the offers of your government, for I can accept nothing from a nation which is the enemy of mine, nor from a government that makes war upon my brother." There was loud cheering, and he put up for the time being at the King's Arms. He had the offer of a country house and was to be watched only so closely as was necessary to prevent his leaving the country.

His revolt against his brother (Lucien would have revolted against anybody) had made him a national hero to the British. At the hotel he accepted for the time being Ludlow Castle, near Salop, at a nominal rent. His landlord was Lord Powis, who was delighted, as a fellow liberal, to have him.

Napoléon, less pleased, struck Lucien's name from the list of French Senators, cut off his French revenues, and outlawed him from France. When Lucien needed money, Mme Mère sent it to him through agents, a form of contraband at which Napoléon winked. Officially it was sent to a Mr. Douglas.

After a short stay at Ludlow Castle, Lucien bought Thorngrove, in Worcestershire. He paid 18,000 guineas for it and furnished it from the *bric-a-brac* he had brought with him, for Napoléon refused to allow the rest of his art collections to be sent on to him.

Here he remained for the rest of the war. He published his first epic and began a second, about the liberation of Corsica from the Moors. "It would be to *Charlemagne* what Homer's *Odyssey* was to his *Iliad*," he said. He was quite wrong. His poverty was relative, since he was able to pay 50,000 francs for a telescope. He corresponded with Herschel. His wife wrote an epic, too. Hers was about St. Clotilda, the Christian who was Queen to Clovis the Frank. It was intended as a surprise.

He lived the life of an English country gentleman, and found it very dull. Surrounded by admirers, he amused himself with amateur theatricals (in every sense—he wrote the plays himself). In late 1813 he offered to escape and come to Napoléon's assistance, but was neither encouraged nor allowed to do so.

That left Napoléon Joseph, as the best of a dubious lot.

T HE problem was to find some member of the family sufficiently trustworthy to act as Governor of Paris in his absence, and to supervise the Regency of Marie Louise. And there was not much time.

Napoléon was the first and certainly the best of the modern dictators, but this did not prevent him from falling victim to the limitations of the type, nor from being overtaken by the madness of the Caesars. He did not know how to govern the world which he had overrun. He could control the army, but he was afraid of the people and had no knowledge of diplomacy or economics whatsoever. Metternich simply outmaneuvered him, and the British, Prussians and Russians so summoned and at last united pounded him to bits.

Around 1809 or 1810 he became corpulent and epicene, though he was only forty. Worst of all, his powers of rapid decision disappeared. Rage replaced punishment, and petulance pride. He could still pull himself together when he had to. But had he still possessed his earlier suppleness, he would not have had to so often.

In addition, he had lost his army in Russia and had very few reserves, either of manpower or of weaponry. And his treasury was close to bankrupt. His marshals were now middle-aged men, longing to retire. And he had traitors in his own government, the most eminent being Talleyrand and Fouché. Talleyrand had been out of office for some years and wished to restore the Bourbons in order to get in again. Fouché, the Minister of Police, agreed with the Vicar of Bray and acted accordingly. He was not so much a traitor as a realist.

Meanwhile, Metternich, somewhat helped by Napoléon's illusion that Austria would never turn against him, since he had an Austrian bride, was carefully arranging the Allies against him. This took him six months. After that, Napoléon was simply outclassed, and his descent became inevitable.

On May 2, 1813, he managed to defeat the Allied armies at Lützen. This so terrified the Austrian Emperor that an armistice was agreed upon on June 4, to run until July 20. Napoléon was offered France's natural territorial limits. Had he accepted, he would not only have defeated Metternich's schemes, but kept his own seat. He did not accept, because he wanted Belgium. On August 11 Austria declared war on Napoléon. On October 17, the Allies won the battle of Leipzig. Since nobody wanted to be confronted with an occupied France, particularly not Metternich, who hoped to use France as a possible threat to the power of Czar Alexander, Napoléon was now offered the natural boundaries of the Rhine, the Alps, and the Pyrenees, Spain to be restored and Holland (at Great Britain's adamant request) independent. This offer was made on October 29. Napoléon did not answer until November 23 and then evaded all reference to the Allied conditions but suggested a congress at Mannheim. On November 25, Metternich replied that nothing could be done unless the proposals of October 29 were accepted. Caulaincourt, Napoléon's new Minister of Foreign Affairs, accepted them on December 2, but it was then too late. His note was merely forwarded to London, for Metternich now had the coalition he required to assure his own direction of the Allied diplomatic negotiations.

On February 3, 1814, the Congress of Châtillon-sur-Seine opened. At this time it was thought that the Allies could reach Paris in two weeks. They had crossed the Rhine at Christmas, 1813. Bernadotte invaded Holland and what is now Belgium. Napoléon had 70,000 men against 260,000. As Mme Mère wrote to Cardinal Fesch, "This is no time to cling to etiquette. The Bourbons lost all through not knowing how to die fighting."

Pozzo di Borgo, an old Corsican enemy of the Bonapartes, now adviser to the Czar, said, "While you go on thinking in terms of battles you run the risk of being defeated, because Napoléon will always be able to fight better than you, and because his army, although dissatisfied, will always be inspired by honor and will fight to the last man as long as he is at hand. . . . But his political power has been destroyed. Times have changed. . . . Touch Paris with a finger and the colossus Napoléon will come tumbling down."

On March 3, the Congress of Châtillon proposed the pre-Revolutionary boundaries of France as a basis for a possible treaty. On the 9th, Caulaincourt accepted them. On the 12th, Napoléon defeated Blücher. Now the Czar pressed for an armistice, but Napoléon decided to ignore what Caulaincourt had done.

Still bent on preventing the Czar from entering Paris and not wishing to overthrow French sovereignty, Metternich urged Napoléon to reach a speedy decision, saying that it was not easy to control 50,000 Cossacks. The Allies demanded a definite reply by March 10.

Neither Metternich nor Caulaincourt could talk Napoléon around. "Are there no means to enlighten [Napoléon] about his situation?" asked Metternich. "Has he irrevocably placed his fate and that of his son on the carriage of his last gun? If the Emperor of Austria could cede Tirol in 1809, why can Napoléon not cede Belgium in 1814?"

Napoléon replied, through Caulaincourt, on March 15, but by then Blücher had defeated Napoléon at Laon on March 9, and the Allies, by the Treaty of Chaumont of March 4, had agreed to prosecute the war in France, if no answer were forthcoming by the 10th, each of them putting 150,000 men in the field for twenty years, if need be, Great Britain alone reserving the right to pay a sizable subsidy instead.

On March 25 Caulaincourt at last agreed to come to the Allied camp to negotiate, but by then it was finally too late. All efforts to make peace had been broken off on the 17th. And on March 20 and 22, the Bourbons were hauled from their bolt holes (though Louis XVIII was still in England). On the 24th Bordeaux went over to them, and the Allies promised to turn over to them the revenues of any province that joined them.

This was Metternich's timetable, by and large planned well in advance, in curious detail, and entirely successful. Napoléon had no timetable. For once events were happening to him, not he to them.

In late October and in November and December of 1813, he tried to bring Joseph round to his own way of thinking. This turned out not to be easy. Joseph was still maintaining a royal court at Mortefontaine. Though not so peculiar as his brother Jérôme's, it had its oddities.

Julie, too, in a quiet way, had had her lovers, but she was extremely discreet. The oddities at Mortefontaine were all domestic. The household consisted of Julie, her daughters, and her sister, Desirée Bernadotte, Crown Princess of Sweden. (Bernadotte himself was marching with the Allies, and had been suggested by the Czar as a possible King of France after Napoléon.) Other residents included the Spanish Grand Inquisitor (though Joseph had abolished the Spanish Inquisition), various Spanish nobility in exile, and Julie's brother, Nicolas Clary, who ran his banking establishments at Paris, Marseilles and Genoa from the house, with the assistance of a full business staff.

Sometimes he would run up to town to visit his mistress, the Marqueza de Monte Hermoso, who was in exile in Paris and who would shortly have to go into exile again.

Joseph was determined to keep his crown. Napoléon regarded pomp as a branch of propaganda and no more, and, as long as he might go first, had no interest in precedence whatsoever. He was willing to allow his brothers to keep their titles as kings, but sensibly insisted that since they had lost their kingdoms, it should not be specified over what.

Moreover he had to disembarrass himself of Spain, as soon as possible, if he were not to have to fight on two fronts. Soult, who had taken over after Joseph's flight, suggested the restoration of Ferdinand VII, with the possible understanding that this degenerate and corrupt prince should marry one of Joseph's daughters.

Napoléon did not speak to Joseph about this. He spoke to Julie, who could both reason and be reasoned with. She had never had any desire to see Madrid. Joseph unfortunately wished to see it again.

"The people don't want him. They know how incapable he is," said Napoléon.

On November 27 the Emperor told Joseph what was being done in Spain and why. To his astonishment, Joseph refused to accept what were, after all, facts. He really did believe there was a party in Spain devoted to him, whereas of course all the Spaniards devoted to him had followed him to Mortefontaine.

Without waiting for Joseph to abdicate, Napoléon signed the Treaty of Valençay on December 11. This restored Ferdinand VII on the understanding that he later marry Zenaïde, Joseph's thirteen-year-old daughter.

Louis now announced that he, rather than the Prince of Orange-Nassau, should represent Holland at the coming peace congress. He said he could not believe Napoléon would prefer a foreign prince to his own brother. He received no reply.

Napoléon concentrated on Joseph. The Allied armies had crossed the Rhine; the Prussians under von Bülow and the Cossacks under the Czar were the most to be feared; and Napoléon would have to leave Paris to defend France. The Empress Marie Louise would have to preside over a Council of Regency, but somebody had to preside over her.

Napoléon's opinion of women was not high, but Marie Louise, on whom he convinced himself to dote, was among his disasters. The doting arose from the fact that she was a Hapsburg, that she was the mother of his son, and that she was the first virgin he had ever deflowered. He also had several reasons for avoiding her. She kept her bedroom so cold that he did not like to go into it, since he was hypersensitive to any temperature lower than that of a furnace. And though he did not care for intellectual women, there are limits the other way, even so. There is not much to be said for a woman who has gone down to posterity as the name of a picture mat (the kind that has watercolor bands around the opening).

In 1814 Marie Louise was twenty-four and her father's eldest and favorite child (the Emperor Francis's favorite *occupation* was boiling toffee on the back of a stove).

The Hapsburgs did not so much conquer territory as marry it. Their princesses were therefore raised to be good breeders and very little else. The Hapsburgs were given to ostentate only on public occasions: their private life was thrifty, prim, and if not proper, at least dull. They were the most middle-class of princes.

There was therefore a lot of cant in Marie Louise's makeup. She was the first Victorian. All male animals were kept out of her presence when she was a child, all references to the sexual act were cut from any book she might choose to read. Her favorite companions, until her mid-teens, had been several pet ducks. It was difficult to wean her away from them. She had no mental interests of any kind, but was good at languages, being fluent in German, French, and Italian. She was inordinately fond of overeating and liked picnics. What she did *not* like was people.

Her French doctors had trouble in explaining to Napoléon that her frequent morning sickness was not pregnancy, but nausea from her habit of gorging herself on whole platters of French pastry with whipped cream.

Her religious education had been deliberately neglected, so that should she have to marry a Protestant prince, she would feel no painful Catholic anguish and thus cause no partisan pain.

She had several traits which were to cause Napoléon pain later. The foremost of these was that she was always obedient and loyal, but to her father, no one else. Another was that she attached herself like a limpet to any man in her immediate vicinity, and though loyal also to him, the loyalty ceased as soon as the man in question was definitely removed. A third was a self-willed, blind hauteur arising from the conviction that whatever she did, though it might not be right, was assuredly never wrong. She was pleased to report to her father, shortly after her marriage, that though nervous at first, she had had no real trouble in making Napoléon afraid of her.

It is somewhat difficult to determine her appearance, for her state portraits were either flattering (if by Gérard) or rather badly drawn (if by Isabey). She had a large jaw, the Hapsburg lip, a nose somewhat too long, an excellent figure (soon ruined by overeating), blond hair, and a pink and white complexion. Her eyes were a Saxon blue, but protuberant. The general effect was of a silly, shallow, vain, and ostentatious woman, willful, shy, awkward, reserved, yet, at unexpected times, gushy.

She did not like babies, and the crime of *lèse-majesté* was seldom far from her mind. She was totally irresponsible, since life for her consisted of the proper forms at the proper times, and nothing more.

She had been told since childhood that Napoléon was the Antichrist and seems to have been agreeably relieved, when she met him, to find that he was not. "I am deeply grateful to him and I respond sincerely to his love. I find that he gains considerably by close acquaintance; there is something very captivating and forceful about him which it is impossible to resist. . . . I cannot thank God enough for granting me such great happiness, and you, dear Papa, for not listening to my entreaties at Ofen," she wrote. He was her first man. Once she had acquired the taste, he was not to be her last.

"She's a beautiful princess," said a spectator, when she drove into Paris on April 2, 1810 (a Monday). "And it touches your heart to see her riding in her carriage with her old governess."

The old governess was Napoléon, wearing the wrong hat. He was extremely jealous of her and kept her as much as possible from male company (he even went so far, eventually, as to suspect Joseph of attempting to seduce her). She was thus locked up with Mme de Montebello most of the time, a pit viper of a woman but her only confidante. Mme de Montebello's chief interests in the world were a rigid etiquette, and her own lover.

Nonetheless, though Marie Louise hated hot rooms and Napoléon could not abide cold, somehow the result was the birth of the King of Rome, after a long and difficult delivery, on March 20, 1811.

"If God has damned the world, then a Bonaparte will not lack a successor, but if, on the contrary, the Divine wrath abates, all the brats on earth cannot save the temple of iniquity from destruction," said the future Louis XVIII, in England, where he was living in exile, when he heard of it.

The Bonapartes did not approve either. It knocked them out of the succession. Apart from this, the King of Rome was popular. No one objects to a royal child. A color for suitings became popular among dandies called *caca de Roi de Rome*. It varied, depending upon whether he had had his spinach or not. Joséphine sent a note to Napoléon to say her sacrifice had not been in vain. 2,526 people received money from the Imperial treasury, to pay for their own wet nurses.

The marriage, however, was not popular. Napoléon got up a stiff Spanish court ceremonial. People preferred the old regime under Joséphine, and Marie Louise hated any public occasion and stayed away as much as possible. She was sometimes tactless and often rude. She had a nasal whining voice, and her habit of calling the Emperor Nana or Popo could not always have charmed him. She was far cheaper to maintain than Joséphine had been, but not nearly so entertaining. She was a hypochondriac, and, like her husband, found it pleasant to soak in hot water. Then there was her aversion to babies.

"Come now, give the child a kiss," said the Emperor once. "I don't know how anybody can kiss a baby," said Marie Louise, and wiped her mouth. She also had the unflattering habit of wiping her mouth after the Emperor had kissed her.

She spent half an hour with the child, in the morning and afternoon, and found it pointless and fatiguing. She was also so lazy that she refused to get up at night to go to the bathroom. The chamberpot, in agate, had to be brought to her. Napoléon visited her at night less and less. At what hours she used her gold tongue scraper we are not told.

She found the burdens of 1813 very heavy. "When you are tired you have to hold a reception; when you want to cry you have to laugh; and even so nobody sympathizes with you."

Whatever her other merits, she was not the woman to be left unguided to preside over a government. But Joseph would not be useful either, unless he stopped calling himself King of a country to which Napoléon must give up all claims if he was to have peace.

On December 27, 1813, Julie and Mme Mère drove down to Mortefontaine. The matter of Joseph's abdication was passed over. He was asked now only to come to Paris as a French Prince, to go to the Luxembourg Palace, his official seat as Grand Elector of the Empire, and to send Napoléon a publishable letter which would announce his arrival.

Joseph had to think it over. On the 29th he wrote Napoléon, "Brought back as I have been to France by the course of events, I shall be happy if I can be of any service," he said, but added, "I know, also, Sire, what I owe to Spain." Fortunately he had brought his Minister of Foreign Affairs with him into exile. Let Napoléon negotiate, then, with the Duke of Santa Fé.

Meanwhile, Napoléon, whose idea of good government was to give orders, was having trouble with the Corps Législatif, whose notion of good legislature was not to obey them. Both houses demanded constitutional reforms. He decided to prorogue them. Joseph offered to come, but on January 2 (when the Allied armies were well across the Rhine), he wrote that he could appear only as the King of Spain, since he had not yet abdicated formally and could not abdicate until a general peace had been declared.

Probably as a result of Julie's persuasions, Joseph came up to Paris on January 5, to the Luxembourg. From there he wrote the Emperor still another letter, saying that, though he had in no way modified his attitude, he wished to be where he could be of service.

Napoléon applied cold water. "You are no longer King of Spain. I have no need of your renunciation. . . . What do you mean to do? Are you willing to take your place beside my throne as a French Prince? You will have my friendship, your income from the civil list, and your position as my subject and a Prince of the reigning family. . . . Can it be that you have not enough sound judgment to take this course? In that case you will have to go to some château in the provinces, forty leagues away from Paris, and live there in obscurity.

If I survive, you will live there quietly. If I die, you will be killed or arrested. . . . Choose at once and take your course."

Joseph, by way of reply, insisted that if he abdicated he would expose the Spaniards who had followed him to France to an unprotected existence. At this point his secretary, Miot, suggested that the Spaniards who had followed him be asked how they felt. Julie, who was Queen of Spain if Joseph was King, was to be present.

A formal council was held, with Julie presiding beside Joseph, her first and last appearance as Queen of Spain. The Spaniards advised the King to do as he had been told. He wrote a publishable letter. "As the first of French Princes, and thereby the first of your subjects, allow me, Sire, to beg you to accept the offer of my hand and my counsels." He asked no favor other than that the relief of his refugees should be administered by the Duke of Santa Fé and that he be allowed to keep the French and Spanish officers who had been loyal to him on his personal staff. One of these officers was a Spanish artilleryman, Colonel de Montijo, whose daughter was later to marry Napoléon III.

On the 9th the two brothers had an interview, at which it was settled that Joseph should keep the title of King and that his uniform should now be that of an officer of the Imperial Guard. On the 16th he gave a reception at the Luxembourg and so formally resumed his old rank of First Prince of the Empire. There was little of the Empire left: Blücher was at Toul, with 30,000 men; by the 20th, Schwarzenberg was close to Langres, advancing on Bar-sur-Aube; Bülow in the Netherlands; and of the Russians, Winzegerode at Aix-la-Chapelle and Wittgenstein near Nancy.

Nor were events in Italy more reassuring. Prince Eugène, at Turin, could be counted on. But Fouché was in Tuscany, trying to persuade Elisa, the Grand Duchess, to desert to the Allies. "The only thing that could save us all would be the Emperor's death," he told her.

Pauline was in the south of France, but Mme Mère was worried about her. "I'm rather concerned at the thought of your being in a place just now so close to the enemy's lines." Cardinal Fesch was trembling in his diocese, at Lyons. The Emperor told him to stay there until the enemy should come too close, at which he was to withdraw to the farthest extremity of the diocese. Actually he joined Mme Mère in Paris. She would have preferred that he fight. "Try to

52

let Pauline know that it's urgent for her to leave the place where she is now."

But it was useless to tell Pauline anything. In November she had offered the Emperor 300,000 francs, but he had not accepted them. Now she sent her jewels to Mme Mère for safekeeping.

"I wish you could so contrive that the Emperor should learn, but indirectly and quite casually, about the losses I have incurred. Emphasize that I ask for nothing," she wrote to Decazes, who helped handle her affairs in Paris. Since she found the news upsetting, she forbade her suite to discuss anything but her health. Whenever the Emperor had a slight success, the guns of Nice were fired. She began to pare her budget, dismissed her surgeon, her private secretary, and the curator of her picture gallery (she had seized part of the Borghese collections, but otherwise never bought any picture unless it was of herself), two grooms and two lackeys, cut back her stable to nineteen horses, and decided to spend no more than 6,000 francs a month on new dresses. Even so, her household expenses were still 500,000 francs for the year. She wrote that her valuables should have been put with the crown jewels. "That would have been the only sensible thing."

Prince Eugène, too, had had his offer. His father-in-law, the King of Bavaria, had written the previous November, offering to protect his interests in Italy and to guarantee him a crown if he would desert Napoléon.

"I am indeed sorry to have to refuse the King," wrote Eugène. "It is not to be denied that the Emperor's star is beginning to wane, but this is only one additional reason why those who have received benefits from him should remain faithful to him." To Napoléon, he commented, "I had a sufficiently high opinion of the King of Bavaria to be sure in advance that he would prefer to find his son-in-law a simple but honest citizen rather than a king and a traitor."

Unexpectedly, this turned out to be true.

Hortense was in Paris; the ex-Empress Joséphine, now Duchess of Navarre, was at Malmaison, making lint bandages for the hospitals, protected by a guard of sixteen wounded men. Sometimes Marie Louise sent on to her (but only through an intermediary) the Emperor's letters.

The Beauharnais could be counted upon. Caroline, Napoléon's most ambitious sister and, as Mme Murat, Queen of Naples, could not. Through Metternich, who had once been her lover, she negotiated to keep her kingdom by going over to the Allied side. She was successful. On January 11, 1814, a treaty was signed, agreed to by England, whereby Murat agreed to turn over 30,000 troops to the Coalition, in return for a promise from Austria that he might keep his throne.

It had not been easy. She had had to provide Murat with a starch his character did not in itself contain, and he had been difficult to control.

Murat, born 1771 at La Bastide, the son of a Gascon innkeeper and estate agent to the Talleyrands, was romantic to look at and romantic by nature. He was also the best man in Europe to lead a cavalry charge, but his abilities ceased there. He was one of those animals in human form who periodically run amok. He was inordinately vain, and dressed accordingly. One of his favorite getups was a gilt jacket, yellow tights, and yellow boots, the whole surmounted by white plumes, for which he had a passion. However, unlike Jérôme, he was not merely a clotheshorse, he was the horse itself.

Caroline, who according to Talleyrand "had the head of a Cromwell on the shoulders of a pretty woman," had been married to him since 1800 and in 1808 had contrived to have him made King Joachim I of Naples. As usual, Napoléon tried to run the kingdom. There were also domestic problems. Murat was unfaithful to Caroline, and she was spectacularly unfaithful to him. She was also so bossy a woman that for a time he had her secluded at Caserta. But he could never do without her for long. When Napoléon discovered that Murat had stolen the Spanish crown jewels, Caroline had to be dispatched to Paris to explain. (She returned most of them.)

Naples is an extremely agreeable place, and the Murats had had six years in which to enjoy it. If all else failed, there was always the joy of restoring Pompeii (the Murats kept 500 workmen there, whereas the Bourbon King Ferdinand had had only the means for fifty).

Russia had been a shock to Murat (he had decamped). The battle of Leipzig was an even worse one. It also presented him with a dilemma he could not himself solve. On the one hand, he had his own code of ethics and did not wish to be *thought* a traitor. On the other, he had his own kingdom and did not wish to lose it. Caroline came to his assistance.

When Murat abandoned his post in Russia, Napoléon wrote, "He is a brave man on the battlefield, but feebler than a woman or a monk when the enemy is not in sight. He has no moral courage." This letter was to Caroline. To Murat himself he said, "The title of King has turned your head. If you desire to preserve it—this title—you will have to conduct yourself differently from what you have done up to the present."

So, under Caroline's tutelage, he did. Metternich, as it happened, was not eager to see a Bourbon restoration at Naples. He preferred to leave the Bourbons in Sicily. Murat was to be compensated for Sicily with territory taken from the Papal States, of not less than 400,000 inhabitants.

There was only one snag. Though England was willing to connive at this, the English Ambassador to, and Commander in Chief of British Forces in Sicily, Lord William Bentinck, refused to obey the orders of his own government and would not sign the agreement. Lord William Bentinck was a difficult man for anyone to deal with, and his plan seems to have been that Ferdinand of the Two Sicilies should return to Naples, but cede Sicily to Britain in return for war aid, so that Bentinck might rule it as Viceroy.

Nonetheless, the treaty had at least been signed with Austria. If the treachery involved disturbed Napoléon, it seems to have upset Murat even more. Or so, at any rate, says Mme Récamier, who was staying in Naples with Caroline at the time.

Murat burst into the room, rushed up to Juliette, took both her hands, and asked her if she thought he had done right.

"Sire, you are a Frenchman. It is to France you owe allegiance," said Mme Récamier.

"Then I am a traitor," shouted the King. He opened the window, pointed to the British ships entering the bay, and burst into tears.

"Joachim, in the name of Heaven, be silent, or at least lower your voice," ordered Caroline. "In the next room there are a hundred ears ready to catch anything you say. Be silent. Have you lost all self-control?" She then gave him a glass of orange water flavored with ether. "Compose yourself, Murat. Remember what you are. You are King of Naples."

Joachim drank the infusion and then left the room to dry his eyes. Caroline turned to Mme Récamier. "You see," she explained, weeping herself, "I am obliged to have courage for him as well as for myself. At a time, too, when courage is barely sustained by my affection for my children—when I am hourly distracted by thinking of my brother, who believes me guilty of treason toward him. Oh! Pity me! I have need of pity, and I deserve it."

But nobody ever seems to have been able to pity Caroline. Napoléon went to the root of the matter with his usual perspicacity. "It is his wife who is the cause of his defection. . . . He is the Bernadotte of the South."

Mme Mère, now a member of the Council of Regency, merely said, "To fall is nothing, when one makes a noble end; to fall is everything, when one makes a dishonorable one." She was speaking of Napoléon, for matters were now desperate. Some of his own generals would no longer obey him. Augereau refused to bring reserves up from Lyons. Napoléon became angry. "I have annihilated 80,000 of the enemy with conscript battalions which had no cartridge pouches, wooden shoes, and uniforms in rags. . . . If you are still the Augereau of Castiglione you may keep your command, but if your sixty years lie heavy on you, give it up." By way of reply, Augereau wrote back, "Where are the men of Castiglione?"

To this there was no answer. They had been killed. Napoléon once estimated he could afford to "spend" 100,000 men a year. But he had been spending them for almost twenty years, and had reached the bottom of the barrel. He had lost over 400,000 in Russia, and was down to 70,000. As he said himself, only General Bonaparte could save the Emperor now.

On January 21 Marie Louise was appointed Regent, with two chief councilors, King Joseph for military matters and Cambacérès for civil affairs. On the 23d Napoléon addressed the officers of the National Guard (a useless and rebellious force). Louis, who had been staying at Lyons with Fesch, came up to town and took enough time off from correcting the proof sheets of a new edition of his novel to wish the Emperor godspeed and say he was sorry he could not be with him in the field. Proof sheets can be most demanding. At thirty-six, Louis had to walk with the assistance of a cane and had an old man's piping voice.

Jérôme, who was at Stains but who had equally unselfishly torn himself away from his mistresses and his masquerades, asked for a final audience, but was refused.

On the 24th, before leaving for Châlons and the army, the Emperor ordered the Treasury to pay Joseph 500,000 francs to meet the expenses of his new position as Governor of Paris. The Treasury was almost empty. But Napoléon, who had always been of a saving disposition as a private person, had saved enough gold bullion out of his civil list to finance the government of Paris. The coin was stored in barrels in the basement of the Tuileries.

He then left to fight the campaign which, though it ended in his defeat, was to be one of his most brilliant, for he was completely revivified by a present danger.

N APOLÉON had held his last reception on January 23, in the
Salle des Marechaux on the first floor of the Tuileries. More
than 700 officers had been summoned there. Marie Louise,
Mme de Montesquiou (the King of Rome's governess), and the
King of Rome arrived late. The Emperor confided them to the care
of the National Guard. He then retired to his study to burn papers
and to study maps, with the aid of his maneuver pieces, chunks of
wood variously colored to represent battalions, regiments and divisions. The King of Rome, who had been let in, meddled with the
pieces. On the top floor and in the attics of Les Invalides across the
river stood scale models of every major town and fortress in Europe,
with its surrounding terrain. But for some time now these had been
gathering dust, and besides, there were no such models for the defense of France, for its invasion had never been envisioned, not, at
any rate, by the present regime. Later, when Paris was occupied, it
was one of the diversions of the Prussians to smash these models of
their once taken towns.

It was hundreds of years since any foreigner had occupied Paris,
more than a hundred years since it had been threatened.

On the 24th, Marie Louise was still weeping, as she had been doing
now for some time. When she was young she wept fluently. There is
no record that she retained the skill into maturity. When she was
particularly disturbed, she sat in Napoléon's lap. Napoléon spent the
day in his study, destroying more personal papers in the fireplace.
Hortense was there. So was the King of Rome. So was Marie Louise.
Everyone treated her like an unnecessary toy, but the toy had to be
constantly reassured. She had to be told over and over again that the
Cossacks were not in Paris yet. To Marie Louise, anything that let
the world in was abhorrent.

On the morning of the 25th, Napoléon went in to take a last look at the King of Rome. It was shortly before dawn, and the boy was asleep. Napoléon left without waking him, and never saw him again. He rode to Châlons to join his troops.

"I remain with you," Joseph said in a proclamation to the people of Paris. Not many found this reassuring.

There was not much Joseph could do. Paris had almost no defenses. Napoléon had deliberately neglected them. And the city had been stripped of troops to reinforce the armies in the field. As soon as new conscripts arrived, they were given three or four days' drill and then marched off to face the Prussians. It was insufficient preparation. "I would fire as well as the rest," said one such conscript, "if only I knew how to load."

In late January and early February, 17,863 men arrived in Paris, but 27,000 were sent to the front. By March 14, there were 19,909 men in the infantry depots of Paris, but of these only 3,899 were available for duty. The rest were ill, untrained, or unarmed. There were 7,000 cavalrymen, but only 3,600 horses to serve both them and the gun carriages. There were several hundred guns in the arsenal at Vincennes, but they could not be moved, for want of carriages, gunners, and horses. Indeed, since mid-1813, it had been easier to find new soldiers than it had been to find horses.

Though there were supposed to be 24,000 National Guardsmen, there were only 11,000 muskets and bayonets in working order. The 30,000 more in store at Vincennes were in disrepair or out of date and condemned. Ammunition was short, and, since cartridges were made by hand, could not be manufactured rapidly. Soldiers sent to the front went with only fifty cartridges and the promise of fifty more to follow. Those in Paris had even fewer.

There were 1,800 competent cuirassiers, but these were detailed to defend the Empress and the Imperial Household. Besides, they were topheavy with show armor. Though they were the best troops in Paris, it does not seem to have occurred to anyone to put them to practical use.

During the winter of 1813 and 1814 it had been suggested to Napoléon that he arm the workmen of Paris. He refused to do so, for, a child of the Revolution, he had a terror of armed mobs. The National Guard (a civilian militia) had been deliberately neglected for the same reason, though in actuality it was mostly made up of parading householders and small shopkeepers who wanted peace at any price. A few volunteer organizations proved more useful; the best was the artillery regiment formed by pupils from the École Polytechnique.

One of Joseph's difficulties was that Napoléon delegated authority only to his Marshals, and not to them if he could help it. Though Joseph ordered the city's fortifications to be put in order, he could not begin until Napoléon approved the plans. Communications were bad, Napoléon was hard to find, and, when found, always disapproved the plans. So it was not until March 23 that construction could start.

Another difficulty was that Joseph was not allowed to give orders directly, but only through the various generals in the area, the best of these—that is, the most certainly loyal—being d'Ornano. Clarke, Duc de Feltre, the Minister of War, was a highly competent bureaucrat, but had had no military experience for years and countermanded everything. He was known as the General of the Pen.

True, a few things could be done. The Pope, for example, had been released from his imprisonment at Fontainebleau, "in order to create a diversion," and was on his way back to Italy.

About the only person in the capital who seemed determined to fight was the young King of Rome, who on January 30 went to mass wearing a National Guard uniform and drawing his toy sword. "I shall use this to defend Papa against his enemies. I am going to beat Papa Francis," he said. He was not yet three.

On the 31st Marie Louise wrote to her husband: "I almost feel tempted to pick a quarrel with you for not writing to me for two days; it really is too bad of you." During February she peppered him with bulletins concerning her medical condition. On February 2 she had sciatica in her right leg. On the 6th it was a backache in the morning and rheumatism in the evening, though on the 3d she had contracted a malady more vague, which had lingered. On the 9th and 14th she had a stomach-ache (overeating again), on the 12th, 15th, and 21st migraine, on the 19th a cold, on the 20th fever, on the 22d a cough. She also took occasion to inform him that Mme Mère "was dying of fright."

This does not sound like Mme Mère. It does sound like Marie Louise. She also relayed information (more welcome) about the King of Rome. He had eaten his spinach. "This may not appear very interesting to you, but it is great news for him, as it means that he has conquered an aversion." Marie Louise herself never endeavored to conquer one. She was relieved that the Tuileries had an enclosed garden, where she could walk without being seen by her subjects. She was in communication with her father, who on February 9 informed her, "Things in this world have changed considerably, and I hope you will never forget it. Only if we remember this fact can we hope to achieve a happy solution to our problems."

Napoléon was in retreat, and a discreet exodus was taking place in Paris, under the name of sending women and children into the country for safety. On the evening of the 9th Marie Louise reported to Napoléon that for some days a crowd had been outside the King of Rome's windows, to see if he was still there. It does not seem to have occurred to her to relieve their anxiety by opening the windows.

Also on the 9th, Joseph received Napoléon's instructions to send Marie Louise and the King of Rome away should the Allies reach the outskirts of Paris. For the moment he kept these instructions to himself.

On the 10th, the Emperor, having been beaten back at La Rothière and Brienne, won a victory at Champaubert. He destroyed twelve Russian regiments, took 6,000 prisoners, forty guns, and 200 ammunition wagons, and lost 200 of his own men. But the Allies could replenish their troops and supplies at any time, and Napoléon could not.

He asked that the victory be announced by the firing of the Invalides cannon and by speeches in the theaters. This was done. Joseph, accompanied by the King of Rome in dress uniform, reviewed the grenadiers of the National Guard. There was some cheering. Parades were kept up. Lights burned late in the ministries and palaces. There were many rumors.

It was proposed to form a commission to control the city in the event of the Empress's leaving. Louis was offered the presidency of it. His reply was a long rodomontade of his theories about Holland. The matter was dropped.

Jérôme came up to the city in early February, commandeered Fesch's house, and asked Marie Louise for an audience. Napoléon, when he heard of it, told her to refuse. Jérôme, who found a general's uniform flattering, asked the Emperor for permission to take up military duties in the capital. It took the Emperor two weeks to answer. He was to give up his Westphalian pretensions, his Westphalian uniforms, and his Westphalian court. If so, he might go to govern Lyons (Lyons fell on the 21st) on condition that "not a musket shall be fired without his being the first under fire." Napoléon, though only in extreme adversity, seems finally to have faced the fact of Jérôme's military incapacity.

Jérôme replied that he would dismiss some of his retinue, but not all of it. Napoléon refused to continue the correspondence. Jérôme was forced to sulk at Cardinal Fesch's house, unemployed.

A great deal of time was lost, because Joseph counseled peace at any price, which was what he always counseled. Depending upon how the battles were going, Napoléon was apt to agree. It was decided to sound out Bernadotte as peacemaker and to attempt to persuade Murat and Caroline to abandon their desertion, which had "revolted even the Allies themselves." Nothing came of either project. The envoy sent to speak to Murat did not reach him until March 20 and was not back in Paris until after the fall of the city. As for Bernadotte, he said he did not wish to push matters too far and was willing to consider a possible peace, but his answer did not arrive until March 13, again too late.

On February 27 there was another parade, with the King of Rome prominently displayed. This was Napoléon's wish. He thought it would rally the people. On February 20 he had ordered Denon, at the Louvre, to have a portrait engraved with the caption: *I am praying for my father and for France.* "If it can be done in forty-eight hours, it should have a good effect."

It was done. It had no effect.

On March 2, Napoléon, complying with a suggestion made by Joseph, allowed a council to be convoked, with the Empress presiding, at which the dignitaries of the Empire were to give their opinions on the matter of an armistice and peace negotiations. All he wanted was their opinions. He did not want a decision. The council did not meet until the 4th. As for Marie Louise's ability to preside, it was limited to being able to sit in a chair. The council, virtually unanimously, opted for peace at any price.

Unfortunately on the 7th Napoléon won another brief and deceptive victory over Blücher, so his answer to peace at any price was a war bulletin, though Joseph wrote, "We are on the eve of a general breakup, and there is no safety except in peace."

At the beginning of March the Emperor had asked Marie Louise to write to her father to intervene. "Imagine my position, dear Papa, if there should be a battle so terrible that I could not go on living afterward. I beg you therefore, dearest Papa, think of me and my son."

But Francis, though an affectionate father when cornered, was cold as bread pudding when politics were involved. Though he sent personally reassuring notes, he had washed his hands of France. "The greatest service you can render your husband, your son, and your present homeland is to support my views [they were Metternich's views actually; Francis had none] and my advice . . ."

Napoléon became jealous of Joseph's relations with Marie Louise. He feared seduction. On March 12 he wrote, "Beware of the King; he has a bad reputation with women and a greed for power which first affected him in Spain. If you wish to please me instead of making me unhappy, show none of my letters, your father's or your replies, to the King, and keep him at his distance. I have been informed that he has conceived the senseless and culpable notion of persuading the people to petition me for peace."

"I am annoyed with myself for having mentioned my father's letter to the King," answered Marie Louise. "I translated some sentence or other for him in order to reassure him, as he had completely lost his head."

On March 9 and 10 Napoléon was pitched back, with heavy losses, by Blücher, at Laon. The position could be repaired, but not the losses. In Paris, there was intrigue among the senators to depose Napoléon and appoint Joseph as guardian of Napoléon II (that is, the King of Rome). Joseph rejected this notion, but agreed to address the Emperor, suggesting he should abdicate if he could not make peace. The Emperor at once decided Joseph was behind a plot to dethrone him and wrote to say that he would consider any pleas for peace addressed to him as an open act of rebellion. "Remember I am the same man I was at Wagram and Austerlitz." It was becoming patent that he wasn't. He added that if any such peace proposal was drawn up without his permission, he would have King Joseph, the Ministry, and all those who signed the petition put under arrest.

Then, marching toward the Aube, he passed out of contact with Paris.

On March 20 the King of Rome observed his last Imperial Birthday. To celebrate, Napoléon captured Arcis-sur-Aube from

Schwarzenberg's troops and wrote to Marie Louise to tell her so. He added he was going to make for the Marne. The letter was intercepted by the Allies and their troops were redisposed accordingly. Blücher then sent the letter on to Marie Louise, with his compliments and a bouquet of flowers.

Another intercepted letter informed the Allies that Napoléon had been asked to return at once, as the royalists were busy plotting to overthrow him. On reading this, the Czar persuaded the Austrians and Prussians to join him in an immediate march on the capital.

As a result, on the 27th, the King of Rome saw his last French parade, which lasted three hours.

On the 28th Napoléon began to double back, via Troyes, toward Fontainebleau. Mortier and Marmont reached the outskirts of the city in full retreat. Communications were completely disrupted. Refugees were pouring into the city from the eastern, northern, and southeastern fronts. Panic had begun on the 27th, and reached its peak the next day. There was a demand for masons, to wall up valuables in cellars. Royalist proclamations announcing the downfall of "The Usurper" went from hand to hand. Shops closed. The theaters played to empty houses. The rich began a scamper west, rumbling out of the city in carriages.

On the 28th, news reached Paris that the enemy had reached Claye and Meaux and that there were Cossacks at Bondy. Hortense sent a note to her mother advising her to leave Malmaison for Navarre, which Joséphine did.

The 28th was the decisive day. The last Council of the Regency was called. Marie Louise presided. Joseph was there with Cambacérès, the Chancellor; Lacépède, the President of the Senate; Clarke, Minister of War; Savary, Minister of Police; and Talleyrand. Clarke suggested the Empress and King of Rome leave the capital. The suggestion was opposed. If she left she would be nothing but a fugitive. If she stayed, she would be an inconvenience, but with an inconvenience the enemy must sometimes strike a bargain. The bargain proposed was to exchange the abdication of Napoléon I for the installation of Napoléon II. It was known that the Czar, the most powerful member of the Allies, would have agreed to this, for he had a low opinion of the Bourbons. It was voted that the Empress and the King of Rome should stay.

Joseph, however, had the sort of prudence which defeats large causes. He now stood up and read a letter from Napoléon, in which Joseph was ordered to send the Empress and King of Rome to Rambouillet, together with the Senate, Council, and such troops as might be available, should Paris be threatened. "I would rather see my son's throat cut than see him brought up in Vienna as an Austrian prince; and I think highly enough of the Empress to feel sure she feels the same way, insofar as a mother and a woman can. . . . I have never seen a performance of *Andromaque* without pitying Astyanax, who outlived the rest of his house, and without feeling that it would have been better for him not to have survived his father."

The reading was followed by silence. Savary then begged Marie Louise to ignore the letter and to remain. The letter, he pointed out, was seven weeks old. Joseph countered by reading a later letter of March 16, in which Napoléon repeated his orders and said the government should leave as well. Another vote was taken. The result was a disastrous compromise. The King of Rome and Marie Louise were to leave, but part of the government was to remain behind.

The meeting had gone on until midnight. As Talleyrand was getting into his carriage, he said, "So that's the end. They had a good hand and they threw it away."

Sometime during the night of the 28th and 29th, Marmont, who controlled the only considerable body of troops near Paris, sent up a note to say the enemy was gaining ground and that "we may be surrounded this evening."

Hortense had tried to induce Marie Louise to stay. For by leaving she would lose her crown.

"Perhaps you are right," said the Empress, "but so it has been decided, and if the Emperor has any reproach to make, it will not be to me."

Jérôme also arrived to protest. The distant bombardment of cannon could now be heard, and the flashes seen. Marie Louise had made up her mind.

It was not until the morning of the 29th that the more reliable members of the National Guard were posted along an eight-mile line east and northeast of the city. Defense works had scarcely been begun here, and there were only a few guns emplaced. The line stretched as far as Vincennes and in the other direction to Montmartre, then outside the city. There was a second, inner line, but the defense hinged upon the defense of Montmartre itself.

On the evening of the 29th, Joseph slept at the Luxembourg for the last time. He did not sleep very well. The Allies had reached the Marne. At three in the morning he got up, put on the uniform of a general of the Imperial Staff, and rode out through the dark streets toward Montmartre. At four the National Guard began to beat the call to arms. At the Clichy barrier Joseph found Marshal Moncey, his staff, and some citizen troops waiting. With these he rode up the hill to a small country house at the top of it. He reached this at about five. It was still three-quarters of an hour before dawn, but the light was deceptive and gray. Nothing could be heard, but there were reports that the enemy had begun to move up.

Montmartre is not only the highest but the only real eminence in that part of Paris. Joseph had summoned all available generals, and they had come in full dress uniform. But there were almost no troops. To make matters worse, Jérôme had arrived, in the most gorgeously ornate of his Westphalian getups and with his equally outrageously accoutered Westphalian, which is to say Franco-Westphalian, staff. He wished to offer his services.

Among those present were three Marshals of the Empire and Clarke, the Minister of War; Decrès, the admiral who was Minister of the Marine; the Governor of Paris; General d'Ornano; Joseph's chief of staff, Mathieu-Maurice, whose credentials consisted of his being Queen Julie's cousin; and, oddly enough, Colonel de Montijo, father of the future Empress Eugénie.

Jérôme promptly quarreled with Clarke and rebuked him for not arming the workmen out of the Vincennes arsenal, whose contents as it happened were useless.

"The Emperor has not directed me to take my orders from your Majesty," said Clarke.

"And lucky it is for you," said Jérôme, and ostentatiously turned his back. "Surrounded by men like the Minister of War, what do you expect but failure," he shouted to Joseph. He was being helpful, as usual.

Before much could be done about this gratuitous insult, a cannonade opened up on the right, and as the sun rose, the Allied armies advanced. The Marshals and generals went off to their units, and Joseph, Jérôme, and a crowd of lesser officers rode to the crest of the hill. This sector was quiet, for Blücher's orders to attack were not to reach him until seven. However, everyone else was attacking. It was not merely a besieging army, it was all Europe come to put down the capital.

At ten the extreme right gave way, but was not pursued. The Czar had given orders to avoid street fighting in the Faubourgs. Allied strategy was merely to engage the French, as a cover for the taking of Romainville and the heights of Belleville and Montmartre. The attack on Montmartre's defenses began shortly before eleven. It was now clear that the entire main armies of the Allies were moving on Paris.

Joseph had early decided a defense could not be long sustained. At eight A.M. he sent orders to his wife to follow the Empress, who had already left. Julie preferred to stay. At ten he ordered her once more to leave. At noon she left.

The Czar sent a message to say that if the Allies were forced to storm the barriers, it would be difficult to restrain the troops from sacking the city. He sent it because he was by no means sure he could storm the barriers, but Joseph had not enough military experience to recognize a bluff when he saw one, and at eleven called a council of war. The Marshals were too busy fighting to attend, but the Ministers of War and Marine and the Governor of Paris did not see how 28,000 regulars could hold out for long against an enemy of at least 100,000. Nor did anybody put much faith in the National Guard, a corps of 12,000.

So it was decided to capitulate, as soon as the outlying positions became untenable. This was done by sending Marmont and Mortier orders that they might enter into negotiations independently, so soon as they saw fit.

At one, Joseph sent orders into the city that the chief members of the government were to follow the Empress into exile. He had lost heart.

At about one-thirty he was riding down Montmartre hill toward the Clichy barrier and Paris. Jérôme went with him. It took them some time to cross the city, but, with the aid of a cavalry escort, they went along the boulevards and the Champs Élysées, through the Bois de Boulogne, to the Sèvres bridge. This was reached at about four. He had not bothered to visit the Luxembourg, his seat as Military Governor, where he would have found a message waiting for him that the Emperor had reached Fontainebleau (an exaggeration) and if Joseph could hold out for four more hours would relieve him.

The message caught up with him at the Bois de Boulogne, but he continued on his way. Behind him, Marmont and Mortier agreed to evacuate Paris, and their armies were marching toward the Loire by sunset. The National Guard was supposed to preserve order in the city until the entry of the Allies.

By ten that night Napoléon had reached the Cour de France, ten miles south of Paris, and had discovered what had happened. "If I had arrived four hours earlier, I could have saved the situation," he said.

Joseph and Jérôme reached Rambouillet late that evening. The Empress, King Louis, and Queen Catherine of Westphalia had gone on ahead to Chartres, with Fesch and Mme Mère, but Julie was there. Hortense and her children arrived during the night.

Bᴜᴛ the first Bonaparte to suffer immediate retribution at the hands of the Allies had been, curiously, Elisa, supposedly safe in Tuscany. She had been turned out on March 13. Nobody seems to have been particularly sorry. The Grand Duchess of Tuscany was a shrewd, scheming, sly, and lascivious woman, with the soul of a libertine in the body of a spinster.

She was the eldest of the Bonaparte sisters, having been born in 1777, the best educated (at St. Cyr, an academy for the daughters of impoverished noblemen, abolished in 1792, during the Revolution), and the least attractive. "There is no malice in her," said Napoléon, when she was fifteen. "In this respect, she is less advanced even than Paoletta [Pauline]." He was quite wrong. She was proud, ambitious, resolute, and took what she could get. She was also a bluestocking, firmly convinced women were the equal if not the superiors of men, and she meant to prove it. Her expression was described as "animated but severe." According to the Duchesse d'Abrantès, who had a sharp eye, "never had woman renounced as she had done the grace of her sex; one was tempted to believe that she wore it as a disguise." She had changed her name from the less pleasing Maria-Anna to the more aristocratic Elisa, apparently on Lucien's advice. Perhaps because she most nearly resembled him in character, she had more trouble getting things out of Napoléon than had her other brothers and sisters. But get them she did. In her case, a second-rate mind was accompanied by a first-rate will. She was clamorous but not shrill, persistent but not noisy, a Caroline without the shriek, a Pauline without the beauty. Like the others she had her little physical defects, mostly a tender stomach, which she alleviated with goat's milk. She was a specialist in the sudden tears of the autocrat, and greatly enjoyed tragedy, Racine for choice (Napoléon preferred Corneille). The Emperor had once had to rebuke her for posing publicly in flesh colored tights.

There had not been many suitors for the hand of this paragon. She had to make do with Felice (Felix) Bacciochi, a fellow Corsican, whom she married in 1797. He was nominally a military man, but since it took him sixteen years to rise from sublieutenant to captain, it would seem not a very good one. What he did have was a small amateur talent for the violin. He was a handsome, indolent, good-natured, bullyable drone. Elisa's dowry was 35,000 francs cash, two vineyards, and a small estate at Corsica, to which Napoléon relegated them both as soon as he could.

This did not suit Elisa. She had Bacciochi moved to Paris, with the 16th Division, and set up in the capital as a *saloniste*. She was not a very good *saloniste*. If she wished to meet anyone of any eminence, she usually had to have herself asked to Mme Récamier's. In time, as Napoléon rose, she managed to attract David, Gros, Isabey, Lethière and Fontanes to her salon. The first three are painters of varied excellence, but of the literary merits of Lethière and Fontanes (editor of Napoléon's official gazette, the *Moniteur*) there was less to be said. To cut the leaves of their latest books, even then, must have been a labor more of diligence than of anticipation.

When the Empire was proclaimed in 1804, the wives of Joseph and Louis became princesses. The wives of Murat and Bacciochi did not. There was a scene at the Tuileries. Caroline continuously drank glasses of water in order to keep her anger down. Elisa, in better control of herself, contented herself with a sarcastic tone and a haughty manner. "This," says Mme Rémusat, who was there to watch (in France there is always someone there to watch), "gave me new notions of the effect produced by ambition on minds of a certain order. It was a spectacle of which I could have formed no previous conception."

It was a shock, if not a surprise, to Napoléon, too. Caroline and Elisa were made Imperial Highnesses in their own right. Murat was made Duke of Berg-Cleves; Bacciochi, with whom not much could be done, a Senator of the Empire, which got him out of the army, where "he had not even troubled to dissimulate his military incapacity." Bacciochi received a gratification of 240,000 francs, and Elisa had her allowance increased to the same sum.

Not even an ambitious wife could do much to camouflage Baccio-chi's innate ineptitude. Since she could not remove him she decided to remove herself to Italy, where she could retire him to a back room without arousing comment. Napoléon, who seems to have reached the same conclusions, not only about Bacciochi but about his sister as well (he once told her she was a caricature of the Duchesse du Maine), made her Hereditary Princess of Piombino, on March 18, 1805.

Piombino did not satisfy her. It had only 20,000 inhabitants. So she intrigued, successfully, to have Lucca as well. Unfortunately Lucca would accept a male prince but not a regnant female princess. This was displeasing so far as the title went, but she contented herself with the knowledge that she would rule in fact, no matter who might do so in name. And so it turned out.

She had a genius for unnecessary organization and soon had a top-heavy court. When it became necessary to retrench, instead of dismissing any of these supernumeraries she merely reduced their wages. Next she built a palace. Since Lucca is a small city, she had part of it torn down in order to make room. The building had reliefs by Thorvaldsen, timepieces by LeRoy, and sculpture by Bartolini and Canova. Since she was in a hurry, most of the decoration was stucco or plaster. Inside, dominating everything, was a heroic statue of Elisa as a neoclassical goddess. Outside stood a somewhat confused work, showing Napoléon standing on a globe of the world, on which were carved the exploits of Themistocles, Alexander, Hannibal, Scipio Africanus, Caesar, Clovis, Charlemagne, Gustavus Adolphus, Prince Eugène, and almost everybody but the later kings of France.

She also opened two theaters, a bathing establishment, and a gambling hell, from which she derived enormous profits, but Napoléon ordered her to shut it down. Elisa had many ingenious ways of making money, some of them reprehensible, all of them cunning.

On the one hand, she built roads, drained marshes, abolished brigandage by the simple expedient of having all the trees cut down so there was nowhere for bandits to hide, introduced silkworms, revamped the judiciary, reorganized the police, reformed the prisons, and put convicts to work. On the other, feeling an income of merely 800,000 francs a year to be inadequate, she imported the mouflon sheep from Corsica, bought an alum mine, established a personal monopoly on the tunny catch, opened forges, and, against Napoléon's wishes, sacked a private company on Elba (it was established to finance the Légion d'Honneur) for ore.

But her stroke of genius was to discover a means of making money out of Napoléon in an entirely new way. She reopened the marble quarries at Carrara and started to manufacture busts of the Emperor. No official in the Empire dared to refuse one, and some were even ordered spontaneously. When everyone had one, she changed the pose and issued another model. She impressed Bartolini, a competent hack, as director of the works and saw to it that he kept producing, by the gross lot.

"The models . . . multiply under my eyes," she wrote the Emperor, "to be transmitted to the kings whom your Majesty has made, and to nations which owe to you their happiness. These monuments of gratitude, erected to immortal genius, will be the first thought of my heart." Then she put the prices up.

Once everybody had a bust and statue of the Emperor, she went on to engineer an artificial boom in Marshals, Senators, and so forth, founded a sculpture school, and proceeded to tables, vases, chimney-pieces, tombs, and clocks. What with one thing and another, she marbleized Europe. Her finest thought was to commission from Canova that superb nude of the Emperor whose original is now in the courtyard of the Brera and whose plaster maquette is at Apsley House, London. Of course she reserved the right to manufacture copies of it.

On June 3, 1806, her daughter Napoléone was born. Later, as the Countess Camarata, she was to prove almost as difficult to control as her mother was. Elisa had not much time for the child. She was busy scheming to annex Tuscany, which took her several years. She was not entirely successful. Napoléon issued a decree which made her "governor-general of the Departments of Tuscany, with the title of Grand Duchess." So she was not to be an absolute ruler, but only his resident lieutenant. He had decided to limit her ambitions.

There was the consolation that Bacciochi was not to be made Grand Duke, but merely commandant of her troops, under her direct orders and those of the French Minister of War, which were given to her, not him, so it came to the same thing. Bacciochi, who had all the independence of an aphid, was quite content with the arrangement, so long as he was adequately fed.

Elisa moved into the Pitti Palace in the middle of the night and with speed. Her husband was put in the Palazzo della Crocetta, where the Medici had lodged distinguished visitors in the old days. This was because Elisa, though yellow-skinned and masculine in appearance, had taken to lechery by the back stairs.

At the Palazzo della Crocetta Bacciochi ran a small court of his own and organized what amounted to a private brothel for his own amusement, except that no one had to pay. In public the couple always attended the theater together, and they indulged in those public shows of affection which more than satisfied both of them and which do so much to counteract scandal.

There was quite a lot of scandal. Though always a believer in the proper forms, Elisa, at thirty-two to thirty-seven, had added a considerable lust after the accompanying bodies as well. Her lovers included her equerry, Cenami, a page, a merchant called Eynard, a nephew of the Marchese Lucchesini, Baron de Capelle, and others.

She was not popular with the Florentines, because she insisted upon asking husbands and wives to the same functions, which discommoded their *cicisbei*. Also she had banished Louisa Maximiliana von Stolberg-Gedern, Countess of Albany, for no worse offense than running a rival salon. This frumpy woman was a Florentine sacred cow, not so much because she was the widow of the English Young Pretender as because she was the surviving mistress of the national poet Alfieri.

Napoléon not only entertained himself with detailed reports on Elisa's bedroom adventures, but when her lovers became a public hazard, had them banished. In addition, he threatened to seize the marble quarries of Carrara unless she paid over the usual levies he demanded from all his relatives' territories. Nor would he let her rule Tuscany directly. If she wished to pass new legislation, she had to go to Lucca to do it. This did not make her popular in Lucca, where, on February 17, 1810, she presented an already overburdened populace with thirty new laws of her own concoction. Elisa, so the saying went, "combined the despotism which she copied from her brother with the despotism natural to her sex."

To cope with her inordinate taste for publicity, Napoléon forbade her name to be mentioned in the Paris newspapers. "The less one speaks of her, the better it will be," he said. That left her the Italian newspapers. She made the most of them.

By 1812 she had gone bald as well as yellow, restricted herself to two dresses and some hats sent from Paris every month, and kept an eagle chained to a rock in the garden. The events of 1812 and 1813 do not seem to have made much impression upon her. The relentless work of self-immortalization absorbed her more. In 1813 she had herself painted by Benvenuti, surrounded by her court. The painter shows her husband, her daughter, and no fewer than three of her current lovers. They stand up. She sits down. In front of Bacciochi, and blocking his view, is a large, accusing bust of Elisa, which he is endeavoring to admire. Behind him the younger Lucchesini glances at the spectator knowingly.

Elisa, no less than the other regnant members of the family but with even less excuse, seems to have been persuaded that she was beloved of the people. Nonetheless, when it became evident that all her French officials who could were fleeing the country, and after an Austrian raid on her territories, she began to intrigue to keep her throne and to negotiate with Murat, who was negotiating with Austria.

In January of 1814 the French garrison, what was left of it, was transferred to Pisa. Murat's army appeared and demanded admittance to Florence. Elisa made a purely formal refusal, in case Napoléon might after all win out over the Allies. Then, protesting that she did so only in order to avoid bloodshed, she had the gates opened. She had overplayed her hand, convincing the Florentines that she wished French tyranny continued, so a mob stormed the Pitti and threatened to throw her out bodily and her household with her. It was with difficulty driven back by the Mayor of Florence, on the plea that she was leaving anyway.

This she did, though a guard was forced to cut her out with sabers and her carriage was pelted with excrement.

Reaching Lucca, she announced her treason and formally severed all connections with the Empire, while at the same time trying to annex a few ex-French possessions in the neighborhood. Masson, the French historian, in his monumental work on the Bonapartes says that this was "like a sailor who, on a sinking ship, steals his captain's pocket handkerchiefs."

She might well have succeeded in holding at least Lucca, had it not been for Lord William Bentinck, who had landed at Leghorn on March 9 and marched on Lucca with 2,000 men. To an embassy sent by the Luccans, on behalf of Elisa, he said, "If you do not send that woman away at once, I will have her arrested and conducted to the frontier."

Since the Lucchese would do nothing to defend her (they had nothing against the Code Napoléon, but the Code Elisa had depressed them), this was the end of her career as a bluestocking and a busybody. On March 15 she left Lucca for Genoa, where her husband was commander of the garrison. Bacciochi prudently resigned his command (he was always willing to resign—it was one of his pleasant traits, both as a husband and as a public figure), and on they fled from Genoa to Turin, Chambéry, and Montpellier, and then, since Napoléon had abdicated, back to Italy again.

Now she no longer had Carrara, she was quite poor. Bacciochi, however, had been investing in Corsican real estate for some time, in his quiet way, so though they could not spend as formerly, neither did they starve.

Metternich allowed the Bacciochi to settle at Bologna. There, in July of 1814, Elisa gave birth to a son, "at a time when she had ceased to need an heir to her power," as Mlle Avrillon says in her memoirs. The son, called Frédéric, died in 1834 at the age of twenty, after a fall from his horse.

Bologna was Austrian territory, and Elisa was closely watched. Since she was known to be intelligent, it was feared that she might also be active. She took the title of Contessa di Compignano, after a country house she had owned, kept herself in touch with any possible revolutionary uprisings in her favor in her old territories (there were none), and amused herself as best she could by giving archaeological masquerade parties (the subject of one: the Marriage of the Sabine Women). A determined woman, she proposed to go to the Congress of Vienna to fight for her rights, a move which earned her the applause of Mme Mère, who was not normally given to approval of the activities of her eldest daughter.

T<small>HOSE</small> who had had to flee from Paris were not so fortunate and had found the flight quite terrible.

At dawn on March 29 ten big green carriages stood in the Cour du Carrousel, outside the Tuileries. They were lumbering state vehicles, the coronation and christening coaches, as a matter of fact, their gaudy outsides camouflaged with green canvas. Nothing could disguise their silver-plated axles. There was almost no one about to watch.

Marie Louise did not wish to leave and wrote once more to Napoléon. "God's will be done, but I am sure that you will not be pleased. . . . Apparently it is thought better to be captured by Cossacks than to remain quietly in Paris! But everyone has lost his head except myself. . . . So I intrust myself to Providence, convinced that no good will come of this."

She had her hat on, when some men came from the National Guard to beg her not to leave. She sat down on a chair, wept, and asked for *anybody* to decide and put an end to the agony. She meant well, but did not know how to give orders, except to servants.

At ten A.M. Clarke, who was afraid Cossacks might arrive in the city at any moment, insisted the order to depart be given. It was given, but the King of Rome refused to leave his rooms. He clutched the uprights of a chair. "Let's not go to Rambouillet, it's a horrible château. I don't want to leave home. And since Papa's not here, I'm master."

Nobody could reason with him, so it was necessary to use force. He even clung to the door on the way out.

He was put into his mother's carriage. So were a good many other things, including over a hundred pairs of shoes and several pairs of boots. Marie Louise's ideas of traveling light were scaled to her notions of what was necessary. The King of Rome traveled with his governess, Mme de Montesquiou, and her staff, not with his mother. The coronation coaches were a jumble of saddles. Other wagons contained the crown jewels, coronation robes, Imperial sword, plate, a silver gilt table service, and the treasury, thirty-two small barrels of gold which Joseph had had fetched up from the basement and which represented Napoléon's personal savings.

It was raining, and there were not more than eight spectators. These watched in silence. Marie Louise said later that if anyone had cut the traces she would have stayed. But as usual, she was weeping, and it did not occur to her to order anyone to turn back.

By evening, she was at Rambouillet. Just before ten P.M. a message came from Joseph, advising her to push on and make for the Loire. Paris was on the point of falling, he said (it had already fallen that afternoon). Mme Mère and the Queen of Westphalia had also reached Rambouillet.

On the 30th King Louis arrived, so frightened, said Marie Louise, "that he wanted us to take refuge in a fortress. He has lost his head so completely it is embarrassing." The party moved on toward Chartres. A letter arrived from Napoléon, written on the 29th but dated the 28th, saying he was making for Paris and was at Bar-sur-Aube.

That night King Joseph and King Jérôme caught up with the party. "Joseph lost me Spain and now he has lost me Paris," was Napoléon's comment. "And the loss of Paris means the loss of France." He was right. It did.

On April 1 the refugees were at Chateaudun, where they had to put up at the Hôtel de la Poste. There being no toys, the King of Rome contented himself by throwing pebbles into the Loire. It was still raining. In fact it rained so hard, and the roads were so muddy and the carriages so heavy, that the twenty-mile journey from Vendôme to Blois took nine hours. A spring broke in the chief Imperial Coach. The procession took the wrong road and had to turn back, except that it was no longer a procession, it was a rout.

On the 2d they reached Blois. Since the château was being used as a prison hospital, there was no place to put everybody. Nonetheless on the 3d it was possible to hold a state banquet. All the etiquette of the Tuileries was reestablished. The local inhabitants demanded to see the King of Rome and were allowed to do so.

In Paris, on this day, the Czar made it clear to Caulaincourt, Napoléon's envoy, that there would be no objection to his son's coming to the throne if the Emperor were far enough away to create no anxiety in Europe. The Allies, he said, had no desire to impose on France either a government or a sovereign she had not herself chosen. Talleyrand, on the other hand, wanted the Bourbons, and the Czar was staying in Talleyrand's town house.

Napoléon seems to have felt Talleyrand was right to espouse the Bourbon cause: "They are the only ones who can accept the humiliation inflicted on France, for they have nothing to lose." He was at Fontainebleau, reviewing the National Guard and trying to exhort them to march on Paris. But the Marshals of France were tired of fighting, and the Senate had already voted Napoléon's deposition.

The Emperor asked if it would accept his son and handed over an abdication in favor of the King of Rome. It was dated and signed April 4, on heavy notepaper, upon which, while writing, he could not have failed to observe the watermark, his own profile, crowned with laurels, with the usual N, and the motto "Emperor of the French."

The Senate might have accepted, had not Marshal Marmont, who controlled the only considerable body of troops (12,000) in the area, that morning agreed to desert Napoléon's army with his men on condition that he be allowed to retire into Normandy as a private citizen, unmolested, and that the Emperor be provided for "in some circumscribed locality."

Marmont's change of sides totally destroyed any possibility that the King of Rome might ascend the throne.

"I would give my right arm to undo what has happened," said Marmont, on the 5th.

"Why not your head? It wouldn't be too much," said Marshal Ney.

On the 6th the Senate declared Napoléon to have forfeited the throne and joined the deputies in summoning Louis Stanislas Xavier, brother of Louis XVI, to it. It took him a while to come. He was in England suffering from gout ("Either his legs are chamberpots, or he has chamberpots for legs," said the Duchesse d'Abrantès). He did not arrive at Calais until April 25, five days before the final peace agreement was signed.

There was one final thing Napoléon could have done: send for

Marie Louise and the King of Rome. He did not do so. His behavior
was withdrawn and uncertain. He was suffering from a venereal disease and did not want her to see it. In his letter to Marie Louise of
April 7, he did not even tell her of his abdication.

On the same day the Emperor Francis wrote to his daughter, "I
doubt if it will be possible for me to give much help, since I have
obligations to my Allies."

Napoléon announced his abdication to Marie Louise on the 8th
and said that she might possibly be given Tuscany, but was no longer
Empress of the French. He added that he himself was to be sovereign
of Elba.

Marie Louise had thought of going to Fontainebleau, but had been
prevented by her confidante, Mme de Montebello, who had always
found the Emperor vulgar (she found everybody vulgar, including,
on one later occasion, Marie Louise herself). Mme de Montebello
wished to stay in France, where she had a lover (Saint-Aignan), and
discouraged any attempt to join the Emperor, since, as lady in waiting, if Marie Louise went into exile, she would have to go herself.
She told her the climate on Elba was bad.

Marie Louise seems to have felt herself betrayed less by Napoléon
than by her father. When she was brought news of the abdication,
she said, "My father will not allow it to happen. He has told me
twenty times, when he put me on the throne of France, that he
would always keep me there, and he is an honest man." She recommended the raising of 150,000 men.

On the following Sunday, which was Easter Sunday, the words
Domine salvum fac imperatorem were omitted from Church services
for the first time. Mme Mère had a mass said privately for Napoléon
and the King of Rome.

On April 8, Joseph and Jérôme attempted to abduct Marie Louise.
She prevented it with the help of those officers of the Imperial Guard
she still had about her. Apparently they had some cloudy idea of
ransom and resistance.

Marie Louise decided to appeal to her father, before trying to join
the Emperor (not a very vigorous attempt). "I am not asking you to
intercede [for Napoléon], but for me and my son, and especially the
latter. I am convinced you do not wish the Isle of Elba to be his sole
inheritance. . . . this unhappy child who is innocent of all his father's errors." She was beginning to change her tone.

"Oh, the sooner this is over, the better I shall feel. Oh to be sitting quietly in my little house in the rue d'Enfer," said Mme de Montebello, who had at least chosen an appropriate address.

"That is a cruel thing to say to me, Duchess," snapped Marie Louise. Since Napoléon had suggested Orléans as an ultimate retreat, she directed the court in exile, what was left of it, to go there. The coronation coaches were laid up for repairs, which they did not get, at Chambord, and six Cossacks tried to steal the treasury along the way. All they got was Marie Louise's hats and bonnets, which had a carriage to themselves.

Marie Louise reached Orléans on April 9. Here she was greeted by a man called Dudon, an agent of the Provisional Government sent to collect the diamonds belonging to the crown. He not only took the diamonds, he also demanded the pearl necklace the Empress was wearing, and got it, as well as the silver plate, the tableware and all the Emperor's handkerchiefs (which had been brought by mistake). It was necessary to borrow dishes from the Bishop of Orléans.

On the 10th, Anatole de Montesquiou, the governess's son, arrived with two letters from Napoléon. Mme de Montebello was the first to receive him (she was in bed), and asked if the Emperor was dead, and if not, why he did not commit suicide.

Montesquiou went on to King Joseph (also in bed). Joseph seemed in a good mood. "It's over," he said. "Now all we want is the King of France to allow us to go on living in France as private citizens." He was thinking of Mortefontaine.

Montesquiou did not succeed in seeing Marie Louise until eight that evening. She too asked if he thought the Emperor would try to commit suicide. She did not want to go to Elba. Nor did she get Tuscany, but, as Napoléon wrote her on the 11th, she was to have Parma (400,000 people and a revenue estimated at 3,000,000 to 4,000,000 francs), with possible reversion to her son.

Marie Louise, much enheartened, set out for Rambouillet to meet her father, taking the new Prince of Parma along with her. It was at about this time that the gush of her letters to Napoléon begins to become cloudy, overemphatic, and insincere. She was a prisoner, and yet she now gave the order to go. She wished to see her father.

On the night of April 12 and 13, Napoléon actually did try to commit suicide, using poison given him by a Dr. Ivan, which did not work and merely gave him hiccups. The hiccups in turn made him vomit. He begged for more poison, but Dr. Ivan refused to give it. So everybody was up all night. At four A.M. he wrote to Marie Louise, a suicide note in which he said he approved of her trip to Rambouillet.

"It seems I am condemned to go on living," he said in the morning.

Marie Louise arrived at Rambouillet in tears. The Prince of Parma, unaware as yet that he was no longer King of Rome, handed out candy to the children of the town. When the box was empty, he said, "I should like to give you more, but I haven't any left: the King of Prussia took all I had." The Emperor of Austria turned out not to be at Rambouillet and did not plan to arrive for three more days.

Napoléon lost patience, and on the 15th of April ordered Marie Louise to come to Fontainebleau with the ex-King of Rome. She did not go, for her father forbade it and suggested two months in Austria first, then a visit to Parma, and, perhaps, later, Elba. . . .

She confided her intentions of going to Elba, eventually, to the Czar, who rather spoiled the game by saying, "But Madame, no one is going to prevent you, though it may be a mistake."

Marie Louise finally saw her father on the 16th, but Metternich had made it his business to be present, so it had not been possible to wheedle anything. She could only reproach, and did so, pushing the ex-King of Rome into his lap. Francis contented himself with the remark that he could see his own features in the boy's face.

Led back to his room, the ex-King of Rome announced that he had seen the Emperor of Austria and that he was not pretty.

Francis sent a letter to Napoléon, drafted by Metternich (who wrote all his letters), explaining that both Marie Louise and the ex-King of Rome would be taken care of in Austria, for the time being.

On the 18th, most of the court at Orléans got passports at the town hall and dispersed, as rapidly as possible. On the 23d, Marie Louise set out for Austria. The Emperor Francis had offered Mme Mère asylum, but this was refused.

"I hope you will always have benevolent feelings toward me," said Marie Louise.

"That will depend on you and your future conduct," said Mme Mère.

Marie Louise did not depart alone, but in a party of sixty-four people, including forty-three servants and what was left of her entourage. She wore a medal of the Emperor, a very large one, around her neck, and kept her servants in the Imperial livery, even at Schön-brunn. Her carriages (twenty-four) were emblazoned with the eagle and Imperial arms.

At Innsbruck, on the way, the citizens took the horses out of the shafts, pulled her carriage, and presented a memorial congratulating "His Majesty's august daughter, who acquired deathless rights to her country's gratitude by an act of self-sacrifice [her marriage] rarely equaled in the annals of history."

When she arrived at Schönbrunn, a crowd came into the garden under her windows, to cheer her. Marie Louise did not care for that sort of thing, but the police reported that she graciously consented to appear at the window and even went so far as not to wear a hat. In fact, she was reading a letter, and went right on reading it while allowing herself to be seen by the people. Such behavior, which shocked those who had come to applaud her, explains why José-phine, even though now only Duchess of Navarre, had had no trou-ble whatsoever in remaining the most popular woman in France.

The better, which is now to say the Austrian, half of the Prince of Parma was favorably commented upon, however, and he too was well received. The present and future popularity of the ex-King of Rome, based entirely upon his appearance and charm, was to incon-venience the Austrian government from now on.

On April 28, Napoléon left Fréjus for Elba. On May 21 Marie Louise was given an enthusiastic reception ten miles from Vienna. "Tormented by care and loving you more devotedly than ever, I am spending whole days in despair at being unable to see you," she wrote to Napoléon. She was embroidering some tapestry covers for chairs, a sofa, and a footstool.

The old Queen of Naples, her grandmother, who on her marriage had said, "All I needed to complete my misfortunes was to become grandmother to the Devil," did not altogether believe in the intensity of Marie Louise's yearnings and delivered herself of a tirade in front of the Prince of Parma, of whom she was very fond, and the Prince of Parma's governess.

"What about his mother? Why isn't she here? And why that big portrait of her husband round her neck, if she doesn't keep his pic-ture in her heart? Why isn't she on Elba?"

"She isn't the mistress, and they refused permission."

"Permission? Oh come now. What difference does that make?

You escape. . . . Hasn't she got sheets in her bed and curtains at the windows? You escape out the window. There was a time when she ought not to have become his wife, but now she is his wife, she must go on being his wife."

Such was the opinion of an eighteenth-century woman.

Marie Louise was not made of such firm material. She was sincere about Napoléon. The trouble was that she was equally sincere about following the instructions of any man who gave her any, at the moment, her father. Left to herself, she merely became evasive.

This characteristic had not escaped the attention of Metternich. The Emperor, of course, knew of it already. Something must be done to wean her from Napoléon and attach her to someone else. Prince Schwarzenberg proposed Count Adam Adalbert von Neipperg, a soldier and diplomat reputed to be able to talk any woman around. Neipperg had recently managed to put aside his wife in order to marry his mistress, but being a loyal servant of the Empire, when told what he had to do he obediently set aside his mistress, in order the better to perform his task, which turned out to be neither a pleasant nor an easy one.

H ORTENSE, somewhat more practical than her husband Louis or ex-King Jérôme, spent the last weeks of March making bandages and directing the schoolgirls of Écouen at the same employment. On the 28th her maid had come to tell her that the enemy was approaching the city. Wishing to see for herself, she got dressed and rode along the boulevards. There she saw the hospital wagons taking the wounded off to Versailles. That evening she had gone to the Tuileries, but not to the Council of Regency meeting. After the meeting she had asked Joseph what had been said about her and her children. Apparently nothing had. Nor had anyone thought to warn Joséphine, so Hortense did this, advising she retire to Normandy. Hortense did not get home until one in the morning. She was wakened by a letter from Louis. In all, he sent three. They commanded her to leave Paris with the children. Though he had himself been supposed to flee with the Empress, he had stayed on to make sure Hortense did not remain behind. He put a guard at her door, to watch her movements.

At eight in the evening of the 29th, she ordered her carriages and got the children into them, and her companion-secretary followed, carrying her jewels in a bag. She went first to Versailles and then to the Trianon. The bombardment could be heard from there. There she learned that the city had finally been occupied and that Joseph, Jérôme, and the officials of the government had passed through Versailles that afternoon.

She went on to Rambouillet, where she found Joseph and Jérôme. The brothers were eating dinner, but offered her none. Her secretary managed to get hold of a loaf of bread. The brothers went off to Chartres and advised Hortense to follow.

Instead she went to bed. While she was in bed another letter arrived from Louis. He was at Chartres, was furious not to find her there with the children, and complained bitterly. She sent him word she was going to Navarre instead. She reached Navarre on April 1, planning to sell her diamonds and take ship for Martinique, where Joséphine still had property. Nothing came of this plan. From Paris word arrived that the Czar wished to visit the Beauharnais at Malmaison and that they had nothing to fear.

Navarre was an impractical, drafty barn of a house. It was known as La Marmite because of the shape of its sliced-off dome (the owner had designed to erect a colossal statue of his ancestor Marshal Turenne on the roof, but had been forbidden to do so). The whole house was nothing but a pedestal, with a circular hall surrounded by triangular rooms. It took twenty-one cartloads of wood and a dozen sacks of coal a day to heat it.

Joséphine hated it, but was passionately devoted to Malmaison, whose gardens were so famous they have left an aroma behind them to this day. She accepted divorce, she accepted banishment, she accepted everything, but she would not accept removal from Malmaison. In the end Napoléon had allowed her her way. After his fall, he had advised her to return there, in order to protect her children's interests and, of course, her own. So she went.

Malmaison is one of those houses which should be ugly, but instead have enormous charm. And then there was the garden. Joséphine had a passion for gardening, particularly for exotic plants, of which she introduced over 180 to the continent, and for roses. The rose gardens of Malmaison were enormous and had the soft pink drifting scent of the variety named after them. There was also a menagerie of Swiss cows, merino sheep, parrots, parakeets, cockatoos, black swans, white swans, ducks from China and Carolina, gazelles, kangaroos (there had been an attempt during the Directoire and the Consulate to colonize Australia), chamois, an ostrich, Moluccan pigeons, monkeys, flying squirrels, storks, a seal, a king vulture, trumpeter cranes, two hocco fowl, and an Imperial eagle with an eight-foot wingspan; also the patter of those little dogs which, in the days when she had been Empress, always made it their purpose in life to bite the Emperor. The estate covered 300 acres, most of them landscaped, complete with farms, copses, formal gardens, and paths.

Before joining her mother there, Hortense felt constrained to pay a duty call on Marie Louise at Rambouillet. At first Marie Louise refused to see her. But then she changed her mind. Her father was coming and she wished to see him alone. "I think he would be vexed if he found you were here," she said cordially. She also said she was afraid her father might force her to go to Elba, an unfortunate admission which later Hortense was to enjoy putting in her memoirs. "You are luckier than I am," the Empress explained, "you haven't been abandoned, and I—why I haven't even my own guard of honor left."

Farewells were cool, on both sides. As she was leaving, Hortense passed an open calèche containing Metternich and the Emperor of Austria, arriving.

When she got back to Malmaison, she found the courtyard full of Russian soldiers, and the Czar already there, walking with her mother in the rose garden.

For Joséphine was a legend, even in her lifetime. No matter what she did, the legend survived. During the Continental Blockade English officers had sent her plants from the Antipodes. The world of fashion had deserted her promptly upon her divorce, only to find that the Emperor had ordered it to come back again. Marie Louise complained, but Joséphine was the one tie he refused to break. He even insisted that she maintain Imperial state, going everywhere with fourteen troopers, a trumpeter, a guard of twenty-five cuirassiers, and a dozen pages and equerries in full court dress. She was generous to everyone and found herself cheated left and right. There were even those, which is most unusual in the social world, who were genuinely fond of her.

She was a light woman, with no interest in politics ("I am too lazy to take sides"), and criticism of her ranges from the bad state of her teeth to the number of her lovers. She sometimes stooped to very womanly tricks indeed (it was she who spread the rumor that Napoléon was committing incest with Pauline). She was invariably in debt, and her dress bills were outrageous (at the time of her death she had 700 dresses and 250 hats). She was undeniably ignorant, but she had a talent for the smoothing of human relations.

She lived in an eternal present, which she tried to make as agreeable for others as for herself, and she knew how. She never dropped an old friend (Napoléon had to order her to avoid Mme Tallien) and always pensioned off old lovers or got them profitable positions somewhere in the army or the bureaucracy. She had a genius for instilling calm.

She had not been born with this grace. She had arrived a gawky girl from the provinces (Martinique). But while separated from her husband she had taken rooms at the Convent of Pentemont, where good company had taught her how to animate instinct.

She had been married to Napoléon for so long that if anything their divorce had brought them closer together. She went (surreptitiously; Napoléon arranged it) to visit the King of Rome, and though she never met Marie Louise, she had Napoléon's most important mistress, Countess Walewska, and his child, Count Alexandre, to stay with her.

She had been at Malmaison since the 14th of April. Since Hortense did not take to this sudden fraternization with the enemy, Joséphine briskly explained the whys and wherebys of making powerful friends. She did sometimes have to explain these things, though she did not like to. The explanation proved effective.

The Czar brought to Malmaison, after him, most of the German princelings and the King of Prussia. The Austrians did not attend. On the 20th, Charles de Flahaut, Hortense's lover, arrived and asked her to marry him. But Hortense decided a divorce from Louis would mean losing custody of her children, as well as the settlement made on her by the Treaty of Fontainebleau (400,000 francs a year, never paid).

The Czar was a myopic half-German giant with red blond hair and blue eyes, benevolent and slightly mad (the madness took a mystical turn). He had the sort of character which is splendid in youth, but time will darken it. Such decent treatment as the fleeing Bonapartes received they owed to him, and to the Pope. He now took a liking to Hortense. It was semiromantic. It might have been more, but neither circumstances nor Hortense would allow of that.

On the 9th of May Prince Eugène arrived. A slight squint and other facial characteristics made him resemble a Mad Hatter of much dignity. After an honorable surrender of his forces in Italy, he had taken his wife, the Bavarian princess Augusta, and their children back to Munich. The Treaty of Fontainebleau stipulated that he was to be given a principality outside France, but which one depended upon the outcome of the coming Congress of Vienna. So the Czar and Eugène made friends.

There were now family parties, consisting of the Beauharnais and the Czar. "I came to Paris full of hatred for your family, and it is only with you that I feel at ease," he said to Hortense, during a picnic at St. Leu, part of which had already been given back to the Duc d'Orléans, its original owner.

There was a rumor that Joséphine was giving money to stir up the workers in the suburbs. Alas, there was no money to give. The 600,-000 gold francs deposited by Napoléon at Blois for the use of Joséphine and Hortense had been confiscated by the Duc d'Angoulême. However, at the end of May, Hortense was confirmed by the new government in the estate and Duchy of St. Leu, with revenues planned to make up the 400,000 francs guaranteed to her by treaty. To Louis's fury, this gave his wife a higher rank than he had, for he was only Comte de St. Leu. He need not have worried. The formal letters patent were never issued, because of the difficulty of knowing how to address Hortense, since she could not be called Queen of Holland, or Bonaparte. The Bourbons were in some ways incredibly petty. A preliminary patent was made out in the name of Mme Hortense Eugénie (the last name left blank), "as described in the treaty of April 11."

Joséphine, too, had been allowed to keep her estates (as a Beauharnais), but she was as extravagant as ever, and her income had diminished by two-thirds, since she no longer received any Napoleonic pension from the civil list. In addition, her own pensions to various people amounted to 300,000 a year.

During the expedition to St. Leu she caught a cold. Now that she no longer had to travel about with Napoléon, her health had improved. She no longer had migraine headaches and had grown plump enough to wear a corset. Nobody was worried by her cold, but she could not shake it off, and it depressed her. The name Napoléon made her cry. She was worried about what would become of her children, in particular of Eugène.

There were other annoyances. Malmaison is about an hour out of Paris, by carriage, from Étoile. The parade of guests going out there profoundly annoyed the Bourbons, or rather their ultraroyalist émigré hangers-on. Impotent to do any real harm, they proposed to dig up the body of Hortense's son, Napoléon Charles, eject it from Notre Dame, and bury it in a public cemetery.

Joséphine was upset. But on the 24th she not only presided at dinner, but walked with the Czar in the damp grounds afterward. Hortense said she would have the child reburied at St. Leu (which was done). Joséphine could by now scarcely speak, and Eugène, too, had come down with a fever. It seems to have been diphtheria, in both cases. Joséphine became more and more ill. By the 28th of May, it was necessary to put off the Czar, who was to have come to dinner before departing for England. He came anyway, but Hortense was afraid Joséphine might overstrain herself by getting up to receive him and diverted him to Eugène's room.

On the 28th, Redouté, whom she patronized and allowed to sketch in the gardens, brought Joséphine two watercolors of plants from the conservatory. She could only wave him away, afraid he might catch her infection. By the morning of the 29th it was evident she was dying. She sank into a coma, had nightmares about Elba, Napoléon, and the King of Rome, and at noon, stopped breathing.

Two hours later Eugène and Hortense left for St. Leu, in order to avoid the lying in state, which was to last three days.

It was the custom to put up black mourning drapes, emblazoned with the arms, or at any rate the initials, of the deceased. This the Bourbons refused to allow, being terrified of some sort of public demonstration. For the same reason, they forbade a state funeral and as much as possible tried to discourage anyone from going out to Rueil (the village where Malmaison is). It was forbidden to give the corpse its formal titles, and in the end, even the nameplate on the casket was left blank.

Nevertheless, everybody knew who she was, and 20,000 people came out to her lying in state. Hatchments and achievements turned out not to be necessary. Appropriately, mourners entered through the Court of Honor, but left through the gardens, which, that summer of 1814, were at their best.

The coffin was closed at noon on the 2d of June. The Czar provided a detachment of Russian guardsmen, and there were four pallbearers: the Grand Duke of Baden, who had married Stéphanie Beauharnais, the Marquis and the Comte de Beauharnais, and the Comte de Tascher. In front of them a footman carried a silver gilt casket on a black velvet pillow. This contained the heart.

The police, in their report to Louis XVIII, put the matter this way: "The death . . . of Mme de Beauharnais has caused general regret. . . . Desperately unhappy during the reign of her husband, she sought refuge from his brutalities and neglect in the study of botany."

The King sent a letter of condolence. Hortense and Eugène did not attend the funeral; the customs of the time allowed one to be absent from this barbaric rite. Neither did the Czar. Instead he spent the day in the gardens at Malmaison, stayed overnight, and did not leave until the evening of June 3. The cortege consisted of representatives of the Czar and of the King of Prussia, and of Hortense's children, Napoléon Louis, ten, and Charles Louis Napoléon, six (Joséphine had called him Oui Oui and had once given him a gold hen that at the touch of a spring laid silver eggs). There were drum rolls and the bells tolled. Twenty girls sang hymns. The Archbishop of Tours, with the Bishops of Evreux and Versailles and the choir of the Madeleine, commenced the service. It was anonymous, for she could not be referred to other than as the widow Beauharnais. But every dignitary of the Empire left in Paris attended. She was buried in the parish church; for the time being, without a monument.

Eugène had wished to join his family at Munich, but Joséphine's estate was difficult to settle. It consisted of Malmaison, Navarre, a house at Pregny in Switzerland, a plantation on Martinique, the contents of all four, very valuable in the case of Malmaison and Navarre, a few government bonds, and a great deal of jewelry. Her debts came to 3,000,000 francs. The business managers suggested an auction, which would appeal to souvenir hunters. Hortense and Eugène refused.

So the stocks were given as dowries to those of Joséphine's servants who were not yet married, and the shawls and personal belongings were distributed. The pensions had to be trimmed, but were continued in her name. What Hortense finally got was half her mother's pictures and half her diamonds, to the value of 2,000,000 francs, but far from the fortune reported by the royalist press. Eugène got the other half. It was decided not to sell the house just yet, as there was no danger of its being confiscated.

Eugène left for Bavaria the end of June. Hortense went to Baden, where she had the misfortune to encounter Mme Krüdener, who was to plague the Czar the next year. She was a religious fanatic who had been converted by her shoemaker in 1804, when her beauty had begun to fade. Later she was to exalt the Czar's innate mysticism. For the moment, she merely offered to tell Hortense where Joséphine and Hortense's dead son Napoléon Charles were at the moment and to communicate with them, if Hortense wished. The offer was firmly refused.

Hortense returned to France, where, somewhat awkwardly, people still addressed her as Queen of Holland, which disturbed the police. Her life until Napoléon's return from Elba was enlivened by a lawsuit brought by Louis for exclusive custody of the children. He was living in Switzerland, where he published a rejection of the Treaty of Fontainebleau in the local newspapers, and was meditating a divorce.

Hortense thought it wise to be presented at court, which was done on October 1. Nothing had been changed at the Tuileries as yet, except the occupants, who sat on Empire furniture, surrounded by such Napoleonic emblems as they could not reach, though lilies in cloth had been sewed over the Napoleonic emblems on the carpets. The King seemed much impressed by her. Secret police were detailed to watch over her daily activities.

Both Eugène and the Czar advised Hortense not to contest Louis's suit. The King, when appealed to, said he could not interfere, and helpfully added that if her sons left France, they would automatically lose their inheritance.

An effort was made to confiscate Hortense's personal property, on the theory that it had belonged to her husband and therefore came under the decree issued in December of 1814 declaring all Bonapartist holdings in France confiscate.

The only member of the family not to suffer by this decree was Caroline, who owned no property there, since Napoléon had forced the Murats to cede their French holdings to him in exchange for small properties in Italy and a reduction in the tribute levied on Naples.

Hortense smuggled her diamonds out and asked the Duke of Wellington to dinner. He was now head of the military commission in Paris. The dinner was reported to the police, and her possessions were not seized.

She was still closely watched. Her favorite flowers were unfortunately violets, which had become the emblems of Napoléon's possible return (because it was said he would be back in the spring).

91

And then, though she did not herself plot, she received many who did.

Louis won his suit, but on March 8, 1815, by which time Napoléon had returned.

Like Hortense, Eugène came out of the debacle with the least ultimate disturbance. Eugène's perfections were so complete that he was a hero even to his own valet. "I was delighted [to serve him]," said Constant. "His features were not handsome and yet his expression was very pleasing. He had a good figure, although he did not hold himself well, owing to an ugly trick he had of twisting his body about when he walked. He was about five feet three or four inches tall. He was kindhearted, cheerful, amiable, very witty and generous; we can safely say he bore his character in his face." The Duchesse d'Abrantès, who could always be counted upon to notice the wrong thing (it was her specialty), was more severe: ". . . he already showed signs of what he became later: a charming, amiable and handsome youth, with the exception of his teeth, which, like those of his mother, were dreadful."

"You mustn't be afraid," said Eugène to Mme d'Abrantès once, at a ball; "my mother and my sister are so kind." "Eugène," said Hortense, "was the only person who made life worth living."

1813 and 1814 presented Eugène with more problems for his conscience than came the way of the rest of the Bonapartes. His father-in-law was Maximilian Joseph of Bavaria, and Eugène got along as well with the Wittelsbachs as he did with everybody else. But he was also an Imperial Prince and Viceroy of Italy and loyal to Napoléon. The difficulty was not to be too loyal.

It was his duty to hold North Italy against the Austrians. The King of Bavaria wrote in October of 1813 tactfully to suggest that Eugène make his peace with Austria.

Eugène, who had a conscience that ticked like a clock, would not do this. Instead, he remained at his post until April 11, exerting himself, but not too strenuously, until the Treaty of Fontainebleau was signed. That released him from his obligations. On the 14th he signed a peace and disbanded his armies.

On the 20th a mob sacked the Senate in Milan and tortured the Minister of Finance until he yielded up the Treasury (1,600,000 francs). This left Eugène and his wife Augusta bankrupt. She had just borne a child. The family made their way through the Tirol to Munich, with an escort of twelve.

After his visit to France, Eugène got back to Munich on June 17, bringing with him some 800,000 francs in gold, which the Emperor had once left with Lavalette against a rainy day. Lavalette had had them hidden in boxes bound as books and put on the top shelf of his library. Since Eugène did not feel his conscience allowed him to spend this money (he eventually doled it out to the Emperor, at St. Helena, at the rate of 20,000 francs a month), for the time being he and his wife were poor. On the other hand, they were safely lodged in Bavaria and protected by the King, who made provision for them both.

The Provisional Government and the Restoration of the Bourbons made a great many people intensely uncomfortable. The painter David, whose artistic dictatorship had begun to collapse at about the same time the Emperor's did, eventually fled to Belgium, though he was pursued by no one. He had lost his vogue. Some curious projects had to be abandoned. For instance, Morghen's huge engraving of *Bonaparte Crossing the Alps*, on which 40,000 francs had already been spent (the total price was to have been 110,000), was destroyed, the Bourbons preferring to lose the money rather than accept the plate. The Prince Borghese, who had been tricked by Napoléon into handing over the best part of his picture collection in exchange for an illusory 18,000,000 francs, began to put machinery in motion to get it back. And there were foolish idiocies. Louis XVIII's government had inserted in the *Gazetier de France*, "Naples, see Sicily, Kingdom of," as a comment on the Murats.

The Murats retorted with a gazetteer of their own, whose index included, "France, see Elba, Island of."

But worst of all, the dignitaries of the Empire were deprived of both their properties and income and forced to disgorge. During his Portuguese campaign, for an instance, Junot, Duc d'Abrantès, who had gone mad of general paresis in 1813 and was now dead (of septicemia, contracted when he broke his leg in two places while jumping out a window, under the illusion that he was a bird), being a bibliophile, had stolen the Bible of Belém, one of the national treasures of Portugal. It was in seven volumes, the covers heavily studded with precious and semiprecious stones, and had been a gift from Julius II to Dom Manuel in exchange for part of the treasures of the Indies remitted to Rome by that pious monarch.

The Duchesse d'Abrantès was now asked to hand it back. Since she had no money, and Junot had left 1,250,000 francs worth of debts and his properties in Prussia and Italy had been seized, she did not wish to do so. Finally Louis XVIII gave her 80,000 francs to return it. But it took over a year to make her yield it up.

She also had other troubles. She had Lord Cathcart, the English Ambassador to the Russian Court, General and Lady Cole, and Elizabeth Bathurst, daughter of the British Secretary for War, quartered on her. When the Coles left, it was discovered that they had taken the pictures in their bedrooms away with them. Later, she lost the house too, for one-third what it was worth. Eventually—but only ten years later, when in ultimate extremity—she was forced to become the mistress of Balzac and to take up hack writing to make both ends meet, a circumstance to which we owe her memoirs, the liveliest of the period.

Her experiences were no worse than those of many, rather better if anything, for she was presented at court and given small pensions from time to time. All her petitions to be pensioned as the widow of a general of France were turned down, because of course he had been a Napoleonic general, but when finally she was persuaded to put in her request merely as a member of the lesser pre-Revolutionary aristocracy (to which her claim was shaky, though her mother was a Comnenus, and as such a registered member of the Corsican petty nobility), Louis XVIII allowed her 24,000 francs a year.

Louis XVIII had entered Paris on May 3, to a distinctly apathetic reception. The day was splendid, but the appearance of the royal family was not. He had been persuaded to sign the not very liberal charter on which his reign depended only if he might point out that he was not so much complying with it as granting it. He persisted in dating his reign from the execution of Louis XVI.

He drove through the city in an open carriage drawn by eight white horses, with his niece the Duchesse d'Angoulême at his side and the Prince de Condé and the Duc de Bourbon sitting opposite him. He was a widower of fifty-nine who weighed 242 pounds and could not move without assistance. Though intelligent and personally tolerant, he was so indolent that all business had to be siphoned through his favorite of the moment, and he did not choose his favorites well.

His niece, the Duchesse d'Angoulême, the daughter of Marie Antoinette and Louis XVI, was ugly as a board fence and twice as stiff. "If she ever had beauty, she has lost it now," said a Scottish observer. She had very bad manners, too much pride, and no charm. She was childless, reactionary, and vengeful. Her husband was thirty-nine, shy, awkward; he had a variety of facial twitches and a lurching walk which people found disconcerting. He was stupid, devout, honorable, and given to fits of ungovernable rage. His brother, the Duc de Berry, fancied himself as a military man, and to prove it, never spoke without an obscenity. He liked to fraternize with the troops, but had no military ability. The Prince de Condé was in his dotage and showed it. He "looked as though his head might drop off." One day, meeting Talleyrand, he took him for his uncle and denounced the nephew (Talleyrand himself) to him. He mistook Marshal Berthier for a marshal of the *ancien régime* and asked him how the Revolution had affected him, and had he been able to get along all right? It was necessary to keep him out of sight as much as possible. His son, the Duc de Bourbon, had only two interests, neither of them strong—sport and low life.

The only competent member of the family, the Duc d'Orléans, belonged to the younger branch, was known to be ambitious, and was kept out of public view. He was also, now he had his estates back, enormously rich. But he did not plot against the government; it was the King's brother, the future Charles X, who did that. Louis Philippe well knew he had only to wait.

This was the royal family, and the Parisian crowds did not like the look of it. As the carriage jerked along, the King, insofar as his enormous bulk would permit, was so gracious as to point out to the Duchesse d'Angoulême, who sat tight-lipped, ramrod-straight and unforgiving at his side, buildings of historic interest along the route. His smile seemed entirely automatic. Nobody else in the carriage paid any attention to what was going on whatsoever. They might just as well have been in a tumbrel. Monsieur, the King's brother, who rode alongside, merely looked haughty.

The silence was so heavy that only the marching of the troops could be heard. These people looked like carpetbaggers. Napoléon had been so diligent to keep all mention of the Royal Family out of the press that nobody knew much about them. There were misunderstandings on the diplomatic level, too. Louis XVIII insisted upon taking precedence over Czar Alexander, who had just restored him, and installed the rigid court etiquette of eighteenth-century France, which, though only slightly more onerous than Napoléon's efforts to outdo the Hapsburgs at the Tuileries, was considerably duller and infinitely more objectionable to a country that had done without it for twenty-five years.

It was not promising.

O<small>N</small> the 20th of April Napoléon had called Baron Köller, the Austrian set over him as one of the Allied commissioners deputed to turn him over to the British at Fréjus, and railed against Austria first for taking the Empress from him and second for having seen to it that the Isle of Elba was denuded of its fortifications (as a matter of fact, Austrian bureaucracy being what it was, this had been established in principle but not done). He said he thought of consenting not to leave. He was persuaded to alter the tenor of his thoughts. At eleven-thirty he got up, dressed, and shortly thereafter delivered himself of that hortatory farewell to the Old Guard which subsequently became a favorite subject of sentimental nineteenth-century painting.

He had been allowed to take 400 of the Old Guard with him, though they were to come after him, not accompany him, since it was desirable to get him out of France with the minimum of attention and fuss. A few days later 600 of them marched down through France, bringing his favorite horses and flying the tricolor. Their number soon swelled to 1,000. Nobody had the stomach to interfere with them.

Napoléon's journey was disordered but comfortable until the last detachment of the Imperial Guard left him at Villeneuve-sur-Allier, on the 22d. There were even loyal demonstrations in his favor. These abruptly stopped as soon as he reached Avignon, on the 26th.

Though courageous in every other way, Napoléon was timid before the people, if only because during the Revolution he had seen exactly how quickly they become a mob and how omnivorous a mob can be. The south of France has always felt itself to be another country, there were many royalists there, and until recently Avignon had been an independent Papal State; he had himself abolished it. So he was now insulted as he went by, and filth was flung at his carriage. In one or two places he was hanged in effigy. He had an unpleasant conversation at a coaching inn with a serving girl who, not recognizing him, treated him to a description of what a real lynching of the Emperor would be like, and how enjoyable.

It shook him. It was thought best that the ex-Emperor leave his carriage and ride a horse, disguised in a blue redingote and wearing a hat with the white cockade of the Bourbons. The horse had a bad saddle, which chafed him, and he still had his venereal complaint. Indeed he made no bones about treating it in full view of the commissioners, several of whom were shocked, particularly the English one.

The mob continuing dangerous, Napoléon next disguised himself as an Englishman, Lord Burghersh. It is indeed curious what names the French will chose as typical when wishing to appear British. But he did not wish to appear British. He was in tears.

It was necessary to send the Austrian commandant, Graf von Clam-Martinic, ahead to round up enough guards to subdue the population of Aix. Napoléon changed disguises again, this time for a uniform of Köller's, to which was prominently attached one of the military orders founded by Maria Theresa. He added an Austrian kepi and a cloak. A crowd pushed around his carriage, and the gendarmes had to be called out. He pushed on to St. Maximin, on the coast, which he reached on the 26th—it was a rapid tour down from Avignon.

At St. Maximin he learned that Pauline was close by, at Le Luc, under the guard of two squadrons of Austrian hussars, and wished to see him.

When Napoléon arrived the next day, she felt herself too weak to rise from her couch. She was a neurasthenic, accomplished at these fits, which were those of a lonely child at three A.M. asking for a drink of water. It almost always took a new lover to make her rise, a phoenix out of her own tidy bed of ashes. But at thirty-four the phoenix was already beginning to tire.

Napoléon, still in his Austrian disguise, was conducted upstairs. Pauline was instantly upset. "What kind of coat is that? What is that uniform?" she demanded.

Napoléon asked if she would rather have seen him dead.

"I cannot embrace you in that coat. Napoléon, what have you done?"

And of course, like many a vain and foolish woman before her, she was quite right. The prisoner is a defeated man only when he has been cowed into someone else's clothes. That is why prisoners must have their distinctive uniform, too. Otherwise they might still be generals. Pauline was expert, when she chose, which was only in an emergency, at going straight to the root of the matter and pulling it up.

Napoléon went into an anteroom to change. After that, the reunion went much better, and he felt himself again. She was the first member of the family he had seen in three months, and the only one, apart from Mme Mère, who was, as always, unchanged. There were excellent reasons why Paulette was his favorite sister.

Crowds had collected around the château and in its courtyard, and Napoléon so far revived under Pauline's attention that he lost his fear of them and was able to bring them around and to charm them. This so upset the Austrians that he was asked to go indoors. He did so and remained with Pauline until evening. She then went to stay in a nearby villa, so that he and his suite might have hers.

The next day he went on to Fréjus, where he remained two days. He seems to have written Marie Louise from there, though the letter has been lost. What has not been lost is a letter from Marie Louise to her father, dated May 4, from Basel. From this, we know that Napoléon had only 10,000,000 or 12,000,000 francs* with him, a quantity of plate, some snuffboxes incrusted with brilliants, and not much more. He had been stripped of his personal possessions, his library and his writing materials. Marie Louise asked her father to see that he got them back and that he got the 2,000,000 francs a year guaranteed to him under the Treaty of Fontainebleau. In the end, he received part of his library, but he never got his guaranteed pension, though Metternich allowed it to be pointed out to the French government that to withhold it was as unwise as to provoke a tiger by removing his meal.

On the evening of April 28, Napoléon embarked on the English frigate the *Undaunted* for Elba.

Pauline had promised to follow shortly, but her latest lover,

* An exaggeration or one of Marie Louise's vagaries. See chapter X.

Duchand, had arrived. So instead she lingered. When Duchand left on the 15th of May, it was with instructions to her comptroller in Paris to "Hand over to him the dressing case which belonged to M. de Forbin (her previous and most hectic lover) and which has his initials on it." Of course the initials would have to be shaved.

Then she went aboard the frigate *Laetitia*, in order to visit the Murats at Naples. As immediately she got off again, for her terror of the sea was extreme. She was not to arrive at Naples until June 1, putting in to Elba on the way, but only for the afternoon. One of her reasons for delay was characteristic of her. Knowing both her vanity and her neurasthenia, a doctor had told her that her health would be improved if she wore the new lace ruffled muslin panta-lettes, and she did not wish to stir until a double dozen of these could be made up for her in Paris.

---------------------------- ❧{ VIII }❧ ----------------------------

T HE first Diaspora of the Bonapartes was not a drastic flight.
They were stripped of their money, but not otherwise hunted
down, and though they were to be watched by the police, they
were not, on the whole, closely confined. It was Napoléon who had
advised the family to scatter. He had even suggested where they
should go, Jérôme to Bourges or Brittany, Mme Mère to Nice, Julie
and her daughters to Marseilles, Louis, "who has always liked the
South," to Montpellier.

None of them did anything of the sort. And they were worried
about money. Mme Mère's pension from the civil list was six months
in arrears, she said, and Jérôme, as always, was short of cash. Fesch
and Mme Mère were not, for both had been prudent to bank their
money abroad.

The family began to scatter on April 9. Mme Mère and the Cardinal left for Italy, with no one in her suite but Saveria, her Corsican
body servant, for her ladies of honor had tendered their resignations
at Orléans. After a not too difficult journey, under the circumstances, they met the Pope at Cesana, outside Rome. Pius VII ex-
tended them asylum.

Jérôme fled to Switzerland, having sent back Catherine to Paris to
intercede for him with her father, the King of Württemberg,
through her brother, the Crown Prince, who, as it turned out, refused to see her. She was told she would be welcome in Württemberg if she consented to a divorce. She put up at Cardinal Fesch's
house and got from the Czar, who was her cousin, a passport for
herself and another for Jérôme, which she sent on to him in the name
of the Comte du Hartz. With this, when it caught up with him, he
was able to reach Neuchatel, then a Prussian enclave, by way of
Pontarlier.

101

Catherine, who was pregnant, thought it best to leave Paris, where the police were objecting to her continued presence. She sold up everything at a loss and took with her only her diamonds, Jérôme's diamonds, and 84,000 gold francs. With the Countess Bocholtz and the Fürstenstein (Lécamus), she fled the city in four carriages, taking the road for Switzerland via Sêns.

Outside Sêns she was stopped by twenty chasseurs under the direction of a man she recognized as Maubreuil, a former member of the court at Westphalia who had been flung out for having tampered with one of Jérôme's many mistresses. Maubreuil said he had an official order to seize her baggage. He did seize it, but it has never been clear whose was the order. He took the diamonds and gold francs, but left her a hundred napoleons, worth twenty francs apiece, when she complained she would be otherwise destitute.

There was nothing for her to do but return to Paris. Once more the Czar intervened. Finally he granted her a pension. But though her jewel basket was retrieved, there were only 2,000 francs left in it, and it was possible to recover only a few of the diamonds. Though detected and his whereabouts and guilt established, Maubreuil was never punished. Something always intervened. In short, he was being protected, nobody knows by whom. When Napoléon returned from Elba, Maubreuil escaped in the confusion and disappeared. By his raid, Jérôme and Catherine lost between 3,000,000 and 4,000,000 francs, most of it in jewels.

Catherine set out for Switzerland again, financed by the sale of the first few diamonds recovered. She met her husband at Berne, from which city Jérôme sent his father-in-law a tart note: "Your Majesty knows better than anyone I did not seek the hand of your daughter. . . . I made her a Queen and Your Majesty yourself was made King by the Emperor, my brother. Your Majesty did not dream of separating your daughter and me during the days of my prosperity." This did not accomplish much. As Count and Countess of Hartz, Catherine and Jérôme made a tour of Switzerland, visited Joseph, and bought the huge château of Ekensberg, near Gratz. It bored Jérôme, and he was not encouraged to linger, so he went on to visit Elisa, but stopping at Trieste on the way, he was so charmed by it that he bought there the Palazzo Romano, a château on a cliff. Catherine joined him there and on the 24th of August, gave birth to their first child, Jérôme-Napoléon-Charles. Catherine wrote to Elba, asking the ex-Emperor to stand as godfather, which he did.

The delights of having a male heir so improved Jérôme's spirits that he acquired a new mistress, Rosa Pinotta, a singer at the Opera. Then, tiring of Trieste, he applied for permission to live in Rome. The Pope, whose ability to shelter Bonapartes was great but not infinite, turned a deaf ear, and Metternich demanded that nothing be decided until the Congress of Vienna had finished its sittings.

Though he had no money, Jérôme amused himself by buying more property, two houses, furniture, and sycophants. At the same time he tried to sell his French properties, which he had never entirely paid for. His chief complaint was that he could not afford new livery for his servants. His baggage was impounded by the French police at le Havre. It had consisted of a hundred crates of family loot. Stains was confiscated, under the decree of December 1814, directing that the Bonaparte's estates and holdings in France should revert to the government.

Jérôme was saved by Napoléon's return from Elba. Pretending to be ill, he locked himself in his house, then sneaked away and escaped from Trieste by boat, only a few hours before Metternich's agents arrived with orders for his removal to a fortress at Prague. So only Catherine was made a prisoner. Jérôme made his way to Naples, Mme Mère, and Fesch.

Joseph got to Switzerland without difficulty and there bought the estate of Prangins, near Nyon, not far from Geneva. From there, with Julie's assistance, he endeavored to sell Mortefontaine and to get his art collections sent on to Geneva.

Julie, whose ability to avoid the proximity of her husband was an acquired but adroit skill, had stayed in Paris with her daughters, on a plea of ill health and to be near her mother, who was, as it happened, dying. The Bourbon government did not interfere with her. No conservative regime is apt to molest the sister of a prominent banker and of the Crown Princess of a friendly state.

In Geneva, Joseph soon had his house in order, complete with the Empire furniture and family portraits. Exile and defeat had made him a statesman, and he served as a clearing house for Bonaparte activities between Elba and the mainland. One morning, while he was having breakfast with Talma, the tragedian and, though nobody knew it, one of Pauline's former lovers, Mme de Staël arrived. Napoléon's defeat had converted her into a Bonapartist. She came to announce a plot to assassinate the Emperor at Elba. Joseph had two of the plot-

ters arrested by the Geneva police, which rather cramped Mme de
Staël's style. She had hoped to descend on Elba with a dramatic announcement. (Both Mme Mère and Joseph had a Corsican terror of
assassination, mostly that of the Emperor. But in fact there were a
good many such schemes in the air.)

When Napoléon landed in the south of France the following
March, Joseph buried his papers, and a few other things, in the forest
of Prangins and set out for Paris by night, accompanied by his
daughters, who were visiting him. He too evaded arrest by only a
few hours.

The most fortunate of the Bonapartes was, of course, Lucien,
who, on the Emperor's fall, behaved with his usual gaudy equanimity. England had begun to bore him. As soon as he was informed that
he was no longer a prisoner of war, he broke up his household at
Thorngrove and started back to Rome, where his properties were
untouched and his relations with the Pope, to whom he had dedicated *Charlemagne*, unimpaired. He wrote to Napoléon, saying that
he had forgotten and forgiven everything, and to the Pope, asking
for a Papal title, which was granted.

"I am so glad to hear that you have been created Prince of Canino,
and that you have accepted," wrote Mme Mère. Since he had arranged the matter himself, he could scarcely have refused. On her
advice, he adopted not the Imperial but his father Carlo's arms. He
thus became a member of the black nobility, protection enough, so
long as he stayed within the Papal States, from all but his fellow
black nobles.

At Rome he soon settled in, received Louis (though not for long)
and Mme. Mère, and devoted his considerable practical energies to a
recent interest in iron smelting. This in turn brought him into correspondence with Elba, whose pig iron he bought and so conciliated
Napoléon, who had need of the market.

Mme Mère arrived in Rome, with Cardinal Fesch, on May 12, at
the Cardinal's house, the Palazzo Falconieri, on the Strada Giulia.
Both were rich, but Mme Mère was concerned to sell her French
property while there was still time, though she had about 13,000,000
francs with her and more on deposit here and there.

Her French property consisted of the château and estate of Pont and her town house in the rue St. Dominique. Pont had been deliberately fired by Frederick-Wilhelm, Prince of Württemberg, who had placed sentries to prevent anyone from controlling the flames. Some of the contents were saved despite him, and on September 4 she was able to sell the ruins to Louis Boigne, a local landowner, for 100,000 francs, half of it cash down.

"I hear with sorrow that Elisa has been to Vienna," she wrote, and advanced her not a penny. Though she was willing to lend out on interest (among others, to Joseph and Pauline, who paid it back), the only people to whom she ever gave money were Napoléon, who needed it, and Jérôme, who was, within limits, able to wheedle it out of her.

She also managed to sell her town house to Dupont, the Bourbon Minister of War, for 800,000 francs, an extortionate sum, though about what it was worth in what was not at the time a seller's market. She wanted to sell him the valuable furnishings too, but since he could not afford them, she had them crated and sent on to Rome and Elba. The French Ambassador to the Papal See duly reported to Paris that someone unknown had bought the house, rather foolishly, since his own government had paid for it, in Dupont's favor. Such are the hazards of counterespionage practiced under the guise of diplomacy.

Pauline was also trying to sell off property, through intermediaries and her comptroller in Paris and from Naples, where she was staying with the Murats. Her properties consisted of Montgobert, in which she had a three-fourths interest from her first husband, who had died in Santo Domingo; her town house in the rue St. Honoré; and her estate at Neuilly. With Montgobert and Neuilly she was unsuccessful. On the whole the Bonaparte estates were much too regal and expensive for the new regime. Both were confiscated the following December. But she succeeded in selling the Hôtel Charost to the British government, as an Embassy, for 300,000 francs in cash and 500,-000 francs in interest-paying securities. So, though she had lost Guastalla, which had been given to Marie Louise, and was having difficulties with her husband and the allowance he was legally constrained to make her, she was not poor. In addition, she had taken 120 cases of furniture out of the Hôtel Charost (which still is the British Embassy) before closing the sale.

At the same time she was endeavoring both to annoy and to cheat her husband, Prince Borghese, a man ideally designed by nature to rouse the scorn of rambunctious women. She proposed to blackmail him with his own picture collections, which he was trying to get back, in order to get a larger yearly allowance out of him. They had been separated for years, and he had made no effort to communicate with her since the collapse of the Empire.

Louis had settled at Lausanne on May 15, in a quite pleasant house on the outskirts of the city, from which he contemplated a divorce and directed legal proceedings against his wife in order to get his children away from her. He was furious she had been made Duchesse de St. Leu, which gave her rank above him, and not pleased that though she used his coat of arms, she had added the motto of the Beauharnais (*Autre ne Sert*) and a ducal coronet to them. For his own part, he continued to use the arms of Holland, to which he had added the collar of the Légion d'Honneur and the blue ribbon of his own short-lived Order of Union. Such ostentations were more important to Louis than to Hortense.

He deposited with a Swiss notary a proclamation protesting the "usurpation" of the crown of Holland by the Prince of Orange, and when the Emperor asked him to return to Paris during the Hundred Days, pleaded ill health and requested an annulment of his marriage. In this he was unsuccessful. He did finally get custody of his elder child. Instead of going to Paris, he moved on to Italy.

Eugène left Munich on September 25 in order to attend the Congress of Vienna, lodging with the Duke of Saxe-Teschen, an unsuccessful military commander who had turned to art collecting as a way of life. He was received with a modulated cordiality, some remembering that he had been an adopted Bonaparte, others that he still was the son-in-law of the King of Bavaria and by birth a Beauharnais, a family whose sole distinction, when looked at closely, was that it was not Bonaparte. For the Beauharnais and the Tascher de la Pagerie, though members of the *ancien régime*, had not, at the time of its abolition, been members of it long.

But since Bavaria was in those days a powerful kingdom, something had to be done for him, particularly as the Czar was his advocate. (In those bright days, the Czar was everybody's advocate. He liked to pose as the Friend of Reason.) The trouble was that no-

body wanted to do it. The Ionian Isles were proposed as an appanage. So was Genoa. In February of 1815, Metternich relieved them
all by allowing himself to suggest that the Emperor of Austria would
not offer any objections to anything the King of Bavaria might wish
to do for Eugène, and so tactfully shirked off the responsibility on
behalf of the other Allies.

Eugène's modest schemes for settling down were almost ruined
when the police intercepted some letters from Hortense, in which
she described the Czar, their protector, as having no wit, no character, susceptible to flattery, and easy to twist around the finger. The
Czar delivered the letters, opened, and the resultant unpleasantness
was somewhat difficult to patch up. But if he had no wit, he was at
least good-humored, and Eugène managed him.

The Congress now offered Eugène the Principality of Ponte
Corvo (it had belonged to Bernadotte) and the half-ruined castle of
Bayreuth. Eugène sensibly rejected Ponte Corvo (in the Kingdom of
the Two Sicilies, which was to say, at the moment, Naples), but
accepted Bayreuth as being a house to live in until something better
turned up. On the 7th of April, 1815, he returned to Munich.

Napoléon had made him a Peer of France, *in absentia*. Despite this,
he was offered a principality in Naples, on the condition that he refuse it in return for an indemnity of 12,000,000 francs. He complied
and was even able, with much trouble and the assistance of the Pope,
to collect half of this sum.

Eugène plays no part in future Bonapartist activity. He contented
himself with giving 1,000,000 francs to help the victims of the White
Terror of 1815, adding another 600,000 in 1816. The rest of his life,
which was not very long, for he died in 1823 at the age of forty-
three, was uneventful. He and Hortense visited each other. He saw
none of the other Bonapartes. The King of Bavaria gave him the
small state of Eichstatt and made him Duke of Leuchtenberg. He
built the Luitpold Palace in Munich. He was given command of the
6th Regiment of Bavarian cavalry. The only interesting thing about
him is his singular success in marrying his children off well. One
daughter married Prince Oscar of Sweden, another Prince Frederick
of Hohenzollern-Hechingen, another the Emperor of Brazil, the
youngest Count William of Württemberg; his sons married Queen
Maria de Gloria of Portugal and the Grand Duchess Marie of Russia.

He was an early Victorian. He left behind him such pieces of piety as that painting of five of his children as winged cherubs, floating in clouds and utterly perfect, which hangs at Arenenberg, and his own tomb, by Thorvaldsen, at which marble women impersonating History, Life, and Death mourn a Roman warrior. As all the Bonapartes felt, Eugène was perhaps too admirable to be admired, a thoroughly upright man, with no splash of grandeur about him anywhere.

THE other true Victorian was, of course, Marie Louise. We are accustomed to seeing the members of the Bonaparte family as they were painted by Frenchmen—David, Gros, Gérard, Isabey—or sculptured by Italians. The French give everything an elegant touch, indeed, they are interested in nothing else. The Italians provided a marmoreal if empty neoclassicism.

German artists saw them differently. There is a miniature of Marie Louise by Kreutzinger, done about this time, which shows her with a slack jaw, a loose wobbly mouth, and affronted eyes. She looks mussed, and is wearing a ruff in the manner of Mary Queen of Scots.

Her behavior in Vienna had pleased no one. She had acted as though she were on a well-earned vacation, which delighted the populace not at all. She kept up Tuileries etiquette and tried to keep her Parisian dressmakers (and pastry cooks), which did not charm the court or her father. She emphatically did not wish to be deprived of regal, Imperial status, though she preferred to live without Austrian ceremony.

So Marie Louise was packed off to Aix-en-Savoie, with the promise that she could go on to Parma afterward, and with Neipperg. On June 29, Marie Louise set out, accompanied by Mme Brignole (a personal lady in waiting), two readers, Bausset and Meneval, Frenchmen attached to her suite, a doctor, two surgeons, a quartermaster, two chambermaids, a laundress, three couriers, a man to repair the carriages, and seventeen serving men. She traveled as Duchess of Colorno, a Parmesan title.

Neipperg went separately and arrived first. His orders were to watch the ex-Empress, though discreetly, and turn her away, though with the necessary tact, from the idea of going to Elba. He was to try *every* means to dissuade her. Such things do not have to be explicit to be understood.

Marie Louise was not at first attracted. She had hoped to attach herself in her usual limpet fashion to Mme de Montebello, but Mme de Montebello was two weeks delayed. Neipperg on the other hand was already there, and she was thinking it over. She was also thinking Napoléon over, and much worried about the possibility of losing the Duchy of Parma. Whatever else she might lose, she was determined to keep her duchy.

"I am in a condition of cruel incertitude," she wrote. It was her habitual condition. She behaved, said her then mother-in-law, Maria Ludovica, like a child of twelve.

"You know how I want to obey the wishes of the Emperor [Napoléon]," she wrote, "but must I do so, if that goes against my father's intentions?" She added that she wanted to die, another habitual reaction when any decision had to be made.

Neipperg progressed so far as to be asked to walk and ride with her, and tried to separate her from Mme de Montebello. It was not easy. When the French wished to divest her of Parma, since the ex-Queen of Etruria, a Spanish Bourbon, had claims against it, she decided to go to Vienna, though she expected to find the Congress personally humiliating. She would leave the 9th or 10th of October.

She also let it be known, quite casually, that she had asked Count Neipperg to come with her on a trip to Switzerland, explaining that he could be useful to her in many ways. By which we may gather she had by now conquered her aversion, even if he had yet to conquer her. This was in August.

Neipperg, for his part, asked to be relieved of his post. Perhaps he had a premonition of what was to become of him. But his request was not granted, and the party moved on to Switzerland.

From there, Marie Louise wrote an odd letter to Mme de Montebello (who had gone back to her lover in Paris) in which she reported that Napoléon had asked her to run away, *without any attendants except for Mr. Hurault* (an emissary). The lack of protocol involved in such a suggestion seems deeply to have offended her. She added that she would give her solemn word to the Congress of Vienna not to go to Elba for the time being, and "that I never will. You know better than anyone, that I have no desire to. . . . The Emperor," she concluded, "is truly of a light and inconsequent temper." She herself was firm as a rock. "Know also that the object is not seductive to me, and that it takes no effort to resist."

In her slow way, she was thinking it over. King Joseph came to pay her a visit, since she would not visit him. "That which vexed me even more than the rain, was a visit from King Joseph."

From the 21st to the 24th of September she was at Berne, visiting glaciers. She now flatly refused to go to Elba, but her desire to return to her "dear Vienna" was not very strong either. She had dismissed all the French members of her suite she could get rid of. She was beginning to look at Neipperg in quite a new way. For one thing, he never left her alone to make a decision, the one thing in life she feared most. She was upset to learn that he had been appointed Minister Plenipotentiary to Turin. What would she do without him?

At this time Meneval, an Imperialist who served as her secretary, seeing correctly how things were going, applied for leave to depart. "I cannot hide the fact," said Meneval to his wife, "that she is no longer the angel of purity and innocence I lately left."

But Marie Louise never liked to give up anybody, and offered to make him her chamberlain and his wife a waiting woman. He stayed on.

On the 24th, Marie Louise climbed to the first level of the Rigi. That night bad weather forced her to stop at the Inn of the Golden Sun. Usually, in rooms organized on the salon principle, a footman slept in front of her door. But the Inn on the Rigi had separate rooms opening on a corridor. So his services were not required.

Downstairs, Meneval found a little note from Marie Louise to Neipperg, in a map of Switzerland left carelessly on a table. Next morning he once more asked to be allowed to depart.

Marie Louise was extremely disturbed finally to have achieved what she now wished. She does not seem to have wanted this ever to happen again, at least not for the time being.

She had been caught out, though unconscious of having done anything that could make her blush. As a matter of fact, she never did anything that could make her blush, except occasionally, when she *was* caught out, and then the reaction was less a blush than a dithering indignation. She went on to the Congress of Vienna.

Unable to mention her new preoccupation, she dwelt, instead, on her health ("The Archduchess," said her father, "is never so well as when she feels ill.") and on how embarrassing she found the Congress of Vienna. "I am very sad: this reunion of sovereigns, this noise, these fêtes at which I am not obliged to assist, but of which I hear the description, afflict me. I lead a most retired life, I see no one, and I would even more readily avoid the visits by the sovereigns if I did not believe them to be necessary to the interests of my son."

She does not add that it was her habit to watch the state receptions through a peephole in the ceiling of the great ballroom at Schönbrunn. She still kept her footmen in the Imperial livery and drove about with Neipperg in those carriages which still bore the Napoléonic coat of arms. Some laughed, others booed. So in December she gave orders for Napoléon's arms to be replaced by her own.

The Emperor Francis might well congratulate himself (as he did) on having picked the right escort. Neipperg, still trying to wriggle out from under, announced that he had conquered his emotion, though that made him most unhappy, and asked Marie not to write to him at Turin. Too many people opened letters, he said.

Marie Louise became abandoned and heroic. "With time, courage and health," she wrote to Mme de Montebello, "I hope I can conquer a feeling I do not wish to avow even to myself, and which will turn into a good friendship."

As Meneval commented, "The Empress has developed the fault of dissimulation and lying to an extreme pitch." Not only to others, but to herself.

The truth of the matter was that Napoléon had been clumsy and abrupt and that Neipperg was her first real lover. Marie Louise, like her father, was both lecherous and extremely proper, a problem they both solved in the same way. All told, the Emperor Francis literally wore out four wives. Marie Louise used up three husbands and Baron Werkheim, a stopgap between husbands two and three. But for the moment she combatted her feelings as best she could, which was not much.

She had much to vex her. Spain, egged on by France, persisted in objecting to the execution of the Treaty of Fontainebleau. Marie Louise was not to be sure of her duchy until mid-March of 1816. She had probably been told that Napoléon was suffering from a venereal disease, and she was certainly told that he had received Marie Walewska and his illegitimate son at Elba (he had himself written her a charming description of the village where this meeting took place, though he had omitted to mention the reunion itself). In addition, the Papal Nuncio was amusing himself by circulating a document which pointed out that since the marriage between Joséphine and Napoléon had never been annulled by the Church, Marie Louise's marriage was null and void and the ex-King of Rome a bastard. Since the ex-Empress Joséphine had died that summer, the pamphlet went on to urge felinely that Marie Louise should have her marriage to the ex-Emperor validated by a church wedding. She was "the innocent victim, the spouse of a monster whom, from a Catholic point of view, she could only marry now that he was in truth a widower."

Marie Louise allowed herself to become upset. She was not sufficiently upset to insist or even to suggest an ecclesiastical marriage. Besides, other of the ex-Emperor's infidelities had been reported to her. "The Emperor had all your ladies in waiting for a shawl. Mme de Montebello alone held out for three."

When told of this, Mme de Montebello, that hardened campaigner in other people's boudoirs, said she was upset only at the low standard of propriety to be found in Marie Louise's salon and at her "poor respect for etiquette in allowing such remarks to be made in her presence."

This brisk exchange ended Marie Louise's one close female friendship, and General Neipperg was forbidden to play with the ex-King of Rome, who liked his hussar's uniform. Neipperg, for his part, liked the ex-King of Rome and was often to prove his friend in the future. Neipperg, in fact, was an admirable man. His only fault lay in getting trapped in his duty.

In order to secure Parma, Marie Louise consented that her son should not succeed to it. When challenged about this by Meneval, she said he might have a little annuity out of money set aside from the revenues of Parma, and that that would make everything all right.

"Our little company," said the child's governess, "is often to be found weeping over his cradle."

Correspondence with Elba began to dwindle, and behind her back, Marie Louise was known pretty widely in Vienna as Mme Neipperg.

THE Bourbons were not popular. Violets blossomed in lapels, and the following exchange became customary in Paris between Bonapartists.

"Do you believe in Christ?"

"Yes, and in the Resurrection."

All of which did much to cheer Napoléon at Elba.

The Isle of Elba is eighteen miles from east to west and about twelve from north to south, and had a population of about 12,000. A large mountain seven miles from the mainland of Italy, it was backward but beautiful, a Corsica in miniature. But it had never aroused either enthusiasm or interest in anyone.

The Treaty of Fontainebleau is careful to state that the ex-Emperor had *chosen* it to be a separate principality during his lifetime. This was a euphemistic sop to his feelings. Elba offered little scope to a man of his ambition and capacity.

He had not come unprepared. He had found a little book entitled *Notice sur l'île d'Elba,* a comprehensive treatise which even so only ran to 130 pages. He also took along a library containing the *Moniteur Universel* for 1789 to 1813, which included his decrees, all but the last ones, and copies of Cervantes, Fénelon, La Fontaine, Voltaire, Rousseau, Bernardin de St. Pierre (Louis's favorite reading), and Plutarch. Two of the four Commissioners set to guard him, Colonel Sir Neil Campbell and the Austrian General Köller, had sailed for Elba with him.

The trip had taken five days, and the boat passed Corsica on the way (Napoléon was affected).

The ex-Emperor, at this time a potbellied little man of five foot six, aged forty-five but looking older, and untidy in his dress, which was dribbled with snuff, did not open his mouth very often, for his teeth were beginning to go. His eyes seemed fallen in. But he was insistent upon his own dignity of demeanor and was beginning to recover from the shock of defeat. At first his reception was unpromising. The islanders thought it was the British come to attack and fired on the ship. It was necessary to hoist a white flag and to stay on board until an enthusiastic welcome could be arranged.

He landed on the 4th of May, at about three in the afternoon, having already provided his new kingdom with a flag of his own design (white, with three golden bees on a red diagonal), and now he handed it over and was given a twenty-one-gun salute. He was lodged at the Town Hall of Porto Ferraio, the only building large enough to accommodate him. Not knowing of his distaste for noise, a string quartet serenaded him during his first audience, and a girl's choir sang below his bedroom window all through the night. Nevertheless, he managed to keep his temper.

Next morning he went in search of a house. What he found was the Casa Mulini, overlooking the sea on the one side and the town on the other. Napoléon had grown so stout he could no longer get on or off a horse without assistance, and the streets of Porto Ferraio are mostly stairs. It was 135 steps up to the Mulini. Since he stayed on the island for 299 days, his health profited enormously.

The worst of his problems was money. The Bourbon government refused to fulfill the terms of the Treaty of Fontainebleau, and the revenues of the island exactly paid for the cost of running it, no more. Nor could much by way of additional taxes be extracted from a population of 12,000, including children. So on the 6th Napoléon paid a visit to Rio, to inspect the iron mines, his progress cheered by a band of hired applauders paid for by General Bertrand. These were always to follow him everywhere, and though in time Napoléon came to recognize the same faces, he pretended not to.

The mines were well managed by a man called Pons d'Hérault. He was a prickly democrat, and his miners were descendants of slave gangs settled at the works by Cosimo de' Medici, 250 years before. They were tough, quarrelsome, and devoted to Pons. The path to Pons's house was lined with lilies (the Bourbon flower). Nothing was meant by this, it was merely that they were in season, but Napoléon thought it a deliberate insult.

"When Napoléon arrived on Elba he was weary of great power

and wanting a quiet life. Undoubtedly, this weariness and longing could not last for a man like the Emperor, but at the time they were genuine," wrote Pons. He was right. They were genuine, and they did not last long.

The ex-Emperor began to revamp the Casa Mulini, into which he moved on the 21st of June, though the work was not finished until September 1. It became a pleasant country villa of the standard Mediterranean type, of two stories, in a small garden, with windows to the view. Downstairs it had eleven rooms. Napoléon furnished it by sending a boatload of workmen across to Piombino, where Elisa had a villa, and having them dismantle it, right down to the sycamore parquet flooring and the shutters. The *pièce de résistance* was Elisa's ample bed. For it was a curious feature of Napoléonic furniture, the family being of slight stature, that the beds were too short for sleep, let alone for intercourse.

"What did my sister do in Tuscany?" Napoléon asked a Piombinese one day. "She made love," said the man.

Elisa's furniture took care of the ground floor. By an accident, Prince Borghese provided the furnishings for the first. He had fled from Turin and shipped his furniture to Rome via Genoa. A storm blew the ship into Elba. So Napoléon had commandeered the cargo. Borghese's furniture and pictures were of much better quality than Elisa's. "At least it hasn't gone out of the family," said the ex-Emperor.

The top floor had nine rooms, arranged in two suites, one for the ex-King of Rome, the other for Marie Louise, with a large anteroom between. Neither of them arrived.

The island was somewhat encumbered by a thousand members of the Old Guard, light infantry, Polish lancers, artillerymen, sailors, and gendarmes. What Napoléon achieved was a small military patriarchal state, extremely well—perhaps *too* well—run. There was nothing for any of these people to do, yet they had to be paid and fed. There were forty-eight carriage horses and twenty-seven carriages, but almost no roads. The farthest one could go in any direction, was about fifteen miles. Napoléon organized customs and excise duties, a stamp tax, salt *étangs*, tunny fishing, a hospital, defense works, public entertainment, vineyards, land redistribution, a silkworm factory, paved roads for the capital, more roads for the island, and the development of a small abandoned flat neighboring island into a grain field. But still there was no money.

On leaving France, Napoléon had had 488,913 francs in hand. At Orléans, Marie Louise had handed over what was left of his savings, 2,580,000 francs saved by hiding them in dung barrels. She had also added another 911,000 francs later. Altogether this gave him 3,979,-913 francs, but out of it he had to pay the fees for the Treaty of Fontainebleau, which came to 30,000. The journey to Elba had cost 60,000, and the men who unpacked his personal baggage had stolen an additional 64,295. To rebuild the Mulini (very cheaply) had cost 80,000. The revenues of the island amounted to about 300,000. 200,000 francs held by Pons in favor of the Légion d'Honneur were, with difficulty, confiscated.

"Ah, how small my island is," Napoléon sighed one day, but he persevered. His first budget showed a revenue of 64,954 francs and an expenditure of 62,285. But this was only for the administration of the capital, Porto Ferraio.

The French government, apparently unaware that it is dangerous to come between an animal and its food, continued to default. Instead of providing him with a sloop, it sent a brig. It had sixteen guns and was called the *Inconstant*. To this Napoléon added the *Caroline*, one gun; two transports; a three-master which cost him 8,822 francs; and a longboat, which had been given him as a gift. These boats were manned by 120 local fishermen under the command of a Sublieutenant Taillade, who unfortunately lost his head when a storm blew up. His crews found him amusing.

Napoléon, who feared assassination or attack, added an army and opened an officers' training school (ten cadets). In addition to the navy, he had 1,030 men and forty gunners. They ate him (literally; they went into the crops as they ripened and left him only the stalks) out of house and home.

The island became a tourist attraction. The English, in particular, wished to see the ex-Emperor in his cage. So hotels were enlarged and new ones opened. The ex-Emperor received with pomp, but there were shortages. At one luncheon the guests could not eat the dessert, because there were no fruit knives to be found, until he provided a set of his own.

Pauline had promised to visit. At the beginning of June she arrived, inadvertently, having been blown in by a storm while on her way to Naples. She refused to land, but Napoléon came aboard at four, after having had a twenty-one-gun salute fired. The people thought she was Marie Louise.

Napoléon persuaded her to visit the Palazzina de Mulini. It is warm on Elba in June. There was a sirocco blowing. She told him he couldn't possibly stay at the Mulini (there were also mosquitoes) and that there must be some place in the countryside that would be cooler during the summer. He said there was, in the forest of San Martino, five miles away, but it would cost 180,000 francs, which he did not have.

Pauline gave him a cluster of diamonds. She had an understanding and generous heart, so long as nothing more than a trifle were involved. She then left for Naples, promising to return, which, in five months, she did, much to Napoléon's surprise.

His next visitors were his mother and his mistress, Marie Walewska. Inconveniently, the two visits overlapped. Before they came, he turned Pauline's diamond spray into the villa at San Martino. Its pleasantest feature was its bathroom, reached by a trapdoor in the floor of his study. The chief decoration of the bathroom was a large explicit female nude painted over the tub. She held a mirror, on which was inscribed "He who hates the truth, hates the light." One of the inconveniences of Elba was a shortage of appropriate and suitably accessible young women at the proper hours.

Upstairs, a Council Chamber provided a splash of color, for everyone sat on a differently hued chair, gold for the ex-Emperor, blue, yellow, white, and red for the other officials of his household. On the ceiling was that pathetic fresco of two doves tightening a knot by flying in opposite directions, his own idea, to symbolize himself and Marie Louise.

It was at San Martino that he learned of Joséphine's death. "Ah, she is really happy now," he said, and seemed sad.

He planted a young elm tree in the garden. "When it is tall enough," he told Campbell, "I shall use its trunk for the mast of a ship in which I shall set off to conquer the world." He was getting restless. And then, the Italian word for elm tree also means practical joke.

Apart from his infatuation with and intimidation by Marie Louise, Napoléon seems to have been truly fond of only two women, Joséphine and the Walewska. She had attempted to get to him at Fontainebleau, but not being admitted to his presence, had spent the night in an armchair and then left. The specific reason for her arrival was that Napoléon had deposited 170,000 francs at Naples, as a nest egg for Alexandre, his son by her. She was afraid Murat might seize this and so went to Naples, from which she crossed to Elba on September 1.

Mme Mère had arrived in early August, from Leghorn, on an English boat, the *H.M.S. Grasshopper*, which arrived at Porto Ferraio on the 2d. It was only a day's sail. Mme Mère, unlike her son, was stately both in nature *and* appearance. "The old lady is very handsome, of middle size, with a good figure and fresh color," noted Campbell, adding that she was pleasant and unaffected. She was also, for a woman of her age (sixty-four), nimble when she chose to be. When Elba came in view, with the Mulini on its cliff above the town, she "mounted upon the top of a gun with great activity," the better to see the view.

She was a woman who had only a few small vanities, one of them an upstanding lace collar to conceal the age of her neck. A long nose, high cheekbones, a good mouth, and enormous, sad, but snapping eyes did much to enhance a firm but kindly reserve. She had been looking forward to this visit very much and was as unaffected by her family's fall as she had been unimpressed by its rise.

Elba has a wild smell, not unlike that of Corsica. She must have noticed it. When she arrived it was night and Napoléon was not there to meet her. He had gone to Marciana, to prepare for the arrival of the Walewska. Mme Mère was extremely upset and agreed "with great violence" that Generals Bertrand and Drouot should be sent for. These, who seemed to be upset themselves, arranged for a small procession to take her up to the Mulini, with mounted torchbearers and an escort of the Old Guard. Only then did she consent to go ashore. Since the Mulini was still a decorators' shambles, she stayed next door, at the Casa Vantini, which had been made ready for her.

Napoléon arrived next day and was so obviously glad to see her that the contretemps of the previous day was overlooked. Mme Mère prepared to settle in. Elba suited her exactly, for it was to the right scale. Her pretensions were amply satisfied by the chatty deference of her immediate neighbors; the language was her own, not French; and she had seldom been happier. She prepared to stay.

Mme Mère was a woman of the eighteenth century, and she brought to everything the calm of reason. Marie Walewska was more in the Romantic style, and Polish besides. Her visit turned into a three-day opera, in the *Sturm und Drang* of Weber at his best.

It was to be kept secret, and to keep a secret on a small island is not easy. The secret had to be kept, because Napoléon had announced, for political reasons, the imminent arrival of Marie Louise and the ex-King of Rome. He did not want the Walewska and her child to be mistaken for the Imperial Family (they were anyway), or Marie Louise to learn that his mistress had visited him (she learned of it all the same).

So he proposed to hide out at a monastery on Monte Giove, concealed in a forest and normally visited only once a year for religious pilgrimage. Mme Mère was to stay at the village of Marciana Alta, a thousand feet up along the way, as a camouflage for the visit.

Marie Walewska's character and position were alike unusual. She was a Laczynska who had been married while very young to the elderly Count Walewski and had been persuaded to become Napoléon's mistress so as to further the cause of Polish independence. She was a righteous woman who would not have made the sacrifice for any other reason. Her husband had abetted her, so had her brother, and so had the Poles. The Poles, a histrionic and somewhat muddled people, still regarded Napoléon as their savior, even though he had not saved them but merely carved out the Duchy of Warsaw for his own purposes. In Poland all lost causes are sacred, not just the Polish. Marie Walewska's husband had recently died, and she hoped to become if not the wife, at least the heroine of the Prisoner of Elba.

She landed dramatically, at nightfall, swathed in a tulle veil, leading her son by the hand, and accompanied by her brother and sister. There was already rumor at Porto Ferraio that the ex-Empress had come.

The climb up the mountain took most of the night. A marquee had been pitched between the monastery and its chapel, and in this, at one in the morning, a party of ten sat down to supper, by candlelight. Countess Walewska was blond, and might be described as an attractive, if somewhat fuzzy, version of Marie Louise, crossed, perhaps, with a dash of Byron's Teresa Giuccioli (whom she knew). She called Napoléon Sire, he called her Mme la Comtesse, and his illegitimate son called him Papa Emperor. Napoléon was extremely fond of children.

That night Marie and her sister slept in the hermitage, Napoléon in a tent. It was raining. There was also lightning. It was possible to observe that Napoléon did not spend all the night in his tent.

In the morning the men went off to the sacristy to shave. News came that the loyal inhabitants of Porto Ferraio were getting ready to receive the ex-Empress and the young heir.

So Marie would have to be smuggled away. "Love making was rarely a need with him, and he probably derived no pleasure from it," Caulaincourt wrote once. "Mme Walewska had pleased him in Warsaw, and he had happier memories of her than of any other woman. But such passing fancies never at any time took his mind off affairs of state."

Napoléon spent the day playing hide and seek with Alexandre. In the evening dinner was followed by dancing, and dancing by separate sleep. Next day she left, in the middle of a storm so bad that it was eight days before news came of her safe arrival on the mainland. Napoléon stayed on at Porto Longone, not daring to return to the capital, where the islanders had refused to allow "Marie Louise" to leave the island. He did not get back to Porto Ferraio until September 26.

Life settled down again. Mme Mère, contrary to her Parisian custom, received every afternoon. "She received her guests with great dignity," said Pons. "I have seen eminent people more intimidated in front of her than in front of the Emperor." Each Sunday Napoléon held a levee at the Mulini and then went in state to Mme Mère's levee, next door.

To maintain this small pomp, Mme Mère began, which was unlike her, to spend money. All told she spent some 2,805,000 francs on the upkeep of Elba. She even sent for her diamonds and offered them to Napoléon, who gracefully refused everything but a jeweled buckle for his sword belt. She paid his pensioners. She allowed him to cheat at cards. Indeed, she could not have stopped him had she wished to; it was the only way he knew how to play cards.

"You're rich, Mother," he would say. And so she was. She was also, for the first time in years, happy.

On November 1 Pauline arrived from Naples, as insouciant as ever, on an English brig but with an escort provided by Murat. One of those sent to bring her was Taillade, who somewhat earlier had been suborned to kidnap Napoléon but had funked out at the last moment.

Pauline was welcome, for life with Mme Mère was reverent but a little dull. She was to have Marie Louise's quarters at the Mulini.

When Napoléon tried to lead her to a barouche, "I have my own

121

carriage," she said, and while they waited for it to be unloaded, distributed sweets among the Porto Ferraio children. Carriages were important to Pauline. Her marriage contract with Borghese had stipulated she might have two, and she never traveled without one of them. She had also brought furniture, cosmetics, and a great many clothes. Since she was as extravagant as ever, Napoléon made her pay both for her horses (240 francs) and her window blinds (72 francs 30 centimes).

Until her arrival, one of the entertainments of the evening had been Bible readings by Marshal Drouot, a devout bachelor with a pained face, good for everything except marriage and light entertainment (to a young lady who fainted when told of his aversion to womankind, he had explained that he would do anything to prevent her dying except marry her: it was the only one of Napoléon's orders he ever disobeyed). Pauline soon put a stop to that. She told her mother to put some makeup on. (Mme Mère seriously damaged her health, as did all women of the day, by using lead oxide as a cosmetic, but did not stoop to rouge. Lead oxide as a cosmetic was one reason the women of the time had such bad teeth and were so often indolently ill.) She gave masked balls. She appeared in amateur theatricals. She induced her brother to play blindman's buff. She got him to pour live sardines into Marshal Bertrand's pockets. She provided such entertainments as the Baroness Skupiesky. This woman developed a passion for Napoléon which was to change her life, for, after Waterloo, acting on inaccurate information, she emigrated to America to be with him, landed somewhere near New York, and after various vicissitudes, for her knowledge of geography was hazy, wound up as the proprietress of a boarding school for girls in Lima, Peru. A woman Pauline did not encourage was the self-styled Countess de Rohan-Mignac, one-half a very old name, who had kept a brothel in Paris and now tried to open a branch at Elba for the use of a loyal but transplanted clientele. She had finally to be expelled from the island.

One way and another, Pauline changed everything, except, of course, Mme Mère, who continued to do tapestrywork by an open window.

N APOLÉON appears first to have begun to plan his escape from
Elba in December of 1814. Though the Allied governments
did everything to search his mail and to keep him misinformed, he had his own network of informers, and a good deal of
information filtered through Joseph, one way and another. He was
aware that Talleyrand, in order to ingratiate himself with the Bourbons, was trying to have him removed to some remoter rock, either
in the Azores or at St. Helena. And of course his pension had not and
would not be paid. He knew the Bourbons were not popular and
that the military were discontented. Those French officials who had
administered Napoléon's conquests were without employment. In
November there had been a plot to throw the King and the Royal
Family into the Seine. There were many plots.

He did not realize that the floor had moved beneath him, that the
social structure had changed, and that the temper of the times was
now against him. Though his faith in his own legend had inwardly
diminished, it was impossible for him to understand that the French
no longer wanted a hero and that the rise of middle-class liberalism
and of the professional politician, who was shortly to abolish states-
manship as a means of government, made a new military dictatorship
of France an impossibility. Also, though he had been an excellent
ruler when he had had the time to rule, he had been a military dictator, and few dictators survive the defeat of their armies.

Colonel Sir Neil Campbell left for the mainland on February 16
and was expected to be gone for twelve days. An amiable, clubbable,
but rather silly young man, to the English preference, he had wished
to see his mistress, the Signora Bartoli, at Florence, as well as to confer with the Austrian chargé d'affaires there. It was his belief that all

British gentlemen never break their word and that foreign gentlemen must be of the same persuasion, since, if they are gentlemen, they must in some way also be British, for there was no other kind. In short, any but an insular cunning was beyond him, and he forgot that he was on an island, since clearly it was not Great Britain.

Before his ship was out of the harbor, Napoléon had ordered the *Inconstant* to be refitted and supplied for a voyage of three months. The supplies were a blind, for he does not seem to have trusted his staff, to whom he gave contradictory instructions. On the same day he closed his accounts and drew up a military budget for 1815. He told Drouot, whom he did trust, "The whole of France wants me back. I shall be leaving here, a few days from now, in response to the nation's wishes." Drouot did not think the invasion would succeed and tried to prevent it. He was right, but he was overridden.

There were alarums and excursions. On February 23, the *Partridge*, Campbell's ship, was sighted coming in to harbor. It turned out not to be Campbell, but six English sightseers who wished to view the ex-Emperor. He received them amiably, and after they had left decreed an embargo on all shipping. One spy did try to take the news to the mainland, but was forced back.

Napoléon had proclamations printed up for distribution in France, one to the French people, the other to the French army. They were in his rhetorical style, which now sounded hollow.

His mother was told of his plans. Pauline, who was a gossip, was not. When he asked his mother for her advice, he was told to go and fulfill his destiny, that he was not born to perish on Elba.

On the 25th a theatrical ball was held. On the morning of the 26th (a Sunday), he announced his departure to the chief dignitaries of the island. "France wants me back. The Bourbons have ruined the country. Several European countries will be pleased to see me return." He then attended mass with Mme Mère and Pauline. He settled the administration of the island during his absence (it was promptly seized by Ferdinand of Tuscany). Pauline, who had finally been told what was to happen, gave him a casket containing all her jewels, with the exception of the Borghese diamonds. They were captured by the Prussians when his traveling coach was found empty at Waterloo. What became of them is not known.

At five Sunday evening the troops were mustered and marched down to the quay. The Polish lancers had to march lugging their saddles, for there was no room aboard the boats for their horses. Only those of officers were taken. The Old Guard had dust covers on their busbies, the plumes of which were carried in leather belt cases. Napoléon rode down to the boats. Beside him his valet carried Pauline's jewels in a black leather box.

In Italy, on the 26th, Elisa looked at her watch and said, *"Le coup est fait."* She could not possibly have known of the ex-Emperor's intentions. Nonetheless, as soon as news came that he had escaped, the Austrians bundled her off, under an escort of hussars, to the fortress of Brünn, in Moravia.

Napoléon had seven ships, the *Inconstant,* the *Saint Esprit* (the brig provided by the Bourbons), a transport, and four others, all small.

As he set sail, Edward Cooke, of the British Foreign Office, was informing Campbell at Florence that Napoléon was quite forgotten in Europe, "as much as if he never existed."

It was not an easy voyage. At first the little flotilla was becalmed, then it was sighted by a French ship, which was told the ex-Emperor was at Elba, wonderfully well, and sighted in its turn a British one, fortunately hull down. On the last night of the voyage, the lookouts mistakenly reported their own fleet's lights as those of someone else.

March 1, at one in the afternoon, at Golfe Juan, Napoléon reached France, but was himself the last to disembark. What he wanted was a bloodless revolution. He issued three more proclamations (there was a printing press aboard).

He marched first to Cannes, which he was not allowed to enter. He did not dare to take the usual route toward Paris, up the Rhône valley, for that area was royalist. Instead he took the mail roads through the mountains, now called the Route Napoléon, after him. "I am not here to talk politics, but to ask for rations," he said when he reached Grasse. Grasse not having any ammunition, he was given rations.

The Bourbon government deliberately kept the frontier and provincial defenses understaffed and undersupplied, because it feared revolt. This made things easier for Napoléon. As he went on, the road grew too narrow for carriages, so he packed his treasury on mules and abandoned his cannon. There was snow. He lost part of his treasure when a mule stumbled into a gorge. He was thus left with 263,000 francs in cash and Pauline's jewels, only.

By March 5, he had reached an area of better roads. The royalist troops he encountered had no powder. At La Mure the soldiers sent out from Grenoble were told to fire on Napoléon, but refused to do so and ultimately joined him. It was his first victory. At Grenoble itself the soldiers began to desert their commander. He marched on the city, whose five regiments went over to him.

"Up until then I had been an adventurer, from then on, I was a Prince," he said. Earlier, on the road to Cannes, he had met the Prince of Monaco.

"Where are you going?"

"I am going home."

"So am I."

From Grenoble he advanced to Lyons. Lyons was to have been defended by the Comte d'Artois (the future Charles X), but since Lyons owed its recent prosperity to Napoléon's creation of a silk industry and was not royalist, the Count had been forced to flee. Napoléon reached the city by nightfall of March 10, stayed at Fesch's Archepiscopal palace, resumed the title of Emperor, and confiscated the Bourbon estates. From Lyons he wrote to Joseph, asking him to inform the Ministers accredited to Austria and Russia that he wished peace and had no territorial ambitions.

The last force between the Emperor and Paris was commanded by Marshal Ney. Ney had been snubbed, and what was worse his wife had been roundly snubbed, by the Bourbons. Ney sent word to Louis XVIII that it was time to come to lead his troops, on a stretcher if need be. There was no answer, and as his troops, the 76th Line Regiment, went over to Napoléon, he followed, after having received two notes from the Emperor, the one saying he would be responsible for civil war if he didn't, the other welcoming him back.

Napoléon now marched on Paris, unopposed, at the rate of fifty miles a day.

THE news of Napoléon's escape from Elba reached Vienna at six in the morning of March 7. Since Metternich was asleep and had not gotten to bed the previous night until three, at first he did not read the letter. He had done so by seven-thirty, and at eight he sent his name in to the Emperor Francis. At eight-fifteen he saw Czar Alexander, at half-past-eight King Frederick William of Prussia. At ten the Ministers of the four Powers (Austria, Russia, Prussia, England) met in his study. One of the aides of the King of Prussia shouted, "Now he has escaped, we must hang him." The King of Prussia said that to do that they would have to catch him, which would not be easy. It seems to have been Talleyrand's idea to outlaw the Emperor as a criminal.

The news was kept private until evening, when it got out at a reception held by the Empress. Marie Louise had been told earlier, by the indispensable Neipperg.

In the ex-King of Rome's nursery, his attendants celebrated by waltzing around the room. Then they thought of telling Marie Louise the good news. Back came the answer. "Thank you. I was already acquainted with the news you send me. I feel like going for a ride to Merkenstein; do you think it is fine enough to risk it?"

"Will they kill my father?" asked the ex-King of Rome (now called Franz even by Marie Louise) of his new governess, for Mme de Montesquiou was being supplanted on the grounds that she was French and he was far too fond of her.

On the 12th, with the assistance of Neipperg, Marie Louise sent her father an official letter, for publication, in which she begged him to shelter her and, by implication, disowned Napoléon for good. To Mme de Montebello she wrote that she "was exceedingly vexed with *that person* who has thus placed the future of myself and my son in danger."

To the Emperor Francis, she added that Franz was "doing his best to become a very good little boy. . . . I have promised him that when he knows [German] fluently I shall ask you, on his behalf, for an Austrian regiment." She was quite content. On June 10 the Congress had ratified her accession to the Duchy of Parma, with Piacenza and Guastalla thrown in, the total revenue 1,200,000 francs a year.

However, to do her justice, she had asked Papa to see that no harm came to the Comtesse de Montesquiou (the dismissed governess); she had refused to ride publicly in the state processions which drove through Vienna to the Dom to ask God to defeat her ex-husband; and when word came that Napoléon was to be transferred to St. Helena, though pleased that he would never again be able to disturb either her or the peace, she did ask that he be treated with clemency and kindness. "I owe him a debt of gratitude for allowing me to live in a calm indifference instead of making me unhappy," she explained. Calm indifference was all she ever asked for.

On the 13th, Talleyrand produced a paper proclaiming Bonaparte's escape "a crime against the social order," by which he had "deprived himself of the protection of the law and proved to the universe that there can be neither peace nor truce with him." "The Powers therefore declare that Napoléon Bonaparte has placed himself outside the pale of civil and social relations, and that, as an enemy and disturber of the tranquillity of the world, he has rendered himself liable to public vengeance."

"One can always deal with an enemy, but there is no remarrying a convict," he explained.

On the 16th, the guard was doubled at Schönbrunn and the servants replaced by policemen in disguise. The removal or abduction of the ex-King of Rome was feared. On the 19th he was transferred to the Hofberg, which was easier to guard. On the same day a letter arrived from Napoléon, asking Marie Louise to join him. She did not receive it, the ministers at the Congress did.

On the 20th, Mme de Montesquiou was hastily dismissed, with the gift of a sapphire necklace chosen at random and delivered unwrapped.

Marie Louise forbade her courtiers to discuss the news from France. As usual, she was very much upset. "If I were sure that no one thought it wrong of me not to have gone to Elba," she began one day, and did not finish the phrase. It was better to be an Empress than a Duchess. But she was afraid of losing Parma, as a result of the Emperor's return, and then there was Neipperg.

She told *him* that she would not return to France at any price.

There was a scare when the police announced the arrival of J. L. David, court painter to Napoléon, and one of the regicides who had voted the death of Louis XVI (actually he had merely added his assent to a vote taken during his absence). After several days of bureaucratic trembling, it was discovered he was quite another J. L. David, the director of the royal porcelain factory at Ludwigsburg. Several letters from Napoléon had been confiscated, but his handwriting was so bad that it took the combined efforts of the Allied Ministers to decipher what it was they contained.

On May 6, Meneval departed for Paris. Marie Louise told him that though she would never consent to a divorce, she flattered herself that he would consent to an amiable separation, which had become indispensable. She added that she felt esteem toward him and had her pleasant memories. Then she took Neipperg, who had returned from defeating Murat at Tolentino, off to Parma with her. He had accepted to be her chief adviser, chamberlain, First Minister, and, of course, lover. The Emperor Francis was both surprised and disappointed in him. "I shouldn't have thought you would want to get mixed up in that affair again," he said, but did nothing to prevent departure.

But Neipperg, whom Marie Louise was literally to wear away to death before his time, seems to have felt it was better to rule Parma, though himself ruled, than merely to take orders for a smaller reward by continuing his usual services in Vienna.

In Paris no one was equipped to withstand the return of the Emperor. Louis XVIII's government was popularly known as "Paternal Anarchy." This was because, in Wellington's phrase, it had "ministers, but no Ministry." The head of each department was in absolute control, and since there never was a cabinet meeting, was never under the necessity of cooperating with anybody else. The only time the Ministers ever met was by chance in the King's anteroom. There was no Prime Minister, only the King's favorite, the Comte de Blacas, who, as Minister of the King's Household, was the only person who had access to his master at all times. Blacas was not a venal man, but he was more reactionary than the King and totally ignorant of French affairs, having been out of the country for twenty years.

A Charter (or constitution) had been forced on Louis XVIII. It guaranteed a legislature, which sat continuously from June 4 to December 30, 1814. Its chief legislation, however, imposed a stringent and unpopular censorship and allowed for the restoration to the émigrés of those properties which had not been sold in the twenty-four-year interim. An act to guarantee Revolutionary land settlements had been written into the Charter to reassure purchasers of national property. It did not succeed in doing so.

Disaffection centered around the salons of the hostesses of the day, Mme de Souza (the grandmother of Hortense's illegitimate child), Mme de Hamelin, and the Duchesse de St. Leu (Hortense herself). Mme de Staël was back from Napoleonic exile and received liberals at dinner three times a week.

Next door to Hortense (they shared a garden wall), lived Fouché, Duc d'Otrante, the ex-Minister of Police. He was fifty-five. He had not been able to get back into office under Louis XVIII, but his opinion was as respected as his person was feared. His fortune of between 12,000,000 and 15,000,000 francs had been made on the stock market, with the aid of secret information gathered by spies. He was without scruples, but he was also without prejudices and in any crisis did the most reasonable thing. He had always been extremely good at getting inconvenient people out of the way, rather than making martyrs of them. In short, he was astute.

But he looked horrible, even worse than Talleyrand, whose chief defect, so long as he was sitting down and relatively motionless and seen from in front, was merely a rouged, pert and haughtily supercilious expression. Fouché was gaunt and untidy, pale, unhealthy, white-lipped, and bloodshot and shifty of eye. Oddly, he had always been popular with women and with the émigrés, for whom he had done many small lifesaving favors from time to time in the past (he was to do the same for the Bonapartes in the immediate future). Though wily, tricky, and devious, Fouché was not a bad man, but he had a bad reputation. "Behold," said Chateaubriand one day, as Talleyrand and Fouché entered the room, "Vice on the arm of Crime."

Fouché early foresaw (and pointed out to Blacas in a paper to be read to Louis XVIII) that the mistakes of the new regime would lead to revolution. He had thoughtfully asked Hortense to allow him to lean a ladder against their common wall and was to play not only a leading role but several roles in coming events.

The liberals in the legislature, as usual, undermined the government by dwelling upon its mistakes and questioning its motives. The extreme monarchists were equally destructive of public confidence. Under the guise of supporting King and Charter, some Bonapartists led by the Duc de Bassano ran a spiteful satirical review, the *Nain Jaune*, which denounced the Ministers, émigrés and the clergy so wittily that even the King read it and refused to have it suppressed.

One of the most unpopular measures was the King's attempt to impose upon France the rigors of an English sabbath. All grogshops were closed during divine worship. This caused so much discontent that the Sabbath had to be discontinued. There is nothing worse than an English Sunday, particularly in France.

The government cannot be accused of bad intentions, but it was incredibly inept. For example, it retired the military on half pay, which amounted to five francs a week, which was not enough to live on, while at the same time reviving the household troops of the time of Henri IV, 6,000 of them, 5,000 of these officers. Instead of being judiciously broken up, regiments known to be Bonapartist were sent intact to the provinces.

If Napoléon could not understand that the nineteenth century had superseded him, the Bourbons found it impossible to remember that the eighteenth century had been for some time over. It was a disastrous illusion. In Fouché's opinion, if Bonaparte returned, if the first regiment went over to him, so would France.

His remark to André, the present Minister of Police and one of his previous subordinates, that "let Napoléon be moved farther away, or watch the coasts carefully, otherwise we shall have him back in the spring, with the swallows and the violets," was not reassuring. Neither was the King's removal of 60,000 men to the region of Grenoble to counter Murat's rearmament projects in Italy.

Fouché retired to his country house at Ferrières and began to shape a military plot to throw out the government. The plotters all wished for a different substitute, one Napoléon, another the Duc d'Orléans, another someone else, but this did not disturb Fouché. The only reason the coup did not succeed was that on the night of March 5, Fouché learned, at the house of the Princess de Vaudemont, that Napoléon had left Elba.

He therefore so managed matters that all the chief plotters were arrested except himself. If Napoléon was defeated, he could make himself a leading member of the provisional government. If Napoléon succeeded, he could present his plot as a useful diversion on the Emperor's behalf.

At first the Bourbon government was not unduly concerned at the news of Napoléon's escape. It was thought there were enough troops in the south to take care of him. The Comte d'Artois was sent to Lyons, with the Duc d'Orléans.

Unfortunately Napoléon took Lyons without opposition, Ney defected, Monsieur (the Comte d'Artois) and the Duc d'Orléans returned to Paris, Soult resigned as Minister of War, and the government turned to Fouché.

Fouché was not to be lured into an office he deemed would be so temporary, but consented to advise, for he did not expect the new Imperial regime to last long either. On the 15th he had a private conference with Monsieur. At the end of it, he is said to have said, "Let your Royal Highness look after the King, I shall look after the Monarchy." It seems likely he agreed to stay on, but to betray Napoléon to the royalists.

The next day an attempt was made to arrest him. It may have been a contrivance to reassure Napoléon later. He paid no attention and drove home. When the police came to arrest him there, he escaped by means of Hortense's wall and his own ladder. It is interesting that a few days later, as Imperial Minister of Police, one of his first acts was to promote the man ostensibly sent to arrest him.

On the same day, the King spoke to the assembled Chambers and told them he could not end his career more fittingly than by dying for his country. The assembled Chambers then rose and shouted, "Long live the King. We will die for the King. The King forever."

Everyone then did exactly the opposite. At the Collège Henri IV the headmaster told his boys to stop shouting *Vive le Roi* and cannily took the bust of Napoléon out of the lavatory, where it had been stored. In the Faubourg St. Germain the aristocracy denounced the Duchesse de Duras for having fled the day before, and then themselves began to pack. Officers of the Gardes du Corps (who were supposed to dress in the style of Henri IV) canceled their orders for new uniforms.

There were several schemes proposed to the Royal Family. One was that Louis XVIII drive out to meet Napoléon surrounded by the

Peers and Deputies, and *shame* him into withdrawing. Another was that he fortify the Tuileries and send the Royal Family out of the country, for should Bonaparte storm the palace and kill the King, there would still be heirs. For obvious reasons, Louis XVIII found this plan inacceptable. However, it would certainly have severely embarrassed Napoléon, had it been put in force.

On Palm Sunday, March 19, crowds began to gather outside the Tuileries. Louis XVIII reviewed the troops, but was so badly received by the populace he thought it better to spend the rest of the day indoors.

Though he had fled France, during the Revolution, made up with burnt cork, Louis XVIII was a believer in good taste. So he tried not to show alarm. "He preserves nothing of his former state except the pride and vices that robbed him of it," said the Abbé Montgaillard, unimpressed by those dinners in the style of Louis XIV, served by 140 servants.

A believer in diamonds, he had had his packed into ammunition boxes and shipped north toward Belgium, together with 4,000,000 francs in cash. His shirts were to be stolen before he reached the frontier, as were the only pair of slippers that could be found to fit his gouty feet.

For the King was difficult to move, both because of his bulk and because of his decrepitude. The latter was extreme. His valet once fainted because bits and pieces of his toes came off when his boots were removed.

At midnight, he was gotten into a closed carriage, which made off for the Belgian border. Monsieur followed. Both left so secretly that the Ministers did not know of their departure until later the same night.

"The King," said Chateaubriand, "was stored away at Ghent like a battered farm wagon."

At six in the morning of the 20th, the Comte de Lavalette, who had been one of Napoléon's mamelukes—the word is Talleyrand's—went to the Post Office to confirm that the King had fled. There he found Ferrand, the Postmaster General, preparing to flee himself. Lavalette took over and sent a messenger to Napoléon, by now at Fontainebleau, to announce the King's flight. By afternoon posters were up in the streets, announcing the Emperor's return.

There now began a gallop to the Tuileries on the part of every

Bonapartist with nothing to lose and much to gain. A crowd had already gathered by ten o'clock. One of the first to get there was General Exelmans, in full dress uniform, wearing the tricolor cockade and moving in a cloud of half-pay officers. He took command of the palace. By two the tricolor was flying from the Hôtel de Ville and from the Vendôme column. The *rentes*, which had gone down on the news of Napoléon's landing, went up from 68 to 73. His stock was rising. Workmen marched through the streets, cheering the Emperor, and shopkeepers began to paint out the fleur de lis on shop signs and paint in the eagle or the bees.

Hortense had been in hiding, fearing arrest as a hostage and in particular the arrest of her children. At seven in the evening she went in her carriage to the Tuileries. She and Julie were the only members of the Imperial Family in France. Julie arrived at the palace an hour later. Hortense was greeted with cheers as she drove up.

She found the palace crowded with the former dignitaries of the Empire and their wives. They had been arriving all afternoon and did not much like what they saw. The Bonapartes were clean. The Bourbons were not. The place was a pigsty. With a great deal of giggling and some assistance from Hortense, the women began to rip the Bourbon lilies from the carpets. This was not difficult. They had merely been sewn on. In half an hour the throne room, at least, was back to Imperial shape.

Still Napoléon did not come, and the crowds began to get nervous. Some withdrew. Hortense and Julie waited.

At a little before nine a sound of distant cheering could be heard. Napoléon's carriage rattled into the courtyard, driven with extreme rapidity and surrounded by Polish lancers and an assortment of men and officers of all ranks, regiments, and costume. He himself was wearing his customary gray field coat. When he got out, he was carried up the great staircase on the shoulders of the crowd, with his eyes closed, his hands stretched out in front of him, and a smile on his lips. It could not be done, and yet he had done it. He was back. It was the fourth birthday of the ex-King of Rome.

On the first-floor landing Caulaincourt and Lavalette met him and swept him off into a private room. Downstairs the crowd became quiet. The escort tied their horses to the railings of the Place de la Carrousel and went to sleep in their cloaks. Upstairs the lights burned all night. Napoléon had no illusions left. "They have let me come as they let the other go," he was to say next day. There was much to be done.

Hortense tried to see him. He was angry and kept her waiting. He felt she had gone over to the Bourbons by staying in Paris. She said she had stayed to help her children. "How could I refuse? Did anyone refuse the Duchy of Parma for your son?"

This brought him around. He said he wanted to move Joséphine's body to St. Denis (where the royal tombs had been), not immediately, but later and without fuss.

Hortense was put to work to write an enticing letter to Marie Louise and, by the same courier, another to Eugène. These were intercepted. As a result there was some talk of removing Eugène to a prison in Hungary, but the Czar was able to prevent this.

Mme Mère, when she arrived in June, also at first refused to receive Hortense, for similar reasons, but when Napoléon intervened, was to find she liked Hortense a lot better than she had before.

At midnight of that first evening, an important personage arrived. It was Fouché. As usual, he could not be trusted, and as usual, he could not be dispensed with either. He had an hour's audience and left disappointed. He had hoped for the portfolio of Foreign Affairs, but was reinstated as Minister of Police instead.

Napoléon moved quickly, but so, in the opposite direction, did the royalists. Louis XVIII crossed over into Belgium on the 23d. At the border Marshal Macdonald said to him, "*Au revoir*, Sire, in three months' time." The same day the Duc d'Orléans sailed for England to join his wife and family, who had gone across even sooner. He had left behind him a letter to his generals canceling all orders he had given and leaving it to their judgment to act as they thought best for France. So they hoisted the tricolor.

Monsieur and the Duc de Berry, pursued by Exelmans's cavalry, also crossed the border, accompanied by 300 men and Marshal Marmont. In the west, the Duc de Bourbon fled to Spain by boat from Nantes, on the 27th. In the south, the Duc d'Angoulême, who had been held as a hostage while Napoléon meditated upon trying to exchange him for the crown jewels, which Louis XVIII had taken with him, was released and sailed, also for Spain, on April 16.

Public order had been restored with commendable alacrity. What could not be restored was international amity. All ambassadors to Paris asked for their passports. Messages sent abroad were refused delivery and returned unopened. England had pledged herself to an annual subsidy of 5,000,000 pounds sterling until the Emperor could be defeated.

Napoléon's only hope was to create disunion among the Allies. He had to hand what seemed a useful instrument with which to achieve this. In the confusions of flight, the government had left behind a copy of a secret treaty (of January 3, 1815) signed by England, Austria, and France and directed against the ambitions of Russia and Prussia. Means were found to bring this to the attention of the Czar, who though made appropriately furious by it was prudent enough not to allow it to alter his plans.

So it was necessary to raise troops. When he returned, there were only 200,000 men under arms, many of them either on semipermanent leave or else deserters. Louis XVIII had abolished conscription, but in Napoléon's opinion this did not apply to the conscripts of the class of 1815, so he had them mustered. Of course they were only raw boys. He had 25,000 veterans, and mobilized 230,000 members of the National Guard, a relatively useless force. Arms were in short supply.

The Minister of War, so soon as the fourth day of the new reign, was asked to supply 400,000 muskets by the end of the year. Uniforms and clothing were scarce, and 5,000 cavalry horses had been let out to farmers, as a Bourbon economy measure, and now had to be got, with difficulty, back.

Napoléon had earlier introduced standardization of military equipment (he had cut the types of artillery wheel from twenty-two to eight) and soon had things in order again. The Vincennes factory produced 2,000,000 cartridges in two months, enough for a hundred rounds for each man. This was for the Army of the North. 56,000 horses were rounded up, and 6,000 muskets reconditioned. In a short while, it was possible to make 2,000 new muskets a day. It was not enough. You cannot lose half a million men in two years, with most of their equipment, and restore the loss immediately. His new army was impromptu and its leaders were tired. He tried to reintroduce conscription, but was persuaded that to do so would be too dangerous. "I find the hatred of the priests and nobles as widespread and violent as at the beginning of the Revolution," he said. The mob would have followed him, but he was afraid of it.

In addition, he had to grant a liberal constitution, abolition of censorship and of the slave trade, and pretend he was a constitutional monarch. This tied his hands.

His only real supporters were the soldiers. On the 2d of April he held a large banquet on the Champ de Mars. 15,000 soldiers and militiamen were fed, while 1,000 officers dined at the nearby École Militaire. This was followed by a procession to the column in the Place Vendôme, its leaders carrying a bust of the Emperor. But discipline was bad, because the rank and file suspected their officers of disloyalty, since most of them had consented to serve under Louis XVIII.

In the theaters things went better. Mlle George, as a former Imperial mistress, was always applauded when she appeared.

Napoléon left the Tuileries for the Élysées, since court life was impossible without the presence of Marie Louise. That neither she nor the ex-King of Rome ever did arrive did much to undermine the security of his regime. He continued to use the Tuileries for receptions and religious rites. He tried to fortify Paris.

The calling up of troops was unpopular. There were uprisings in Brittany and the Vendée. In Amiens a notice was distributed in the streets, which said "Who recalled Bonaparte? The army. Then let the army defend him. His enemies are our friends." Marseilles was rebellious. Fouché was caught out in secret negotiations with Metternich at the end of March. Fouché explained it in his own way. "I ought to have you shot," said the Emperor. "I can't agree with you, Sire," said Fouché, and since he had a large following, he was left unmolested.

Though Napoléon had been greeted with joy, his continued presence produced gloom. It seems to have been felt that he was bad for business. During April and May the theaters were ill attended, the shops empty, and the *rentes* fell once more, this time to 56. The general feeling was that war was coming. On April 13 it had been necessary to publish a report on foreign relations, in order to justify military preparations and to prove that the coming war was none of his making.

With no one else to fall back on, he had to summon the family. Caroline was a traitor, Elisa was a prisoner, Eugène refused to stir, and Louis stipulated he would consent to arrive only on condition that he might divorce Hortense and have total custody of the children. It never seems to have occurred to him that his making of conditions was rendered futile by the fact that nobody wanted him on any terms. Pauline, also, was a prisoner. Joseph had arrived, however, and was made a Peer, to steer the upper house, and Lucien had come and was placed at the head of the Assembly. Jérôme, Mme Mère, and Cardinal Fesch turned out to be less useful.

Joseph and Lucien, having had their experience of exile and a diminished stature, not to say income, were more cooperative, if no more helpful, than they had ever been before.

But there was something hesitant and sad about this return. It was haunted by empty rooms. Napoléon had taken to visiting time past as though he no longer had a future. In April he told Hortense that he would like to visit Malmaison. She had not been there since Joséphine died, and went ahead to open the house. When he arrived, he locked himself up in Joséphine's room, and when he came out, it was plain he had been crying.

Joseph was installed at the Luxembourg, Lucien, at last an Imperil Prince, at the Palais Royal. Lucien found the Emperor, whom he had not seen for years, much changed. His health, too, was bad. His cancer had probably begun, he had kidney trouble, his venereal diseases had been checked but not cured. He had trouble staying awake. Lucien urged him to abdicate in favor of L'Aiglon. Napoléon sometimes considered it, but always rallied. He had become pettily quarrelsome. "Men have grown very daring in his presence since his misfortunes," wrote the diarist Viel-Castel, and "despoiled him of his former prestige."

On April 20, the Swiss closed their frontiers. On May 2d, Ferdinand VII of Spain declared war. The British sank French shipping, even though Napoléon had his own boats fly the Bourbon flag to prevent this.

And the government was unruly. He was forced to grant a constitution. Since the Assembly was more given to oratory than to effort, it had been drawn up by Benjamin Constant. The result was a hasty botch satisfactory to no one. The Bonapartists thought it made too many concessions to the liberals, and the liberals thought it did not make enough. The people as a whole treated it with indifference. Napoléon made the mistake of ordering elections to take place. The result was that of 629 deputies elected, only eighty were Bonapartists, 500 were liberals who could not cooperate with each other, let alone with anyone else, and forty were Jacobins. This result had largely been rigged by Fouché, who wished to cause embarrassment all around.

The Acte Additionnel, as the constitution was known, was proclaimed on April 23 and was practically identical with the Charter of Louis XVIII. Napoléon's opinion of it was that "I am asked to allow the men I have loaded with wealth to make use of their fortunes to plot against me abroad," which was true enough. The ambitious politicians who had at first supported him now tried to limit his power and to defeat him. It was absurd. Only as a military dictator could he give them support, but only if he were stripped of all real power would they support him.

On the 1st of June occurred the ceremony of the Champ de Mai, which was to inaugurate the Acte Additionnel. 1,228,257 citizens had voted for it, and 4,802 against. Most of the 5,000,000 entitled to vote had not voted at all.

It was a mad ceremony. 600 guns were fired at each salute, and there were many salutes. 50,000 soldiers assembled. The Emperor's departure from the Tuileries for the Champ de Mai was signaled by one hundred guns.

There were heralds, eagle banners, and state coaches. Napoléon and his brothers appeared on a large platform built out from the École Militaire. Two pyramids of trophies had been set up, together with an altar. He and his brothers entered public view from the École Militaire. At first they were greeted with a shout, but then the crowd became utterly silent. This was because of their costumes. For Napoléon, Lucien, Jérôme, and Joseph were dressed in outrageous getups of white satin trimmed with rosettes and diamonds, ermine, and purple cloaks. It was unreal.

John Cam Hobhouse, who was present, described them with that accuracy available only to the malicious. "The Emperor looked very ungainly and squat," in purple mantle and black hat looped up at the side with a diamond brooch; "Joseph and Jérôme, caparisoned in fancy dresses of white taffety, as ill as the princes of any legitimate House in Europe." Napoléon did not help matters by staring at the people through opera glasses to relieve the tedium of the public prayers. He also gave a very bad speech, only part of it audible.

But the shocking thing had been their appearance. Napoléon had held back fashions and designed an age. But now the continuity had been broken, it could be seen that the national leader had become, overnight, an uncertain anachronism.

"*Empéreur, consul, soldat, je tiens tout du peuple,*" was all that could be heard of the speech. "*Je tiens tout du peuple,*" was to become the incessant motto of the next generation of Bonapartes, as they ceaselessly strove to ride to power again on the backs of the newly fashionable proletariat, by emulating the politicians of the day who had so successfully done exactly the same thing.

The ceremony ground on. A few shouted, "*Vive* Marie Louise." This created an awkward silence, until some soldiers had the wit to shout, "*Vive l'Impératrice. Vive le Roi de Rome. Nous irons les chercher.*"

Napoléon then climbed to the top of one of the pyramids and sat down, surrounded by his followers and with his trophies below him. His hat had gone askew, and he looked very much like a white satin and purple velvet Aunt Sally. He then distributed the Imperial eagles.

Afterward Fouché said to Hortense, "The Emperor has just lost a good opportunity. I urged him to abdicate today. Had he done so, his son would reign and there would be no war."

On May 3, Neipperg had defeated Murat, Napoléon's only ally, though his efforts to seize a bigger kingdom for himself had ruined Napoléon's chances of making peace with the Allies, at Tolentino. Jérôme, Mme Mère, and Fesch had gotten out just ahead of the invading Austrians, after a wild ride over back country lasting twelve and a half hours.

The fiasco of the 1st of June had been Lucien's idea. And like Murat's, it had led to trouble. Four days later Napoléon prepared to leave for Belgium. It was a Sunday and a public holiday. Thirty-six fountains in the Champs Élysées were made to run with wine. There were twelve outdoor buffets, and theatrical performances and mountebanks to amuse the crowd. At night there was a concert and a fireworks display. The set piece showed a ship, the brig on which Napoléon had returned from Elba, the Emperor himself, and a bright star over his head. He watched this from a balcony of the Tuileries. After a while the star waned.

The Allies were beginning to mass on the Belgian border. They had 210,000 men to Napoléon's 124,000.

On the 7th the Emperor attended the opening of the new French parliament. So did Mme Mère. The disastrous white costumes were worn again.

"Today my dearest wish is accomplished; tomorrow I begin my reign as a constitutional monarch." It was clear from his expression that he did not like the sound of it. It was also clear that he was ill.

In return, four days later, again on a Sunday, the two Chambers addressed the Emperor at the Tuileries. They dwelt upon their rights, not his.

That night Napoléon dined *en famille* for the last time. Mme Mère, Hortense, Joseph, Lucien, and Jérôme were there. At the end of the meal Hortense's children, Napoléon Louis and Louis Napoléon, ten and seven respectively, were brought in and made much of.

He had already had printed and sent ahead proclamations issued as from the Imperial Palace of Laeken, outside Brussels. But he was traveling encumbered, for he took with him cash, diamonds, his personal gold plate, eighty Arabian horses, and a traveling library of 800 volumes. He left Paris on the 12th of June, at three-thirty in the morning.

His parliament began to intrigue against him even before he had departed, a particularly vociferous voice being that of Lafayette, the self-proclaimed Friend of Liberty, whom Napoléon himself had asked to enter the new Chambers (and at that he had had to persuade him; Lafayette was vain, not to say girlish, of political rectitude).

The battle of Waterloo began Sunday of June 18. Napoléon had been suffering from hemorrhoids since the previous Friday, and was thus paralyzed from divided attention and an inability to make a clearheaded decision about much of anything. Sometimes he contradicted himself.

THOUGH the battle lasted long enough to be sometimes in doubt, and though Jérôme, for the first and last time in his life, surprised everyone by his intrepidity, it was, of course, the final blow to the regime.

Napoléon fled, and had a nightmare journey back to France. Even his personal treasury of some 1,600,000 francs was scattered across the road and into the ditches, where soldiers and townspeople fought for it. He rode alone, with two carriages behind him, containing Bassano, Bertrand, Drouot, Gourgaud, Flahaut and Labédoyère. These made for Paris via Laon.

On the battlefield, the Prussians captured, near the village of Genappe, Napoléon's famous traveling carriage, built for the Russian campaign. In it they found, among other things, the state mantle, diamond coronet, and so forth he had intended for his triumphal entry into Brussels. In a flap in the berlin, which had also been abandoned, was Pauline's diamond necklace. The diamonds went to the King of Prussia; the rest, including a gold as well as a silver table service and more plate of one kind and another, was anybody's booty. Blücher took charge of the traveling carriage.

At first the battle had been announced in Paris as a victory. Cannon were fired from Les Invalides. It was a bright sunny Sunday morning (the news came by heliograph). But by Monday it was known that there had been two battles, not one, and by evening of the same day a dispatch rider came in with two letters written by the Emperor. One was to be read to the Council of Ministers, and said that the battle had been lost. The second, to his brother, said that all was not lost yet.

Napoléon himself arrived at eight A.M. on Wednesday, June 21. By then everyone who was awake knew that there had been a disaster. If he had gone straight to the Chamber of Deputies, as Lucien advised, and had dispersed both Chambers, he could still have saved something by proclaiming a dictatorship. Instead, in agony from an inflamed bladder, he went straight to a hot bath, in which he sat beating the water with his palms, crying he was defeated, defeated, defeated. This was at Caulaincourt's house. Lavalette, who was there, says he laughed like an epileptic.

Joseph and Lucien arrived. Lucien had learned of what had happened at about noon on the 20th. Fouché had been better informed and sooner, during the night of the 19th and 20th, and had immediately begun to pay visits and make disruptive proposals to both Deputies and Peers. To Bonapartists, he had advocated abdication in favor of L'Aiglon; to the liberals, such as Lafayette, he explained that Napoléon would try to impose a dictatorship, which must be opposed at all costs. Then he went off to intrigue by messenger with the Allies and the Bourbons.

When the Minister of War came, Napoléon was still in the tub. Fouché, having made his preparations, came next, to reassure Napoléon, so that the Chambers could meet undisturbed.

At ten Napoléon, after a walk in the Élysées gardens, during which he was cheered by the crowd gathered there, held a meeting of his Ministers. Lucien advised him to round up what troops he had and march on the Chambers. Napoléon refused, for though the mob was clamoring for arms, he did not think it safe to trust it. On the 10th, he had warned both Chambers not to follow the example of the Greeks, who had continued to squabble about abstractions while the enemy was at their gates. It was not a warning heeded. He would have done better, from his own point of view, to arm the mob. As Benjamin Constant said, "The wretches who were eager to serve him when he crushed liberty are abandoning him now that he is establishing it."

But of course he had had no desire to establish it. What he wanted to do was decree a universal mobilization. "In the public interest I could seize that power [dictatorship]; but it would be better for it to be given me by the Chambers."

He had hesitated too long. Fouché informed both Chambers that Napoléon proposed to dissolve them. And Lafayette could always be counted upon to raise a clamor in the name of liberty, which to him was a goddess, rather than a condition.

Both Lucien and Joseph appeared before their respective Chambers, but without effect. On the motion of Lafayette, the Assembly declared itself in permanent session and decreed that anyone endeavoring to dissolve it would be guilty of high treason. In the streets the crowds were shouting, "*Aux armes! Aux armes! Vive l'Empéreur!*"

Lucien, who reached the Chamber at six P.M., had the galleries cleared and very nearly swayed the house, but concluded his remarks with the unfortunate phrase that if France abandoned Napoléon, the other nations might "brand her with levity and inconstancy."

This was Lafayette's chance to play to his preferred audience. He was fifty-eight and a professional liberal, popular with the mob, scheming and muddleheaded, an antidynastic aristocrat, of a kind by no means unknown. As the Comte d'Artois said when he became Charles X, "The only two men in France who have not changed since 1789 are Lafayette and myself." His chief characteristic, in Thomas Jefferson's phrase, was "a canine appetite for popularity." He was vociferous, self-righteous, and fantastically long-lived, and though none of his plots ever succeeded, he spoke always for the underdog, even when there was not one.

He spoke now. "That is a calumny," he said. "How can anyone charge the French nation with inconstancy and levity toward Napoléon? They have followed him through the sands of Egypt and the steppes of Russia, and that is why we now have to mourn the loss of 3,000,000 Frenchmen." He was much applauded. Lucien was booed.

Lucien went back to the Élysées, where the Emperor was having dinner with Hortense. Another council was held, at the Tuileries, this one lasting from eleven at night until three the next morning.

Next day the Chambers decided to send commissioners to the Allies, to negotiate a peace, thus bypassing the Emperor. Napoléon thought of a *coup d'état* but dared not attempt it. He was given the choice of abdicating or being deposed. At about noon of June 22 he dictated his abdication to Lucien. It was in favor of the reign of his son. The crowds were still shouting, "*Vive l'Empéreur,*" outside the windows.

The Chambers ignored the accession of Napoléon II, though according to the constitution and the Acte Additionnel it was legal.

Once more Lucien had to intervene, and was denounced for his pains as not being French. The crowds outside, however, were for the Emperor and against the Deputies. Fouché advised the Chambers to recognize the claims of Napoléon II, for as he pointed out, they could as easily vote for another sovereign when the time came.

This was on the 23d, the day Jérôme arrived from Belgium. He stayed with Cardinal Fesch. The crowds in the city hailed Napoléon II and again demanded arms. Fouché asked Napoléon to withdraw.

Napoléon had said to Benjamin Constant, "If I abdicate today, in two days' time you will no longer have an army. These poor fellows do not understand your subtleties. Is it credible that metaphysical axioms, declarations of rights, harangues from the tribune, will stop an army disbanding? To reject me when I landed at Cannes, that I can conceive possible; to abandon me now is what I cannot understand. A government cannot be overthrown with impunity when the enemy is only twenty-five leagues away. Does anyone imagine that the foreign powers will be won over by fine words?"

With something much like this in view, Fouché had had himself named president of the commission which would treat with the Allies. He was hampered by the intransigence of the Chambers (he had sent Lafayette and other troublemakers on a fool's errand to get rid of them), by the refusal of the Allies to agree to an armistice, and perhaps a little by his own desire to see the Duc d'Orléans on the throne rather than Louis XVIII.

On June 22 Louis XVIII moved to Mons, where he was finally persuaded to divest himself of his favorite, Blacas. On the 24th, Wellington suggested that His Majesty's presence on French territory was again desirable, so he entered Cambrai. That he was moving directly behind the Allied baggage wagons made him no more popular. On the 28th the Proclamation of Cambrai was signed. It provided, among other things, for the punishment of those who had joined in or promoted the Hundred Days. The Chambers were to hand these offenders over to the law, an attempt to shift the odium of prosecution from the Royal Family to the government.

In Paris, Fouché was endeavoring to negotiate with Wellington, but Wellington refused to negotiate. Some Bonapartist generals spoke of surrounding the Tuileries, where Fouché now was, and having him shot in the courtyard. Davout, who had resigned as Minister of War, presented a protest against the recall of the Bourbons.

Two things saved Fouché. Davout reached the conclusion it was better to accept Louis XVIII, and on the 30th of June the Prussian bombardment of Aubervilliers, a mile from the capital, shook every window in the city.

On the 24th Joseph and Lucien left Paris for Malmaison. Napoléon left the Élysées Palace (by a side door) on the morning of the 25th, for the same destination. Hortense had once more gone ahead to open another wing of the house, for he did not wish to sleep in Joséphine's old quarters. Mme Mère also left the city for Malmaison, arriving the late afternoon of the 25th.

As for Paris, it behaved much as it did in 1940, though there were crowds kneeling at the Vendôme column. All the theaters were once more well attended, the cafés of the boulevards were popular, and there were an unusually large number of well-dressed women to be seen about. The Bourse continued to prosper, and all important *rentes* continued to rise, the closer the enemy got to Paris. They stood at 63 when Le Bourget was occupied, at 64 after the fall of Aubervilliers. The town council waited on Fouché, to beg him not to defend Paris. Sismondi, the historian, complaining of the forthcoming capitulation, was told "that it was easy to see that he had nothing but his writing table to lose." Pamphlets appeared with such titles as "Let us have done with him," and sold enormously.

But this capitulation was not to be so uneventful as the previous one. The Allies now wanted revenge. On June 28 Blücher sent a cavalry regiment to capture Napoléon. Its efforts were frustrated only by blowing up the bridge at Chatou.

Though Paris was not to capitulate until July 3, Fouché ordered Napoléon to remove to the relative safety of the port of Rochefort, where two frigates would be put at his disposal.

At Malmaison, where the gardens had never been lovelier, and the Scottish and English gardeners still moved among the roses, it was a time of farewells. "My life ended with the Emperor's fall," said Mme Mère, afterward. A page slept on the threshold of Napoléon's bedroom, both to protect him and to prevent another suicide attempt. Various people came to say goodbye, Cardinal Fesch, Countess Walewska and Alexandre, even Napoléon's other illegitimate son, Léon Denuelle, turned up. He distinguished himself by saying he was on Louis XVIII's side, because he didn't like the Emperor.

As usual, both Joseph and Lucien ignored Hortense. Times may have changed, but she was still a Beauharnais. Mme Mère was scarcely more hospitable. But Napoléon seemed glad to have her there. She went walking with him in the gardens, which both found haunted by Joséphine. There was a rumor that 500 royalists were marching on the house, to assassinate the Emperor.

"How beautiful it is," said Napoleon. "How happy we would be if we could stay here forever." He could not bring himself to leave.

Hortense advocated escape to America, and so did his brothers. She gave him a diamond necklace, for which he gave her a receipt to the value of 200,000 francs.

On the 29th, as he was about to depart, the Emperor suddenly changed into uniform and persuaded General Beker, who was there to guard him but was also his jailer, to go to Paris to offer the Imperial services to the government, simply as those of a general. Afterward, he said, he would leave for the United States, once the enemy had been defeated. Fouché went purple with exasperation, and Beker was sent back to Malmaison to say no. The Emperor did not protest, took off his uniform, and after saying a remarkably monosyllabic farewell to his mother, drove off for Rochefort.

The family began to disperse. Hortense, walking through the Malmaison picture gallery, looked at everyone she had ever known, and realized that now the pictures would have to be packed to prevent confiscation. She then started back for Paris by a roundabout route, to avoid the Prussian troops in the neighborhood.

At Paris, all demands for an armistice were refused. The Prussians were crossing the Seine. Davout had to shift troops from the north to the south side of the city. The march of troops through the streets panicked the inhabitants. Nobody wanted to resist, but nobody wanted to assume the responsibility for capitulating. By calling a meeting at midnight and holding it until three in the morning of July 3, Fouché got answers sufficiently ambiguous from his advisers to enable him to open negotiations for surrender. On July 1 Wellington had been informed that Napoléon was on his way to the United States, and he had declared that this news removed the great obstacle to an armistice, or would, if the French would agree to the military evacuation of Paris. He did not wish to attack, for should he be beaten back, he would lose what prestige he had gained at Waterloo. Blücher, however, wished to sack the city, and it was difficult to restrain him. On the third, fighting began. It did not last long. Fouché had ordered Davout to agree to the occupation of the capital. Conferences took place at St. Cloud. The French army was to retire behind the Loire.

At nine on the evening of the 3d Fouché had the articles of capitulation in his hands. Changing the word capitulation to convention, he sent them over to the Chambers. He had had a busy day. Among other things, he and his fellow members of the Provisional Commission of Government had divided up the 140,000 francs expense money on hand among themselves, as a self-granted gratuity. The Chambers made no difficulty about the convention (or capitulation). Its members were much too busy discussing the rights of man, decreeing the abolition of titles of nobility, drafting constitutions, and in other ways disporting themselves to consider such matters as the enemy at the gates.

Napoléon II had been forgotten. "This has reassured me about a lot of stupid rumors which have been in the air here," wrote Marie Louise to her father, when Louis XVIII entered Paris again. The stupid rumors had been about her being one of the Regents should Napoléon II's claims be recognized.

On the 5th, Fouché went out to Neuilly to confer with Talleyrand, Pozzo di Borgo, the Czar's Ambassador to Paris, and others. He wished to talk himself into office again. Wellington helped. On the 6th Talleyrand and Fouché had an interview with Louis XVIII, at St. Denis. Louis XVIII agreed to retain him as Minister of Police. "I have told him [Wellington]," he wrote, "to do whatever he may think best in my interests, but he must be tender with me, *c'est mon pucelage.*"

Fouché's reinstatement turned out to be a very good thing for such Bonapartes as were left in the vicinity.

Fouché had borrowed 2,000,000 francs from the banker Laffitte with which to pay off the troops. So they left the city relatively quietly. He also wished to preserve the tricolor as the national flag (a sensible suggestion: it would have saved much face with many people), but this was refused.

On the 7th, while he was trying to induce the Chambers to dissolve themselves, without much success, a Prussian detachment with two guns arrived in the courtyard below the conference room. The Chambers dissolved, but it was necessary to have the National Guard turn them out in order to get them to do so. This happened on the 8th, the day Louis XVIII entered the city, which he did by the St. Denis gate.

It was a raggletaggle procession, for behind him came an endless file of cabs, country carts, and wagons, filled with English officers and sightseers. There was little cheering. At the Tuileries, some Prussian troops were hanging out their wash on the railings of the palace. They went right on doing it, before and after he had entered the building. There was no one to meet him.

Napoléon had reached Niort on July 2, where he was joined by Joseph, who had gone to Paris to arrange about money. Napoléon's private fortune had been deposited with Laffitte, and Joseph had withdrawn enough gold from it to take care of emergencies. On the 3d the two brothers went on to Rochefort.

The two promised frigates, the *Saale* and the *Méduse*, lay at anchor, still flying the tricolor, but the British were patrolling the harbor mouths. This made Napoléon a virtual prisoner, since there was no way of getting past the blockade. Joseph, with the aid of an American, arranged to have him run through the cordon on a blockade runner, concealed in a cask marked brandy. Napoléon declined. It seemed desperate, and his dignity was offended.

He tried to board the *Saale* on the 8th, but since the Provisional Government no longer ruled and the Bourbon government was now restored, permission to sail was denied. As Rochefort was Bonapartist, the authorities asked the ex-Emperor to withdraw to the Île d'Aix.

Joseph had chartered an American vessel at Bordeaux for his own flight. He now proposed, for the two looked somewhat alike, that he masquerade as the ex-Emperor, and that the ex-Emperor sail for America in his stead. Proscription had begun. Unless he left soon, the ex-Emperor would be hunted down as an outlaw. Napoléon refused the offer and proposed instead to throw himself on the mercy of the English. Joseph offered to do the same. The ex-Emperor said he would be of more use in America.

So Joseph escaped in a fishing boat on the morning of July 4, appropriately enough, and boarded his American schooner (the Pike).

Napoléon opened negotiations with the British on the 9th and on the 15th surrendered to Captain Maitland, of the *Bellerophon*. Maitland, from no motive, apparently, but good will, promised more than he could guarantee. The thought was that Napoléon would live within twelve miles of London, incognito and closely watched.

Getting the ex-Emperor aboard was not easy. There was a good deal of luggage, and since he had been refused permission to return to the mainland, he had to be taken off the Île d'Aix. Loading began at midnight of the 15th. At three A.M. the ex-Emperor came aboard the sloop which was to take him out to the *Bellerophon,* dressed as a colonel of chasseurs. Since he arrived before dawn, Maitland was absolved, by naval regulations, from firing a salute, which relieved him, for the departure was a clandestine operation. During the morning fresh vegetables and fruit were brought out. Then they set sail.

The British government was embarrassed at his having sought asylum and did not know what to do with him. Lord Liverpool, then Prime Minister, even went so far as to write to Castlereagh, the Foreign Secretary, suggesting that the best solution would be for Louis XVIII to have him shot. At any rate, he could not stay in Great Britain, where he was apt to become "an object of popular compassion."

On the 28th of July, it was agreed to send him to St. Helena.

─────────────── ❧{ XIV }❧ ───────────────

Aꜰᴛᴇʀ Napoléon left Elba, Pauline and Mme Mère were left holding a very large and very empty paper bag. On the morning of the 28th of February Sir Neil Campbell arrived back from Leghorn. He came ashore at a little after noon, found out what had happened, and went straight to the Casa Mulini, where he demanded to see Pauline. Since he was somewhat frightened, he attempted to scare her. His rage took a typically British form.

"Your brother has broken his word not to leave the island," he said.

Pauline managed to keep her composure. So did Mme Mère. They both belonged to a tradition in which the giving and taking of words is a tricky business. But Sir Neil Campbell's equanimity had been disturbed and his manner was threatening. Pauline was upset, and when Campbell went once more to the mainland, to report the escape, she escaped herself, on the night of March 3, in a felucca, with four servants and her sedan chair, landing next morning at Viareggio, where she was recognized but encountered the Marchese Mansi, an old admirer. He did not dare to help her.

The countryside was in Austrian hands, but remembering that Elisa, who was at Bologna, had a villa nearby, Pauline had herself carried up to Campignano in her sedan chair. From there she hoped to go on to Rome, where Lucien would arrange for her immediate future. But her luck had run out. Lucien went to Paris, and Pauline was to be detained at Campignano until October 11.

Mme Mère's departure was more stately and longer delayed, and her luck was better. She wrote to Caroline, at Naples, asking for a frigate to come to take her off. Instead she received a small squadron, led by a seventy-four-gun ship of the line, the *Joachim*. The Murats

151

wished to conciliate her. In view of their recent treachery, a ship of the line did not seem too much. She went aboard with Mme Bertrand and Mme Bertrand's children, and the guns of Porto Ferraio saluted her as she left the harbor.

At Naples, she at once rebuked Caroline for her treason. Caroline pleaded remorse. Since the Murats were still in power and the Bonapartes had not gotten theirs back yet, things were patched up somehow, with the assistance of Fesch, who had arrived in search of his half sister. Jérôme arrived overland, after a hazardous trip, and Fesch, Mme Mère and he set out for France, by way of Corsica. Jérôme rode ahead from the south of France, but Mme Mère and Fesch did not reach Paris until June 1, which left them scarcely time to get ready to flee again.

Pauline was trapped at Campignano. She did not at first think so. Instead she had a mass said in her bathroom, for she did not wish to interrupt her bath, for her fortunate escape from Elba.

A Colonel Wercklein, the Austrian governor of Lucca, who took his duties seriously, had Campignano surrounded by cavalry. Pauline promptly evolved a scheme to dope the guards with opium. It proved impracticable. So she appealed to her husband and to the Grand Duke of Tuscany. This had no effect either. Murat was induced to intervene, and Napoléon tried to. Colonel Wercklein remained adamant.

Pauline fell back on the precarious state of her health, never better. With the aid of a hot-water bottle, makeup, a darkened room, a half-blind specialist, and a doctor dazzled into acting as her accomplice, who provided false blood and urine samples, she managed to convince the world that she was indeed dying. Wercklein allowed her to move to the baths at Lucca, where she set up, eventually, at the Villa Fatinelli, in San Pancrazio, nearby. Just as things began to go better, Wercklein intercepted some of her correspondence. She was at no time political, but she did have her opinions, which she expressed vividly, and she was a Bonaparte. She was watched more closely again. The Hundred Days passed. Wercklein took pleasure in describing to her Waterloo, the second abdication, and the exile to St. Helena.

She had other worries, and much time to think of them, for her treasury was empty. This meant giving a little thought to her previous treatment of Borghese, her vehemently estranged husband (the vehemence was hers; there is no record that Camillo ever felt strongly about anything), for somehow she would have to wheedle or threaten money out of him.

She thought of selling her furniture, which had arrived at Elba, but was offered so little for it that she paid her doctors' bills with it instead. Some were given pictures, some small tables, and some chairs. Vacca, the doctor she had used as an accomplice, got her state bed.

Pauline's attitude toward her husband (it resembled everybody else's except in intensity) is best summed up in a brisk exchange she once had with the Emperor, whom she was nagging for a position for Camillo. Napoléon said angrily that he was good for nothing. Pauline agreed instantly, but asked what that had to do with it.

In 1803, which is when she had first met him, he was 28, the head of his family (he had a younger brother), slender, rich, and beautiful in the Italian way. He was also completely empty-headed, his father's educational program having been based upon his belief that as future subjects of the Pope, his sons "would have known too much, if they had known nothing at all." In 1798 Camillo had taken up the new fashionable French principles and had danced around a bonfire of cardinals' hats in the Piazza di Spagna. This, his only recorded political act, though it endeared him to the French, did not disturb the Pope, who knew him merely to be a rattlebrain. But Camillo had not felt happy in Rome and in the fall of 1802 had set out on his own version of the Grand Tour, arriving in Paris in March of 1803. He knew no more of the world than can be acquired at billiards, and was not equipped by nature to cope with a highhanded woman. For a while, he lived in retirement, studying French with, oddly, his concièrge. His interests in life were bric-à-brac, art dealers, practical jokes, and being a gentleman not so much jockey as coachman. He was quite content to fritter his life away. He had nothing else to do with it.

Pauline was then the widow of Leclerc and had to be married again to cover up her extramarital behavior, which was careless and scandalous. Prince Borghese was introduced to her, and then literally conned into marrying her. Pauline was delighted. Borghese was upset. The Borghese family, however, thought the marriage would protect them from future Napoleonic depradations in Italy. The marriage contract was signed. Its terms were to be the basis of all Pauline's future legal assaults on her husband. It provided that any income from her first husband's estate (sizable) was to be exclusively hers, that she and Borghese should have separate establishments and property, that her allowance from him should be 50,000 francs a year, her place of residence left to her own choice, and that should Borghese die, her dowry would revert to her. The dowry itself was 800,000 francs, Borghese to keep the interest and use of the capital, but out of it to give her 20,000 francs a year pin money. Since Pauline spent almost that much a year for pins, it was not much. The wing of the Borghese palace in Rome she was to occupy was to be hers for life. She was to have two carriages.

Pauline was always ruthless with her husbands. It did not take her long to get to the bottom of Borghese. For one thing, there was not much to him. For another, he was a bundle of good manners, nothing more, and somewhat disappointingly had a very small penis. Pauline, whose nymphomania was periodic but intense, scorned all but very large ones. There is a diverting medical correspondence about the matter, pointing out that her neurasthenia was based on nothing but undue friction, mostly brought on by M. de Forbin, who was endowed with a usable gigantism and very hard to get rid of.

To a natural antipathy toward her husband, therefore, Pauline added an exasperated and clinically specific scorn. Rome bored her. And when Pauline was bored, she acted. Her terrorism of Borghese spread over twelve years. It took her about two months first to remove Borghese from her bedroom and then to remove herself from him. And of course since she *was* married, that meant she must have a new lover.

Camillo became hysterical. He spoke to Mme Mère. He spoke to Cardinal Fesch. He wrote to Angiolini, an abbé who had arranged the marriage. "Even though any denial was out of the question, it seems to me she might have made everything good again by a confession," he said. "This, however, she did not do. I did not even wish it: all I wish is that all the people we brought from France would return there."

He spoke to Lucien. He asked that *someone* speak to Joseph. He got Fesch to write to Napoléon.

Napoléon rebuked Pauline, and Joseph sent Camillo advice. "Women, especially before they have reached the years of discretion, insist on having what they want, and they are to be brought to their senses neither by force nor authority." This, though true, proved unhelpful. Pauline never reached the years of discretion. "Give Paoletta a son, and you will have done much to become happy," concluded Joseph.

Borghese wasn't up to administering this sovereign remedy. Besides, Paulette already had a son, Napoléon Dermide, by her first husband, and that hadn't done any good either. Pauline began to express herself volubly about the tenor of her husband's tenor and the insufficiency of his calves. She then went off to pose for Canova, thus producing a famous nude. As a matter of fact, there were two nudes. Camillo had the large or recumbent one relegated to a dark gallery at the Palazzo Borghese, where it was shown only to privileged cognoscenti. Like most libertines, he was a prude.

Relations with the Borghese worsened, the Roman Bonapartes taking Pauline's side, and the no less Roman Borghese Camillo's.

On the 18th of May, 1804, Napoléon proclaimed himself Emperor and Pauline an Imperial Highness. This gave her precedence over her husband, a position she was born to make the most of and enjoyed heartily. She treated men as she treated clothes: she spent a great deal of money on them, and unless she liked them, she wore them only once. If she did like them, she wore them out.

On becoming an Imperial Highness, she changed her name to something more mellifluously regal. Paoletta became Pauline. She was scheming to get back to Paris, but needed an excuse, in order to obtain permission.

This was provided by her son Dermide, who died on August 14, at the age of four. She was appropriately grief-stricken, and certainly Borghese was not apt to provide more. ("To give oneself to him, was to give oneself to nobody," wrote the Duchesse d'Abrantès.) The need to take her son back to his father's family burial vault at Montgobert gave her the pretext she needed for a return to Paris.

Unfortunately Camillo came with her, in the hope of getting a few new distinctive titles out of the Empire. He was given honorary citizenship, and the Grand Cordon of the Légion d'Honneur, which pleased him very much, and was made an Imperial Highness himself. But he did not find the life easy. In 1805 he reported that he could get through life only by taking a hot bath every morning: "It calms me and allows me to get through the rest of the day, which is always the same, with patience. . . . Her condition remains the same, and there is need of much patience."

Being part vegetable, Camillo had patience to spare. Being entirely animal, Pauline had none. She proclaimed that the sight of her husband was injurious to her health and asked Napoléon to get rid of him. Napoléon gave him the Golden Fleece, which he had always wanted, and had him posted (as a captain in the mounted grenadiers) to Boulogne. Camillo was overjoyed. He was thus enabled to avoid both the battlefield and his wife.

Pauline was also relieved. She had a relapse when Camillo returned after the Peace of Pressburg, but as the relapse drove him to return to Rome, she soon recovered. Napoléon made her Duchess of Guastalla in her own right, but when she found out how small Guastalla was, she traded the property, keeping only the title and allodial estates, to the Kingdom of Italy (a temporary Napoleonic creation) in return for 6,000,000 francs. All of which gave her an income of 550,000 francs a year, which was not enough.

Camillo was once more sent off to the wars, though well behind the lines, and Pauline acquired the most medically unfortunate of her lovers, M. de Forbin, a competent society painter who had studied under David and gone to Rome with Granet, was not yet thirty, and hung like a horse. He became indispensable, which distressed her doctors, Peyre, and the gynecologist, Halle. Halle's medical report makes harumphy reading.

"The twitching of the arms was hysterical. . . . The general state is one of depression and exhaustion. The inflammation is not of the ordinary sort. . . . The permanent state is one of stimulation of the sexual organs, and if this were to continue, would be of lasting disadvantage. . . . I blamed the internal douches, and spoke in general of anything, of whatever nature, that stimulates the abdomen; I think she understood. . . . One cannot always blame the douche and the hose. . . . and whatever the cause, it is high time to eliminate it. . . . We must do all in our power to save a young and interesting woman from destruction. . . . If there is anyone who shares the fault for these indulgences, this person . . . would not accuse himself. . . . We would be blamed for seeing nothing and permitting everything, however. . . . If we cannot speak as masters the only thing to do is to withdraw."

But Pauline, like many suffering from the results of overindulgence, would give up anything to cure her ailments but their cause. There was also the difficulty of breaking the news to the family.

Finally Peyre told Mme Mère, Mme Mère summoned Pauline, and
Fesch was persuaded to deliver a moral-medical lecture. Pauline obediently dismissed Forbin, and immediately took him back again on
the sly. By now she was being carted around in a litter, an eminent
example of vaginal exhaustion, and her nerves were so exacerbated
that she had all dogs shot who barked within sound of her lodgings.
Her circulation, always bad, broke down again. She had her own
way of warming cold feet. At Nice, the Prefect found Mme de
Chambaudoin lying on the floor with her dress undone. Pauline ran
her toes under the breasts while she talked to the Prefect. This was
a habit she had picked up in Martinique. It was how she received
guests.

"Your position must be uncomfortable," said the Prefect, watching the breasts flop back and forth at the touch of Pauline's very
white exploratory feet.

"Not at all," said Mme de Chambaudoin, from the floor, "I am
used to it."

Pauline inquired if the Prefect enjoyed the theater, and if so, what.

"Tragedies," said the Prefect.

"I too," said Mme de Chambaudoin, indistinctly, trying to peer
around at him. "They elevate the soul."

The conversation continued.

Deprived, temporarily, of Forbin, Pauline acquired Blangini, a vio-
linist whom she promptly took into her household as director of an
entirely imaginary orchestra. He had the added advantage that he
was cheaper than Forbin, who had at last begun to bore her. Sometimes they would sing duets together. Afterward a mass table was set
up near the music racks. Thus piety was invariably brought to the
assistance of song. In addition, Blangini composed romances and noc-
turnes. He was extremely handsome in a puppydog way.

This idyll was disrupted by the Emperor, whose moral sense
sometimes brought him into conflict with his favorite sister, though
true, most of the time, he also had the sense to laugh. He made Camillo governor general of the five departments into which the Kingdom of Sardinia had been converted, with a capital at Turin. Pauline
was ordered to accompany him, and Borghese would pick her up on
the way.

This unwelcome news was announced to her during dinner, and

Camillo, with his suite, arrived shortly thereafter. Pauline's reaction was to entertain Camillo with duets with Blangini—to be exact, following Mlle Mello's rendition of *Armide, vous m'allez quitter* with *Sempre sarò costante, sempre t'adorerò*. Camillo, who was as bored by music as he was by everything else, does not seem to have been aware of the byplay involved in the choice of piece. Blangini was carted off to Turin with the other baggage, behind the dresses in a carriage by himself, like a small but notable trophy. It made him nervous. He was afraid the Emperor might find out.

During the journey, Pauline insisted upon taking precedence over her husband and gave speeches in his stead. It was necessary to threaten her with the Emperor's name. Camillo was beginning to turn pale. At Turin, and later at Stupinigi, which she preferred, she went on a hunger diet to get permission to return to Paris. Recollecting that she had an annuity of 20,000 francs, drawn against the estate of her first husband, and tiring of no food, she decamped to the capital during July. Borghese, who had control of it, cut off her income. Pauline promptly borrowed money from the banker Laffitte. Napoléon gave in, and in October of 1808 granted her 600,000 francs a year from the civil list, permission to separate from Borghese, and the domain of Neuilly, which had been remodeled by Murat into a sixty-room palace and which he had been forced to give up to the French crown when he became King of Naples. The following February Napoléon enlarged Pauline's pension to 1,300,000 francs and at the same time raised Borghese's to 1,000,000. Since even this was not enough to keep her going, he canceled her debt to the Treasury, which amounted to 5,000,000 francs, and again raised her yearly income to 1,500,000. Since Pauline spent over 298,000 francs during the first quarter of the year at one jeweler's alone, this did not go far. But she had the merit of being extravagant but not greedy, and this, as far as Napoléon was concerned, made her the most restful of his brothers and sisters.

By now Pauline's distaste for her husband had become both a mania and a crusade. When he made the mistake of coming to Paris for the wedding of Marie Louise, a thing he did only because he had been ordered to do it, though she could not prevent his staying at her house, the Hôtel du Charost, she did charge him for his board and room. If he refused to pay, he might have his meals sent in from Very's. Nor did she stop there. She had the document in which Napoléon separated her budget from Camillo's read to him in the presence of her ladies-in-waiting. She sent down a message when he moved a chair or coughed, to complain of the noise (though the Hôtel du Charost was thickly built). If he wished to see her, he had to make an appointment several days in advance, by messenger, and then she kept him waiting. If he addressed his notes to the Princess Borghese, she returned them as improperly directed. The correct salutation, he was told, was to her Imperial Highness, Pauline, Duchess of Guastalla, etc.

The visit coincided with one of her nymphomanic periods. Borghese made himself so scarce that one day Pauline's dentist, who always came to the house, drew the teeth of one of her lovers under the mistaken impression that it *was* Borghese.

Borghese retired to Turin but had to come back for the birth and christening of the King of Rome. This time Pauline thought of a subtler refinement: he might stay at the Hôtel du Charost but only on condition that neither he nor his suite use the bathroom and toilet facilities, and all chamber pots were removed from his quarters.

This proved effective.

They were reconciled, so far as public appearances went, at the Emperor's orders. But when the Parisians one day saw them together in a carriage whose horses had bolted, the jest was made that it would be amusing if two persons who found it so impossible to live together should happen to be united in death.

In any event, they lived apart. Borghese went back to Turin. He was a dreadful snob and much too vapid to bear grudges, which after all requires a certain energy. But he preferred not to see his wife again. In a little while he found a duchess who exactly suited him, Lante della Rovere, who was not only as dull as he was, but as beautiful and only a little stronger.

Though incapable of regretting anything she had ever done, Pauline began to worry, for in September of 1815 she learned the extent of her reduced income. It amounted to 250,000 francs in cash, 250,000 more from the sale of the Hôtel du Charost, the bonds involved in that sale and the interest accruing from them, what she had inherited from the estate of her first husband (but Montgobert was sold out from under her), the furniture from the reception rooms at Neuilly, spirited away from the Bourbons before they could seize it as well as the house, and of course, silver plate, gold services, her enormous jewel collection, and the allowances from Camillo set forth in the original marriage settlement. In her view, this left her impoverished, so she decided to have the Holy Office intercede for her, in an effort to readjust and enhance her settlement from Camillo. She started toward Rome, and arrived there on October 15, the same day Napoléon reached St. Helena.

Charles Bonaparte

Mme Mère
(Letizia Ramolino Buonaparte)

Cardinal Fesch

The young General Bonaparte

Bonaparte
at the time of the Consulate

Napoléon I, in his coronation robes

THE EMPEROR

Joséphine

Hortense de Beauharnais,
Queen of Holland

Eugène de Beauharnais,
Viceroy of Italy, Duke of Leuchtenberg

Marie Louise

Marie Louise

Opposite and above, Napoléon François Charles Joseph, King of
Rome and, later, Duke of Reichstadt. The later picture, above, shows
him in Austrian uniform.

Joseph,
King of Spain

Lucien,
Prince of Canino

BROTHERS

Jérôme,
King of Westphalia

Louis,
King of Holland

Elisa,
Grand Duchess of Tuscany

Pauline,
Princess Borghese

Caroline,
Queen of Naples

Prince Camillo Borghese,
Pauline's husband

Joachim Murat,
King of Naples,
Caroline's husband

The Empress Eugénie

Prince Louis Napoléon,
later Napoléon III

The Prince Imperial,
their son

Napoléon Joseph Charles Paul, Prince Napoléon ("Plon Plon")

His wife, Princess Clotilde

Princess Mathilde

Elizabeth Patterson
(Mme Bonaparte)

Jerome N. Bonaparte,
Elizabeth Patterson's grandson

Jerome Napoleon Charles,
the last American descendant,
who died in 1945,
shown here with his wife

Charles Joseph Napoleon
(Secretary of the Navy)

T HE second Diaspora of the Bonapartes was much more severe
than the first, for now the Allies wanted vengeance, and so did
the followers of Louis XVIII, and followers can be well-nigh
impossible to control.

Jérôme had been given 100,000 francs in cash by Napoléon, before they both left Paris. It was Jérôme's only capital. At first he
thought of going back to America (and Elizabeth Patterson, pre-
sumably), but was denounced, though not recognized, while trying
to find a boat near Niort and had to turn back. He returned to Paris
and went into hiding.

Fouché, who was a man totally free of any vengeful spirit and
who did not wish the Bonapartes to be caught, for fear of a political
incident, persuaded Wintzingerode, the representative of Württemberg, to give Jérôme asylum in the Württemberg legation, where he
would be protected by extraterritoriality. The ex-King of Württemberg was then shamed into offering him refuge, on condition that he
give his word not to try to escape Württemberg. Then, in order to
cover his tracks, Fouché informed Louis XVIII that Jérôme was to
be smuggled out of the country and told him when and how. Louis
XVIII, goaded by Talleyrand, who *was* vengeful, though only the
better to keep his own seat, ordered a message to be sent to the borders by heliograph. Fouché, whose secret reports also included fore-
casts of the weather, seems not to have been surprised that a rainy
overcast made the use of heliograph impossible for twenty-four
hours.

So to everyone's relief, Jérôme crossed the border on the 21st of
July and reached Karlsrühe the same evening. But if Jérôme ex-

pected that his troubles would now be over, he did not know his father-in-law, who detested Jérôme and who was as ingenious as he was ill-natured.

Catherine, who did know what her father was like, at first refused to take refuge with him, but had been talked into doing so by Metternich, who pointed out that the only alternative was imprisonment in a fortress at Prague. "Very well," she said. "I cede only to force." And off she went to Göppingen, the particular preliminary hell her father had prepared for both her and her husband. She was happy enough there until Jérôme arrived.

Jérôme had been met at the border by Count von Zeppelin and forced to sign a long declaration which, among other things, stripped him of the title of Graf von Hartz, forbade him to have any French, Italian or Westphalian retainers, to communicate with his family on any subjects but those of their common health, and constrained him to obey the military and civil officials of Württemberg. Jérôme signed. He and Catherine were then relegated not to Göppingen but to Ellwangen, which was smaller, less agreeable, and easier to guard. The jailer was instructed to construct bastions and dig a fosse. As soon as he arrived, Jérôme was asked to provide a balance sheet of his remaining fortune. He refused, so the guard was doubled, and nobody was allowed in or out.

"Remember," said the King to Catherine, "it is not an asylum which I have granted to your husband, but a prison less disagreeable than the fortress at Wesel." (There had also been a plan to immure Jérôme in Russia.) The doors to Jérôme's quarters were forced and his private papers examined in his presence. The inspectors found only 20,000 francs in gold and twenty large gold medals. Catherine had prudently hidden in her bosom the deposit slips from the banks in which they had deposited what was left of their fortune.

Blocked in this direction, the King of Württemberg arranged to seize Jérôme's personal furniture and movables, having them sent to Stuttgart from France and sold over his head. Though worth 3,000,-000 francs they brought in only 700,000.

The result was a family quarrel so intense that the King of Württemberg finally let Jérôme and Catherine go. On condition that they drop the title of Hartz, Austria consented to receive them. The King of Württemberg was compelled (by the Austrians) to grant a new title (Comte de Montfort). Unfortunately the Count and Countess stayed first with Caroline, who had taken shelter at Schloss Hain-burg and who, being hard up, suddenly remembered she had once lent Jérôme 500,000 francs and demanded her money. It was neces-sary to move on.

Caroline could outshout Jérôme any day.

Catherine was pregnant again. On October 30, 1816, her father died, calling out for his favorite daughter, so we are told, but also disinheriting her. All she received was 150,000 francs due her as her part of her mother's dowry.

Jérôme, who always spent his credit freely, whether he had any or not, bought an estate at Erlau. Metternich ordered him to sell it, which he did at a loss, buying Schönau for 400,000 florins and hiring 200 workmen to put it in repair and to have it lit with hydrogen, an expensive, novel, and fashionable new mode of illumination which had caught his fancy. Catherine's pretensions had altered, too. She now refused to go for a drive unless her carriage had at least six horses.

1816 was not a good year for Bonapartes to borrow money. All the family were busy realizing property and retrenching. Jérôme left his French estates of Stains and Villandry in the hands of an old drinking crony, Hainguerlot. Hainguerlot, as Napoléon had earlier advised, was a con artist and embezzler of long standing and much ability. He so contrived matters that Jérôme received not one penny. The brothers Girard, who owned a linen-weaving establishment founded with Jérôme's money, sold out and put everything into a firm to navigate the Danube, which went bankrupt, though the brothers Girard seemed no poorer.

The Montforts were now very poor. Cardinal Fesch relieved mat-ters by forwarding 150,000 francs he had owed to them. Fesch never gave money to the Bonapartes, only to charity, but he was scrupulous about his debts.

Jérôme managed to borrow 40,000 francs from the Arnstein bank in Vienna, and removed to Trieste, where he bought still another house, being, it would seem, an artist of the small down payment. This one had been built twenty years before by the treasurer of the Pasha of Egypt, who had had to remove himself from the Nile some-what hastily and had thought Trieste a likely place to pause. It had an enormous park, with fountains and orange groves.

The colony at Trieste now included Catherine and Jérôme, who were to stay three years, Elisa, and, oddly, Fouché, who had not only been turned out of office but had thought it wise to flee the country. He had his fortune and a very young wife, Ernestine de Castellane, but died a few months after his arrival.

By the 1st of May, 1820, Jérôme had to pay over 80,000 florins toward the purchase of the palace he had bought. Jérôme's contribution was to spend money he did not have on the hiring of too many servants, the purchase of pictures and furniture, and the keeping of two ballerinas from the opera. Catherine extracted 25,000 rubles, paper, as a yearly pension from the Czar, and 50,000 florins a year from her brother, the new King of Württemberg. On the 27th, she gave birth to her daughter, Letitzia Mathilde Fréderique Aloisia Elisabeth, the future Princess Mathilde of the Second Empire.

Jérôme divided his efforts between conspiring with a crony of his called David to have himself elected King of Greece and endeavoring to seduce his friend's wife. Nothing came of either project.

When Napoléon died in 1821 and security measures were relaxed, Jérôme applied for permission to move to Rome in order to be near his mother (Catherine had applied for permission, though without success, to join Napoléon at St. Helena). He did not get it until after the Congress of Verona (1822) and could not leave until March of 1823, because Catherine was pregnant again, this time with Plon Plon, born September 9, 1822, and christened Napoléon Joseph Charles. As his sister was to be the chief ornament, so was he to be the principal nuisance of the Second Empire.

The Montforts lived in Rome from 1823 to 1831, when Jérôme was at last asked to leave. He bought the Palazzo Nuñez from Lucien, though there is no record of how or if he paid for it. His life was devoted to cadging money and visiting Mme Mère. Every morning Jérôme's children were taken to see her, a visit which lasted six minutes. They were then taken off to Cardinal Fesch, at the Palazzo Falconieri, a call which seldom lasted longer. Cardinal Fesch was benign, but did not like to bend down to play with children. Then everyone went on to the Palazzo Ruspoli, Hortense's residence when she was in Rome. Here the atmosphere changed, for if Hortense managed, without difficulty, to restrain her enthusiasm for Jérôme, she was fond of children. Mathilde in particular had always grateful and pleasant memories of her. Plon Plon, who took after his father with scrupulous ingratitude, was more reserved. But at Hortense's they met Louis Napoléon, the future Emperor and their future patron.

The arrival of Mme Patterson-Bonaparte and her son created only a slight disturbance. "With what grace she would have reigned, had she been Queen," Talleyrand said once. This was her own view, exactly. "My American wife," Jérôme called her in 1821, while pointing her out to Catherine. His American son was now sixteen.

His American family caused him less embarrassment than his Italian. He had to sell his country house at Formio because his niece, Elisa's daughter Napoléone Camarata, while staying there liked to drive down to the Neapolitan border to curse the customs inspectors. She had an obscene tongue, the Court of Naples complained to Metternich, and Metternich forced the sale of the house, which stood on then Austrian territory. This was a great inconvenience, for Jérôme had bought it only in order to have a provincial headquarters from which to conduct his latest attempt at seduction.

Mme Mère and Cardinal Fesch had had an easier time out of France and back to Italy. Mme Mère fell ill as soon as Napoléon left for Rochefort, and she returned to her town house in Paris. Fesch remained with her. On July 10 he wrote to Louis XVIII, explaining that now he had done his duty to his family, he felt he should devote himself entirely to his diocese. This infuriated Mme Mère, the French government, the church authorities, and the Pope, none of whom wished a Bonaparte relation as Archbishop of Lyons. But there was no way to remove him from his Archbishopric, and he refused to resign. A tug of war went on about this for years. The Bourbons were forced to appoint the Abbé de Rohan over his head, and the Pope forbade Fesch from exercising spiritual jurisdiction. Nevertheless he continued to regard himself as Archbishop of Lyons, and under canon law nothing could be done, except to keep him away from it.

Sometimes, while they were in Paris, Hortense came to dinner. Mme Mère had revised her view of Hortense during the Hundred Days. An annoyance was that her former secretary, Decazes, was now Minister of Police, knew more than he should, and set spies on her. She decided to leave, and on the 19th of July, protected by an escort provided by Metternich, she and Fesch left Paris for the last time. He had managed to save his collections, his library, and his house in Paris by putting it in the name of his bookseller. He insisted upon saying mass publicly along the way. They went first to Geneva, to Prangins, now deserted and shut up, and then on down toward Rome. The Paris papers announced her departure as that of the widow Ramolino. This was not so much studied discourtesy as the fear of the name of Bonaparte in print.

The only member of the family left undisturbed by the second Diaspora was Louis, though that was not his own view. He had been slightly inconvenienced, though only mentally, by Murat's maneuvers during the Hundred Days and sufficiently alarmed by them to leave Rome hastily for a place of greater safety. In 1816 he ventured back and bought the Mancini Salviati palace (until 1801 the seat of the French Academy at Rome, before it moved to the Villa Medici). In order to put a stop to police surveillance, he pointed out that he had always been devoted to the government of Louis XVIII.

He had before shown signs of having a taste of a seemingly platonic sort, for young girls, both in his imagination and once, but only once, with an actual woman, Émilie Beauharnais, now Mme de Lavalette. In 1816, he felt himself to be in love with a sixteen-year-old girl, Vittoria Odescalchi, the sister of a friend whom he admired. The results were both embarrassing and funny. He had a new seal made up, for use on letters to her only. It showed a crowned lion emerging from the sea. He had himself painted in his Dutch regal robes (by Vogel), as a gift. He pressed for an annulment of his marriage to Hortense.

Vittoria Odescalchi's relatives, particularly Monsignor Odescalchi, a member of the Rota, promptly pressed even more firmly the other way. The matter became the incredulous giggle of Rome, and was put a stop to.

Next Louis demanded of Hortense the return of such of their community property, furniture and portraits mostly, as she still retained. He wished them to furnish rooms for Vittoria. For the first time the family was on Hortense's side. Mme Mère denounced Louis publicly. Joseph and Lucien would have nothing to do with the ridiculous affair. Queen Julie sent him a letter so sharp it caused a nervous collapse. Elisa sent one even sharper. Only Jérôme (who hated Hortense) abetted him. The annulment was shelved.

Louis bought the domain of Civitanova for 642,000 francs and sold his hotel in the rue Cerutti in Paris to Prince Torlonia for 535,-000 francs. The banker Torlonia had an agreement with the Bonapartes from which he made large profits. He took over their French properties, to prevent confiscation, advanced them ready cash, and when he resold the properties gave them the difference between their debts and the announced purchase price, minus discounts, interest, and so forth.

The next few years were spent by Louis in polishing his *Reflexions on the Government of Holland*, published in 1820, just in time for Napoléon to have the reading of them. They of course blamed the Emperor for everything. He also published his little treatise on versification, dedicated to the French Academy, and for which the Muses are blameless; and some *vers d'occasion*, very gloomy, the titles of which upset the French Ambassador to Rome. "Complaint of an Exile," for example, which Blacas felt was a covert reply to the perpetual banishment of the Bonapartes recently decreed by the Chamber of Deputies.

But Louis had no desire to go back to France. He preferred to stay close enough to the Bonapartes to be able to quarrel. When his sister Elisa died in 1820, he said that he was "astonished at my calm and at not being more upset." Elisa's husband took her demise equally placidly, merely demanding his passport, for "The death of my wife having broken all my ties with her family, it seems to me that I have almost a right to reclaim my liberty." He got it, too.

Louis quarreled with Lucien and with Fesch. Perhaps his masterpiece was a letter to Pauline, who was vain and frightened of losing her beauty. It was to congratulate her on her birthday. "You are now thirty-two," he said. "At thirty-two one begins to grow old."

He never could be made to understand why she took this ill. He had thought she would be pleased.

Hortense had not been prepared for the violence of the ultraroyalists during the second Restoration. On July 6, when Louis le Desiré entered his capital, she was booed, hissed, and threatened as she went by. Fouché told her it was unsafe for her to remain in her house, so she rented the first floor of the house behind hers, moving back into her own only when the Allied armies entered the city on July 10. Schwarzenberg made her house his headquarters, which gave her some protection. She began to pack, and being short of cash, sold off some horses and some paintings. Fouché provided her with passports. Her name appeared in the *Moniteur*, listed as one of the enemies of France, and the Czar, having read her letters and remarks about him, refused to see her.

On July 17 she was told she must leave the city within two hours. She was also warned to take no valuables, as she would probably be robbed along the way. So she left her jewels and most of her funds with her confidante, Louise Cochelet.

She took a house at Aix, where she was visited by her lover, Charles de Flahaut, and by Louis's agents, who took away her elder surviving son, Napoléon Louis, but left her the younger, Louis Napoléon, who promptly developed jaundice. The government ordered her to leave Savoy.

Like the Bonapartes, but unlike her brother Eugène, she was now a stateless person, and she had, of course, lost both her pension and what was left of St. Leu. She went to Constance, then in Baden. Though her cousin, Stéphanie, was Grand Duchess of Baden, she was asked to move on. Instead she lingered, and Eugène, who came for a visit, arranged a credit account for her with the Frankfurt branch of the House of Rothschild, her jewels to be the collateral. This relieved her of her worst worries.

Louis was, of course, trying to have his marriage annulled. Hortense decided to contest the annulment. Her own lover, Charles de Flahaut, had decided to marry Lady Margaret Elphinstone, who was handsome, frigid, rich, and a peeress in her own right. Hortense was thirty-two and wished no more lovers. She approved of the marriage. In 1816 she bought the castle of Arenenberg (Narrenberg). The name means fool's hill, and it was not a castle but a small square two-storied seventeenth-century pavilion, on a bluff over the Bodensee's inlet, in Swiss territory. The price was modest, and she wanted to garden again. Since, however, she could not yet get permission from the Swiss to live in it, she went to Augsburg to be near her brother.

Czar Alexander had so far forgiven her as to buy most of the picture collection at Malmaison for a good sum, and she had sold her gold and silver plate. She stayed at Augsburg off and on for several years.

While she was at Augsburg, the son Louis had taken was allowed to visit her. Louis's educational regimen had not been a success. For one thing, very little of it had been devoted to education and entirely too much of it to obedience to Louis's crochets, which were many. The boy had been isolated from anyone of his own age and made to serve in the mornings as acolyte at mass. Soap and Eau de Cologne had been forbidden, and the use of a shoe of Louis's design, made to fit either foot impartially, encouraged. Washing was done with dry bran. The boy had been allowed a quarter of a square of chocolate a day, exactly measured, and all rules had to be obeyed, particularly if they seemed unjust. Tutors were hired, but seldom stayed long. The result, as one might expect, was a sickly, taciturn little hypocrite, afraid to say what he thought of anything. Louis was only moderately satisfied. "If I have not been able to correct all his bad habits, it is not because they have developed since he has been with me," he wrote Hortense. He was also displeased by his younger son, whom Hortense had educated, though so far, it must be admitted, not very well. "His wilfulness, his extreme talkativeness, his puns and bad jokes—in this he is much worse than Napoléon [Louis]—pained me." In short the future Napoléon III was a lively child.

It is pleasant to know that when Napoléon Louis was old enough to get away from his father he was sturdy enough to throw off these traits and revert to his own innately sound character.

Hortense hired a new tutor for Louis, a M. Le Bas, who was extremely thorough. Lessons ran from six in the morning until nine at night, but included outdoor exercise as well as Latin, arithmetic, German, Greek, history, geography, and, of course, the works of Napoléon I.

The outcome, as Hortense seems to have planned, was a Napoléon III, though not for some time to come.

After Napoléon's death, Hortense spent her summers at Arenenberg and her winters in Rome. Since she was the only member of the family to have any political ambitions, Arenenberg thus became the center of Bonapartism, in all its various forms, both in her lifetime and in that of Napoléon III, who used it as a refuge before the Revolution of 1848 and as a summer home afterward.

It was (and is) a charming small building of ground floor and two stories, attic rooms in the mansards, and a reception room added to the garden front. But in the winter it was devilish cold.

Here Hortense devoted herself to a woman's accomplishments, which in her case meant sketching, watercolor landscapes, and the writing of romances and art songs. She published a collection of these, *Romances Set to Music and Dedicated to the Prince Eugène by His Sister*. One of them was "Partant pour la Syrie," which was to become the acknowledged unofficial anthem of the Second Empire. She also began to put together her memoirs, which she finished in 1820 but polished for another ten years. Though she claimed she had no literary skill, they are skillfully composed memoirs. They leave out whatever she did not wish to put in and concentrate upon Napoléon. It was her announced theory that he had been a social messiah, which turned out to be the right tone to take, considering the temper of the times and of the future, which she had considered. In her own way, Hortense was a remarkably clever woman. Though the memoirs were not published until the twentieth century and so did no public good, they were effective when she gave selected readings from them.

After the Hundred Days, Elisa was released and allowed to settle at Trieste. Though Austrian, the city was agreeably international in character. Here she bought a house in town and a country house, the Villa Vicentina. The Austrian government had returned her Italian property to her in 1819. This she now sold, and was able to live comfortably on the proceeds. She was content to settle down, and Istria suited her. What was important to Elisa was not a country but a court. She soon had her second-rate artists, musicians, and French exiles back again. Sometimes Caroline came to visit her. She bought another estate in Istria.

She died of malaria, unexpectedly, in her forty-fourth year, at the Villa Vicentina, August 7, 1820, leaving her money, most of it, to her children, of whom two survived infancy and one youth.

Her husband took her death with his usual peripheral poise. As Duke of Lucca and Piombino in his own right, he went on playing the violin. He was known as *ce bon et rebon Bacciochi*. He sold her villas and settled in Bologna at the Palazzo Ranuzzi. The Austrian government made him an allowance, and the Pope, with some prodding, made him a Roman prince. He died in 1841, an object of apathy to all.

He had erected a sugary monument to his family, at San Petronio in Bologna, in a side chapel he had purchased for the purpose. In the center is a medallion showing the three children who died in infancy, supported by marble women weeping. An inscription felicitates the children on not having known the misfortunes which befell the family. On the *back* is another medallion, showing Elisa and explaining who she was. Beneath this a somewhat idealized man and woman hold hands beneath the Genius of Conjugal Love, who is somewhat conveniently looking the other way. It was the best the bereaved widower could do. To judge from his portraits, plump Bacciochi had the most complacent thighs of any man then living. Nothing disturbed the sedate repose of that plummy mediocrity.

Jérôme was at Elisa's deathbed. She had lent him money. Mme Mère refused to. "Do as I do. Retrench," she said. Mme Mère took Elisa's death calmly, too. "You have reason to feel your loss, but it is not irreparable," she wrote to Elisa's daughter Napoléone. Napoléon took the news more ill. "I thought death had forgotten the family, but since Elisa has been taken I shall soon follow."

Elisa's two most lasting monuments are probably those marble busts with which she seeded Europe and her own statue in the Palace at Lucca, which turned out to be both too large and too heavy either to move or to destroy. There she sits, on top of a marble tea canister some ten feet high, ample and easy, whereas in life she was a small woman, shriveled round the bone. It does help to have one's own sculptor in the house.

But the most histrionic and hectic adventure was Caroline's, for though she was good at telling Murat what to do, she was unable to prevent his doing precisely what he shouldn't. At first, of course, she had been able to keep her throne, and she and Murat continued to improve their surroundings. Ferdinand, when restored to Naples, said, indeed, that Murat had been an excellent upholsterer. His palaces were better furnished than he had ever seen them. Caroline, when Mme Mère reproached her, pleaded her husband's influence. "If you could not control him, you should oppose him," Mme Mère had snapped. In the event, she was able successfully to do neither. Though she manipulated him, she could not always be sure of her effects.

They would probably have been able to keep Naples if he had not, on March 30, exhorted the Italians to rise against the Austrians and drive them out. This was done against her advice. He was overly ambitious, insufficiently skilled, and hoped to put himself on the throne of a United Italy. Then he went off to join his troops, where she could not get at him. He invaded the Papal States and Tuscany, but his troops were raw and he was good only for cavalry charges. Neipperg decisively defeated him at the battle of Tolentino, on May 3, and his armies simply ran away.

He had to flee back to Naples. Caroline had been regent in his absence. There was nothing she could do now he was back. The Austrians refused to deal with the Neapolitans unless "Marshal Murat" was excluded from any possible peace. On the night of May 21 and 22 the rabble rose at Naples. Caroline had to get the English to defend her palace. She had sent her children for safety to the fortress of Gaeta and had been forced to surrender her fleet. Now she had to take refuge on an English man-of-war, the *Tremendous*. From it at night she could see the city illuminated against the return of Ferdinand, and sometimes her former subjects put off from shore in small boats to hoot her. This went on for several days.

Murat, disguised as a sailor, fled Naples via Ischia for France, on a boat flying the English flag in order to run the blockade. On the 2d of May he landed at Cannes, where he offered his services to Napoléon, who did not accept them. Murat then crossed over to Corsica.

Caroline had wished to join Murat in Provence. The English refused to allow it. No provision for her or for her children had been made in the convention concluded with the Austrians. She appealed to Neipperg, who had just entered Naples at the head of the Austrian army. He consented to take her to Trieste, for which she sailed on the 8th of June. It was not deemed safe to allow her to travel overland. On the way, her ship passed that bringing Ferdinand back to Naples. A salute was fired, and she was told not to be nervous when the guns went off. "The sound of cannon is neither new nor unpleasant to the ear of a Bonaparte," she said.

Murat, who had waited for her before crossing over to Corsica, seems to have believed she had deserted to the Allies.

Caroline, calling herself the Contessa di Lipona, an anagram of Naples, was not allowed to stay at Trieste but was hustled off into the interior of Austria, first to Hainburg, twenty-five miles south of Vienna, then to Frohsdorf, which was to be her home, or at any rate place of detention, for some time to come.

There, in October, while and by reading a Viennese newspaper, she learned of Murat's death. It seems unlikely she was deeply

172

moved. Her affection for Murat had not long survived her marriage to him, and she had brought into exile with her General Macdonald, her ex-Minister of War, who was both handsome and devoted. The death of Murat was a political, not a personal, shock, for it deprived her permanently of Naples.

Murat had hoped to appeal to the Allies for protection, but was caught in the White Terror, which raged at its worst in the south of France. So instead of waiting for an answer from the Allies (the Emperor Francis had offered him Austrian asylum), he had crossed over to Corsica, landing at Bastia on August 25, 1815. If he had counted on Corsican support, he had miscalculated. Those who came with him were arrested, and he himself escaped into the hills only with difficulty.

The Austrian offer had been contingent on his renouncing his claims to the Neapolitan throne. Instead, acting on misinformed reports and in emulation of Napoléon's return from Elba, he decided to invade Calabria, and from there once more to "liberate" his former kingdom. On the night of September 28 and 29 he set sail on six ships, accompanied by 250 fellow adventurers. A storm separated his ships, and on the morning of October 8 he found himself opposite a little town called Pizzo, with none of the other boats in sight. He would have abandoned the attempt then, but his boat was so leaky that he had to run in to shore.

Murat, gorgeous as ever in an emergency, put on a full dress uniform with a diamond buckle in his hat and landed with twenty-six men. It was a Sunday, which happened to be the local market day. "Long live our King Joachim," shouted one of his followers. The villagers ignored the disturbance and went on buying their weekly vegetables. They did not love their former King, for Murat had tried to suppress Calabrian brigandage, which they regarded both as a legitimate industry and as their livelihood.

Murat retreated, followed by the townspeople throwing vegetables. An armed captain of gendarmes, Trentacapilli, caught up with the former King and since the crowd began to beat him up, knocking his hat off, got him away and locked him up in the castle of Pizzo.

On the 13th, he was shot as a public enemy, at the order of the Neopolitan government. "Aim at my heart, not my face," he said. So one member of the firing squad made sure a ball went through his right cheek, tearing it open. He had had time to write Caroline a highly rhetorical letter of farewell. "I leave you without a kingdom and without means," he said.

This was not quite true. Caroline could no longer pay 15,000 francs for a dress and 500 for a hat, and Ferdinand of the Two Sicilies had confiscated all her Italian property, but she still had the moneylenders, General Macdonald, and some of her jewels. So she did not entirely starve.

It had been a stagy death. Murat wore a large cameo portrait of Caroline around his neck and held miniatures of his four children in his hands. His advice to his children was, "Remember what you *are*, not what you have been." He was buried unceremoniously in the cemetery at Pizzo.

Caroline had exchanged her French estates for cash and a reduction of the monies Naples had been supposed to pay Napoléon. What else there was in France the Bourbons now confiscated. Mme Mère not only refused to make her a loan, but refused to receive her. She was told she must either resign herself to living in Austria or emigrate to America. She chose Austria, where she was closely watched, for she was regarded as the most dangerous of the family because of her political abilities.

She was a peacock woman and now all her tailfeathers had been pulled out. She took it ill. In particular, she took Metternich ill. She was not a libidinous woman and had always taken her lovers for sound practical reasons—Junot so he might help her to seize the French government for Murat if Napoléon died (nothing came of it); various statesmen, Italian and Austrian, in Naples so she might gain control of the Neapolitan government, and keep it despite Murat; Metternich, just to be on the safe side, because he was the leading diplomat of the day. As a matter of fact, he tried to help her when he could. But this was not enough for Caroline. "During the nine years I spent at Frohsdorf I followed all his counsels. What is the result? Incessant persecution."

When Napoléon died, she was allowed more freedom and moved to Trieste, where she bought the Villa Campo Mars. She saw none of the family except Jérôme, who would visit anyone. Mme Récamier paid her a visit. The amiable Juliette, who had married her father, had an exacting sense of the proprieties and was not altogether pleased. She had come to pry. Caroline, she found, "was fat, and since she was not tall, her figure had not gained in elegance." Her complexion had faded. Caroline laid herself out to be agreeable. She needed powerful friends, for she hoped to extract a pension from the French government, and Mme Récamier, who had formed a dishwater alliance with Chateaubriand, who fancied himself as a statesman, could be influential.

General Macdonald was introduced. Caroline's manner to him, Juliette noted, was "affectionate, but mixed with a slight shade of domination." It meant nothing: this was Caroline's manner toward most people. But it was rumored that Caroline had married him secretly, though she never let him forget she was his Queen. Caroline got on well with her ex-War Department. Though poor, she was probably the happiest of the exiles, except Lucien, who had always been protected from life's buffets by the cotton padding of his own smugness.

Caroline was a woman totally undisarrayed either by truth or conscience. One of the larger salons at the Villa Campo Mars was fitted out with Imperial souvenirs and dominated by an equestrian statue of Murat, but everyone else was there, either on canvas or in the form of one of Bartolini's ubiquitous busts. It was a museum. Caroline never appeared in it. It was always General Macdonald who showed people around.

In the autumn of 1831 a cholera epidemic swept down through Germany toward Trieste. Caroline was allowed to move on to Florence, where she was permitted to settle and where she was to remain. "All Florence visits me, and foreigners come in crowds." All Florence, that is, except Louis, who preferred not to see her.

In the summer of 1838, Caroline, taking advantage of Louis Philippe's policy of posing as himself a Bonapartist in order to take advantage of the new liberalism, which had made a cult of the dead Emperor, visited Paris, where she managed to wring a pension of 40,000 a year out of the Chamber of Deputies. She did not live to enjoy it long, but died on May 18, 1839, at the age of sixty.

Of her four children, the two girls married minor Italian noblemen and sank into obscurity; the two boys had more decided characters and lived to figure both at the court and in the civil list of Napoléon III.

Of the remaining Bonapartes, Joseph had emigrated to America, and Lucien, whose life was better to live than to read about, merely applied for and was given passports under an assumed name and set out for Rome. On the Italian side of the Mount Cenis pass, he was arrested by the Piedmontese government, the King of Sardinia hoping thus to please the Allies, and spent three months as a prisoner at Turin. Pius VII got him released, and as usual received him once more at Rome, where his life was undisturbed by any interesting event and where he went on as before, devoting himself to his children and to Etruscology.

THE Restoration of the Bourbons was followed by that persecution of the Bonapartists called the White Terror, which in its turn followed upon the horrors of the occupation of Paris. These were considerable.

As soon as he had entered Paris, the Prussian war leader, Blücher, had become possessed of a desire to blow up the Pont d'Iéna. Iéna had been his worst defeat, and the name bothered him, though the bridge itself was handsome. He also wished to extort a crippling indemnity for the benefit of Prussia. Talleyrand protested both. Blücher said that not only would the bridge be blown up, but that he hoped that Talleyrand would be standing on it at the time. It is some measure of Talleyrand's popularity that this rejoinder appealed to almost everybody. Louis XVIII riposted by threatening to be wheeled onto the bridge in his chair, which had casters. Wellington was asked to intervene. He was the only military leader who could control Blücher. It was finally agreed that the bridge might be left standing (it was, after all, useful for crossing the river) on the condition that its name was changed. It was to be called the Pont des Invalides. As for the indemnity, Wellington contented himself by pointing out that if it was collected, it would have to be divided equally among the Allies. Blücher gave up the idea of an indemnity.

He had other projects, however. He wanted to blow up the as yet unfinished Arc de Triomphe and the Pont d'Austerlitz, planned to seize the Banc de France, and though thwarted in these ambitions, was the first to take down and have sent back to Prussia those twenty pictures and pieces of sculpture which Napoléon had stolen and put in the Louvre, in that Musée de France of which he had been so proud. Earlier Blücher had amused himself by shooting up Malmai-

177

son, and it was he who wished Napoléon executed as a common prisoner. His troops, billeted on the French, were encouraged to be as
objectionable as possible.

"You eat a great deal," said one Frenchwoman.

"Madam, these are our orders," said the soldier who had requisitioned her house. Blücher knew how to hit the French in the only
place where it would hurt.

Indeed, the behavior of the French was outwardly too irrespon-
sibly effervescent for the Allies. "I hate cheering," said Wellington.
"If once you allow soldiers to express an opinion, they may on some
other occasion hiss instead of cheer. However, I cannot always help
my fellows giving me a Hurrah." His attitude to civilian cheering
was about the same.

It was difficult to know what to make of the latest theatrical sensa-
tion at the Opera. It was a ballet in which the battle of Waterloo was
danced. Wounded members of the Imperial Guard formed dejected
groups, and smart English officers made brilliant entries. As a finale, a
French officer, a *danseur noble*, was presented to his mistress, who
had believed him lost. *Pas de deux. Bourrée.* Grand finale with the
entire company. It was much applauded. It was not too different in
spirit from the ballet Lady Morgan had seen in Milan, when it was in
French hands, where the company had danced a Papal Consistory,
with satiric and lightfooted stage cardinals, a comic Pope, and a real
chimney.

The Louvre had been left unmolested in 1814. In 1815, however,
all the Powers insisted on getting their pictures and sculpture back.
The Prussians, indeed, removed theirs forcibly. The Louvre had not
too many, for of course the French have never had a taste for German art and had taken mostly Italian and French pictures from Dresden and Potsdam.

That left 1,400 looted pictures and a good deal of sculpture, as
well as the Egyptian collections, which remained, and any odd bits
and pieces of classical Rome that had appealed to the Emperor, including a good many things from the Vatican.

One reason Paris was flooded with tourists was that there was a
desire to see this haul before it was dispersed. Admission to the
Louvre was free, and many came. The place was a clutter. The English cognoscenti were particularly numerous. The two cant art-
appreciation phrases of the day were "crisp bits" and "buttery
tones." A Scottish traveler, a lawyer called James Simpson, got so

tired of hearing both that he would ask cognoscenti to breakfast and then use them of the toast. "Have a crisp bit," he would say, add marmalade, and then admire the "buttery tones." Sir Walter Scott (then Mr.) had been brought over too, and could be seen at a table in the Palais Royal, placidly ignoring the tarts, whose beat that was.

Dictators usually have, not surprisingly, a reactionary aesthetic taste. Napoléon is unique in encouraging a style to arise. He once complained of the absence of good prose and ordered his Minister of Police to make inquiries as to why there was not any. But the architectural and decorative arts were another matter. The Bourbons were now forced to move among this lumber, which was difficult to remove. Themselves, they brought back with them a fussy taste for bad imitations of Louis Seize, and for even worse society painters. Neoclassicism was abolished, and a neo-Gothic style arose overnight. Everything now had to be in the manner of Charlemagne or Clovis. Merovingian jewelry came in. It was not very convincing, but Romanticism arose to fill the gap.

Those of the old court painters of sufficient mediocrity to adapt did well. Gérard and Isabey changed and softened their styles and went right on working. Baron Gros, though commissioned to do the ceilings of the Panthéon, committed suicide, because, unable to adapt, he lost his patronage. He was really only good at Marshals and generals.

But Hortense, at Arenenberg, was soon patronizing Ary Schaeffer, who brought the Landseer touch to Christ, wearing pinched-in medieval waists and posing beside lamps with Gothic frets at a piano disguised as a cathedral organ.

That was the lighter side. The heavier was the White Terror. Fighting in the provinces was not subdued until September. Prussian troops were often garroted in the streets at night. If the Austrians and Russians were better controlled than the Germans (the Russians had not been told they were outside Russia, in order to prevent their looting), the behavior of the Belgians and Württembergers was shocking.

The country was clamoring for scapegoats, as any defeated nation always does, and the task of choosing them fell to Fouché. It was not a duty he wished to perform, but he submitted a list of one hundred names. "In justice to himself," remarked Talleyrand, "we must allow that he has omitted none of his friends."

The reduced list was published in the *Moniteur* on July 25, probably with the intention of giving those on it time to escape. Though the émigrés wished revenge, Louis XVIII definitely did not. The proscribed were divided into two classes. The first, with nineteen names, was of those to be court-martialed and executed. The second, with thirty-eight names, listed those to be banished. They were ordered to withdraw from Paris within three days.

Despite Talleyrand, Fouché wished no one apprehended and the list was an odd one. Some persons were listed under their titles, others under their given names, and Fouché handed out passports under the counter, lent money to those who needed it, and saw to the safe removal of others.

The royalists were more royal than the King and did not share his common sense. Members of the Gardes du Corps beat up Bonapartists in the streets, and the aristocratic ladies of the Faubourgs St. Germain and St. Honoré claimed to be ravenous for blood and attended all trials. They were delighted with the execution of Labédoyère, and much anticipated that of Marshal Ney. Both men were national military heroes of enormous prestige. To put them in prison would have destroyed their glamour; to shoot them merely made them the martyrs to an unpopular government. So they were shot.

It was not at Louis XVIII's request, but he had to bow to the common bay for vengeance, as that was reported to him by a bigoted brother, a frightened middle class, the clergy, and all those who wished to prove their own loyalty by the denunciation of someone else.

Still, one can scarcely complain that, in the face of a terrified bureaucracy and a spiteful horde of émigrés, only seventeen men were executed and thirty-eight banished. The real horrors of the White Terror took place in the provinces and may be laid at the door of the émigré royalists, the gangs they raised, and the clergy. They were inspired by unreasoning terror and by a desire to settle old private scores. The terror was of a widespread Bonapartist plot, which did not then exist, though there were many small ones. The desire to settle old scores under the guise of putting down underground activity is unfortunately a permanent trait of man.

There had been civil war in the Vendée and Brittany. It was put down, but gangs of ruffians, egged on by the rural clergy, sacked the houses of and threatened to murder the purchasers of national property, that is, of estates seized by the government during the Revolu-

180

tion and long since sold off for the profit of that government to private owners. Carriages were stopped, and rape and riot were the order of the day. The worst excesses took place in the south. Once the Imperial troops evacuated Marseilles, the royalists, on June 25 and 26, rose and slaughtered 200 people in the streets. The movement, if such it can be called, spread west to Languedoc, Gascony, Avignon, Montpellier, Nîmes, Uzès, and Toulouse. At Avignon Marshal Brune was butchered in his house. At Nîmes Protestants were cut down as well as Bonapartists: the Church was strong there. At Toulouse General Ramel had his penis and testicles hacked out. But the royalists did not always have it their own way: in the Gard, the Protestants fought back successfully. Civil war there was averted only by Neipperg, at the head of an Austrian division.

This state of affairs continued until the end of the year and was accompanied by judicial murder. The most famous case was that of the brothers Faucher, at La Réole, near Bordeaux. They were condemned to die for having defended themselves against the mob. "Inciting their countrymen to civil war by collecting an armed force [themselves] at their own house," was the charge. They took their condemnation with Socratic calm. "We are about to die owing to a judicial error [a rigged jury], for which a time of great popular excitement must be the excuse," they wrote in a joint letter, just before they were shot.

Later in 1815, in order to placate the new royalist majority in the Chamber of Deputies, the government got rid of both Fouché and Talleyrand. Fouché had never been trusted anyway. One of his own underlings had been instructed to keep a secret dossier on him. This had turned up nothing except a report that on his wedding night he had behaved in an athletic manner. But the Duchesse d'Angoulême found his deportment offensive, so out he went. It was the custom at the time to send sacked ministers off to be ambassadors. He was offered Dresden (Talleyrand was given London). For some reason, he lost his nerve and fled to Brussels on October 4, and then on to Italy. Talleyrand was not precisely sacked. He made the mistake of offering his resignation only to have it accepted.

The royalists were thus able at last to obtain the dismissal of the two most competent men in France, a great victory for the reaction. There remained only the occupying troops of the Allies and the war indemnity to be gotten rid of.

The final treaty with the Allies was agreed to on October 2, and signed on November 20. The Duke of Wellington was to direct an occupation army of 150,000 men, who were to remain for not more than five years. The indemnity was to amount to 700,000,000 francs. Savoy was to be returned to Sardinia, Landau to Bavaria. The Allied sovereigns themselves had left toward the end of September. Among their other multiple agreements was that odd document the Holy Alliance. It had been the work of Mme de Krüdener, and made a bad impression on almost everyone.

Mme de Krüdener was a Slavic hysteric with a mission. She came from Riga and was about fifty years old. Marriage had not interfered with her love affairs until one day, from a window, she had seen one of her lovers raise his hat to her and then drop dead. Obviously God had stricken the adulterer. Mme de Krüdener experienced a religious conversion. She was also getting older and was heavily in debt.

So she advanced on Czar Alexander. It is difficult to tease out the various strands of self-delusion, self-interest and exaltation in her nature, but for a while she got what she wanted. The Czar was a mystagogue by nature. He also had some odd habits, one of which was to give audience between one and three in the morning. Mme de Krüdener stayed up and came in on him just as he was reading, in Revelations, that passage which begins, "And there appeared a great wonder in Heaven, a woman clothed with the sun." We are not told the color of the dress Mme de Krüdener was wearing at the time, but thus prepared for, her intervention produced a considerable impact.

She said a voice tormented her to enlighten him and to induce him to prove himself worthy of the sacred Russian race. She also told him that more earthly relationships must be sacrificed to this end. "If you can advance without me I will go away," she said. "But where would you find the being who could be to you what I am?"

So she was set up in a house in Paris next door to the Czar's, and her debts were paid. She held prayer meetings and wore a blue serge dress and a straw hat, and had nothing whatsoever to be ashamed of, for she was saving a soul.

She induced Alexander to erect eight altars, hold a military review, and dedicate them and himself to a holy crusade. In the view of Alexander, "The French are a race of 30,000,000 beasts with the gift of speech and nothing more." The altars seemed to help. "This day . . . my heart was filled with love for my enemies," he told her.

He fasted, performed light penances, and together they wept in ecstasy, mostly over *her* sins, though she was not a selfish woman. Her approach with converts was charming: "I have hopes of you," she would say, "but so often I am disappointed." People were persuaded to live up. The Czar obediently dismissed his mistress of some sixteen years' standing.

The result was a foggy, irrational, impracticable document in which the signees pledged themselves to regulate their public acts by Christian doctrine. It was signed by the sovereigns in person (Prussia, Austria, Russia), which was unfortunate, for it roused suspicion in every clerical, anticlerical, liberal, and Protestant breast. England abstained, with the excuse that the Prince Regent was not empowered to sign national treaties.

On December 8, behaving in a Christian manner, the French government asked for a bill of amnesty. Like most such bills, its important feature was the list of those to be exempted from it. The Bonapartes were to be permanently banished. So were the more prominent among their followers. The bill of amnesty was passed, with considerable opposition, which sufficiently delayed legal proceedings so that a good many people could be arrested who might otherwise have gotten away. In 1816 the *Moniteur* published the text of a law depriving all banished Bonapartes of the protection of French embassies, forbidding them to travel in France or any allied country without a permit from an Allied Committee (which sat in Paris and sometimes took up to three years to reach a decision), and barring them from communication with Corsica. One of their followers, Santini, was arrested and lengthily imprisoned for carrying their messages. As a reward, some forty years later, Napoléon III made him keeper of Napoléon's tomb, at Les Invalides. All Bonaparte property in France was confiscated at the end of 1815.

In addition to the Allied indemnities, various governments put in their claims against France. By July of 1817, these, if admitted, would have amounted to 50,000,000 pounds sterling. Some of them were anachronistic and absurd. One small German princeling demanded payment for 4,000 knights supplied to Henri IV during the Wars of Religion, for example. Wellington was appointed arbitrator, and being a man of common sense, whittled the claims against France down to 9,000,000 pounds. So on February 11, 1818, an attempt was made to assassinate him as he was turning into his house. It failed.

The assassin was a former army sergeant, Cantillon. The jury acquitted him, and Napoléon left him 10,000 francs in his will. "Cantillon had as much right to assassinate that oligarch, as [the oligarch] had to send me to perish on the rock of St. Helena." What is more, the money was eventually paid over, though Napoléon's executors did not do so until the time of Napoléon III.

By the Treaty of Aix-la-Chapelle, October 9, 1818, the occupying army withdrew the following November 30, or two years ahead of time. France, though watched, was left to its own devices.

These turned out to consist chiefly of intramural warfare in the Royal Family, in the government, and in the country as a whole, where secret societies and liberal and Bonapartist plots followed each other in disorderly succession.

It was a period of unrest, and the Austrians and Bourbons were by no means foolish to keep such close watch on the Bonapartes. The causes of the unrest, primarily the new distribution of wealth and landed property among the social classes brought to the top by the Industrial Revolution, the rise of the modern opportunistic middle-class politician, and the inability of the traditional governments to cope with change, were badly understood.

The Austrian police in Italy, and the French everywhere, concentrated their attention upon the first generation of Bonapartes. But these had no political ambitions left. The real danger was to come from the second generation, to be exact from the sons of Hortense, who was deliberately educating them, insofar as she was able, to play their part in world affairs.

Napoléon was closely guarded, too, at St. Helena, "An extinct volcano, where . . . men seldom reached the age of fifty or even sixty," as Mme Mère called it. But extinct upon his extinct volcano, Napoléon had no political ambitions left either. In fact he several times evaded offers of rescue. What he was doing, as were the Bonapartists in France, each independently, though Joseph endeavored to supervise, was to create a liberal Bonaparte myth.

This legend, which was to prove far more politically potent than any number of small doomed military insurrections and faultily placed bombs, began to be put together about 1818. It has not died yet. On the part of Napoléon, who began work on it as soon as he arrived at St. Helena, it was a deliberate creation, in which he presented himself as a misunderstood figure, half Christ and half Prometheus, the savior of mankind, crucified, or chained to his rock for his liberal opinions. Which, needless to say, had never existed.

In France, among the Bonapartists, it was more the product of nostalgia and partook of the flavor of the King Across the Water, though Napoléon, unlike the later Stuarts, had the advantage of an illustrious career behind him.

In popular iconography, the Emperor was shown in his plain gray greatcoat, chatting with his soldiers around their campfires, planning the happiness of his people, and thwarted only by the hostility of the reactionary Allied sovereigns or the perfidy of Albion. Curiously, this view came to be popular in Albion itself. Two enormously popular writers did much to help. Béranger, a most unwilling conscript soldier during the Empire, began to produce such pieces as *Le Vieux Sergent* (1815), and *Le Vieux Drapeau* (1821). These lamented the fallen greatness of France and dwelt upon the glorious lot of the Napoleonic soldier. The government imprisoned him for three months, which greatly added to his vogue.

Paul Louis Courier, on the other hand, who had been an absentee officer of the Imperial army and who was a relatively well-to-do Greek scholar, while not a Bonapartist, indulged himself in posing as a vine dresser and speaking always in the character of the ordinary peasant and common man. His specialty was anticlericalism.

Bonapartism, then, shifted from being the party of one highly intelligent dictatorial man to become an ideology in which the absent Emperor and his equally absent family became the protectors of the new proletariat, and, skillfully, of the new enlightened, advanced, liberal and prosperous bourgeoisie, who wished both to control and to change the social system in order to gain the upper hand over the old aristocratic dispensation so that their own desires might not be thwarted.

All of which the future Napoléon III, throughout a bumbling career of twenty-eight years of much trial and more error, was to come to understand very well indeed, and daily to exploit to his own profit.

Rome had been as much changed by Napoléon, though from a distance, as had been the rest of Europe. He gave the Pincian Hill its gardens and the Tiber its embankments. He had had the Piazza del Popolo cleared. For Rome had been intended as the appanage of the King of Rome.

But the palace designed for him was never built, and now he would never come. Instead, Mme Mère ruled her family from there. That is, she tried to scare them into their best behavior, usually without much by way of a favorable result. She and Fesch annoyed no one, except, of course, by their continued existence.

The Palazzo Falconieri, which at first they shared, was majestic but gloomy, having been built during the Thirty Years War. It was Fesch's seat at Rome. They divided housekeeping expenses between them, the division being made, rigorously, by Mme Mère, who occupied the ground floor. The first floor and every other empty room were cluttered with the Cardinal's 30,000 Flemish and Italian primitives. Mme Mère disapprobated both the habit and the resultant bulk. He went on adding more and had finally to take space in adjacent buildings to house the overflow.

It has always been fashionable to assume that this collection was mostly junk. Nothing could be farther from the truth. Certainly there must have been a good many false attributions, but there were a great many Flemish and Italian primitives. Fesch never bought later than the cinquecento if he could help it, and there was no market for such things in his day, the only other collector of note to buy them being, oddly enough, George III. In Fesch's case mania was accompanied by a discriminating eye. He liked Botticelli forty years before anyone else in modern times discovered such virtues in that painter.

His collections were dispersed after his death, all but about a hundred of the best, which went to Corsica. They are still there, in the museum at Ajaccio, and they are unimpeachable.

Unlike his nephew, he specialized. Also unlike his nephew, he frequently paid, and always got a bill of sale. So nothing had to be returned.

Fesch was a worldly prelate, pleasant, plummy, and expensive. Mme Mère was not a prude, but she abhorred expense. In 1818, when she was finally paid the purchase price of the Hôtel de Brienne, she moved out and into a palazzo of her own, the Rinuccini, at the foot of the Corso, facing the Palazzo Venezia. It had been a bargain at 27,000 piastres, and she was to live in it for the rest of her long life.

Her style was as compressed as her lips. Her memoirs, dictated to her companion at the end of an exhausting career, run to a tart and sufficient six pages. Those of her children Lucien and Louis ramble through as many volumes, to less purpose.

"Everyone called me the happiest mother in the world, yet my life has been a succession of sorrows and torments. I never let myself be deluded by the grandeurs of flattery at court, and if my sons had taken more notice of what I said they would be better off than they are."

All this has the smack of Roman annals. And that was certainly her style. The only thing she missed was the theater, "my one distraction." She refused to go, because she would have to attend as a commoner and also, perhaps, because the theater at Rome has never been very good. As a young bride, fresh up from the country, she had been given her audience with Louis XVI and Marie Antoinette, at Versailles. Twenty years later, as mother of the Emperor, she gave audiences there herself. Now she was in exile again. She was sixty-six, but that does not seem to have bothered her. Neither did anything else.

She was accused of distributing millions to raise a revolt in Corsica. She replied that if she had millions, she would use them to arm ships to rescue the Emperor from St. Helena. She had already asked to join him, but the Allies had refused to let her do so.

She tried to track down her family. Only Lucien, Pauline, and Louis were available, and Louis was not very available. He quarreled with Lucien, who had committed the offense of putting him up, and with Fesch, for having put up with him. "Not a day passes without

Your Eminence finding some way of insulting me, and either because you have spent too much time in the company of uneducated people, or because . . ." Louis' denunciations were always long.

So matters went until 1818, when there occurred the deplorable affair of the Clairvoyante. Her name was Mme Kleinmuller. Though a devout Catholic, she had visions and could communicate with the spirit world. She may possibly have been an Austrian spy. Her spirit control was the Virgin Mary.

In their later years both Cardinal Fesch and Mme Mère became more devout. Mme Mère always had been, but with the onset of old age she began to believe more desperately in the existence of Divine Intercession. As for Fesch, once he had made his fortune, he became pious. Once he said to Marie Louise of the Emperor, on a fast day, "If he eats meat, throw your plate at his head." As Cardinal, he backed Pius VII against Napoléon and took his duties seriously. With age he became ascetic besides. He fasted more than he should have and liked to head penitential processions to the Colosseum, barefoot through the dirt and horse dung, in a gray habit, carrying a cross. These have been described by Mme de Staël in her novel *Corinne*. He spent an increasing amount of time on his knees, and his sister joined him. So did Mme Kleinmuller. She earned her living off such people and had a sharp eye for the symptoms.

Mme Kleinmuller's ultimate revelation occurred about the 15th of January, 1819, when she claimed that Napoléon had left St. Helena, that the British had moved him somewhere else, that he had been Called Higher (though still corporeal) and wafted away by authentic angels (incorporeal). She was believed. Fesch took to writing in this vein: "Although the gazettes and the English always insinuate that he is still at St. Helena, we have reason to believe that this is no longer so, and although we do not know where he is, nor when he will appear, we have sufficient proof to hope we shall soon be told those with certainty. There is no doubt that the jailer of St. Helena forces Count Bertrand to write as if Napoléon were still there.

"Everything about his life is miraculous, and I am inclined to believe in yet another miracle."

It was hinted that he might be at Malta.

Communications with St. Helena were bad, and made no better by the Allies. In May of 1818 Bertrand wrote to Fesch, explaining that Napoléon's *maître d'hôtel* had died and that the climate was so bad that they felt the need of a priest. "Send us a Frenchman or an Italian. Please choose a cultivated man, under forty, with a mild character and not Anti-Gallican." A doctor and a French or Italian cook were also requested.

Since, in Fesch's opinion, this letter was a forgery and Napoléon was not there, he chose as a cultivated man one Abbé Buonavita, who was antique, and who, as the result of an apoplectic stroke, could no longer speak distinctly. He had spent most of his life in Mexico and Paraguay and was an ignorant backwoods priest. His assistant was even less well informed than he, though a little more knowledgeable than the doctor selected. Foureau de Beauregard, who had been chief physician to the Emperor in the days of the Empire, volunteered but was refused. Pauline, Catherine of Württemberg, and even Louis tried to intervene, but were not allowed to do so. Mme Kleinmuller said no. The physician chosen was Antommarchi, who, so Louis discovered, was not even a doctor, but merely an assistant at the autopsy tables of Florence.

The climate of St. Helena was not so bad as the Emperor liked to make out. What was wrong there was that sanitation was not a subject the English were willing to recognize as a necessary adjunct to survival, with the result that dysentery and hepatitis were widespread and usually fatal. The East India Company had some notions of what must be done about such matters, but the British military garrison on the island had, of course, none whatsoever. And neither had Antommarchi. Though Napoléon was, in fact, dying, Antommarchi was sure that his illness was merely political. To give him credit, he was therefore willing to assist, though totally incapable either of diagnosis or of cure.

Fesch sent out these people as a blind, with no thought they would arrive or that if they did arrive they would find anyone there. At the last moment Pauline threw in her own cook, who had been a spit boy in the kitchens at the Tuileries in the old days but who was by now well trained in more exalted culinary arts.

Napoléon, who could not stand Buonavita's habit of gumming his mass and his generally uncouth manners, sent the priest back. He felt angry and abandoned. He kept Antommarchi and the cook.

It was a triumph for Mme Kleinmuller, to whom Mme Mère continued to give regular and more than adequate sums of money. Despite everything Pauline and Louis could do, Mme Kleinmuller (she conspired with Mme Mère's confessor) lasted two years. Apparently she even forged letters from the Emperor, who had been "transported to an island where his health was very good." Mme Mère felt happier and began to look healthier.

Cardinal Fesch tore up and hid all letters received from St. Helena. But when Buonavita came back in 1821, he also brought a letter for Pauline. Thus armed, Pauline marched on the Palazzi Rinuccini and Falconieri and had such a fight with Fesch as never to wish to see him again, but finally managed to convince her mother that Mme Kleinmuller was a spy, a liar, and a leech. It took her four nights of argument and evidence.

The Abbé Buonavita maintained that Napoléon had said that if the Pope would not find a place for him, the family was to provide a pension of 3,000 francs a year. The thought of paying 3,000 francs a year had Fesch more firmly convinced than ever that the Emperor could not have been at St. Helena and that the Abbé Buonavita could not have seen him. Finally, since no one else would do anything for him, Pauline paid his pension.

Buonavita had left St. Helena on March 17, 1821. He brought bad reports of the Emperor's health. Pauline wrote at once to Lord Liverpool, the English Prime Minister, asking for permission to go out to the island. But by then Napoléon was already dead.

Mme Mère became herself again. She had wasted two years. Now she, too, began to write petitions and letters for the Emperor's release or relief. She even wrote to Marie Louise, for the first time since 1814, though there was no answer. She in her turn petitioned the British Prime Minister. She even wrote to Jérôme.

None of this could accomplish any effect. It was too late.

THANKS to Napoléon, St. Helena has remained a much maligned island. Yet it is beautiful, a subtropical Tristan da Cunha, expansive, mountainous, isolated, and, in its protected parts, somnolent with foliage, for it is well watered. Its death rate arose not from its climate, which was good at sea level and excellent on the heights, but from its faulty sewage disposal and from its army of rats, who carried typhus. No real effort was made in those days to put down the rats.

Even so, the death rate was 35 per thousand, as compared to 18 for Malta, 75 for Ceylon, 668 for the Gold Coast, or, for the matter of that, 81.5 for the West Indies and 21.6 for the London Foot Guards. (These death statistics are for the military installations only.) Among the civilians the rate was lower. Among the East India Company, which maintained tauter standards than the garrison on the island, it was much lower. Its employees averaged three deaths per year, as opposed to the thirty-five for the British government. It was not only the plumbing that made the difference, it was the food. In the midst of an island rich in fresh greens, good vegetables, fruit, and sheep, the government troops were reduced to salt beef, salt pork, stale bread, and a pint of Cape wine a day. And, brought up to such a diet, it did not occur to the troops to eat anything else.

On a better diet, and with his own privy system, Napoléon had little to fear. Both Old and New Longwood were at an elevation, with few houses above them, and therefore with an adequate supply of uncontaminated running water; and proper drainage reduced the chances of dysentery and hepatitis. And in truth, he had neither. Both his houses stood well above the habitual sea fog belt. He could not have asked for a better climate. But of course he was dying of defeat, boredom, lack of exercise (he did not like to be seen by the English), undulant fever contracted as a child in Corsica, ill-treated venereal complications, and incurable progressive cancer of the pylorus, the disease to which male Bonapartes were prone.

Life on St. Helena was life under a microscope, which enhances faults, but merely blurs greatness. There were many petty squabbles during the six years he spent on the island. At one time, Napoléon, Montholon, Bertrand, and Las Cases had to dine each alone in his room, because they could not solve problems of precedence at table. All three aides were jealous of each other, and Las Cases himself intrigued to have himself deported. Delays in getting him off "prolonged the conflicts of my mind and lacerated my wounds." He wanted to get away and publish his *Mémorial de Ste. Hélène*, but could not do so until 1817, was detained six months at the Cape, and could not publish, in French and English, until 1823. It is the first great piece of Napoleonic propaganda.

Napoléon had holes cut in the shutters so he could watch what was going on without being seen. Of his staff, only Las Cases spoke adequate English, and he left early. Most of the others did not speak it at all and did not wish to. Efforts were made to make the Emperor, always referred to as "the General," forget his French and speak only Italian instead.

It was to Napoléon's purpose to present himself as a mistreated martyr. But most of the friction between himself, the Allied Commissioners, and Sir Hudson Lowe, the jailer set over him, though at a distance, was of his own making. He threatened to shoot anyone who entered his apartments. The Commissioners and Lowe were only allowed to enter the main halls, and then under special circumstances. It was part of his plan to exhibit himself as the persecuted and fallen savior of Europe.

Oddly, the miscellany of incompetents sent out by Fesch worked a temporary improvement. The auxiliary priest, Vignali, had begun to study medicine, Fesch hoping he might qualify as a consulting physician. As a matter of fact, he helped to check some of Antommarchi's wilder notions. Only the cook was perhaps superfluous. Napoléon had always bolted his food and ate mostly mutton and overdone cutlets and overrich pastries. He refused to eat fruit or vegetables, which might have done him more good, but had the sense to water his wine. Even at the Tuileries meals had not been supposed to last longer than half an hour or forty-five minutes (a custom Napoléon III was to reintroduce); on St. Helena they lasted less than fifteen minutes.

There was no conversation.

But Fesch's little company at least had the merit of instituting a routine, and everyone agreed that life went better after their arrival (September 20, 1819).

Napoléon put Vignali to work copying twenty pages a day of Rollin's *Ancient History*, to cure his ignorance, and forbade him to speak of medical matters. Vignali spoke of these to Antommarchi instead. He also forbade him to offer his medical assistance to anyone, even the Chinese coolies.

Antommarchi at least recognized that the Emperor would be the better for some exercise, and encouraged him, therefore, to make improvements in his garden. This worked. In no time Napoléon had put everybody to work and had three acres landscaped in imitation of Malmaison. Seeds were sent from Rio and Calcutta. There were eleven gardeners.

Napoléon perked up sufficiently to take potshots at passing livestock, rabbits, goats, and chickens. Eventually he winged a cow. When the East India Company gardener refused to make more bullets, the Emperor put his staff to work to make their own. This sort of thing was an Italian custom. Pope Pius VII, at the Vatican, often amused himself by shooting sparrows from the windows, and in palmier days Napoléon had liked to pepper Joséphine's pet dogs from the Malmaison French doors and upper casements.

There was another incident when Napoléon planted *haricots verts* instead of *haricots blancs* in the kitchen gardens. Lowe wondered whether this was not a rebellious act, green being the color of Napoleonic livery, white that of the Bourbons. It wasn't, it was just a distaste for *haricots blancs*, but such was the level at which life on St. Helena was usually conducted.

Antommarchi's regimen of exercise did Napoléon much good. He began to believe it might cure his cancer and so took to riding for the first time in four years, and when that was no longer possible because of his condition, he would go out in a phaeton.

He did not really want to die, but he was losing energy. His habit of taking long hot baths further debilitated him. By the winter of 1820 and 1821 he was sinking. "I vegetate; I no longer live," he said.

193

And sometimes he would drag himself to the window when he got up, saying, "Good morning, sun, good morning, sun, my friend." This, unlike the pathos he generated for public consumption, was how he really felt. (Years later, dying and blind, Mme Mère used to say, "The sun comes to me like a friend, though I can no longer see it." They were a Corsican family after all. Unlike the Parisians, they lived in light and could not do without it.)

By December he could no longer tolerate nourishment. It was even thought to send to the Cape for the celebrated Dr. Barry, not then known to be a female transvestite and so at the top of his (or her) profession. Elisa, of whose death he now learned, had kept herself alive by will power. He decided to try the same thing. Antommarchi was not much help. Vignali had been forbidden to give any. Buonavita had another attack of apoplexy, before leaving, and the cook Pauline had sent out developed fainting fits. Napoléon had taken to hiding in darkened rooms. New Longwood was now ready for occupancy, and it would have been easier to nurse him there, but he refused to move into it.

The final illness began in March of 1821. He lay in a room so dark, it was hard to make him out. The oddity of his case was that he was so enormously obese, whereas cancer has usually an emaciating effect. Since he refused to go down to the new house (which indeed he was never to occupy), he was moved into the drawing room of Old Longwood, as his bedroom was too small for his attendants to be able to attend him there.

His staff began to think of departure. Montholon sent down to Jamestown, the port, to inquire about the availability of large trunks. Mme Bertrand cast about for a female servant willing to make the voyage to England (where they would all have to go, in order to secure their manumission).

On the 21st of April Napoléon gave orders for the preparation of his mortuary chapel. He then wrote out and added to his will, and dictated his own death notice (with the date left blank). On the 4th of May there was a squall outside the windows. It rose to a tempest. On the 5th everyone came in to be present at the deathbed (which had to be moved to make enough space). At 5:41 P.M. the sun sank. At 5:49 Napoléon died. He was only fifty-one.

An autopsy was necessary, to disprove the rumor that he had been poisoned. He himself had asked that one be performed, to see if he had died of cancer, and if so, if something could not be done to save L'Aiglon from the same disease. The autopsy was marred by Dr. Short's attempts to twist the evidence and to destroy the organs, to support his own diagnosis of liver disease. This diagnosis proved to be so patently false that to his chagrin he did not succeed. It was an eminently healthy liver. Everyone was astonished by the excessive amount of fatty tissue. The autopsy lasted six hours and was performed in the presence of six doctors. It proved cancer of the pylorus.

Antommarchi tried to take a death mask but failed. In the process he used all the available plaster of Paris. But there was a deposit of gypsum on the island, and sending out a longboat and grinding and mixing his own powder, Dr. Burton tried and succeeded. The body was by then so decayed that he could take only the one cast. The cast was in two parts, face and back of the head. Mme Bertrand then stole the facial half and refused to return it. She took it back to England with her.

On the 7th of May the funeral took place. On the 9th, the Emperor was buried in the valley below Hutt's Gate, under some weeping willows and beside a favorite spring. The grave itself was made of portland stone, obtained by dismantling a battery mount. The willows were stripped for cuttings as souvenirs (the banks of the Avon, at Christchurch, in New Zealand, are lined with willows grown from cuttings of these trees). Later some cypresses were added. There was no name on the grave slab. Montholon insisted on Napoléon and Sir Hudson Lowe on Napoléon Bonaparte, and no compromise could be reached, so they left it blank.

After the interment there was a scamper to flee the island. On the 27th the entire society at Longwood left for England, on the storeship *Camel.* The furniture of the three houses, Old Longwood, New Longwood, and Bertrand's house, was sold at auction on the 26th. The sale lasted until the 3d of June and brought in 2,577 pounds, seven shillings and ninepence.

Sir Hudson Lowe and his family took their departure on the 25th of July.

Napoléon left a complicated will. The executors tried to keep its provisions secret, but on the 10th of December, 1821, it was proposed in the Prerogative Court of the Archbishop of Canterbury, though not probated until August 5, 1824. Property held in England was sworn to a value under 600 pounds. In April 1822 a copy was published in Paris, where, since Napoléon had been proclaimed a rebel and a traitor, it was decided the Emperor had no property to assign. The executors ignored this decision.

It was a fantastic document, less a will than a manifesto directed against his enemies, fancied or real. He claimed to have deposited nearly 6,000,000 francs with the banker Laffitte in 1815. Actually he had deposited 4,200,000, on which he had drawn while at St. Helena, leaving 3,418,785. The will, however, disposed of public legacies of 200,800,000 francs and private ones of 10,010,000. The odd 10,000 was for Cantillon, the man who had tried to murder Wellington.

The will began with eight political clauses. 1. He was a good Catholic. 2. He wished to be buried on the banks of the Seine "in the midst of that French people whom I have loved so well." 3. Sentiments to Marie Louise, with a hair watch chain and a bracelet of the same material, never made and certainly not wanted. 4. L'Aiglon must remember he had been born a French prince. 5. He died prematurely, murdered by the English oligarchy and its hired assassins. 6. Marmont, Augereau, Talleyrand and Lafayette were traitors, but "May the posterity of France forgive them as I do." 7. The family is thanked and Louis specifically forgiven for his *History of Holland*, "full of false assertions and falsified documents." 8. Disavowal of unauthorized memoirs, and self-justification for the murder of the Duc d'Enghien.

Then came the bequests. The King of Rome was to receive no money, but almost all his personal belongings and military souvenirs, including fifty-two snuff boxes, some of them pinched from the Tuileries in 1815, with Marie Antoinette, Louis XVI, and the Duchesse d'Angoulême on their lids. To his mother, his night lamp. To his family, bracelets of his hair (even with his post mortem beard to be shaved, there was not enough hair). Nothing he had owned was ever to be sold outside the family, but a gold snuff box was given to Lady Holland, who had been kind to him.

To his household at St. Helena, 3,000,000 francs. Everyone got something, except Antommarchi. Las Cases got 100,000. So did twenty-one other people. All told these legacies came to 5,600,000 francs; they were to be paid out of the sums left with Laffitte, though the sums left with Laffitte had never been that large.

He next left his private domain (nonexistent), which in his opinion amounted to 200,000,000 francs. It was made up of his savings from the civil list (long since distributed, stolen, or spent), plus his holdings and movables in France and Italy, long since confiscated, plus interest.

One half this imaginary sum he divided among the soldiers and officers who had fought with him, in proportion to their length of active service. The other half was to reimburse towns which had suffered during the invasions of 1814 and 1815, most of them on the Franco-German border.

Then came, first, instructions to his son, a clearheaded document, and then more cockaigne, in the form of codicils. Codicil one: his executors were to take over his personal belongings at St. Helena. Codicil two: distribution of 2,000,000 francs raised against the sale of his valuables in Italy. As Viceroy of Italy, Eugène was expected to pay this sum, but everything in Italy had been seized by the Austrians. Previous bequests were increased, and 200,000 francs were left to those maimed or wounded at Waterloo. Codicil three dispensed the value of diamonds stolen from him by the Provisional Government in 1814, which he set at between 5,000,000 and 6,000,000 francs. Codicil four awarded imaginary monies to the heirs of various military men whose services he had valued, including 10,000 to Cantillon. Codicil five asked Marie Louise to refund the 2,000,000 francs she had taken away with her from Orléans in 1814. It recommended she pay pensions to his loyal followers, for example, 30,000 francs a year to Bertrand. In codicil six he divided up the 2,000,-000 francs she was asked to return in codicil five. Codicil seven gave 300,000 francs to his illegitimate son Léon Denuelle, and in it he also remembered various Corsicans and Elbans who had been kind to him.

To every surviving member of his family he left some personal trinket (such as a pair of gold spurs to Joseph), with the exception of Louis. To none did he leave money.

All the executors could do was to pay out the sums remaining with Laffitte, on a percentage basis, with modifications, and to the personal legatees only. This was done in 1823, after arbitration. The Longwood domestics received ninety-four percent of their legacies, the other personal legatees, about three-fifths, though Montholon got sixty-seven percent, Marchant sixty-two percent and Bertrand fifty-seven percent. Payments were not completed until 1826, by which time 457,336 francs interest had accumulated on the monies placed with Laffitte.

Thirty years later, in 1853, Napoléon III requested the will of the British government, which had kept it, and appointed a commission to report on the practicability of carrying out its terms. The commission decided that 4,000,000 francs should be provided for the individual legacies and another 4,000,000 for the collective. 4,700,000 was paid out in 1855 on the personal bequests, and 4,000,000 on the collective, to the Battalion of Elba, the wounded of Ligny and Waterloo, the towns of Brienne and Méry, the provinces which had suffered most in the invasions, and to the soldiers surviving from the campaigns of 1792 to 1815.

On May 5, 1821, the day Napoléon died, something inexplicable happened at the Palazzo Rinuccini. It is amply attested to by witnesses.

A decently dressed stranger called and asked to see Mme Mère. He did not have an appointment, but was finally able to force his way in. He demanded to see her alone. When he was alone with her, he told her that at that moment Napoléon was freed from his sufferings and happy. He pulled out a crucifix, asked her to kiss it, and told her she would see her son again. He predicted civil war in France and a conflagration in Europe. Then he bowed and left.

Perhaps it was a last bid for continued income on the part of Mme Kleinmuller, with the aid of a confederate. But the coincidence of day and hour is striking. So, it seems, was the man's manner, which was somewhat Napoleonic.

The news of Napoléon's death took nearly two months to reach England. Nine days after Metternich had been informed by means of a courier of the House of Rothschild, Marie Louise found out about it by means of a letter from one of her ladies in waiting, posted from Milan on June 16. Marie Louise was on her way to the Opera when she received the letter. Parma had quite a good little Opera. She went right on, and so was able to enjoy, which she did very much, the *Barber of Seville*. The news had also been printed that day in the *Parma Gazette*, but Marie Louise did not read newspapers, though occasionally, if anything of any importance was going on, she asked that selected bits of them be read to her.

The Austrian Foreign Office had not seen fit officially to inform her. This, she said, in the circumstances, "was her greatest affliction." Nonetheless, "I would have preferred him to enjoy many years of life and happiness, provided they were spent far away from me." She was eight months pregnant at the time, by Neipperg, and had been so badly stung by mosquitoes that she did not like to appear in public.

"I am delighted that my son showed so much feeling upon the occasion of his father's death. Death wipes out one's unpleasant memories, as I found on this occasion."

It also presented the Court of Parma with an awkward point of protocol. It was solved, as was just about everything in Parma, by the indefatigable Neipperg. "The most difficult problem," he wrote to Metternich, "in view of the absolute necessity of sparing Her Majesty's delicate feelings while at the same time respecting the principles generally adopted with regard to the deceased, was how to announce his death in the *Gazette* [of Parma] and motivate the adoption of mourning. . . . I hope that the expedient I have employed, avoiding as it does all mention of the titles of Emperor, ex-Emperor, or the names Bonaparte or Napoléon . . . which would have offended Her Majesty's heart or the political principles at present in force [Neipperg was a realist], will find favor with Your Highness."

It had been decided to refer to Napoléon only as the Most Serene Spouse of Our August Sovereign. This highly amused Metternich. Mourning was established as full mourning from July 25 until September 4, second class from September 5 to October 2, and third class from October 3 until October 24. At the requiem mass, *Serenessimo* had shrunk to *Consorte ducis nostrae*. Which made Napoléon no more than Prince Consort of Parma. Marie Louise's third illegitimate child, a girl, was born August 15, which was Napoléon's birthday and the Bonaparte *fête* day. In September she became Neipperg's wife. She was a little distraught to learn that Napoléon had left her his heart in pickled spirit, and refused to accept it. "My only desire is that it should remain in his grave," she said. "Ill-disposed people would take it as a pretext to make a pilgrimage to Parma, which would pain me exceedingly, for all I wish is peace and quiet."

Her peace and quiet were disturbed by the arrival of Antommarchi in Parma during the period of third class mourning, but after her second marriage. He had come not only to report the details of death, but also with a cast of Napoléon's death mask, which Mme Bertrand had allowed him to take in London. He in his turn cheated her, as she had cheated Dr. Burton, by selling the rights to reproduce it to not one, but two French firms.

Marie Louise refused to receive Antommarchi. A little after this visit, a Dr. Hermann Rollet reports he saw the children of Marie Louise's steward playing with a plaster object attached to a piece of string. They were pulling it across the floor "as though it were a carriage." It was Napoléon's death mask; Antommarchi had left it as a post mortem gift, and it had been put on a table somewhere. . . .

For Marie Louise was very busy. Not only did she have music lessons, feeding, and backgammon to attend to, but she was also *compelled* to attend to affairs of state between nine A.M. and eleven, after which she got dressed. By the time midnight came, she was exhausted, and retired to bed, seldom alone. Before Napoléon's death she and Neipperg had occupied rooms separated by an antechamber. This was no longer necessary.

Chateaubriand, who saw her in 1822, said she was extremely gay, and pregnant again. This was at the Congress of Verona, where she disconcerted everybody by wearing a bracelet put together out of pieces of the Cosmati work of Juliet's tomb. Neipperg, however, also according to Chateaubriand, "was a man of good breeding."

On the whole, Antommarchi had bad luck. Louis, in Florence, would not accept the details of Napoléon's death, either. His health was too delicate, he explained, to withstand the shock of minute description.

Antommarchi had to go on to Rome, where Mme Mère presented him with a diamond.

Mme Mère had received the news on the 22d of July. She screamed once, grasped at a bust of the Emperor, said nothing else whatsoever, and fainted to the floor. She remained speechless for the next two weeks, and would not see anyone, even Fesch. Neither would she answer letters. Fesch answered them in her name.

She then got up and wrote herself to Pauline, saying she wished to ask the British government to return Napoléon's remains to Europe. "Inexorable history is seated on his coffin," she said. The British government preferred not to reply.

The French Embassy in Rome was terrified lest the Pope allow a memorial mass at Rome, in public, at one of the basilicas. So the Pope said three private masses, according to Pauline.

In the words of Plon Plon, then as ever a spiteful child, Mme Mère retreated into an atmosphere of "laurels and snuff."

But the death of Napoléon unleashed more feeling than his captivity had done. Paris was deluged with souvenirs and funeral trinkets. Lafayette demanded that the body be brought home. A play called *Napoléon at Schönbrunn and St. Helena* became enormously popular. Manzoni composed an ode. In England, too, there was a cult. Napoléon's death sparked a Napoleonic revival. The fact that France's second period of greatness, her only period of prolonged successful military greatness, was the work of an Italian from a recent province was conveniently overlooked.

In a way, his martyrdom had been real enough. You cannot put a military genius accustomed to ruling a continent on an isolated rock forty-seven miles square and do much but kill him with boredom and bad food. The only available delicacy at St. Helena was shark's meat, and that the 500 Chinese coolies ate. For the others, including the 1,200 blacks, there was nothing much above the level of cold mutton.

He had been completely surrounded by people writing their and his memoirs. So he had to be careful not only of what he said, but what he showed. The result was a deluge of reminiscences. Antommarchi provided the *Derniers moments de Napoléon* (which he had done little to prolong). But the great book, which swept England, America, and Europe, was the ten volumes of Las Cases's *Mémorial de Ste. Hélène*, which appeared in 1823. Las Cases was a literary artist of considerable ability, a convinced Bonapartist, and the perfect sympathetic ear. True, he had left St. Helena in 1816, but the Emperor had been at his exiled best then. Napoléon edited himself, in conversation, and Las Cases edited Napoléon. More particularly, he had caught the authentic timbre of a voice before that voice turned querulous. In the *Mémorial* Napoléon had his say, from a carefully staged Olympian distance, about everybody.

Pauline received one of the first sets. Unfortunately she got Las Cases mixed up with the *Campagnes de l'Empéreur*, by Montholon and General Gourgaud. "The *Mirroir* praises it greatly. You should read it," she said to Coulman, who presented her with it. When told it was not the same work as the *Campagnes*, she showed more interest, though at the same time calling for a cashmere shawl and a hot-water bottle and asking what was being given at the Opera that night. She was particularly eager to know if Marie Louise was mentioned anywhere in it.

---------------------------------- ❧{ XIX }❧ ----------------------------------

Pauline's later years were those of a society hostess, which is what her earlier years had been, but now she needed money. She got it, of course, from Camillo. Though she had told him in 1812 she wished no more to do with him, what she wanted was half the Borghese palace to live in and an allowance.

Camillo thought not. He had settled in Florence, where he had a palazzo on the Via Ghibellina and his mistress, the Duchessa Lante della Rovere, to amuse him. He forbade Pauline to occupy the Palazzo Borghese at Rome and refused to pay so much as her pin money.

Pauline had settled first with Fesch and Mme Mère, which she found unendurably dull. She had always made it her practice to be kind to the Pope. Now the Pope was to be kind to her. The dispute was turned over to the Holy Office, whose head was a Corsican friend of Lucien's. So the Palazzo Borghese was made available to her. She had rather thought it might be.

Arnault, a friend of her first husband's, had once observed that Pauline had plenty of good nature, "but because she was made that way rather than from intention, for she was devoid of principles, and if she did good, did so from caprice." She now wrote a letter offering, or rather threatening, to live with Camillo again. Camillo began to shake, and made the error of writing her a long letter, saying why he would not accept her offer. Thus she was able to pose as a wronged woman. The letter was turned over to the Holy Office, and the result was a decree of June 25, 1816, whereby she was given a pension of 14,000 scudi a year and the right not only to the Palazzo Borghese, but to the Villa Borghese on Monte Pincio and the Villa Mondragone at Frascati as well, part of the Borghese household goods, and all furniture and jewels bought out of her own money.

So she was no longer poor, and she took to driving about with Negro pages in attendance, for show. The Villa Schiarra, which she had bought, she rechristened the Villa Paolina (all told there were to be three Villas Paolina). Mme Mère would not allow her to call it the Villa Bonaparte because its gardens were not showy enough. She filled it with English furniture and British guests, chiefly because the French daren't attend and the Italians mostly wouldn't. She was busy collecting anyone influential enough to intervene on behalf of her brother. "I have now some enemies the fewer," wrote Napoléon, when he heard of Pauline's system of entertaining.

She had begun to worry about her looks. "I said she had not altered since she had left Paris," reported the Duchesse d'Abrantès. "I lied in this and I lied so well that she shook her head at me with a sad little smile." It was bright-eyed lying, though. Mme Junot noted that Pauline had taken to wearing ten strands of pearls, to conceal the withering of her neck.

Pauline had Canova's statue put away, because "They want to see how the poison works in me." She did not, however, wish it destroyed. Once she was dead, and out of the way of comparisons, it would continue to show her at her best.

But she was as vain as ever. "If you would like to see my feet," she told the Princess Ruspoli, "come and visit me tomorrow morning." The showing of the feet turned out to be an elaborate ceremony.

Sometimes, also, she showed privileged visitors (at any rate, Lady Morgan, another scribbler) her bed. It was white and gold, with a point lace quilt.

She was as given to her own ailments as ever. "She makes a new will every day," said Elizabeth Patterson Bonaparte, over for a visit in 1821, "and has quarreled with every human being on earth, and will finally leave her property to strangers. . . . All that has been said of her is not half what she deserves—neither hopes of legacies, nor any expectation can make anyone support her whims [one of her whims at the moment was to get Elizabeth's son Bo married to Zenaïde, Joseph's daughter], which are so extraordinary as to make it impossible not to believe her mad." Time had made Elizabeth Patterson prim. It had not made her kinder.

Pauline's last lover was, as might have been expected, for she was over forty and as imperious as ever, a humiliation to her. He was

Giovanni Pacini, the composer, then a young Sicilian with his way to make in the world, beautiful rather than handsome, temperamental, and the chief rival of Rossini. Pacini was at first flattered, but he really was more interested in his career than in anything else, and unlike Talma, the actor who had amused her for one whole summer, more apt to drop her than to be dropped by her.

It was a little sad. It was now her turn to undergo those agonies which heretofore she had always caused, not felt. It did not make her bitter, but it left her desperate. For a time she became musical. She called him Nino. She had his opera, the *Slave of Bagdad*, performed at her house. She sang his songs. She tried to wreck Rossini's *Barber of Seville* by distributing free tickets to anyone who would hiss it (she preferred Paisiello's version). Later, they were reconciled. She collected composers, of whom Carafa at least had the merit of having been Murat's orderly in Russia.

Pacini was pleased. The relationship survived his *Caesar in Egypt* of 1822. It was not an outstanding success. But he was becoming famous, she would drag him around like a toy dog, and besides, she was often ill. Her complexion turned yellow. Pacini, being a good Sicilian, brought his sister Claudia to stay with them.

Indeed, she became so ill that it was sometimes difficult to find on short notice a confessor sufficiently indulgent to administer the absolutions she felt to be required.

So her last two years were not happy ones. Pius VII died. He had been her great protector. She felt it necessary to bring a new action before the Rota. She hoped to get a larger settlement from Camillo. Privately she confessed she would have dropped the matter if he had raised her pension to 20,000 scudi. He refused. Moreover, this time he fought back.

Pacini was slipping away. He went through Lucca, where she had gone to take the baths, without even coming to see her. His destination was Trieste. Jérôme was there, and took pleasure in sending Pauline a letter outlining Pacini's infidelities. So, rather pathetically, for he had left her already, she dismissed him.

"I have suffered so much that I feel the need to breathe in your arms," she wrote one month. "I have already forgiven him so often that I am tired at last of being deceived by a man on whom I have rained kindnesses," she wrote the next. It was a blow. She began to avoid mirrors.

The Rota nonsuited her complaints against Camillo. Again she threatened to live with him. This made him so desperate that he applied for a passport at the French Embassy, in order to flee through France to England. Pauline countered with an autograph from the new Pope, Leo XII, ordering him to accept his wife. She did not propose to die alone.

He said she might come, but must leave her "swarm of comedians behind."

To his chagrin, she came.

"Her husband does not know any longer how to act in her company," said Waldburg, the Prussian Ambassador to Florence, in March of 1825. "And he is deeply distressed that he can no longer appear at the French Minister's, who can neither receive Bonaparte's sister nor be seen at her house."

Camillo, by this time, had also lost his looks, had a scraggly moustache, and was beaky. But his life was made of such trifles as being received at the French Ambassador's. He found existence once more unendurable.

So did Pauline. She began to object that her windows did not face south, and moved to a villa a mile outside the walls, the Villa Niccolini. She hired six doctors. Jérôme paid a visit. So, for a wonder, did Louis. In point of fact, she really was at last mortally ill.

On the morning of June 9, she dictated her will, and at one in the afternoon, died, at forty-five, of cancer. Jérôme was the only member of the family present. Camillo closed her eyes. Louis had had trouble starting and met the hearse between Viterbo and Arezzo, so turned back.

She was buried in the Borghese vault in Santa Maria Maggiore, at her request. Also at her request, the coffin was closed and there was no lying in state. She had been revolted at the thought of gossips coming to describe a beauty double dead, so she had prevented their doing so. If anyone wished to see how she looked, let them look at the statue by Canova.

Like Napoléon, she left behind a complex will, but hers was a canny document. Borghese was to be executor of her possessions in Tuscany and Lucca, but Cardinal Agostino Rivarola of everything she owned in the Papal States (most of it). She thus contrived to satisfy Camillo legally, while at the same time keeping most of her possessions for distribution to those whom she wished to have them.

Louis, Jérôme and Caroline got most of her personal fortune, which amounted to 2,000,000 francs. The Villa Paolina at Rome went to Prince Napoléon Louis, Louis's elder surviving son. The Villa Paolina in Monte San Quirico went to Camillo for his lifetime only. Joseph received nothing, because he was rich, and Lucien the same amount, because he had always been critical of her habits. Pauline had always liked young people, so the children of Louis, Caroline, and Jérôme all received small legacies. She even left Bo, Jérôme's American son, something. Lucien's son Paul got 20,000 francs.

To L'Aiglon she left San Martino, on Elba, which Napoléon had left to her (on L'Aiglon's death Mme Mère bought it; on Mme Mère's death Prince Demidoff bought it). Fesch got her English coach. Her brother-in-law, Aldobrandini, got, rather thriftily, a portrait of Camillo by Gérard.

She left something to almost everyone who had sat at her table without complaining. To the Duke of Hamilton, her gilt toilet table, to his wife, two vases. To the Duke of Devonshire, to Lord Gower, to Lord and Lady Holland, and so on down the list, through her servants to the children of her wet nurse.

It was a courageous and considerate way to spend one's last morning, for that is when she dictated her will, while she lay there between two aging fops, her husband and her youngest brother.

For Pauline was spoiled, vain, tyrannical, extravagant, vulgar, exquisite, capricious, and neurasthenic, but almost everyone forgave her. For she was also loyal, generous, and vivid. She has only to enter any memoir of the period and say something silly, and at once the prose springs to life. For the Napoleonic legend, when looked at closely, consists of only three people, the Emperor himself, Joséphine, and Pauline. Of the lot, they alone have given their names to a style, a manner, and an age.

J OSEPH, of course, was in America, where he stayed, except for a
long visit to Europe, until 1832.

He arrived at New York, traveling as a M. Bouchard, with a
suite of four, on July 29, 1815. The captain of the *Commerce* (the
Bonapartes had the knack of traveling on appropriately named
boats) had thought him to be General Carnot traveling under an
assumed name. So did the Mayor of New York, who came to welcome him to the city and to congratulate him upon a safe passage.
Landing had not been easy, as British frigates were patrolling the
harbor mouth. The captain of the *Commerce* was able to outsail one
of these, and so prevent a search. This was a relief to Joseph, whom
the Allies had planned to send to Russia.

Joseph, now calling himself the Comte de Survilliers (one of the
names attached to the Mortefontaine property), stayed at the City
Hotel, as the guest of Henry Clay. Later, he took a house on the
Hudson, and from there went on to Philadelphia, where he rented
another house and held a reception. Though he kept a town house
there, Philadelphia did not satisfy him either, so, after a certain
amount of traveling about, he bought the estate of Point Breeze
("Bonaparte Park"), on the Delaware, at Bordentown in southern
New Jersey. It consisted of a house and 211 acres and cost him
$17,500. When the state legislature passed a special act permitting
him to own American property, he enlarged Point Breeze to 1,800
acres.

Bordentown was on the main New York to Philadelphia road,
being the landing stage for the ferry across the Delaware. So Joseph
did not lack for visitors. The park was laid out with twelve miles of
bridle paths and a great deal of statuary, rustic cots, seats, temples,
and solitary retreats. A lake was made, half a mile long.

The main house was in the standard Federal style, but there was another house, white with green shutters, where Joseph's daughter Zenaïde and her husband, Prince Charles Lucien Bonaparte, lived. The two houses were connected by an underground tunnel with a branch which led down through the bluff to a landing stage. Though Julie, as usual, gave bad health as her excuse for not coming out to America, both Joseph's daughters stayed with him.

Point Breeze became a Bonaparte museum. He also collected both nudes and mirrors, to the distress of his more puritan guests. Of the museum, it is perhaps kindest to observe that the masterpiece was an alterpiece by Raphael Mengs and to say no more. Joseph had not Cardinal Fesch's taste. But he had all his relatives, and one of the fatigues of Point Breeze was an obligatory tour of the house, during which Joseph gave a little lecture on the unique merits of his relatives and, of course, himself, winding up, most generally, with the semi-naked merits of Pauline.

Visitors were brought down on a sixteen-oar barge, from Philadelphia.

All told, Joseph spent about $300,000 on Point Breeze. He could afford it. In 1815, before going back to France, he had buried his jewels at Prangins. In 1817 his friend Mailliard, posing as an English coal expert, had some workmen dig a hole and got them back. They were worth perhaps 5,000,000 francs.

In January of 1820 Point Breeze burned down. He was chiefly astonished that his neighbors managed to save a good deal of the contents and actually returned these to him, instead of looting them. Joseph, who had had considerable experience of looting, on both sides of the fence, was so touched that he wrote the mayor a note of thanks, in which he dwelt upon the moral merits of America, a *new* country. Then he rebuilt the house, though not to the same scale.

One of Joseph's cronies was Vincent le Ray, Comte de Chaumont, who had been born in America and so was permitted to own and did own large acreages in upper New York State. From him, between 1815 and 1828, Joseph bought what eventually turned out to be 26,840 acres in the northern part of the state, 1,200 of them a lake, Lake Bonaparte. It was a complicated financial exchange. The property was to have been 150,000 acres, but as the value of Joseph's security diminished, so did the acreage. After 1828 he began to spend the summers there, building several lodges (one of them with bulletproof sleeping rooms). It was where he chose to keep his mistress (at Natural Bridge).

All the Bonapartes were singularly matter-of-fact about their vices, of which, on the whole, they had only two, a rampant sexuality and an Italianate taste for expensive display. The exceptions were Louis, with his ill nature, and Plon Plon, with his shifty choleric meanness. Joseph's daughters were in no way distressed by their father's habit of supplementing his wife. Charlotte, indeed, after her own husband's early death, took after her father in such ways. Joseph's American mistress was Annette Savage, a Quakeress from Philadelphia, by whom he had a daughter. When he left America in 1832, he left them provided for; though he was too outwardly proper to leave them sums in his will, he left something to his friend Mailliard to be used for this purpose (10,000 francs to the daughter).

Joseph was a man cautious of his dignity, but given to Rotarian pranks while in his cups. In fact he was a Rotarian by nature, which no doubt explains why he stayed in America so long. He liked his private hunting grounds in Jefferson County, which he called "my wilderness." But he was not a very shrewd businessman and was easily outtraded, losing more than he made by investing in American real estate. Just as in Switzerland, in the absence of the Emperor, he became head of the family (though Mme Mère no longer recognized him as such), a role he thoroughly enjoyed. He did not always enjoy its responsibilities, which descended upon him in two clumps, Napoleonic plots and Napoleonic relatives.

Of the former there were almost as many as of the latter. Joseph offered to go out to St. Helena in 1817 and 1819. The Emperor politely refused.

There were plots to get him off the island, though. A Mr. Johnstone was arrested in London for testing a submarine in the Thames designed for this purpose. He was to be taken off at night and transferred to a fast frigate, and thus to the New World. The fast frigate, as a matter of fact, had been arranged for and was waiting in the docks to sail when news came of the Emperor's death. In Philadelphia, Captain Jesse Hawkins and Joshua Wilder, both freebooters, planned another such effort. They proposed to fit out two clippers and to register their voyage for Canton, but to go to St. Helena instead. The clippers were to carry smaller swifter landing craft. Another such plot, launched from Brazil, was to carry aboard small steamships to the same purpose. Stephen Girard was fitting out still another ship at Philadelphia, with rescue in mind, and this was the ship docked at New Orleans, when the Emperor died; and at Rio, a Mme Fourès spent her fortune on such schemes. She claimed to have been Napoléon's mistress in Egypt.

A house was built for the Emperor's use at New Orleans, and a fast vessel, the *Séraphime*, was constructed at Charleston. Any of these plans might have succeeded, had the Emperor been willing to cooperate. But on at least two occasions he hesitated and then said no. He must have known the game was up, and besides, he was working on his legend. "If Christ had not died on the Cross, He would not have become the Son of God," he said, on turning down one such scheme, though only after considerable agitated pacing back and forth and much irresolute thought.

Lucien at one time thought that it would be a good idea if he came to America and joined Joseph and Napoléon in an attempt to conquer Mexico, a country about which they knew virtually nothing, and that wrong, a country moreover much more lethal to the conqueror than even Spain had been. Connected with this dream, in a murky way hard to make out, was that unfortunate experiment in exile, the Champ d'Asile, a colony of Bonapartist officers, under the direction of Lallemand, who tried to settle in Texas, six days from Galveston, on an island made by "a river as wide as the Seine, but full of crocodiles." The colony was a failure, and had to be rescued by Jean Laffite, the pirate.

In August of 1817 occurred the Lakanal affaire. Lakanal was a regicide and a defrocked priest who had come to settle in America, and later became President of the University of Louisiana, though not for long. In 1817 he was trying to farm in the Midwest. The Lakanal Packet was a sealed collection of documents sent to Joseph, but intercepted by the American government. It turned out to contain: 1. An ultimatum, stating that "The King is to have nothing to do with the mysterious enterprise . . ." That is, King Joseph. 2. A report asking for 65,000 francs for expenses. 3. A petition, requesting crosses, ribands, marquisates, and a Spanish distinction of some sort for Lakanal. 4. A vocabulary of the languages of the Indians on the Mexican frontier. 5. A list of Indian tribes in northern Louisiana. 6. A cipher, so contrived as to make secret messages resemble Latin prayers, which would have a good effect on the Spanish Mexicans, "who are generally attentive to religious forms."

The contents of this packet greatly agitated both the American government and the French and Spanish Ambassadors, until President Monroe decided that Lakanal was so impotent, and the scheme so nebulous and absurd that the matter was best laughed at and then forgotten.

Some time after Napoléon's death, revolution having broken out in Central America, a deputation waited upon Joseph to offer him the crown of Mexico. He refused it. "I have worn two crowns. I would not take a single step to obtain a third. Nothing could be more flattering to me than to see the men who, when I was at Madrid, were unwilling to recognize my authority, come today to see me, in exile, to place the crown upon my head. But I do not think that the crown which you wish to erect anew can promote your happiness. . . . Imitate the United States and seek from the midst of your fellow citizens a man more capable than I am to act the grand part of Washington."

By which it will be gathered that Joseph believed in buttering up his hosts. But he thus saved himself from the fate of the Emperor Maximilian forty years later, another Napoleonic scheme, but in the second generation.

Joseph's relatives were more difficult to deal with. Elizabeth Patterson and her son he managed to keep at a distance most of the time. But it was otherwise with the Murats, who not only descended on his doorstep, but set up a colony for a while at the foot of his bluff, at Bordentown.

They were Caroline's two sons, and combined all the rowdier features of both parents. But they were at least lively. Prince Lucien Murat arrived first, but did not turn out well. He was a drunkard and a gambler, and was soon borrowing money from his uncle. Since Joseph did not like to lend money, there were quarrels, followed by coolness. Lucien Charles, born in 1803, stood six foot two, enormous for a Frenchman, and was built accordingly. He was extravagant and indiscreet, spent his wife's fortune (he had married Miss Carolina Georgiana Fraser, the daughter of one of Joseph's Southern planter guests), and lived below the bluff, where, to keep them both, his wife opened a day school. Joseph gave her money he would not give to Lucien. The school operated until Napoléon III ascended the

French throne, at which time everybody emigrated to the Tuileries, and Carolina Georgiana Fraser Murat became Princess Murat, and her daughter Anna, Duchess of Mouchy.

Lucien Murat's chief fault was his own heartiness, and a tendency while drunk to knock other people down. His elder brother, Napoléon Achille, born in 1801, who arrived shortly after Lucien, was downright eccentric. He paid only a short visit to Bordentown, and then went on to Florida, where he married Catherine Willis Gray, a grandniece of Washington, and settled down to be a planter, becoming Mayor of Lipona (a town named after him; he was Prince of Lipona), near Tallahassee, Florida. Among other oddities, Achille Murat had a shaggy dog he used as a spittoon. He was also a diet faddist; he nearly killed his slaves in an effort to see whether or not man could live on a diet of cherrywood sawdust. Another of his inventions was alligator-tail soup. He had an aversion to bathing, and would drink water only when it had been suitably diluted with whiskey. Prince Achille wrote two books about America, both salty. Indeed he was the best of the writing Bonapartes. Here is his remark about temperance societies: "The members engage never to drink any distilled liquor, nor to permit its use in their families. But nothing hinders them from drinking wine. In that they mistake the Creator for a bad chemist." His exegesis of the dilemmas of a puritan brewer is not bad either: "They are in this respect so scrupulous that a brewer was reproved in church for having brewed on a Saturday, by which the beer had been exposed to work on the Sabbath." This is from the *Exposition of the Principles of Republican Government as Brought to Perfection in America*, which ran into fifty editions. "North Carolina is a bad imitation of Virginia" is another of his helpful apothegms. Among other unlikely things, he struck up a friendship with Emerson. "His soul," said that worthy, "is noble, and his virtue, as the virtue of a Sadducee must always be, is sublime." The friendship prospered. Achille wished Emerson to evangelize Florida to Unitarianism, in order to save it from Methodism, which "augments every day and will probably in a few years be the only religion among the ignorant classes of the people."

It is easy to see how Achille's liveliness grated upon Joseph's pomposity. They seldom saw each other. Achille died at Tallahassee on April 5, 1847, too soon for him to take advantage of the excellent terms offered by the Second Empire. However, Napoléon III gave an annuity to his widow, whom he called "Cousin Kate." When Florida seceded from the Union in 1861, Catherine, whether as a Murat or as a Washington, was on hand personally to fire the first cannon, which turned out to be quite a nice little noisy ceremony. She died unreconstructed in 1867. The Achille Murats enjoyed life heartily and had a very good time.

By comparison, Joseph seems increasingly to have partaken of the family fudge. With the Emperor, he could quote, he said, and did, from Zaïre, "*À revoir Paris je ne dois plus pretendre.*" But also like the Emperor in his later years, he worked hard on Bonapartist propaganda. "My sentiments are as invariable as yours and those of my family. *Everything for the French people.*" "Doubtless I cannot forget that my nephew, Napoléon II, was proclaimed by the Chamber which, in 1815, was dissolved by the bayonets of foreigners. Faithful to the motto of my family, *Everything by France and for France.*"

This was the new line, and brought him violently into conflict with the old one of Lafayette, who complained that he could not remember this doctrine's being much whiffed about at the time of the Revolution and Consulate. Joseph replied, unanswerably, that Lafayette had been imprisoned in Austria in those days, and so knew nothing about them. "I remember one day my brother, coming from an interview with you, my dear general, said to me . . . 'The Marquis de la Fayette does not know the character of these people in whom he interests himself. He was in the prisons of despotism when these people made all France to tremble. But France remembers this too well. We are not here in America.' My brother . . . was forced into war by the English, and into the dictatorship by the war."

This was the line Joseph was unswervingly to pursue. But he was getting restless in America. In 1830 he wrote to Marie Louise asking for custody of the Duc de Reichstadt. He got no answer. In 1832 he wrote to the Duc de Reichstadt himself, and removed to London. In 1835 he sold his Black Valley properties in upper New York State. And though he came back to America in 1837, and stayed two years, London was from now on to be his headquarters, until such time as he was permitted to go to Italy. The only outcome of his American adventures was his daughter, later Mrs. Benton, who also was to take advantage of the Second Empire and also to receive her pension from the civil list. When both the Empire and the pension ended, she returned to America, where, when her husband died, she supported herself by teaching the piano at Utica and Watertown. She died at Richfield Springs, New York, in 1891.

Joseph came back to Europe the second time to supervise the disposal of Mme Mère's property. But from London he took some interest, most of it highly disapproving, in the schemes of his nephew, Louis Napoléon.

Jérôme's American wife, Elizabeth Patterson Bonaparte, was not dead, only dormant. She had been waiting. Now she planned to erupt again. She was not her father's child for nothing, and had a well-developed sense of real estate and property. As the daughter of the second richest man in America, she intended to grow no poorer. But unlike her father, she had ambitions on a European scale.

She had come back to Baltimore after her son's birth, but she did not enjoy herself. Neither did her father or family once she had returned. Betsy was a difficult woman. To great beauty she added vigor, gumption, a contempt for all things American, and a sharp tongue. She was socially much in demand, *at first.* When she was not in demand, she went off to rusticate at any of several houses her father owned in Maryland. One of her enterprises was to get her portrait out of Gilbert Stuart, not an easy thing to do, for he hated to finish anything. She got it. "It looks like myself," she said. "The others look like any other woman."

She consented to remain in America, to placate her father, to supervise her son's early years and education, because Napoléon had barred her from the Continent, and to receive the latter's pension of $12,000 a year, money she managed herself, with her usual shrewdness. But she had kept up her European correspondence, and two months after Waterloo, leaving her son behind at Mount St. Mary's College in Maryland, she came to England and then crossed over to Paris.

"Everyone wishes me to educate my child in England, and they are good enough to flatter him by saying that Bonaparte talents ought to have an English education. He would indeed be much more highly considered in Europe than in America, where unfortunately he possesses no rank; and could I combine with the interest he excites here, the solid advantage of a large fortune, I should be too happy! . . . America and its institutions are yet in a state of infancy —nor is there, from the commercial complexion of all its pursuits, the same field for successful exertion of the kind of mental superiority which your grandson [she was writing to her father], happily or unhappily, possesses. . . . My conduct in leaving America was the result of much previous reflection, nor do I see any reason yet to regret it; on the contrary, my most sanguine expectations have been exceeded."

In 1813 Elizabeth divorced Jérôme, by act of the Maryland legislature, because, as the wife of a European citizen, she could not own her own property in America in her own name, and did not wish Jérôme to be able to get at it. This did not prevent her from claiming such notoriety and position as she could achieve as his wife.

On September 2, 1815, Mme Bonaparte was again explaining things to her father. Indeed, describing to him the merits of life as far away from him and from America as she could get was among her many pleasures. "I perceive, with much regret, by your letters . . . that you announced . . . that I *conceived* myself ill. . . . The physicians of England are willing to give a certificate of their opinion that there is an accumulation of bile on my liver, which would have killed me, or produced the last stage of hypochondria in three months, had I not gone to sea and tried a change of climate. . . .

"As for leaving America without the consent of my friends, it appears to me that, if indeed I have friends there, they would have wished me to come to a country where I am cherished, visited, respected, and admired. It appears to me that, if I have friends in America, their friendship might have been shown in some more agreeable mode than finding fault with me for being miserable in a country where I never was appreciated, and where I never can be contented . . . I acknowledge that the standing I possess in this country [England] is highly flattering, and that it is not surprising I should prefer people of rank and distinction who are willing to notice me."

This explains both Betsy's travels and Betsy's health. The following explains Betsy's preference:

"I have taken a house beside and under the protection of my amiable friends, Sir Arthur and Lady Brooke Falkener. The family with whom I came over remain in a boarding-house. My friends advised

me to move, as people of fashion never live in boarding-houses. . . .
Adieu, my dear sir. I am going to dress for a ball at Lady Con-
dague's, and am then obliged to go to one at Genl. Trivin's. I expect
the Americans in Europe who cannot go out will write lies about
those who can. . . . All my conduct is well calculated."

Father William, a worldly man, replied, "I cannot say I am satisfied with the attentions you seem to receive from great people in
England; they cannot be lasting; they must arise chiefly from curiosity and compassion. Your regret and disappointment hereafter will
be in proportion to the elevated notions you may entertain at present
from those attentions."

This did not go down at all well. Betsy to Father William: "I
every day find new reasons to think we succeed best in strange
places, since human infirmity seldom stands the test of close and perpetual communion. . . . The Portuguese Ambassador, Count
Tonsall, sent me, through Viscount Lord Strangford, late Ambassador to the Portuguese court, an invitation to a grand ball given by
the nobility of Cheltenham. . . . The count la Chatre, ambassador
from France, has just sent me my passport for Paris. . . . In this
country [Betsy was now thirty], the term *old*, which is so often
repeated in America, is completely banished from the polite vocabulary. Women of forty, even of fifty, are more cherished and as advantageously married as chits of sixteen. They are not here cheated out
of their youth, as with us, but retain the glorious privilege of charming until at least sixty. . . . Since I am so happy as to be in the best
society, I much deplore the absence of American friends to witness
the estimation in which I am held. . . . The British are, as they
modestly confess, the greatest nation in the world. We must acknowledge that their monstrous vanity is excusable. . . . All the
Americans in Europe, except Mrs. Mansfield, have been very civil.
Aunt [Mrs. Mansfield's mother, a Patterson relative] ever was an old
hypocrite, and her conduct on this occasion proves that deceit and
wickedness will go with her to the other world. . . . As to Mansfield, he is only afraid that I will write to Baltimore a true account of
his entire insignificance in London. I know no one who has ever seen
him, and they are in *no* society."

If this sounds like a manifesto, it was. But Betsy was not in the best
society, only in the second best, the professional, and the titled bohemian. Her chief pusher in England was Lady Morgan, an ex-

governess who had risen by her pen and wits to the top of Upper Bohemia. Great men, if in politics, received Betsy once as an interesting political anomaly. Great families did not receive her at all. She had to make do with the likes of Sir Arthur and Lady Falkener. She found that sufficient.

She crossed to Paris in the winter of 1815 and 1816. Wellington was civil and Talleyrand praised her wit. Mme de Staël admired her beauty, and Louis XVIII offered to see her at court, an offer which *she* refused. As a Bonaparte, and as a pensioner of the ex-Emperor, she did not wish to show ingratitude or, for that matter, to stoop. Others she met in Paris were Sismondi, Chateaubriand, Humboldt, Canova, and the Duchesse de Duras. The Faubourg St. Honoré and the Faubourg St. Germain were closed to her. But then they had been closed to everyone for years. Even Louis XVIII was not received *there*.

"I form no plans, I try to hope that some unexpected happiness may continue me where alone I attach value to existence," she explained to her father. This was the *Night Thoughts* side of her. "The ex-King of Westphalia is now living at the Court of Württemberg. He has a large fortune, and is too mean to support his own son. He ought to pay you your money." This sounds more like Rochefoucauld.

In 1816 she returned to Baltimore, for a visit of three years, until such time as her son should ripen and she could finish his education there and release him into the midst of his Bonaparte connections, out of whom she hoped he would get something.

So she arrived at Amsterdam on the 25th of June, 1819, accompanied by Bo, her son, and went on to Geneva, where the boy was to continue his education and Mme Bonaparte her social career. Both did well. Bo was a diligent scholar. Betsy managed to bag a stepson of the Duke of Kent, the Princess Potemkin, the Princess Galitzine, and, oddly enough, Prince Demidoff, whose son was later to marry Jérôme's daughter Mathilde.

Using John Jacob Astor as an intermediary, Pauline Borghese asked the Patterson Bonapartes to come to Rome. Betsy accepted. "I have made every inquiry concerning her circumstances, disposition, and mode of life," she informed her father. "She has, perhaps, some fortune of her own. . . . My opinion is that I should go to the Princess myself in the autumn for three months, that Cricket [her name for Bo] should be left at his present boarding school, . . . that he should remain ignorant of the expectations which are held out to him. . . . She is perhaps sincere in her present intentions [she had offered to help Bo along and leave him a little money], but the fortune of a pretty woman of thirty-five is a bad object of calculation for nephews. . . . If I were to take the child to a palace, he would naturally prefer pleasure to study: the habits of the Italians are delightful, but do not lead to personal distinction."

Betsy's ideas of education were of a Hapsburg rigor. Bo was to have "a tincture of Greek," Latin and mathematics, French, English, chemistry, physics, etc., jurisprudence, history, mythology, geography, drawing, equitation, fencing, and dancing. In addition he was to be sent to a ball every Saturday evening, to polish his "*usage du monde.*"

As for Pauline, "They say she is good *au fond,*" but "I cannot say I have the least reliance upon that family. . . . They are less wealthy than is supposed. . . . I believe some of them are amiable; but when there is a question of parting with money, good will is generally exposed to a great trial."

"The King of Westphalia spends everything he can get hold of, and will keep up kingly state until his expended means leave him a beggar," added Betsy. "Joseph is said to be the richest, and is a man of sense. . . . Bo has written to you for money to buy a horse, which I beg you *not* to send him. He pretends it will be more economical for him to keep a horse than for me to pay nine francs per week for riding lessons; but I prefer paying twice that sum rather than allow him to ride about the country." For Betsy was a jailer of a mother. She had him write to Mme Mère. "I must make him write a letter to the old lady, to jog her memory." And: "There is a son of Sir Robert and Lady Wilmot going out [to America] with the British Ambassador. . . . If you should be giving a family dinner, you might invite him; but I do not advise people to take any trouble about strangers, as they are very ungrateful in general, and their acquaintance of no great advantage unless one has daughters to get rid of."

Such was Betsy's wisdom at thirty-five. As she got older, it increased, but along the same lines. In Geneva she limited her own expenses to $3,000 a year, by living in a boarding house for $60 a month. As Bo wrote to his grandfather, "Mama lives in town, in the cheapest way possible, on account of the troubles now in Baltimore [a slight recession in the value of her real estate]. She has no man-servant, but one single woman. . . . Her meals are furnished by a woman for a certain price per month."

It is true that it was only in her later years that Mme Bonaparte's attention turned exclusively to the making of money (she died a mil-lionairess, in her nineties), but even in 1820 her poverty, like her ill health, existed chiefly for her own convenience.

She was inclined to take Lady Morgan's advice. "Lady Morgan is one of the shrewdest women in Europe, and her opinion is perfectly to be relied on. She knows the value of money as well as anybody, and when it is worth while to put oneself in the way of getting it." Lady Morgan's opinion was that Pauline would spoil Bo and give him nothing, and that "he would be ruined for every purpose of life if taken to her."

In Betsy's opinion, the only Bonaparte in Rome with any sense was "the old lady," for "she is very sensible and very miserly, and probably will leave all she can save to her children, who are all spendthrifts."

This was Betsy's essential side. The other side is reported by her son: "Mama goes out nearly every night to a party or ball. She says she looks full ten years younger than she is, and if she had not so large a son she could pass for five and twenty years old. She has a dancing-master and takes regularly three lessons a week, and has done so for the last six months; is every day astonished at the prog-ress she makes, and is fully determined to dance next winter. . . . She is not fully satisfied with Geneva for the laws are very severe. Among others, it is positively forbidden to dance after mid-night. . . ."

Father William got rather fond of Bo, who did not take his moth-er's view of the superior advantages of Europe, and told his grandfa-ther he "missed the roast beef and beefsteaks of home." As soon as his education was finished, he said, he would hasten over to America, "which I have regretted ever since I left it."

Finally Mme Bonaparte did go to Rome, for the winter of 1821 and 1822, taking Bo with her. She had heard that Mme Mère and Pauline might not live much longer, and though she expected nothing, still, there was the chance that something might be wrung out of them. She was upset about money, for "The English have doubled the price of everything on the continent [by overpaying]."

What she was hoping to do, was to marry Jerome (Bo) off to one of Joseph's daughters, though as she pointed out, Joseph's Swiss property brought in no income. Jerome was sixteen; Joseph's daughter Charlotte, of a suitable age, was in America with her father. The Bonaparte family was not averse. Mme Mère was kind. Pauline, now forty, gave Betsy a pink satin cloak, a bonnet, and a ball dress. She also chose new clothes for Bo and promised him $400 (2,000 francs) a year clothes money, and a capital gift of 40,000 francs when he married.

"Bo," wrote Betsy to her father, "feels the propriety of doing what I please on the subject of the marriage, and has no foolish ideas of disposing of himself in the way young people do in America. . . . I shall esteem myself fortunate in being able to dispose of my son according to my views, instead of his choosing before his judgment is matured, and probably encumbering himself for life with a poor wife and clamorous offspring [Betsy hated children]. Marriage ought never to be entered into for any other purpose than comfort, and there is none without consequence and fortune; without these it is more prudent to live single."

As it turned out, Betsy knew very little about Bo, who was a throwback to his grandfather, whom he admired and whose opinions he secretly shared.

Bo's only reason to applaud the proposed marriage was that it would get him back to America, and to his grandfather. Mme Mère, Cardinal Fesch, and the rest said he should return to America, to accost Joseph in person, advice he was delighted to take. He sailed from Leghorn on February 23, 1822, leaving Mama behind him, which filled him with only a very little grief. He had had a lifetime to form his views of Mama. She intended to return to Geneva, "her health being too delicate (as she thinks) to support the American climate." He also left behind him a bill for 600 cigars. Mme Bonaparte paid it, with the remark that she foresaw nothing but poverty and solitude, and how were her finances?

Though both William Patterson and Joseph seemed to approve of Bo's marriage to Charlotte, it did not take place. "She is in size a dwarf and excessively ugly," wrote Mme Toussard, a friend of

Betsy's. One reason it did not take place, was the extremely large settlement Mme Patterson Bonaparte demanded ($100,000 from Joseph, half of it to be settled on Bo—in today's money, about half a million).

In default of marriage, Bo went on to Harvard, where he did well, though he had to have a special dispensation from attending chapel, since Mme Bonaparte had had him made a Catholic, for dynastic reasons.

Meanwhile, in Europe, discovering Mme Mère had made a will (in the autumn of 1822, after Napoléon's death), Betsy enterprisingly hired an undercover agent to find out what was in it. The result was not encouraging. Everything had been left to L'Aiglon, except for a sum, which Betsy calculated came to $50,000, to each of her sons, and some smaller bequests. "If anything would surprise me, I might say that she ought to have left as much to Bo as to the sons of Lucien [who got 25,000 each]. I must write this to *Bo*, and most sorry am I to be obliged to announce to him the little reliance there is to be placed on appearances. She took such interest, and appeared so partial to him, that he cannot help feeling his faith in virtue shaken."

Lady Morgan got a more spirited letter, in which Betsy complained about the food at her boarding house. "The hosts are too *spirituel* to imagine that their *pensionnaires* possess a vulgar appetite for meat and vegetables, tarts and custards." So she took an apartment in town for six months, "where I hope I shall get something to eat."

In the spring of 1823, she learned that Bo had spent $2,500 in fifteen months at Harvard. She was drastically upset. "Had Bo been born a fool, I should not have toiled to beat learning into him; as he has natural sense, I thought it my duty to give him an education. . . . I may as well spend my income myself, as see it squandered by him." She said she would give him $1,100 a year; "I will not on any pretext allow a farthing more."

Bo had kept up a correspondence with his father since 1821, though he had not met him. Jérôme the Elder allowed his son a pension of $1,200 a year (seldom paid and never in full). Bo's Harvard expenses had been such a shock that Mme Bonaparte sailed for America. Bo was sent down from Harvard for three months, for drinking alcoholic punch at his club, and spent his time with Betsy, in the country at Lancaster, Massachusetts, except for a visit to Lafayette, of whom he thought not much. To his grandfather he wrote: "I am glad to hear that you have got through with General Lafayette. I fear that you must have been very much fatigued with the noise and disorder which accompany him wherever he goes. I think that the general will find that living on *honors* will not agree with his age and broken constitution. The papers say that he is only sixty-eight years old. I am sure he looks near ninety-eight."

Mme Bonaparte liked America no better than ever. "The men are all merchants; and commerce, although it may fill the purse, clogs the brain. Beyond their counting-houses they possess not a single idea; they never visit except when they wish to marry. The women are all occupied in *les détails de ménage* and nursing children; these are useful occupations, but do not render people agreeable to their neighbors."

Unable to stand it, she sailed for Europe again, in June of 1825. Once more there were marital projects for Bo, but Bo would have nothing to do with them. "I am perfectly happy and contented with my present situation and prospects; a wife would be apt to mar the whole, and as I have been brought up to hold the single state as preferable to the married state, my plans have always been formed with a view to remaining unmarried. If I marry I must change them all. This is my way of thinking; but I would submit it all to your better judgment and experience."

In his reply to this, Father William could not help but agree. It was necessary to found a fortune first.

When Pauline died in June of 1825, she left Bo 20,000 francs ($4,000) in her will. Mme Bonaparte sent for Bo to come at once, to claim it. She had another small victory that year. Her sister-in-law, Mrs. Robert Patterson *veuve*, married the Marquess of Wellesley. She had been a Carroll of Carrolltown. The Marquess of Wellesley, who was sixty-five, was the widower of an Italian opera singer, and had many children and even more debts. Mr. Carroll's money would therefore be a distinct advantage. "Mary's fortune is reported in Europe to be eight hundred thousand dollars cash."

"I can only say that if Jerome were a girl, and had made such a match, I am convinced that I should have died with joy." And, "Mrs. Dallas, a widow of the person who wrote Lord Byron's memoirs, lives at Havre. She has lost the use of her limbs, and never gets out of her bed. . . . She is said to be a woman of genius."

The Patterson Bonapartes went on to Rome, where they found a letter from the ex-King of Westphalia to his American son. "My position is so complicated on account of the Queen and the princes, our children, that I do not know how to reconcile their rights with your peculiar position. . . ."

The year was now 1826. Mme Bonaparte had got her son's legacy paid; she complained it was "curtailed and maimed," but "I seldom allow myself to be made a dupe of . . . I have placed the money at four percent, . . . until I can make some arrangement, and at all events I can spend it, and account to Jerome for it out of my property in America, which will save the trouble of any remittances from America (Betsy never transferred much money at any given time, because of the necessity of paying bank charges).

In Florence, Bo met his uncle Louis, and then, on the 25th of September, went on to meet his father at Lanciano. Mme Bonaparte remained in Florence, where she was much agitated by Charlotte's marriage to Napoléon Louis, for she had not given up hope that Bo might somehow marry into Bonaparte money. She had, as usual, made minute inquiries into Joseph's fortune (she had demanded $200,000 for Bo in the end). She found it overrated, being worth $400,000 in French property (held through the Clarys), mortgaged for $160,000 to pay the marriage portion of his other daughter, Zenaïde. The $100,000 estate in Switzerland brought in nothing, and he could find a buyer for neither the French nor the Swiss holdings. He was a bad manager, she said, though his wife was excellent.

Bo got on well with everyone, and was acknowledged (informally only) as Jérôme's eldest son. He was not acknowledged as heir. He was asked by his father to stay with him in Rome, did so, and did not much like his visit.

"I have now been for two months with my father in the country and arrived in Rome yesterday. . . . From my father I have had the most cordial reception, and I am treated with all possible kindness and affection. . . . I have not seen Mama for two months; she is still at Florence. I do not expect to see her before the spring. . . . During this winter I shall have but little leisure for serious study, but will make the most of what time I may have."

As it happened he had no leisure for serious study. In January of 1827 he wrote to his grandfather to complain. "I am excessively tired of the way of living at my father's. We breakfast between twelve and one o'clock, dine between six and seven, and take tea between eleven and twelve at night, so that I seldom get to bed before half-past one o'clock in the morning. My father does not see much company at present, but during much the greater part of the twenty-four hours the whole of his family is assembled together in the parlor, principally for the purpose of killing time. No one about the house does anything, and I find it impossible to read or study; although my time is not entirely lost because I have an opportunity of examining the antiquities of Rome." He added that his father's fortune was "equal perhaps to one-third of his debts." "I was always aware that America was the only country for me, but now I am still more firmly persuaded of it than ever."

No doubt Father William chuckled over this sort of thing, for at the same time Betsy continued to bombard him with details of an elaborated existence of balls, parties, dinners, receptions. When the Grand Duke of Tuscany (An Austrian) condescended to receive her at court, she found it hard to keep back the tears of gratitude. "I observe what you say of my partiality for Europe, and am only surprised that you should wonder at my resembling every woman who has left America. I never heard of one who wanted to return there, not excepting Mrs. Gallatin. . . ." Besides, "I think it is quite as rational to go to balls and dinners as to get children, which people must do in Baltimore to kill time."

Bo joined his mother in Florence, and then sailed for America during June of 1827. Once more Betsy stayed on. In 1829 she got a severe shock, and it cannot be said she took it well. For on November 3, 1829, Bo married Susan Mary Williams of Baltimore. The news was conveyed to Betsy, with sedate glee, by Father William, and produced an immediate breech with her father which it took four years to close again. *All* the Bonapartes sent congratulations. But not Betsy. Betsy railed and Betsy raved.

"He has neither my pride, my ambition, nor my love of good company; therefore I no longer oppose his marriage," she wrote Father William. "I perhaps may think myself fortunate that he was not married even worse. . . . As the woman has money . . . I shall not *forbid* a marriage which I never would have *advised* . . . I hope too that he has not been cheated, which I think very likely, in the settlements. . . . I hope most ardently that she will have no children; but, as nothing happens which I desire, I do not flatter myself with an accomplishment of my wish on this subject. . . . I would as soon have gone to Botany Bay to look for a husband as to have married any man in Baltimore. . . . [postscript] They ought to have given him half of her fortune at least, if he outlived her."

In a second letter, she again explained her absence. "The Americans themselves had sense and good taste enough to feel that I had risen above them, and have always treated me with the respect and deference due to a superior. When I first heard that my son could condescend to marry any one in Baltimore, I nearly went mad. . . ." Nonetheless, she consented to leave Bo her money; and, though she fervently hoped he would have no children, after him, to them. She also determined from now on to spend her whole income (not, of course, a penny of her capital). She had lived a miser for nothing, she said. Unfortunately Betsy had been a counting-house child, and was a miser not to purpose but by birth. She went on getting richer and richer. Money was now her only passion left. It was her belief, she added, that no parent had the right to disinherit a child, so that she would have left Bo her fortune if he had attempted to cut her throat first but had failed in the attempt. It did not mean that she forgave him for so lowering himself as to marry Miss Mary Susan Williams.

"My life, from want of money, has been a disgusting burden," she said. It is hard to see how. At no time did she have less than $12,000 a year, at a time when the purchasing power of that sum was the equivalent of today's $60,000, and there were almost no taxes. And in her prime her income was $100,000 a year, year in year out, of which she spent so little that at least $97,000 a year was ploughed back into capital, which, in turn, merely increased her income. She owned large tracts of the most valuable real estate in Baltimore and Maryland, and many profitable rental houses and warehouses upon them. But in her will, she gave away no personal trinket worth more than $20 to anyone. The residue went to "my *natural*, or most *unnatural* heir."

It had been a blow to her ambitions. She had wished to be the mother of at least a reigning prince. She decided instead to glitter, and sent for her jewels.

On November 5, 1830, Bo had a son, christened Jerome Napoleon Bonaparte, Jr. (his other son, Charles Joseph Bonaparte, was not born until June 9, 1851). Joseph was the first to congratulate his nephew. Jérôme also wrote, and so did Mme Mère and, for a wonder, Louis. Betsy did not.

She had settled down in Florence, where she formed a friendship (it was that and no more; Betsy was in no way a sensual woman, she was American enough in that) with Gorchakov, the future Russian chancellor, but in 1830 still chargé d'affaires to the court of Tuscany. She said he was "the only man she would condescend to argue with." He said she would have made an excellent diplomat. It was her one male friendship, ever. She reopened the correspondence with her father, in order to discuss investments in city bonds, deciding to put one-third of her fortune in city bonds at five percent, one-third in five-percent state bonds, and the other third half in ground rents and half lent out at interest. Thus she risked nothing and made much. She complained however that the customs officials at Leghorn had just robbed her of six sheets. Then she closed communications again.

At forty-seven, she had kept her entire beauty. It did not begin to fade until her sixties, and never went away entirely. "It is a bore to grow old," she said, in a letter requesting some Brazilian white topazes, which she thought would set off her neck. More fortunate if less active than Pauline, she was preserved by her presumptions. She simply did not age. It astonished everyone. From a dynastic she had become a physiological curiosity.

In the winter of 1832 and 1833 she went to Paris, where she met the Duchesse d'Abrantès, who tried to pump her for Napoleonic anecdotes. Betsy refused to be pumped. "She has already published twelve volumes," she said sternly.

"Dear Betsy," wrote Father William, on March 10, 1834, "I have some time since received under cover . . . your letter of 10th October, which is the only one that has come to hand from you for several years. . . . But still it affords me pleasure to have heard from you at length, and to find that you have concluded to return to your native land. Time brings about what we little have expected, and sweet home and the natural intercourse and connection of our family is, after all, the only chance for happiness in this world. We are in great confusion and distress in this country, on account of President Jackson's arbitrary conduct in respect of the Bank of the United States. . . . It may . . . ultimately bring about a revolution. Your presence here is absolutely necessary to look after your affairs and property, and the sooner the better."

So she sailed during the summer. She had been away nine years.

In the winter of 1835, William Patterson died, at the age of eighty-three, as outspoken in his will as he had been in life, but also patiently forgiving. His fortune was very large, but Betsy got little of it. "The conduct of my daughter Betsy," said the will when read, which must thus have entertained many, "has through life been so disobedient that in no instance has she ever consulted my opinions or feelings; indeed, she has caused me more anxiety and trouble than all my other children put together, and her folly and misconduct have occasioned me a train of expense that first and last has cost me much money. Under such circumstances it would not be reasonable, just, or proper that she should inherit and participate in an equal portion with my other children in an equal division of my estate; considering, however, the weakness of human nature and that she is still my daughter, it is my will and pleasure to provide for her as follows: . . ." The provision included the house in which she was born, houses and lots on Market Street, four other new brick houses on the corner of Market and Frederick, two more new brick houses and lots on Gay Street, entailed on her son, and his wine cellar (bang-up port and very good Madeira). The wine cellar seems a curious afterthought. Perhaps they had had something in common after all.

Mr. Patterson had been the last man in Baltimore to wear an eighteenth-century queue. He was also something of a philosopher. Elizabeth was not. His legacy would have made another woman rich. It only made Elizabeth richer, and she commenced to feel very poor. So she touched neither the property, nor, except on rare festive occasions, the Madeira, and then in a thimble. It went eventually to her grandson, Charles Joseph, who had a better palate than his brother.

In 1839 Mme Bonaparte went to Europe again, taking Bo with her. Cardinal Fesch had died, leaving him 50,000 francs, which it seemed to her wisest to extort from the estate in person.

"I never supposed that I had preserved sufficient energy or moral courage to put into effect my inclination to absent myself from the *République par excellence,*" she wrote Lady Morgan. She meant again. "A residence of a few months in the *États Unis* would cure the most ferocious republican of the mania of republics."

Though Bo had no difficulty in collecting his money—like his sister, Cardinal Fesch had always been precise in his accounts—it was Mme Bonaparte's last visit to Europe, for "I have found few of those persons whom I knew and saw habitually five years ago. Death, time, and absence have left me scarcely an acquaintance in Paris. If our friends do not die, their sentiments change toward us so much that really I know not which is most distressing, to hear that they have gone to the other world, or that they have forgotten us in this. . . ." So, in July of 1840, she returned. From now on she spent her summers not in Rome or Geneva, but at Rockaway Beach and Virginia Springs.

It devolved upon Bo from now on to press what claims they might still have upon the Bonapartes.

WITH the death of Napoléon, the hopes of the Bonapartists, and of Mme Mère, turned to the ex-King of Rome. Mme Mère was much concerned about him. He was, after all, her late son's only legitimate child. But to the others, he was an inconvenience, insofar as his existence interfered with the claims of their own children to a nonexistent succession. None of the family had seen him since 1814. His had indeed been the fate of Astyanax, held in a rigorous, affectionate, sumptuous, but relentless confinement close to his maternal grandfather, in Vienna.

Though he had been twice declared and once proclaimed (in an order of the French Senate) Napoléon II, L'Aiglon was to be brought up as an Austrian Prince. All Marie Louise wished from and for him was no bother and a commission in an Austrian regiment. She had left for Parma in March of 1816, saying she would die of grief had she not the hope of seeing him again in a few months, and promptly stayed away for twenty-seven, because of Neipperg. Her visits were to become increasingly infrequent. To Marie Louise, anyone not in the room with her at the moment promptly ceased to exist.

In 1815 L'Aiglon was turned over to Count Maurice Proskau-Leslie-Dietrichstein, his tutor, a gloomy man, chiefly terrified that he might be "compromised by his pupil's progress." Dietrichstein was a musical amateur, to whom the *Erlkönig* had been dedicated, and who later was to produce *Der Freischütz* at the Imperial Theater. He had been chosen with the thought that the child's education was to be retarded as much as possible. Unfortunately the child was preternaturally intelligent.

"What do you mean by lying down when I'm reading to you for your amusement?" snapped Dietrichstein one day.

"And for *our* instruction," said young Francis, as he was now called, who was five.

Frederick Gentz, Metternich's chief factotum and a member of the Cabinet, said, "If he were given a first-class education he might well become a man of remarkable distinction, but he is doomed to languish in mediocrity."

It was indeed misfortunate, for L'Aiglon was one of those rare cases in which genius, assisted by a dull and unimaginative but robust woman, produced, instead of the usual wishwash of the second generation, a scale model of itself. Charles Francis was intelligent, wayward, observant, stubborn, authoritarian, charming, witty, and gifted with excessive curiosity. He was unaffected, spontaneous, and had early shown an intelligence for and interest in military affairs. And he was more than a little frightening. Fouché had written to Austria, that so disaffected were the French with the Bourbon Restoration, that had the child appeared on the borders on a white horse, no one would have opposed his march to the capital. The Austrian reaction had been to remove Francis's French household and, insofar as possible, the French language itself. He was to be taught German, and surrounded by Austrian cousins and relatives only.

The behavior of these, to a child accustomed to make small talk with men who had fought and won an Empire, must sometimes have been disconcerting. His grandfather the Emperor was absorbed in perfecting a new formula for sealing wax. He was also much taken up with the manufacture of really practical body armor, in particular, of chain mail. There were jolly romps with cousin Ferdinand, the Crown Prince, who liked to jam himself in a wastepaper basket and roll end over end down the corridors. Ferdinand's playfulness arose from the fact that he was twenty-three and feebleminded. Archduke Francis taught L'Aiglon obscenities, not by preference, but because he spoke nothing else. Archduke Rainer, endowed with common sense, presented him with a basset hound. That was a happy day. But most of the court preferred to snub him. He soon became aware of this. One day in 1816 (at five) he was explaining to a Baroness Hohenegg how a fortress should be built. "What next, what next," she kept exclaiming. "Madame, this is not a subject for ladies, so I shall say nothing more," said he. And true to his word, he said nothing more. He became taciturn and watchful, courteous, but remote. It was a great waste. He was as precocious as Macaulay or

John Stuart Mill, but that was the last thing the court of Vienna either understood or wanted.

"I am always afraid," wrote Marie Louise, "that people will forget that it is not his fault that he had such a father." There was some talk of making a monk of him, or if not that, a prelate, to spike his ambitions. He would have none of it. "I shall become a soldier, but my regiment shall march in front of me, because I don't want to die. Does everybody have to die in a war?"

This was at six.

In 1816, the Empress Maria Ludovica having died of exhaustion, the Emperor Francis married for the fourth time, choosing Charlotte of Bavaria, which made Prince Eugène his cousin-german. "At least this one should stand the strain," he said. "I won't risk having another corpse on my hands in a week or two." He was as uxorious as ever.

The new grandmother encouraged L'Aiglon. He had by now learned German, but spoke it in a more distinguished and noble manner than his relatives (according to Archduke Louis), all of whom rattled away in Viennese dialect.

"When the Austrians entered Paris, people shouted, 'Shut up the shops,' " L'Aiglon told his tutor.

"He knows a great deal about past events, but maintains a silence about them extraordinary in a child," said Captain Foresti, his second tutor. "I feel I must tell you again, Marie [it was a warning to his mother], that he knows almost everything there is to know about his father. He has always concealed this knowledge from you."

"I feel," wrote Marie Louise to the tutor, "that you should speak truthfully about his father, and while never saying he was a bad man and mentioning only his abilities, persuade him that it was inordinate ambition which deprived him of his throne and put him in the prison where he is today, so that his son never conceives the idea of imitating him."

"And what if he should turn out to be weak in the head?" asked Napoléon, at St. Helena, and went on reading *Andromaque*, which he described as a "play for unhappy fathers." It is in *Andromaque* that Astyanax appears. "What if he should take after his mother's family?"

Charles Francis, despite his astonishing memory, was after all only a child. He became convinced that his father was poor, because he confused Ste. Hélène with the German word *Elend*, which means poverty. He was most distressed. It took some time to reassure him that matters stood otherwise.

"I feel that every toy of his, everything that interests him, ought to remind him of what he owes to his mother," Dietrichstein informed Marie Louise, who, in 1817, at Parma, gave birth to the first of her children by Neipperg.

"You may be surprised that I should be taking an interest in baby clothes, but the fact is that Mme de Scarampi has just given birth to an heir," she confided to Mme de Montebello.

"Do you know," said Charles Francis to Dietrichstein, "I think my dear Mama is going to stay in Parma this winter to help the poor." Dietrichstein (everybody in Vienna knew the facts of the matter except the Emperor Francis and L'Aiglon) so far relaxed his discipline as to allow the boy to cry, explaining that though tears were odious in some circumstances, in this case they were commendable.

The next domestic occasion was to provide L'Aiglon with a proper title. Several were suggested, but rejected by Marie Louise, for they were drawn from Hungarian and Bohemian estates, whose names she found too difficult to pronounce. Finally it was discovered that one of these had also the German name Reichstadt. So Duc de Reichstadt he became.

In Rome, Mme Mère did not think much of it. "Where and what is Reichstadt?" she sniffed. "Whereas the name Napoléon Bonaparte will ring around the world forever, and the echoes of France will not fail to pick it up."

This was exactly what the Austrians had been afraid of. Hence the new name.

Though Marie Louise kept her title of Imperial Highness, her son did not. He was to be called Serene Highness (Höheit) only, and rank immediately after the Archdukes.

She met her son at Theresienfeld, July 1, 1818. It was to be her first and last visit for some time to come. She did not care for Theresienfeld. Jérôme was nearby at Schönau, Caroline at Frohsdorf, and there were some retired officers from the Imperial Army in the neighborhood. When the Duc de Reichstadt encountered these people, he was so loudly cheered that Dietrichstein was forced to say that his pupil spoke only German. Marie Louise, who refused to leave her carriage, described it as "an unpleasant neighborhood." She had Neipperg hand the boy in through the window.

She left after as brief a visit as possible, promising to return soon, but could not do so, as she was pregnant by Neipperg again. After the child was born, she took a tour of northern Italy. When the news was broken to L'Aiglon that she was not after all coming, he fell into "a fit of absent-mindedness which did him honor." Dietrichstein took occasion to point out to him the difference between this kind of absent-mindedness and the reprehensible kind. Indeed, he had won Dietrichstein over, as he did most people.

Oddly, he never panicked. He merely became silent, and then, when he had recovered, went on as before.

In May of 1821 Napoléon died, leaving to his son (to be given him when he was sixteen) an assortment of relics, most of them associated with battles he had won, the sword he had worn at Austerlitz, Sobieski's saber, the gold dressing case he had used at Ulm, a brace of pistols, the Imperial dagger, glaive, and hunting knife, the campstools he had taken on campaign, thirty-three snuff boxes, his brass collapsible field beds, one of each of his uniforms, his washstand and field glasses, two watches, a chain made of Marie Louise's hair, his medals, spurs, saddles, bridles, plate, porcelain, 400 books from his library, Frederick the Great's alarm clock, the seals of France, the collar of the Golden Fleece, a saber worn at Abukir, a cloak used at Marengo, and the little gilt clock in his bedroom, which had ticked away while he was dying.

Five years later, when the executors tried to deliver these things in person, they were told to leave them at the Austrian Embassy in Paris, where they would be promised a receipt signed by the Duc de Reichstadt. So they were never delivered. On L'Aiglon's death they went to Mme Mère.

On July 13 the news of his father's death was broken to L'Aiglon, who wept. He could be induced to write to his mother only with the greatest difficulty. In the end the letter had to be dictated by his tutors, for no matter whom Marie Louise had managed to deceive (not many), she had not been able to deceive her child.

The Duke's household went into mourning. The rest of Vienna did not. There was a hunting party the next day. It was not canceled. Neither was anything in Parma. "This event," said Metternich, "puts an end to a good many hopes and criminal conspiracies. It has no other interest for the world."

Metternich was wrong. At Lyons and Bordeaux in 1817, and at Paris in 1820, there had been conspiracies to dethrone Louis XVIII in favor of Napoléon II, whose miniatures, showing him dressed as a French sergeant, were being hawked openly in the streets. In 1817 the picture of the son of a Bavarian diplomat, looking mighty like L'Aiglon and holding a bunch of smudged blue flowers in his hands, nearly caused a riot at the Salon. Forget-me-nots were also a Bonapartist flower. The picture had to be removed. By 1821, one could buy in Paris everything from liqueur bottles with the Duc de Reichstadt's portrait on them to trouser suspenders with the same motif. Another uprising in his favor occured at Thouars in 1822.

L'Aiglon, told none of this, was allowed to become a Feldwebel in the Imperial infantry, given a white uniform, and watched. His own view was that he was a young Spartan.

Marie Louise paid him a quick visit in 1823, and then returned to her own children, for so she had come to regard them, and him. He could not, she said, come to Parma. For once the Austrian government heartily agreed, both for its own sake, and, a little, for his. The King of France was now Charles X, who was even less popular than his brother had been ("The future of the monarchy," Louis XVIII once said, "depends upon whether or not I can survive my brother."). Pictures of the Duc de Reichstadt sold in Paris now included the letter *N* surrounded by a halo. Under these circumstances the French Ambassador to Vienna was pleased to note (late in 1824) that all the officials of L'Aiglon's household had been placed in their present positions by the secret police.

Louis XVIII had met a bizarre death. Convinced that "A King of France must die, but must never be ill," and determined to outlive his brother, he sat daily at his desk, and in the evenings went on holding receptions even though his face was battered and bruised, for do what he would, it knocked against his writing table when from pain and weakness he fainted. Then he would recover and go on. His last days were made no easier by the efforts of his family to get him to confess, fearing he was an agnostic (he was), and by the efforts of his last favorite, Mme de Cayla, an adventuress, to get money out of him, though she had had plenty already. She emerged from the deathroom, finally, with a bank draft for 800,000 francs so shakily signed that she had difficulty in cashing it.

There had been some respect in France for Louis XVIII, who though indolent and attentive to bad advisers, was a man to command respect. There was none for Charles X, who was a reactionary bigot, with even worse advisers. So Bonapartism continued to grow.

Of these events L'Aiglon was kept in ignorance, and to outward view was a well-adjusted and agreeable Prince, without ambition. His tutor's diary reveals, however, that he frequently wet his bed about this time. In 1825, he was waked at two and again at five A.M., to prevent this. "We must tame the insolent boy, otherwise we are done for," wrote Dietrichstein.

Having been broken of speaking French, he must now learn the language all over again, for it was the polite language of the court and of the great world. Dietrichstein fussed. The Empress referred to him as L'Aiglon's "wife." Charles Francis was fourteen. In Dietrichstein's opinion, his charm was "varnish." He was restrained in many ways (whom could the son of Napoléon safely marry?).

In 1826 he began to change. He developed a proneness to colds and a weak chest. He took to reading, preferring Corneille to Racine, as had his father. Corneille, after all, is the only writer to be able to make great drama out of politics. He also devoured the eight volumes of Las Cases's *Mémorial de Ste. Hélène*, which could no longer be kept from him, as well as Montholon's account and Antommarchi's memoirs, which contained the ex-Emperor's will.

Napoléon had died thinking L'Aiglon cared nothing for him (any communication had of course been forbidden). Now L'Aiglon became a Bonapartist. He wrote to his mother about it.

"I am therefore trying, dear Mama, to offer you on your return the sight of a morally superior and nobler being, and thus show you the foundations of a character which will remind you of my father's; for a soldier, can there be a finer, more admirable model of constancy, endurance, manly gravity, valiance and courage?"

He was suffering from tuberculosis, diagnosed by the physician Staudenheim as "a tendency to scrofula and a phthisis of the trachea." The cure recommended was constant swimming. So he swam, but he was not cured.

In 1828, Marie Louise, for her father had said "he would send a firing squad to Parma, if she did not consent to come," visited her son again. She found him six feet tall. At her request, he was promoted to Captain of Tirolean cavalry and given a saber Napoléon had used in Egypt, one of her few souvenirs. Neipperg, too, took an interest, and not a bad one, for though Neipperg's body had been engulfed by his morganatic wife, his soul had not. He had, of course, to govern Parma, since she would not, but sometimes he managed to spend a few evenings alone, playing billiards. He now took pity on Napoléon's son, whom he liked, and did his best to smooth things out when he could.

In 1829 the poet Barthélemy arrived in Vienna, to seek an interview with the Duke. He wished to deliver copies of his epic poem, *Napoléon in Egypt*. As he was an indifferent poet, but a loyal Bonapartist, he got no farther than Dietrichstein.

"You must understand that the Prince hears, sees, and reads only what we want him to hear, see, and read," explained the tutor. "He is not a prisoner, *but* . . . he is in a very special position."

The result was another poem, *Le Fils de l'homme*, published in 1829, in which the Duke was described as having "a pale face, in which life and death seemed to mingle," and as a prisoner. The poem swept France, and Barthélemy was sent to jail for three months, which only made the poem sell the better, and much decreased Charles X's already slight popularity.

In the year 1829, Neipperg died, of dropsy and totally worn out. The Emperor Francis said he had regarded him as a model of chivalry.

So he had been, but unfortunately he had left a will, in which he declared himself to be Marie Louise's husband and the father of the two surviving Montenuovo's, his children by her, given the Italian equivalent of his own name, of whose existence Marie Louise had not had the courage to tell her father until the previous autumn.

It was impossible to conceal the marriage any longer. This meant going into how old the children actually were. Marie Louise was caught out, and with much wincing, had to admit to her father that both Albertine and William had been born before Napoléon died, the one in May of 1817, the other August 8, 1819.

The difficulty was to conceal their ages from the Duc de Reichstadt. Unable to face him, instead of coming to Vienna, Marie Louise took a little trip to Switzerland, to be precise, to Geneva and French Switzerland.

"I cannot imagine that any harmful agitation could result from the presence on the frontier of a person so utterly devoid of political importance or personal standing as the Duchess of Parma," wrote the Prefect of the Rhône, with the unconscious brutality of truth. From Geneva she sent her son a collection of cravats and walking sticks.

In the end, it was Neipperg's son Gustav (by an earlier marriage) who told Reichstadt the truth, not because he wanted to, but because Reichstadt trapped him into it.

Reichstadt said nothing to his mother, but in his diary he wrote, "If Joséphine had been my mother, my father would not be buried at St. Helena, and I would not be languishing here in Vienna. Oh, she is kindhearted but weak; she was not the wife my father deserved." He showed his displeasure in other unconscious ways. For instance, he forgot how to spell her name. "I was absolutely dumfounded," complained Marie Louise. "He might at least make his spelling mistakes in his letters, and not on the envelope where everybody can read them."

Her eye had already been caught by an Austrian officer at her court, Wercklein, Pauline's earlier persecutor. He was not quite what she wanted, but for the time being he would do.

At least he had the sense not to marry her, so he survived.

In August of 1830, Charles X was driven out by the July Revolution, which he had done much to provoke. He had never understood the temper of the age and had never tried to.

In the city, it was uncertain who would rule. The Duc d'Orléans, the only intelligent and adaptable member of the Royal Family (Charles X had himself raised him to this status, though he came from the younger branch), was proposed, but Lafayette, who had barricaded himself in the Hôtel de Ville, wanted a Republic. It is claimed that if the King of Rome had known of the Revolution, or had been there, he could have been proclaimed. This seems unlikely. It was both too late and too soon for another Bonaparte.

The American Ambassador, Mr. Rivers, was induced to intervene, and once he had convinced Lafayette that the endorsement of a liberal monarchy would not cost him his popularity in the United States, the Hero of the People allowed himself to appear with Louis Philippe, wrapped in the tricolor, on the balcony of the Hôtel de Ville. This turned the scales, but it did not get Charles X out of the country. He was persuaded to flee, by the simple ruse of sending out a horde to St. Cloud and then telling him that they were sansculottes come to eat him. Charles X then abdicated and took his departure, but slowly, and with much procrastination, making as protest a state progress across France to the nearest port of embarkation for England.

So L'Aiglon had lost out. In 1830 his tuberculosis was again incorrectly diagnosed, first as a skin irritation, and then as a diseased liver.

A trip to Italy might have helped, but he was regarded as too politically dangerous to be taken to Italy.

In the meantime Charles X had got aboard a ship for England owned, oddly enough, by the Bonapartes.

"Where are you taking me?" he asked.

"To St. Helena," said the crew.

Polignac, his chief minister, had saved himself, for a while, only by disguising himself as a servant. His habit of wearing gloves while polishing his mistress's boots led to his detection. He and three other ministers were dispatched to the fortresses of Ham, for a few years.

There had been an ebullition of Bonapartism. *Le Fils de l'homme* was put on the stage, as a breeches part, as *L'Aiglon* itself was to be, eighty years later.

The July Monarchy took eighteen years to fall, primarily because Louise Philippe cleverly put himself forward as patron of Bonapartism, and hence of liberalism, and, so to speak, seized the leadership of it. *Le Fils de l'homme* was revised, to include a speech in which the Duc de Reichstadt declared that as a ward of Austria he could never rule over France. It thus became a tragedy, and Louis Philippe relaxed. Plays about Napoléon I were safer. There were four of them running in 1830, and at one of them, Mlle George, a recognized ex-mistress, was identified and sat in her box and wept.

Louis Philippe managed things very well.

In November of 1830 the Countess Camarata arrived in Vienna. This young woman, Elisa's daughter, was now twenty-four. She was like her mother, only wilder, and had left her husband, after having reduced him to a rubble heap, on the grounds that he stifled her ambitions. She resembled Napoléon, and had gone so far as to drop the last letter of her first name (Napoléone), dressed like a man, and acted as her own coachman. She also enjoyed fencing. She was mannish, masculine, peremptory, and brusque. She had a hearty handshake. It was her scheme to kidnap the Duke and take him to France. Her third letter about this reached him, the second was missing, and the first had been intercepted and turned over to the Austrian secret police.

The Duc de Reichstadt did not know what to do about it. Neither did Prokesch, his aide and only close friend. If she represented the family, the effort was futile; everyone knew the Bonapartes to be politically impotent. If she represented the Bonapartists, that was better, but still folly. It did not occur to either of them that she represented merely herself. Since it was clear her earlier letters had been intercepted, she was given a noncommittal reply. Three weeks later the police asked her to move on, and she went on to Prague, disappearing from public view until the Second Empire.

Various other schemes were proposed for the Duc de Reichstadt. None was proposed to him. The throne of Belgium, the throne of Poland, even Corsica was suggested. All such plans came to nothing. And there were others besides the Austrians who did not wish to see L'Aiglon liberated. Among them was the future Napoléon III, who had ambitions of his own: "What true Frenchman would want as his ruler the Emperor Francis's grandson and Metternich's pupil? . . . No. No. Austrian influence has always been baneful to us." He was upset. Modena had proclaimed Napoléon II King of Italy.

Austria began to use L'Aiglon as a means of blackmailing France. If France encouraged insurrection in Italy, Austria would release L'Aiglon and install him as King at Modena. Unfortunately the Italian revolts against Austria, backed by France, spilled over onto Parmese territory, and Marie Louise was first interned by a mob, and then forced to flee to Piacenza. It soon proved possible to restore her. But by this time the Emperor would by no means have been averse to seeing his nephew on the French throne.

"I shall never return behind foreign bayonets," said L'Aiglon one day.

"Ah, Franz," said the Emperor sadly, "why aren't you a few years older?"

Metternich objected to this scheme, and banished L'Aiglon's one friend, the optimistic and energetic Prokesch, who had done so much to encourage him. Dietrichstein was also dismissed, and Reichstadt posted to the 60th Regiment of the Hungarian Infantry (which was stationed at Vienna).

In 1831, the French Chamber of Deputies decreed that should either the Duc de Reichstadt or the Duc de Bordeaux (the Duc de Berry's son) set foot in France, they would be exiled. This was an improvement on the previous proposal, which was to have them shot.

On the 3d of April Louis Philippe issued the decree that Napoléon's statue should be put back on top of the Vendôme column, which made him most popular. As for L'Aiglon, there was no reason to be afraid of him. He was dying.

241

NAPOLÉON's had been a family in which a great many facile talents never, except in his case, amounted to much. His scientific and literary abilities, which by themselves would have come to nothing, focused by one extraordinary aptitude, allowed him to accomplish more than is within the ambition of most generals. He supervised an age, and had, moreover, enough legal skill if not to frame at least to preside over the framing of the Napoleonic Code, his most lasting accomplishment; and enough aesthetic sensibility to give David his head in creating the Empire style.

The main bents of the family were scientific and literary. Nothing of permanent worth came of the latter. But Lucien's sons made their mark as philologists and ornithologists. Napoléon's genius for propaganda was mastered by Napoléon III after long trial and error.

Hortense's sons, so confusingly named Napoléon Louis and Louis Napoléon, as though they had been each other's mirror image, presented an ambitious and complacent mother with contradictory talents. Her ambitions for them were political, but Napoléon Louis, the elder, was chiefly interested in such projects as the development of the dirigible and the improved manufacture of paper. Such things are admirable, but they do not lead to thrones.

In his will Napoléon had ordered the Bonapartes to inbreed. Napoléon Louis married Joseph's daughter Charlotte. Like her mother she was ugly and had a crook shoulder, but also like her mother, she was intelligent. She had sufficient talent to illustrate her husband's books, which included a translation of Tacitus (the *Agricola* only) and *The Sack of Rome*, written by one Jacopo Buonaparte in 1527.

Hortense concentrated on Louis Napoléon. He was artistic enough to sketch cleverly, but he seemed promising. "With the name you bear," she told him, "you will always be something, either in old Europe or in the New World."

Though there were two claimants to the Bonaparte throne ahead of him, L'Aiglon and his elder brother, this seems to have been his own view. To Napoléon he was ever to play the sedulous ape, with bad results, on the whole. Napoléon had been an artillery expert. He became an artillery expert. He was never much of a soldier, he could not endure bloodshed, but he was an expert at artillery. Later, he was to encourage the introduction of the rifled cannon and of the iron-clad. For the time being, he cast about for some such opening as had allowed his uncle to rise.

Louis Napoléon, also like his uncle, was an enigma. But whereas Napoléon's had been the enigma of genius, the nephew's was that of a politician, which, after the event, seems somewhat more to have been no more than a manner. Moreover, he achieved success late in life, so there were not many to observe him closely during his youth.

He seems always to have been imitating not so much his uncle as himself, and his life was to be a performance. He was a demagogue who did not like to appear in public, and though capable of great charm he impressed most people, even when young, as being both cold and withdrawn. He had blond hair, blue eyes, and the Bonaparte short legs. He swam well and rode even better. He was extremely intelligent and seldom frank. It was his misfortune to speak French with a German accent. He was dreamy, much too short for his pretensions, and at the same time a dandy, invariably watchful and extremely libidinous. He had always about him a transitory air.

He was also, in later years, kindly, and "as great as a man can be without virtue." In short, he was an opportunist who shrank from violence and who was both generous and benevolent by disposition, but sometimes ruthless by act, only, however, until he had gotten his own way. As a child he had been called Oui Oui (by Joséphine); as a man, Napoléon the Little (by Victor Hugo). In the opinion of Talleyrand's niece, the Duchess of Dino, he was "timid and silent as a well-brought-up girl." He had the dignity of a toy lion.

This bundle of contradictions was the only one of the Bonapartes to understand the bourgeois temper of the age and so the only one of them able successfully to take advantage of it. Needless to say, the rest of the family was thoroughly against him.

Since the Bonapartes were still banished from France, he had to begin his adventures elsewhere. So he turned to Italy, which was disturbed both by the July Revolution of 1830, whose unrest had spread to the peninsula, and by the death of Pope Pius VIII, on November 30 of the same year, which caused an interregnum in the Papal States.

Louis Napoléon's first efforts at self-advertisement were puerile. He rode about Rome on a horse with a tricolored saddle blanket. However this was enough to put both the Papal police and his own uncles and aunts in a flap. They were living well, except for Caroline, and did not wish to be disturbed. Cardinal Fesch flew into a temper. Hortense was uneasy. Jérôme's son Jérôme (his eldest, who died in 1847, not Plon Plon) was arrested, so Jérôme was also outraged (the boy was released after an appeal lodged by the Russian Ambassador). Louis, as usual, blamed his wife for everything. Louis Napoléon was deported to Florence.

He left behind him at Hortense's house a political refugee he was giving asylum to. So Hortense was sucked into his conspiracies against her will, though it was her opinion that a revolution at this time could not possibly be successful.

This did not discourage the revolutionists. When, on February 2, 1831, Pope Gregory XVI was elected, there were uprisings in Bologna, Modena, Forlì, Ravenna, and Ancona. Hortense left for Florence on the 19th, with two insurrectionists concealed in her coach, one of them called Fido after Louis Napoléon's favorite pet dog, because he would not give his real name.

On the 20th of February Louis Napoléon and Napoléon Louis went off to join the insurrectionists. The ex-King of Holland, with his usual consideration, tried to trap Hortense into luring his sons to Tuscany, where they could be arrested. Hortense saw through this and refused to cooperate (the plan was for her to pretend to be seriously ill). Jérôme and Cardinal Fesch had an audience with the Pope, to disclaim all part in any such doings, and Jérôme publicly ordered his nephews to desist.

Napoléon Louis then sent home a list of grievances against the Papal and Austrian government, so vague, magniloquent, and grand, that, fearing a stroke, Louis, their father, had leeches applied to his forehead while he read it. Scrawling "This is the work of an adventurer," he had the document sent on to Hortense.

In 1832 Italy was divided, except for a few independent enclaves, among the King of Sardinia (the House of Savoy), the Kingdom of the Two Sicilies (the Spanish House of Bourbon), the Papal States, and Austria (Tuscany, Venetia, Parma, Modena, Istria). Gregory the XVI signed a treaty with Austria effectively condemning a revolt which could not have succeeded anyhow. The revolutionists themselves asked the two Bonaparte brothers to resign from the movement, for of the two powers most potent in Italy—Austria and France—neither could be expected to back any insurrection led by Bonapartes.

Hortense, though a febrile woman, was never at a loss for what to do during a crisis. She prepared to smuggle her children to Corfu, and got two passports from the English Ambassador at Florence, one in her own name, the other in the name of a fictitious Mrs. Hamilton, traveling with her two sons, Charles and William. Armed with these, she set off for Ancona, the usual embarkation point for fugitives. To her inconvenience, when she arrived there she was publicly cheered as the mother of Napoléon.

The provisional revolutionary government was in retreat. The Napoléonids were at Forlì. On her way to collect them, Hortense learned that Napoléon Louis had measles. Actually he had died two days before, on March 17th, after a five-day illness complicated by pneumonia. The persistent rumor that he was shot by his fellow revolutionists seems not to have been true.

The last act of the revolutionary uprising was a state funeral at Forlì cathedral. As soon as it was over, everybody else hid his tricolor rosette, and Hortense her grief. While the others dispersed, she sat down to compose the official obituary, a thing she would allow no one else to do. In some ways Hortense resembled Mme Mère.

Louis Napoléon had caught measles from his brother. Somehow Hortense got him to Ancona, where Eugène de Beauharnais's son, the Duke of Leuchtenberg, had inherited a town house. The weather was stormy. Hortense gave out that her son was to flee to Corfu, and then, when he was well enough to be moved, departed with him in the opposite direction, for France, having first sold up some land she owned in the area, for the relief of other refugees.

The Austrians had occupied Ancona. Nonetheless, taking along a refugee named Zappi, since her passport was made out for two sons, Hortense managed to reach the Gulf of Spezia (where Napoléon Louis had hoped to build a naval base).

She had had, as might be expected, a letter from Louis, blaming her for the death of their elder son and asking her to save the life of the other. This she intended to do. The Bonapartes were proscribed, but Mrs. Hamilton and her children Charles and William were not. Hortense made for Paris, and once there (April 23, 1831), as Duchesse de St. Leu, asked to be received at court. On the way, though with her veil discreetly down, she had taken Louis Napoléon through Fontainebleau, to inspect her old rooms and the chapel where Cardinal Fesch had baptized the future Napoléon III. It was an illicit guided tour.

Like her mother before her, Hortense kept a foot in both camps, not so much out of policy as because she had friends and relations in both and so saw no reason to deny either. In 1815, during the Hundred Days, two of Louis Philippe's female relatives, both aged, had been unable to flee Paris, because one of them had broken her leg. Hortense had protected them. For this and other reasons she expected a civil reception from the King.

But she had not chosen her moment well. To be benevolent toward Bonapartism was not the same as to be amiable to a Bonaparte. The government was not yet stable.

So though Louis Philippe received her, he did so surreptitiously, by a back entrance, and in a small room containing nothing but two chairs, a table, and a bed. Hortense sat on the bed, the King on one of the chairs. He had no objection to Hortense's being in Paris, but many to the presence of young Louis.

Hortense and Louis were the first Bonapartes to appear in Paris in sixteen years. When she went out publicly to visit Daguerre's Diorama, which depicted Napoléon's grave on St. Helena, she was recognized and cheered. On May 5th, the crowds come to lay wreaths at the foot of the Vendôme column in memory of Napoléon fell to rioting and had to be dispersed with a fire hose. So Hortense and Louis were asked by the government to move on, and on the 6th, they went to London.

The cult of Napoléon, now he was dead, was also popular in England, in obedience to a natural law whereby the conqueror always comes to admire the leader of the conquered. Some branch of the Bonaparte family or other could always be found in London. At the time of this visit Napoléon's two illegitimate children, Léon Denuelle and Count Walewski, were there, and so was Lucien's daughter,

Christine Egypta (who had married Lord Dudley Stuart), and Achille Murat, on a visit from America. None of these people, with the exception of Count Walewski, of whom Louis Napoléon then thought not much, was particularly civil, but an acquaintance with the Hollands and with their son Charles Richard Fox gave Hortense entrée to the great Whig houses.

Their visit was not a long one. Hortense was short of money. Louis made the most of it, however, laying the social foundations for those future stays of his in Great Britain which were to allow him to plot not one, but three returns to France, two of them amateurish invasions and the third a triumphant return by engineered request. From England, too, he partly learned to phrase his own will to rule as a concern for the rights of the people, a formula which, during the nineteenth century, was indispensable to the success of the dictator.

In late July passports allowing them to cross France were issued, and in August they left London. The return journey turned out to be another pilgrimage to family shrines, to Boulogne, where Hortense had, in 1805, visited the Grand Army drawn up for its aborted invasion of England, to Malmaison (from which she was turned away because she had no ticket of admission), and to the church at Rueil, where Joséphine was buried.

By the end of the month they were at Arenenberg.

247

Bотн Napoléon Louis and Louis Napoléon had been inconvenienced in Italy, insofar as they had had to act in L'Aiglon's name, for he was the Emperor's legitimate heir. On July 22, 1832, L'Aiglon died, oddly enough in the room in which Napoléon had dictated peace to the Austrians from their own palace in Vienna, and with his state cradle nearby. Marie Louise had carried it off to Parma, but had returned it at L'Aiglon's request. It may seem unusual to wish to live on terms of intimacy with one's own cradle. L'Aiglon's explanation to Metternich was that "No one returns to his own cradle once he has left it. So far it is the only monument to my own history, and so I am anxious to keep it."

He had been ill since February. Marie Louise could not come, because she was pregnant again, this time by her Court Chamberlain, the Count of San Vitale. She had become so dissolute that a sentry was stationed at her bedroom door to prevent the entry of lovers, on the order of Baron Marshall, who had taken over Neipperg's duties. One morning the sentry was found in her bed, so after that the guard had to be doubled. She never rose to the excitement of pairs.

By March L'Aiglon was much worse. Unhelpfully, his doctor diagnosed spring fever, though he was by now spitting up bits of lung. He should have been sent to Italy, but Metternich would not allow it. Marie Louise wrote to say she feared a local outburst of cholera would prevent her from arriving. This deceived no one. Marshal Maison, the French Ambassador to Vienna, reported bluntly that "It is said his mother . . . is too far advanced in the task of replacing her dying son, and so cannot decently put in an appearance." In May Dietrichstein wrote to her at least twice, suggesting that she come. She did not come. Instead, she wrote another one of those letters of hers, full of those *underscorings* which one usually associates with the full emotional style of Queen Victoria in spate.

"If you knew, my dear Count, how much I long to go to Vienna, you would pity me, but I *cannot* unless it is *absolutely necessary* [The Paris gazettes had to be kept from L'Aiglon, for they said quite openly he was dying of tuberculosis. They were received in Parma, as elsewhere, if only for their news of the latest mode in dress], and that because public feeling remains so bad and the political condition of Italy so uncertain and critical that my departure would *cause offense*, something *to be avoided at all costs*. Furthermore, we have cholera close by. . . . This is what *the world does not think or see,* . . ." And so on and so forth.

On May 22, L'Aiglon was taken, on a camp bed, to Schönbrunn to die. By June 1 the terminal symptoms were unmistakable. Once more Dietrichstein begged Marie Louise to come. She was in Venice and not feeling well. "They say it is my nerves, but I am sure it is my stomach." She refused to budge until June 4, when her father would be in Trieste and could tell her what to do.

Dietrichstein insisted upon calling in another doctor. By now L'Aiglon had gone deaf in the left ear and could not stand for weakness. "Between my cradle and my tomb there is nothing but a great zero," he said.

At Trieste her father told Marie Louise she should leave for Vienna at once. But it was the 20th before she could bring herself to travel. She claimed she had been delayed by an attack of fever. It seems, however, to have been a miscarriage.

Charles Francis was by now spitting pus as well as blood, but insisted upon being taken for an airing in a carriage, apparently to prove to whoever was watching that he was not dead yet. On the night of the 12th and 13th he had a crisis, but recovered.

On the 20th he confessed, saying he realized the gravity of his condition, but hoped to recover. He also said he was ready to die. The Hapsburg ceremonial of dying was relentless and complex, and involved a procession through the sick man's room of everyone who had anything to do with him. First came his footmen, then the civil and military officers of his household, the Schönbrunn servants, and finally, the clergy. Behind the clergy came the personal spectators, in this case the Archdukes Louis, Charles and Anthony, the Crown Princess, and the Archduchesses Sophia and Clementine.

On the 21st, Malfatti, a thoroughly incompetent physician, tried to magnetize (galvanize) Charles Francis. It was a form of mesmerism designed to put the patient to sleep.

When told his mother was on her way, he said he wouldn't believe it until he saw her. On the 24th she reached Schönbrunn, paused long enough to have a highly public fit of grief, and then went in to see her son. The meeting did not go well. He said afterward that she annoyed him. She did not like sickrooms, and retired to her own suite, where she stayed. On the night of the 27th she sent word that she wished him goodbye "from afar."

"Then she isn't returning?" he asked.

On the 29th, while he was napping, his suite debated among themselves whether or not to sell his cradle for what they could get out of it, but decided that to do so would create too much scandal. There was a seeming improvement in his condition, to the distress of his doctors. "If he recovers," said Hartmann, one of them, "I shall resign." He did not recover. Hartmann did not resign. Instead he presented Marie Louise with a memorandum, requesting post mortem pensions for the Duke's personal staff. She did not feel called upon to grant them.

L'Aiglon tried to talk sometimes. "My heart is empty and I don't know what love is; not only love for a woman, but love of my fellow men."

Möll (one of his staff): "That is the inevitable result of your cold reserved nature, of your mistrust, too, which alienates all who come near you, and whom you consider treacherous or disloyal."

L'Aiglon: "You know me very well."

He died in irony.

Marie Louise wished to return to Parma, but was prevented by court etiquette from doing so until her father returned, or L'Aiglon died. She came three times on the night of July 15, to ask how he was, but he refused to die just yet. Around him his three adjutants were taking inventory of his possessions, wondering how to divide them up among themselves. Marie Louise spent her time in Vienna shopping for gifts for lovers and favorites at home. She had already accumulated three packing cases of these, but, being a stickler for form, had given instructions they were not to be forwarded to Parma until a month after L'Aiglon's death.

"I want to die, I want to die," muttered L'Aiglon on the 21st. One of his doctors recommended that he eat exactly sixty-four live snails. Marie Louise came in with the priest, and wished to leave at once, but L'Aiglon would not allow it. He did not wish to be alone with the priest.

That night he finally did die, saying, "I am going under," though not until dawn. "Call my mother."

Everybody came, even Marie Louise. He died at shortly after five A.M. It was raining. He was only twenty-one years old.

Charles Francis had to be buried in his hat, for all his hair had been cut off by souvenir hunters. Marie Louise did not wait for the state funeral, but left for Parma on the 24th, taking with her all of her son's personal papers and manuscripts, which she burned as soon as she arrived. "I cannot imagine what was so blameworthy," wrote Dietrichstein on the 16th of September. But she had found his diary and miscellaneous jottings revolting.

It was the last she had to do with any Bonaparte. She progressed from San Vitale to the Baron Wercklein, and finally married a French émigré, Bombelles, who ran both her and the Parma government for her. Though the government of Parma had been less reactionary than most, after the events of 1831 and 1832, which had forced her to flee, she reversed, or had Bombelles reverse, her policies. In later years she became a pursy, dropsical old woman with a face the color of blotting paper. She was frequently booed when she appeared in public in Vienna, and in Parma she did not appear in public at all, except at the Opera and the theater, both semiprivate. She died December 18, 1847.

The only person really distressed by L'Aiglon's death seems to have been Mme Mère. She had left him her fortune. Now she must revise her will. "This last way of losing a son has been more painful than the first," she said. Marie Louise sent a sympathetic note from Vienna on July 23. It was her first communication in seventeen years. Mme Mère refused to answer it. Fesch answered it and signed her name.

The person to benefit by L'Aiglon's death was Louis Napoléon. He was now the oldest male heir of the second generation.

L'Aiglon had in his will left Louis Napoléon his sword. More important, his death changed the etiquette at Arenenberg. One of Napoléon's many earlier schemes for the succession was that it should

251

go to the King of Holland's sons. So Louis Napoléon now took precedence over everyone on the way into the dining room—and there were many visitors. Chateaubriand came (to sniff). Mme Récamier came. Alexandre Dumas followed. Anyone came who did not altogether approve of Louis Philippe or who had memoirs to write. On hearing of L'Aiglon's death, Joseph left America for London, the better to gauge the Bonaparte position. Louis Napoléon went over to England to visit him. Lafayette was there. He told Louis Napoléon that only his name, or to be more exact his uncle's, retained any popular significance.

Feeling this to be true, Louis Napoléon acted accordingly. He turned to propaganda and published in 1832 a pamphlet entitled *Political Reveries*. It was by no means an idle publication. It paid tribute to the Democrat of St. Helena, pointed out that Kings broke their promises, and assured the public that Louis himself was both a democrat and an imperialist. Chateaubriand took it well. His father, infuriated by a passing reference to Holland (a general would have been more useful there, said his son), denounced Louis's "frenzied desire for fame." It was not frenzied at all. On the contrary, it was patient, calculating, and cool.

The *Rêveries Politiques* were followed by *A Consideration of Swiss Politics and Military Affairs*, mostly devoted to French, and by his *Manual of Artillery*, which had the advantage of being practical. "What a generous nature he has," wrote Hortense. The book went to most French artillery officers and was designed to prove the nephew had inherited the uncle's skill.

Hortense was equally busy. She edited Joséphine's letters and published her own *Queen Hortense in Italy, in France, and in England,* in 1831. Again, her husband was profoundly distressed, this time because he was not mentioned.

Hortense felt that the time had come to marry Louis Napoléon off, advantageously if possible. The immediate candidate was Jérôme's daughter Mathilde.

The politics of 1831 and 1832 had forced Jérôme to remove to Florence. His life there was much like his life anywhere else. He bought a new and larger palace, the Orlandini. It was the exact opposite of its new owner, being plain without but sumptuous within. In a small room downstairs Jérôme worked at his memoirs and presided over a visitors' book in which any artists passing through town were supposed to leave sketches. He had gathered around himself a picture gallery, filched back somehow from the Tuileries, St. Cloud, the Élysées, and Malmaison. The indefatigable Bartolini had obliged with busts. David, Gérard, Gros, Girodet, Isabey and Horace Vernet provided oils. Jérôme had taken to walking with his hand in his coat, Napoleonic fashion, and had now the profile of a nutcracker. He was getting older. He got a new loan from Zürich and made a state visit to Württemberg, where his elder son, who was to die before the Second Empire enriched them all, was with the army. There was a state entry into Stuttgart, and Catherine was much moved to see her own country again and to be so well received by it. Mathilde also was made much of, but told she dressed too badly and too young for her age. Catherine was a neglectful mother. The King of Württemberg, Catherine's brother, ordered her to dress better and became fond of her.

Mathilde had a sharp eye and an even sharper tongue. One of her recreations was to describe in her journal the minute details of her mother's physical decay, the wrinkling face, the breasts that were beginning to slop down, the increasingly deformed body, and the symptoms of a cardiac condition. "I knew little of her," said Mathilde after her death, "and she, nothing of me."

Jérôme did not enjoy his visit so much as had his wife, for the diplomatic corps refused to present their official respects to him, as King of Westphalia, and there were other slights. So he ordered everyone back to Florence.

Catherine was failing. Mathilde, according to the Russian Minister at Florence, "shone stunning as a diamond." She was fully aware of it, and longed only to remove herself from so inferior a setting.

In the spring of 1835 a cholera epidemic drove the Montforts to Switzerland. They stopped over at Lausanne, at the Villa Mon Repos, for Catherine was plainly dying and could not go on. To distract Mathilde, Jérôme took her in to Geneva to the theater. Catherine, bedridden with circulatory failure in her extremities, was no longer amusing. It was autumn and it rained incessantly. Liszt, who was going through, compared Mathilde to a dove nesting in ruins. In November Catherine began to sink. Her elder son came from Württemberg. During the night of November 29 and 30 she died, protesting that she had always loved only Jérôme. Mathilde thoughtfully wrote out in her diary her clinical observations ("face the color of wax, plumpness fallen in, her face had become grandly noble . . .").

Jérôme was profoundly affected, quite genuinely so, but not for long. "Thus the end came for this noble woman, one of the finest figures of the Imperial epoch," he wrote in his memoirs. What affected him even more was that her income died with her. Both the Czar and the King of Württemberg canceled her pensions at once.

Someone always saved Jérôme. This time it was Louis Napoléon, who offered to take Mathilde and Plon Plon to Arenenberg for the winter. Pretending to be asleep, Mathilde heard her father talking over the chances of marrying her off to Louis Napoléon. Plon Plon was thirteen, Mathilde, sixteen. Louis Napoléon, who never did anything without a precedent, tried to teach Plon Plon mathematics. This was one of the things which had made Louis King of Holland hate his brother the Emperor, and it was just as effective in the second generation.

It does not do to be too hard on Mathilde. She was young, defenseless, spirited, beautiful, fastidious, and more intelligent than any other surviving member of the family, with the possible exception of Hortense. But she could not relax, for she longed desperately to escape from the parental madhouse.

She was also born worldly. Though she was genuinely fond of Hortense, she could see for herself that Louis Napoléon was scarcely a genius. And Arenenberg was a small constricted world which soon bored her. Louis gave her a turquoise ring, a wreath of myosotis inlaid in silver, for her sixteenth birthday, and there was a night regatta on the Bodensee. Throughout her life she kept the ring. But she did not marry him.

Mathilde was a stunning woman who believed in low-cut evening gowns. Louis Napoléon, who had not seen her for two years, was properly impressed. Hortense's private secretary, Valérie Masuyer, was jealous. Plon Plon spied on the supposed lovers. Mathilde sulked and insulted Valérie. Nor did Louis altogether manage to hold her attention, "If I had married him I should have broken his head open to see what was inside," she explained later. She found his constant good temper unnerving (his strongest expression was "*Absurde*").

The ex-King of Holland did not approve. There was no marriage of which the ex-King of Holland could bring himself to approve, but this time he had some reason, for Jérôme was penniless and Mathilde had no dowry. He promptly informed his son that his annual allowance would be no more than 6,000 francs. "Marry," he said, "but with a young woman rich, moral, and wellborn." It did not seem to him that his niece fulfilled any of these qualifications. And Hortense was not pleased to learn that Jérôme planned to live at Arenenberg after the marriage. The King of Württemberg was not charmed either (Jérôme expected him to provide both an allowance and a dowry for Mathilde). He countered by suggesting that Mathilde come to Württemberg, where he would give her a pension of 6,000 florins a year. Mathilde went. Jérôme then denounced the ex-King of Holland for hindering the marriage. The King of Württemberg refused to continue Mathilde's pension if she married Louis Napoléon.

So Louis Napoléon went off to the gaming tables of Baden. In October of 1836, he came home so quiet that Valérie Masuyer thought he must be ill. He was not ill. He was plotting.

Louis Napoléon's first attempt to seize power in France was an ill-conceived *opéra bouffe*, of which the organizing genius was an agitator and journalist called Fialin, later to be Comte de Persigny, whom Louis had met in London.

Persigny was an agitator's agitator. He was persuasive, ingenious, and adroit. What he was not was successful. Louis Napoléon had few scruples. Persigny had none. Among other things, he dispatched his mistress, Mme Gordon, an opera singer of independent means, to seduce the commander of the brigade at Strasbourg. In this she was successful. Vaudrey, who could not hope for promotion under Louis Philippe and who controlled the garrison, was persuaded that a restored Empire would make him a general.

Strasbourg had been chosen because it was conveniently close to the Swiss border, and because it was the center of an area of political discontent. The idea of revolt by proclamation was not so wild as it sounded. There had been Bonapartist uprisings at the garrisons of Grenoble (1816), Vincennes (1820), and Belfort and Saumur (1823). What was in the minds of the plotters was some such exploit as the unopposed march on Paris after the return from Elba. What was overlooked was that in the year 1836 the power in France resided not with the military but with the politicians as spokesmen for the bourgeoisie.

The putsch took twelve months to prepare (from the autumn of 1835 to October 1836) and less than a morning to put down.

On October 24 (in the evening), Louis Napoléon announced he was going on a hunting excursion to Baden. By way of reply, Hortense, *who knew nothing*, gave him Joséphine's wedding ring as a talisman. Louis Napoléon then left in the opposite direction to

Baden, and at Freiberg was joined by Colonel Vaudrey, Persigny, and Mme Gordon. Vaudrey went on to Strasbourg in advance.

Louis Napoléon followed on the 28th, and went into rooms at a private house, taken for him by Persigny, under the name of M. Manuel. (Manuel was a liberal French politician who knew nothing of the plot. Someone at the time described him as "a tiger in the guise of a housecat, with ingratiating manners and the soul of a hyena." He seems to have been on Persigny's mind.)

It was a romantic conspiracy. The chief plotters held a final meeting by moonlight, on a quay by the river. Louis Napoléon explained that the putsch was not a military revolt, but an appeal to democracy. His auditors, all of them military men, dutifully noted the difference. Louis Napoléon then went to still another lodging, to order his thoughts. In a letter to his mother he explained that he was not acting from personal ambition. In three long-winded proclamations, which it took most of the night to read to a few friends, he explained to the French people that they were betrayed, to the army that the shade of Napoléon was looking down from heaven, and to the people of Strasbourg that their trade had been ruined by the treaties of 1815.

The putsch was to begin at six A.M. on Sunday the 30th. The weather was cold, and during the night it began to snow. At five A.M. Colonel Vaudrey reviewed his troops at the Austerlitz barracks, and officers in on the plot tried to explain to their men that the revolt was not isolated, but echoed a revolutionary uprising all over France.

At about six a small group of conspirators were let in to the parade ground. Some of them were regular army officers, others had been appointed as such by Louis Napoléon. All had uniforms. It is difficult to preside over a military uprising in a top hat. Napoléon himself wore a colonel's uniform of the French Artillery, with a tricolor ribbon and the ribbon of the Legion d'Honneur. The only memento of his uncle was a cocked hat.

Vaudrey explained that the revolution had just begun. Louis Napoléon unfurled the tricolor and the eagle. The soldiers shouted, "Vive L'Empéreur!" Parties were dispatched to see that the proclamations were printed (Napoléon I always had his printed in advance), to arrest the Prefect of the department, and to win over the Third Artillery and Pontonniers garrisons.

Louis Napoléon then went to General Voirol's house. Voirol was

Vaudrey's commanding officer. Voirol was not yet up, and was just trying to get into his trousers as Louis Napoléon entered his room.

The moment was not well chosen. Louis Napoléon asked Voirol to recognize him as Napoléon II (he had yet to stumble on the advantages of III as a numeral).

"Silence," said Voirol, and ordered the conspirators arrested. Unwisely, instead of taking Voirol prisoner themselves, the plotters put him in an inner room which had a far door to a staircase. Voirol escaped. He soon had things under control.

The revolt fizzled in two hours. Louis Napoléon retreated to the parade ground. An officer had the presence of mind to shout, "Soldiers, you are deceived. The man they are presenting to you as the heir to the Emperor is nothing but a dressed-up actor—he is only Colonel Vaudrey's nephew." This rapid string of impromptu deceits turned the tide. Colonel Taillander, who was in command of the infantry, ordered his men to arrest the Prince. Louis Napoléon stood with his back to a wall, surrounded by his followers. He had forbidden anyone to use weapons. But one of his followers, Parquin, had used his fists, and his knuckles were bleeding.

"You are wounded," said Louis. "You have shed blood for me."

"I wish there was not a drop of blood in my veins," said Parquin. "I wish you were safe with the Queen at Arenenberg."

"We will be shot. But we will die a good death," said Louis Napoléon.

Some workmen who had climbed over the wall began to throw stones. Louis Napoléon surrendered. Nobody was shot. By eight the revolt was over. All the conspirators had been arrested except Persigny, who had the wit to abandon his uniform and escape to Kehl.

It took the French government a week to decide what to do with them. Rather than make a martyr of a Bonaparte, it was thought better to ship Louis Napoléon into exile, and not to send him, but to take him, on a cruise of the Americas, on a ship called, with the usual felicity of boats chosen for the Bonapartes, the *Andromède*. Chained to this floating rock, Louis Napoléon would bother no one for some time to come.

As for the other conspirators, including Mme Gordon, they were tried on January 6 and acquitted. Popular feeling was behind them. They were given an ovation.

The family took the matter ill, except for Hortense. Napoléon had written her two letters, one announcing victory, the other a farewell. The victory letter was delivered by mistake.

It was a mistake which the morning's newspaper soon rectified. Valérie Masuyer was sent to Strasbourg, and Hortense set out for Paris. She was not allowed to enter the city, but was told that no harm would come to Louis Napoléon. She returned to Arenenberg. The press treated the putsch as a gleeful farce, and her private mail made no more agreeable reading. Joseph and Jérôme publicly disowned their nephew. Louis King of Holland stopped his allowance and confiscated the proceeds from the sale of some of his property. Jérôme informed Mathilde that Louis Napoléon was not a Bonaparte but a bastard.

Jérôme was in London, visiting Joseph, at the time of the Strasbourg coup. "I would rather have given my daughter to a peasant than to a man so ambitious and egotistical as to play with the destiny of a poor child who was almost confided to his care," wrote Jérôme, and looked about for some more reliable source of immediate income than Arenenberg seemed to offer.

He found two. The first of them was the Marchesa Bartolini-Badelli, born Pecori-Suárez-Grimaldi, a widow of forty, rich, handsome, and brainless. She had once been lady-in-waiting to Catherine. The Marchesa, though of older family, wanted a higher title. Jérôme, though of not much family at all, had one. On the other hand, he took his rank seriously, and explained that it could only be a morganatic marriage. By now she was charmed by him, and agreed. The religious ceremony took place in 1840, at Florence, and the civil ceremony as soon as the Second Empire was proclaimed, in Paris in 1853. He continued to be known as Comte de Montfort, though everybody knew he was an Imperial Prince and an ex-King. She continued to be known as the Marchesa, since everybody knew she was a fool. But like Catherine before her, she was a remarkably loyal fool. She kept him going between 1837 and 1840, which was when he found his second source of income. Unfortunately for him, she had a shrewd sense of the value of untouched capital, and being as prudent as she was sensual, consented to dole out sums to him only in exchange for visits to the bedroom. There was no standard fee, but if he did not make the one, he did not get the other. This he soon began to find irksome. So irksome that after each visit he would demand that his valet sponge him down from head to foot. He even sold up some of his own furniture and art objects and a few oriental rugs and some silver plate, in a laudable effort to get the night off. But he was extravagant, so he always had to go back again.

Thus he was delighted when Prince Demidoff, who collected Napoleonic souvenirs, showed signs of wishing to add Mathilde to his collection.

Anatole Demidoff did not have a savory reputation. He was the very rich son of a very rich Russian merchant whose grandfather had been a serf at the time of Peter the Great; and his conduct had made him *persona non grata* almost everywhere. His manners were brutish. That he had recently had his late mistress, Fanny de Montault, dragged by horses for his amusement does not seem to have upset Jérôme or, for that matter, Mathilde, for Demidoff was very rich indeed.

"I am happy beyond belief," wrote Mathilde. "I cannot tell you with what confidence I regard the future."

It took some time to jockey Demidoff into marriage, because Jérôme demanded as the price of it a settlement not only on his daughter, but also on himself, of as much money as possible. He also had other tricks. One of them was to sell to Demidoff a collar of pearls given by Napoléon to Catherine, so that Demidoff might give it to Mathilde, and the Marchesa Bartolini-Badelli might thus continue to use it. He then gave Mathilde a nonexistent dowry of 290,000 francs, 60,000 of it represented by her trousseau, which Demidoff had paid for, and the rest imaginary. Demidoff was to pay Mathilde 200,000 francs a year, of which 40,000 was to be set aside for Jérôme. After these details were settled, the marriage took place in the Greek chapel of the cathedral of Florence, with the Archbishop presiding. Jérôme then borrowed 40,000 francs from his new son-in-law. He proposed to live not so much with as on the happy couple.

Mathilde first had to go to Russia, for Demidoff had been recalled to St. Petersburg for having manhandled the Russian Ambassador at Rome, Potemkin, during a quarrel over the dispensation necessary if Mathilde was to marry a Greek Orthodox Christian.

Demidoff enlivened the journey, which was made in the dead of winter and took six weeks, by forcing Mathilde to drive with the top of the carriage down, in order to study the effects of subzero weather on a pretty woman.

He was not well received in Russia, where his habits were almost as detested as were the interest rates charged by his men of business. Mathilde was more successful. Nicholas I took a liking to her (he was related to her through her mother) and told her, before the Demidoffs set off once more for Florence, that one day she would have trouble with her husband and that therefore she must never forget that the Czar would always be disposed to take her part.

From Florence they went to Paris, where Mathilde became most popular, and Demidoff even less so. This did not please him. So he began to parade his latest mistress before the guests at Mathilde's receptions. They returned once again to Florence, where Demidoff took the Castello of San Donato, which he fitted up luxuriously. Jérôme made a point of appearing there so often, and of asking incessantly for so much money, mostly through Mathilde, that Demidoff began to beat his wife several times a month with a riding crop.

On one of their visits to St. Petersburg, when he had done this once too often, she went to a ball at court in a low-cut evening dress, so that the Czar might see her scraped and bleeding shoulders. But she did not ask for intervention just yet.

The couple continued to spend the next few seasons in Paris. Demidoff was not a penny-pinching man and had no objection to his wife's establishment, but Jérôme's continuing demands for money were beginning to get on his nerves. One evening, when someone said that the tragedienne Rachel had been sold to a man called Véron for 200,000 francs, Demidoff snapped, "Such is the power of money," and pointed out Mathilde to assorted guests. On another occasion, when she was on her knees begging for more money for Jérôme, he rang for his valet, and said to him when he came, "See the niece of Napoléon, who has thrown herself at my feet so I may give her father money." This sort of thing was much harder to take than a weekly whipping. At the end of 1846 Mathilde made her own journey to Russia. The Czar issued a decree of separation and forbade Demidoff to enter Paris without his permission. Mathilde was to receive 200,000 francs a year, of which 40,000 were earmarked for Jérôme. So Jérôme got his money just the same, and, more important, Mathilde was able to get away from her father.

She does not seem to have regretted her marriage, until Louis Napoléon became Napoléon III. After that she regretted it very much indeed.

•   •

Hortense was not to hear from her son until March of 1837. By then she knew she had cancer of the uterus. She did not at once attempt to recall him.

1836 was marked by the restoration of Napoléon's statue to the Vendôme column, by the death of the exiled Charles X, on November 6, and by the restoration of Versailles, which cost 23,000,000 francs and was part of Louis Philippe's "exaggerated love of the trowel." Sometimes he even laid bricks with the workmen.

Having exiled the pretender to the Americas, the French were in no hurry to get him there. He had sailed from L'Orient (Lorient) for Rio, with 15,000 francs given him by Louis Philippe as traveling money. After a longer voyage than usual the boat reached Rio, where it stayed in the harbor for a month. He was not allowed to go ashore, and visitors were not allowed to come out to him. But he was well treated by the officers and crew. In January the boat finally reached Norfolk, and Louis Napoléon went ashore, and went overland to New York, establishing himself at the Old City Hotel, on Broadway. New York was having a cold wave at the time.

His Murat cousins came to see him, and he made friends with General Scott and the (not very good) poet Fitz-Greene Halleck, who says of him, "I thought him a dull fellow, which he certainly was while among men, but sprightly enough when surrounded by young ladies. He would sometimes say, 'When I shall be at the head of affairs in France,' or 'When I become Emperor,' and I then looked upon him as being as mad as a March hare. . . . He was rather a dull man, on the order of Washington."

It was Louis Napoléon's intention to stay a year, though the French government had not stipulated the length of his absence from Europe.

Hortense had already sent out an Italian friend of Louis's, Arese, with letters, personal gear, and a sketch of Mathilde. Now she informed him of her condition (on April 3). Her cancer had turned out to be inoperable, but she was so delighted to avoid the operation that the thought of death did not unduly bother her. She wrote in a more cheerful style on the 7th. Under the flap of that letter, Valérie Masuyer had written, "Come quickly."

Louis left New York on June 6, 1837, first depositing a formal farewell with President Van Buren. It deplored Louis's inability further to study the habits and manners of the United States and pointed out the honorable nature of his own conduct. It was a Napoleonic manifesto of the second period.

On the 27th he sailed for England, in order to get a passport for the continent. Persigny had been so busy explaining what had gone wrong with Strasbourg and how fortunate the French were in having Louis soon to rule over them, however, that no Ambassador in London would consent to issue a passport. So Louis Napoléon had to use a false one, issued in America in the name of Robinson, and franked by the Swiss Consul. Leaving his hotel by explaining he was on his way to Richmond, he went downriver instead, crossed to the continent, and taking a steamer up the Rhine, reached Arenenberg on August 4.

Hortense had the slow sinking unpredictable death typical of her disease, and lingered until October 5. There was a good deal of suffering, but she felt so encouraged by Louis's return that for a while she could get up and take brief walks in the gardens. Her disease had made it impossible for her any longer to control her household, which was one of middle-aged dissatisfied women, so there was a good deal of bickering both in front of her and behind her back.

In her will she asked to be buried beside Joséphine at Rueil. A funeral service was held at Ermatingen. It was rather grand. The mass was celebrated by a bishop, the peasants came in from the countryside, and Mozart's *Requiem* was sung. Since Ermatingen was in neither French nor Austrian territory, names might be named, ranks given, titles honored, and encomiums pronounced. They were. Hortense had been the most popular of the Bonapartes, with everyone except the Bonapartes.

Hortense left nothing to her husband, and he took the news of her death calmly. He attributed it to Louis's coup. "I must profit by the occasion to acquaint you," he wrote to the Princess de la Tour d'Auvergne, "with the wrong my son has done to his mother, but the papers will have told you of it, and I do not like to put myself to the bother of useless formalities."

He refused to communicate with him after Strasbourg, and still sent back his letters unopened. However, he had the grace to send a letter of condolence. "I was not surprised, but I was saddened to hear of your poor mother's death," he wrote, and offered to pay for *one* mass for the repose of her soul, and half the cost of a monument by Bartolini.

Lucien and Joseph, who had explained after Strasbourg that Louis Napoléon no longer had four uncles, sent notes of sympathy. Jérôme did not. Neither, apparently, did Caroline.

Valérie Masuyer had known that Hortense had an illegitimate son by Charles de Flahaut since 1830, for she was Hortense's confidential secretary. Now, perhaps partly to hit back at Mme Savage, for such is the illogic of jealous spinsters, she told Louis Napoléon. He was upset, but not for long. In later years, Auguste de Morny was to be useful to him.

Hortense's body was interred at Rueil on January 8, 1838. Louis Napoléon was prevented by the proscription from coming, but both Charles de Flahaut, her lover, and Auguste de Morny, her son, were there. Louis Napoléon was represented by his cousin, Tascher de la Pagerie. One of the Murat sons represented the other Bonapartes. Such dignitaries of the Empire as still remained alive also attended.

Valérie Masuyer settled down near Rueil, at the Abbaye aux Bois, to tend the tomb. After the Second Empire was proclaimed she was given a suite of apartments in the Tuileries. However, she never *quite* approved of Louis Napoléon, because of his erotic habits and because he would not take her advice.

Over the years the chapel at Rueil became more and more elaborate. Bartolini's somewhat sugary statue of a veiled and kneeling Hortense was installed in 1845. In 1856 it was replaced by something more suitable to a reigning monarch, a monument in which Hortense stood up, still veiled, but regally crowned, to be welcomed by an angel. Both the hortensia and the arms of Holland were inserted in the stained glass of the church windows at the same time.

THE family was now without a female head, for Mme Mère had
died the year before. She had lived surrounded by Napoleonic
souvenirs, and the lamp he had had beside his bed when he died
she kept beside her bed for the same purpose. In 1830 she had slipped
in the garden and broken her hip. But she was a difficult woman to
kill, and though she could no longer move about freely, she recovered. That Moorish-looking wooden balcony still to be seen was
built out from the palace for her, so that she might amuse herself by
watching the crowds at the end of the Corso. Though she was going
blind from cataracts, she liked to be read to. Usually she liked to
listen to Napoleonic memoirs, and she did not like them edited. If her
readers edited, they were rebuked.

"Because Napoléon was not infallible. Napoléon was not the son
of Mary, like Jesus, but only the son of Letizia."

Like most mothers, she opposed everything her son had done
while living and built a shrine to him after he was dead. "The Emperor," she explained, "will only be properly understood in a hundred years."

She could be difficult. When the family wanted to attempt an action against the French government, to recover moneys not paid under the sixth clause of the Treaty of Fontainebleau, she forbade it,
because of the fourth clause (banishment in perpetuity). "I know,"
she said blandly, "you too well not to be certain that you will never
hesitate between honor and money." She was, after all, a million-
airess. She also turned down a proposal to lift the ban of banishment
for herself alone, in the same spirit.

Nor was she given to making capital out of her own memories.
"The details I could give you of the Emperor are too puerile to be

included in his story," she wrote Napoléon Louis, before his death. "He has himself indicated, in his memoirs, how history should be written. The Emperor must appear to posterity in his colossal dimensions."

She took a certain interest in the political schemes of Louis Napoléon, but advised caution. "However, it is better at your age to have too much fire than to have too little."

For though she was an invalid and half blind, Mme Mère, except for the one pitiable lapse with Mme Kleinmuller, had an intelligence which never grew senile. She seems to have seen what Hortense was up to, she had had opportunity to survey her grandchildren, and she began to think better of the ex-Queen of Holland. She had not been "altogether displeased" at the Carbonari plots of 1831.

When L'Aiglon died, she made a new will (September 22, 1832), though she was to live another four years.

Though she had given her various children 10,000,000 francs since 1815, she had an estate formally assessed at 1,700,000 francs, and probably worth at least double that sum, for a good many things had been deposited with Fesch, for distribution after her death.

Her public estate was to be divided among Joseph, Lucien, Louis, and Jérôme, with smaller sums for Caroline and for Elisa's children. Her palace was to go to Joseph, but its worth was to be deducted from his share of the estate. Her busts and family portraits went to Fesch. She annulled all her children's debts to her, except those of Caroline, which debt was to be held by the four brothers equally. She left legacies to her intimates, her servants, and her doctor, and her heart was to go to Ajaccio, a wish not granted at the time. The grandchildren received nothing directly, because they would inherit from their parents, with the exception of Elisa's son and daughter.

She finally died February 2, 1836, during carnival, in Napoléon's bed, surrounded by family portraits, with her husband's likeness at the head of it, and a bust of Hortense in the room.

Those celebrating carnival were asked not to let off fireworks in the Piazza Venezia. Otherwise it was a private death, except for one bizarre irregularity. There was a screen at the foot of her bed, and her death agony was so prolonged that the porter let sightseers come to peer through the joints of the screen, at a scudo a head.

She died at about seven in the evening, at the age of eighty-seven. Fesch, who was in his mid-seventies, was there to close her eyes. It was the year the Arc de Triomphe, which had been mocked up in wood for Marie Louise's entry into Paris, was finally completed in stone, though the four horses which were to adorn it had long since been returned to St. Mark's in Venice.

She was laid out in the large drawing room, for two days, on a bed of state shaded by a canopy supported by four silver eagles. The funeral was to be private. The family display of arms customary in such cases was forbidden by the Church, and a very private mass was allowed only at Santa Maria in Via Lata. She was to be buried, too, as obscurely as possible, at Corneto near Civitavecchia, in the convent church of the Sisters of the Cross and Passion. Since the funeral procession had to wind its way through the carnival, the coffin was sometimes pelted with confetti.

Fesch, who died of cancer of the stomach May 15, 1839, at the age of seventy-six, leaving everything to Joseph, provided 200,000 francs for a mortuary chapel at Ajaccio. Joseph did not carry out the building of this, but Napoléon III did. It was not finished until 1857, but the bodies of Mme Mère and Fesch were moved to Ajaccio in 1851 and into the Imperial Chapel in 1860.

The survivors did not get along with each other, and all continued to ignore Louis Napoléon.

I<small>T</small> took the future Napoléon III a very long time to learn his business. It was four years until he evolved his second and even more ridiculous *démarche* against the legitimate government of France; it was to be twelve until he succeeded in getting himself put at the head of it, and thirteen before he could safely seize it.

For the time being, he was once more reduced to the condition of a paper war. For one reason, his finances were not in order. He had inherited Arenenberg, a few over three hundred shares in a Viennese bank and revenue derived from investments in Spain and Portugal— all told, a capital of 3,000,000 francs and an income of 120,000. This, though a sizable sum, was encumbered by Hortense's various pensions to retainers and was not enough to finance the various newspapers which he felt it necessary either to own or to subsidize for purposes of propaganda. His father, whose capital, exclusive of real estate and personal property, was perhaps double this amount, refused to advance him a penny.

So he had to go in debt, sell Arenenberg (it was an arranged sale, on condition he might buy it back later), and then go deeper in debt. This had the advantage that it was to his creditors' interest that he should eventually succeed in gaining power. As for his ridiculous coups, as Metternich pointed out to the prosecution after the Strasbourg affair, "Be on your guard. This young fool acquires importance by your mistake in making more than one need of everything which has to do with the Emperor Napoléon. You will end by making everyone believe in the future of the Napoléon dynasty."

This was to Louis Napoléon's plan. Already, in France, he was known as the Child of the Column (that is, of the column in the Place Vendôme to which Napoléon's statue had been restored).

And that he should be regarded as an impotent but well-publicized fool suited his book very well.

In the spring of 1838, Laity, one of the Strasbourg conspirators, drew up, with Louis's assistance but published under his own name, an account of the Strasbourg affair called *Prince Napoléon at Strasbourg*. The core of its argument was that France was democratic but not republican, for by democracy the author meant the government by one with the consent of all (out of a population of 35,000,000, only 200,000 Frenchmen had the vote), and by a republic, the government of many in obedience to a system. This was felt to be dangerous doctrine. Laity was prosecuted before the Chamber of Peers and condemned to five years in prison and a fine of 10,000 francs.

Every cause needs its martyr if it is to succeed, and Laity made an excellent martyr. Napoléon put the proceeds of the sale of Arenenberg into two newspapers, *Le Capital* and *Le Journal du Commerce*, both Parisian. They were devoted to pushing what were now known as *Les Idées Napoléoniennes*. Louis Napoléon was perhaps the first modern salesman to create out of thin air a pressing need for an unwanted product, of no value or utility, but with a catchy name.

The French government made a mistake by having its Ambassador to Berne demand the expulsion of Louis Napoléon from Swiss territory. It does not do to stir up the Swiss. Louis Napoléon was an honorary citizen of the canton of Thurgau. The French massed troops on the border. Other cantons voted him an honorary citizen, and the papers made much of his charities to Thurgau (among other things he had founded a school and saved two people from drowning in the Bodensee). Prussia, Austria, Baden, and Württemberg supported the French. It was almost war.

The only result was that Louis Napoléon, in order to spare the Swiss an invasion, removed himself to England, which gave him a much better base. France was unlikely to mobilize troops along the English Channel. He had now become exactly what he wished to be, a persecuted international figure. As the *Courier Français* wrote, there now attached to him a fame which would follow him everywhere. Out of someone whom the public considered a little mad, the French government had made a hero.

He was again short of funds, and an appeal to his father again went unanswered. The ex-King of Holland had a habit of taking to young girls whose fathers he admired. So he had decided to marry

269

the daughter of the Marquis Strozzi, whom he admired very much. Her name was Julia-Livia, and she was a fine-haired blonde of sixteen. Louis of Holland was sixty and in a wheelchair.

What was left of the family was consternated. Joseph wrote to say, "If you decide on marriage, I do not know how sufficiently to remind you that at your age you must find in marriage less the transports of earlier days, than the pleasure of her company and charms." This letter went unanswered. The marriage has been contested, but was announced in the newspapers (*Le Siècle* of June 6). "There took place at Florence, the 22d of May, the marriage of the Comte de St. Leu. The bride, who is sixteen, is the loveliest person in Florence. The husband is so paralyzed that he cannot lift a spoon to his mouth without assistance." On the 6th of July the paper published a retraction. Nonetheless, the couple lived together.

The family tragedies continued. Charlotte, Contesse de St. Leu, Joseph's daughter, the ex-King of Holland's daughter-in-law, and Napoléon Louis's widow, had been misbehaving herself. She not only visited one relative after another, she also slept about. She surrounded herself with Polish refugees (male only), and her chief lover was Count Potocki. Becoming pregnant by him, she hid herself first at the Villa Paolina, which Pauline had left to her husband, and then went to Genoa, which was considered to have the best midwives in Italy. She did not reach it, but died at Sarzana of internal bleeding after a botched delivery. The child did not live either. This death of his daughter-in-law did not seem to affect the ex-King of Holland. He was always rather pleased by deaths: they meant that he had survived.

Caroline also died in 1839. She had sometimes visited Louis, since she now lived in Florence, but he had not cared for the visits, since she did not conceal either her regal airs, or her intention of making it always a *short* visit. These days Louis sat inside his palace, and one of his few pleasures was showing visitors through the Napoleonic portrait gallery.

Indeed, he did not like to receive the French, and much preferred the Dutch. He kept up state as King of Holland inside his own house, sometimes still had himself painted in his now mothy robes, and any Dutchman willing to address him as "Sire" was always sure of admittance and even, sometimes, of a gracious reception.

Caroline died of cancer of the uterus. Her lover, Macdonald, had died two years earlier. Lucien died on the 29th of June, 1840. So Jérôme and Louis were now the only survivors of the elder generation. This, except that Jérôme was still alive, pleased Louis very much.

What did not please him was that though most of Lucien's children were docile as ducks, and had married well, two of the sons, Pierre and Antoine, were holy terrors. The youngest, they had become privileged juvenile delinquents, strutting about Rome dressed as Calabrian brigands and occasionally committing murder. Their father disowned them. Eventually they made the mistake of killing two Papal guards sent to arrest them. Antoine fled to London. Pierre, who had more spirit (and lived longer), set fire to the Castel Sant' Angelo, was condemned to death, had his sentence commuted to fifteen years' imprisonment, and was freed at the intervention of Sir Thomas Wyse, one of Lucien's innumerable sons-in-law; he then went out to America, where his energies found a natural outlet in serving as a soldier of fortune in a variety of South American revolutions and counterrevolutions. Louis had tried to introduce them to a more lamblike form of behavior, and was much put out when they would not listen.

Louis would lend his son nothing. In response to an earlier plea for a loan (in 1834) he had given up one of his tenderest memories: "I remember with pride that one day, by the bed of your grandmother, you were deeply distressed to observe that not only did considerations of pecuniary self-interest mix with expression of affection on the faces of those who were there, but that there were also discussions about money. 'Oh Papa,' you said to me, 'that children should inherit from their parents should not be.' "

Such was the authentic fond paternal tone. Louis Napoléon had to look elsewhere. (To the House of Baring, which made a shrewd investment and got back every penny. Napoléon III was always as scrupulous to repay his debts as he was unscrupulous to contract them, which, considering the well-known advantages of interest, made him an excellent debtor.)

On his arrival in London, with a personal staff of half a dozen, including Count Arese, always a loyal follower, Colonel Vaudrey, left over from the Strasbourg coup, Persigny, as indefatigable as ever, and Dr. Conneau, his doctor and devoted friend, Louis Napoléon became a social lion, at least during his first year in residence.

271

The second year he was less of a novelty. This subsequent fall from felicity allowed him to frequent more raffish and more interesting company, such as that of those who attended the salon of Lady Blessington, who, though *hors de société*, knew everyone of any interest in London, including Benjamin Disraeli, then a dandy bent on much the same course as Louis Napoléon, in order to secure an even more effectual power. It was here, according to some accounts, that he met Miss Howard, who was for so long to be his mistress, a thoroughly respectable woman in every way but one. More probably he first encountered her in 1846.

Louis Napoléon set up housekeeping at Carlton Terrace, in a house crowded with Napoleonic relics, and actually a headquarters from which conspiracies could be directed. They were winked at by the British government, which has always given asylum to useful plotters and whose relations with France had not been improved by French efforts to gain control of Turkey, Egypt, and Algeria.

The Pretender, for he was that by now, was watched by French agents who, to earn their keep, sent back so many and such conflicting reports of nonexistent plots that the government was lulled if not into a sense of security, at least into that boredom produced by the constant starting of false hares. As the historian Kissinger says of similar activities in 1815, "most secret documents are not worth stealing."

Louis Napoléon took part in the Eglinton tournament, dressed in medieval armor, despite the rain, and published in 1839 his *Idées Napoléoniennes*. It consisted mostly of incense, but though Louis Napoléon could never hold a crowd, he could always sway it from the study. It presented Napoléon I as the friend of the people. ("His aim was liberty. Yes, liberty.") "No sovereign sought so much advice. Could he be a despot who by his codes had substituted laws for caprice?" He was never the aggressor: he merely repelled hostile coalitions. And so on and so forth. Rather tactlessly, considering the Pretender's place of asylum, England was blamed for everything. "His ideas live after him. His memory grows." It was implied that though he was dead, the nephew was very much alive.

Next year came a shorter version, *L'Idée Napoléonienne*. "The Napoleonic idea springs from the Revolution like Minerva from the head of Zeus."

In the event, Louis Napoléon himself was to spring from Margate, for it was from there that he proposed to launch a personal invasion of France. It was timed to coincide with the return of Napoléon I's ashes from St. Helena, a ceremony proposed by the politician Thiers to end "the sublime agony of St. Helena, as resigned though more prolonged than that of Christ." "The return of the ashes," wrote Victor Hugo, "was a sort of disappearance trick. The government was terrified of the phantom they had conjured up—and seemed to be trying to show Napoléon and hide him at the same time."

Not only was the French government unstable, but France was threatened externally by opposition to its policies in Egypt and Syria and the rise of Germany. "Already the clash of the brazen bucklers of the Valkyries can be heard, those divine sorceresses who decide the fate of battles," wrote Heine, who though he lived in France was opposed only to that portion of his Fatherland which was opposed to him. "France," said a German general, "represents the principle of immorality; she must be annihilated, otherwise there will no longer be a God in heaven." "They shall not have it, our German Rhine," wrote Becker, a Pole who had written an enormously popular book on Pan-Germanism.

It certainly seemed that France was representing immorality at the moment less than ably. What seemed needed was a Napoléon, and this Louis Napoléon proposed to supply. It was his plan to go to Boulogne by boat, take over the garrison there, and proclaim his own government.

In execution the plan turned out to be another comic opera, though both more expensive and more lavishly performed than had been the Strasbourg putsch. It involved fifty-six people, all of them in uniforms imported from France. Polish and French adherents had been enlisted in Leicester Square and Soho, then even more than now not quite the districts they should have been. Arms were bought up at Birmingham, and Dr. Conneau himself printed up manifestoes on a hand press, during the journey over. It was said that one of the garrison officers at Boulogne was in on the plot. Marshal Causel might be.

The invaders crossed the channel on an excursion steamer, the *Edinburgh Castle*, hired for the purpose. It cruised down the Thames on August 3, 1840, pausing to pick up conspirators along the way. Parquin, another of the Strasbourg lot, seeing a small eagle on sale at a bird fancier's while waiting for the boat, had the happy idea of buying it and bringing it aboard, with the symbolic intention of once more setting the Napoleonic eagle free on French soil.

Louis Napoléon joined his excursion steamer on the 4th. The necessary uniforms, those of the 40th Regiment of the Line, were taken on board on the 5th. The steamer had only been chartered until the 6th, so it was necessary to hurry. The crossing was without incident. The *Edinburgh Castle* dropped anchor off Wimereux, a virtual suburb of Boulogne, shortly after midnight of August 5, some four miles away across the harbor from the target aimed for. Landing parties began to go ashore at two A.M. Some customs officers who came to ask what the devil an excursion steamer was doing there were told it was taking members of the 40th Regiment on their way from Dunkirk to Cherbourg. When the customs officers asked why, they were taken prisoner.

Dawn came shortly before five, and it was a high clear sparkling day. The march on Boulogne began at five. The real eagle had been forgotten on board ship, where the customs officials impounded it, but there was a bronze eagle atop the tricolor carried by the marchers.

At Boulogne, the troops in barracks were asked to revolt. They refused to do so. There was a brisk scuffle, during which Louis Napoléon lost his head and shot one of the soldiers. His supporters induced him to retreat. Some army regulars had come up behind the invaders, shouting, "*Vive le Roi*." The invaders made a run for the beach and their boats, hoping to return to the *Edinburgh Castle*. But the customs officials, who had by now been freed, had impounded this, too. A lifeboat was launched into the low surf, but overturned. Members of the National Guard, who had pursued the invaders down to the beach, began to fire at the men in the water. Louis Napoléon, who had also run into the sea, had his clothes ripped by bullets twice. He and forty-five of his followers splashed up the beach and surrendered. Of the remaining invaders, one was drowned and the rest variously wounded. By eight in the morning all were in jail. It was a worse fiasco than Strasbourg, and in addition, the owner of the *Edinburgh Castle* demanded full hire and damages for the impounding by the French government of his boat.

The ex-King of Holland reacted to news of the Boulogne raid in his customary way, by taking to his bed in a darkened room. On the

24th he wrote to Jérôme to explain that he no longer had a son, and to the French newspapers (not to those controlled by Louis Napoléon), to explain that his son had been misled and had fallen into a terrible trap. If so, Louis Napoléon had dug the hole himself.

As for Jérôme, the raid ruined his attempt to wring a pension out of the French government by taking advantage of the recrudescence of Bonapartism, and he therefore regarded his nephew's political activities as a personal affront.

It took the French government several months to evolve an effective way of dealing with Louis Napoléon, but on September 18 he was indicted by the Chamber of Peers, since the government did not dare to risk a jury trial, in case of acquittal. He did not make a good public impression. His gestures were clumsy, he had never learned to speak well before a large audience, and worst sin of all in French eyes, his French was neither Parisian nor perfect, having now an English and now a German accent. Both were almost imperceptible, but not to the French.

There were 312 Peers, of whom 167 sat, of whom 152 consented to participate in a verdict. One of them advocated a death sentence. All of them found the defendant and his co-conspirators guilty. 151 voted imprisonment in perpetuity. The sentences were read out to the prisoners in their cells.

"How long," said Louis Napoléon with a smile, "does perpetuity last in France?"

On October 7 he arrived at the border fortress of Ham (Hâ), where perpetuity was in this case to be passed. Dr. Conneau had elected to come with him, as had Montholon, one of Napoléon I's companions at St. Helena. The invasion had been badly timed. It was on October 7 that Napoléon's ashes were put aboard the frigate *La Belle Poule*, at St. Helena.

The remains of the Emperor did not arrive in Paris until December 15, coming up the Seine by slow stages. The temperature stood at fourteen below, the sky and air were misty. Toward noon the overcast lifted and the sun came out. The casket was transferred to a catafalque, and then brought down the Champs Élysées and across the bridge to the Invalides, on a gigantic cart rolling on four wheels. There was a grandstand at the Invalides.

"Sire," said the Prince de Joinville, his son, to Louis Philippe, "I present you with the body of Napoléon."

275

"I accept it in the name of France," replied Louis Philippe. There was then a salvo of artillery, and later the coffin was lowered into that vast sarcophagus which lies at the bottom of the well of the dome of the Invalides.

The people persisted in singing

Napoléon aimait la guerre
Et son peuple comme Jésus,

which was not only sacrilegious, but a little dangerous. For of course now there was another Napoléon.

The only way to solve the problem of a political martyr is to persuade him to take office. But nobody dares to try that. Louis Napoléon shot would have overturned the July monarchy. Louis Napoléon, the perpetual prisoner at Ham, became a national folk figure, all the more potent for being invisible. Though there is no real evidence, the absurd raid on Boulogne seems to have been halfway between a gamble and an educated guess. Now the gamble began to pay off.

Sensing this new ground swell of popularity, the ex-King of Holland began to take a more amiable view of his much-denied son. He reopened their correspondence. He had found a new pose: that of the martyred father of a martyred boy. And his temper had been improved by his reception during a supposedly incognito trip to Holland, to settle his private and financial affairs there. Crowds waited outside his hotel and cheered him when he appeared. It was again part of that movement whereby the Bonapartes had become the symbol of liberation from tyrannies they had themselves practiced. And in his atrabilious way, he had, while King, tried to protect the Dutch against the exactions of the man who had made him King over them.

He was further cheered by the death of Joseph, also by now a resident of Florence, on July 28, 1844. Joseph left his diminished but still considerable fortune to his wife, with whom he had at last been again living, but who survived him by less than a year. The Joseph Bonaparte money then went mostly to his only surviving daughter, Zenaïde, who had married the second Prince of Canino, the ornithologist who had succeeded Lucien. Louis did not grieve about the lost money, for after twenty-three years of waiting, now he was head of the family, and Joseph had often burdened him with unwelcome advice.

The succession had, after all, as Napoléon I had once planned, devolved upon Louis and his sons though, true, there was only one son left. Louis spent his time putting the family archives in order, and restored Louis Napoléon's portrait to the picture gallery in his house.

I T cannot be said that the Prisoner of Ham was uncomfortable. Perpetual imprisonment turned out to be five and a half years, and his detention was made agreeable for him in many ways. The fortress itself was an old one, partially dismantled, on the borders of Belgium, and had long been reserved for prisoners of state. Louis Napoléon lived in rooms in the main block, with Dr. Conneau to watch over his health. He was permitted to gather in his library, write, and carry on a large correspondence. He could sometimes receive visitors. There were daily walks on the ramparts, and he amused himself by laying out a garden. He prepared for his third bid for power. He fitted up a laboratory in which to study physics, chemistry, and electricity, with the assistance of M. Acar, the local chemist. He had a mistress—*la belle sabotière*, daughter of the local cobbler, who brought in his meals, looked after his dirty linen, and with whom he washed it; he had two sons by her. Later he made the one consul at Zanzibar, the other a bureaucrat in the Ministry of Finance. Napoléon always took care of his byblows.

He also had pamphlets to write, for the affairs of France were all blowing his way, which is not surprising, since he had grown adept at the use of the fan.

At the reinterment of Napoléon I, the poor had demanded alms not for the love of God, but in Napoléon's name. And Louis Philippe was much criticized for having avoided a war with Germany.

Nineteenth-century attitudes toward Germany are a complex subject. It would not be unfair to say that France and England had been quarreling with each other over spheres of self-interest for so long that they did not wish a third contender.

The patriotism of France had been first diverted and then exhausted by the eighteen years' war with Algeria, of which ten had already elapsed. It was part of that general dismemberment of the Turkish Empire by the European powers which dictated so much policy until 1918. Blocked elsewhere in the Mediterranean by the prior claims of England and Austria, France decided to take Algeria as her own. Unfortunately she did not know how, and the war cost over 40,000,000 francs a year and produced no immediate profit.

"Algiers is like a box at the Opera," said the Duc de Broglie. "France is rich enough for a box at the Opera, but this one is too dear." Though the French refused to colonize the captured territory, suffering from the national disinclination to go anywhere that is not already French, the government had been able to settle 100,-000 Europeans there, mostly Greeks and Levantine Jews. These people make excellent shopkeepers, but very poor farmers.

Nor were the internal problems of France to be solved by a war in Algeria. Early in his career Louis Philippe had fallen upon the phrase "the golden mean." This had been imposed upon the country so successfully, that everyone but the poor grew prosperous, and, in Lamartine's words, "the whole country was dying of boredom."

The poor grew poorer. They were the new industrial poor. At Lyons, 100,000 workers out of a population of 150,000 were destitute. In France 130,000 babies were abandoned every year, and this does not count the number murdered or left to starve. Crime increased. And, since the *nouveaux riches* had not the sense to hide their excessive wealth, so did resentment.

The King, an almost entirely sympathetic figure, was known as the Pear not only because of his shape, but because in French argot of the day the word also meant fool. He was anything but a fool. That he managed to keep his throne through eighteen years of progressive unrest is better proof of that than any document. A good actor, he had the sense to pose as a simple citizen. When, as once or twice happened, someone had the folly to address him as a citizen, the pretense broke abruptly down. As he grew older and less publicly tractable, his popularity broke down too. At the time Louis Napoléon was relegated to Ham, he was sixty-six. His later years were hampered by illness and by the death of his sister, Mme Adélaïde, whose advice and friendship he had always relied on, for both had been of the first quality.

He inclined toward personal rule, but as this was the age of the middle-class politician, he had to work alternately through Thiers and Guizot. Of the two Thiers was the more appealing, but, had a tendency to irritate by giving lectures. He was also venal. Guizot was less governed by self-interest. Thiers was a rabble rouser, full of liberal catchwords and no less liberal trickery. Guizot relied upon the bribe. Nobody found him particularly appealing, though many were fascinated. "I should like to act in tragedy with that man," said Rachel one day. "He is Mirabeau turned into an insect," said Mme de Girardin, the hostess, who kept always at her table three permanently set places for Hugo, Balzac and Lamartine, and really, when it came to Guizot, there was no room.

The words attributed to Guizot himself are, "Get rich." And he did. For the eight years he was in power (Thiers, who was temporarily out of it, spent the time writing his history of the First Empire and intriguing with the Bonapartists), he was one of the world's busiest and most accomplished place sellers, contract jobbers, bribe takers, and pork-barrelers. That he also governed well did nothing to enhance his reputation. Both he and the King wished to maintain a banker's peace, in everything. And from 1840 until 1848 they succeeded. "If that were all the genius required of a statesman charged with the direction of affairs, there would be no need for statesmen— a milestone would do as well," said Lamartine.

What the Milestone and the Pear overlooked was that, in cutting the shape of their government to the requirements of the wealthy parvenue bourgeoisie of the capital, they denied the rest of the country a voice, and so deflected it toward that Bonapartist cult they had themselves done so much to encourage.

The heir, Louis Napoléon, did not overlook this. One of his first acts at Ham had been to write the *Aux Mânes de l'Empéreur*. It was a celebration of that dead body over which he still proposed to steal power.

"Sire, you return to your capital and the crowds salute you. From the depth of my dungeon I can merely catch a glimpse of the sun which shines on your cortège. . . . From your sumptuous cortège, disdaining some of the homage you receive, you cast a glance at my humble dwelling, and, mindful of your caresses in my childhood, you say to me: Friend, you suffer for me; I am pleased with you."

And so on. It is possible he believed some of this. At any rate, the French public believed the rest of it. According to Béranger, who was the best propagandist in Europe (with such little songs as *"Parle-nous de lui, grand-mère, parle-nous de lui"*), Louis Napoléon was the best writer of his sort then living. He was certainly the most effective. In 1841 came his *Fragments historiques*, another apologetic in disguise, this time, that of a history of the English Glorious Revolution of 1688. One had only to change the names. Charles II had been a very good king (Louis XVIII). James II had been a very bad one (Charles X). So the Bloodless Revolution had brought in William of Orange (Louis Philippe, for which read Louis Napoléon).

A volley of pamphlets followed. He revised his artillery manual. He published something called *The Extinction of Pauperism*, which made him friends among the liberals, and a study of the sugar beet. At first the connection seems elusive, until we realize that Napoléon I had himself encouraged the sugar beet and kept a cone of beet sugar on the mantelpiece of his study at St. Cloud. Louis Napoléon never did anything that Napoléon I had not done before him, though frequently he does not seem to have understood why Napoléon I had done it, or that circumstances had changed in the last forty or fifty years.

Imprisonment had begun to irk him. Schiller was the only literature he cared for. It is not difficult to see why. The rest of his reading was devoted to mastering facts. Later, he was to refer to his "years at the University of Ham." He became a well-read man.

Lord Malmesbury, who visited him during April of 1845, found him little changed from his free condition. But then he was not supposed to find him changed. Like other and would-be dictators, Louis Napoléon was an excellent actor, though only of his own part.

Besides, there was the irony that the English backed him in order to defeat the French, whom he in his turn wished to raise to preeminence over them. He never succeeded. Britain had an economic stranglehold on France, because of the cheapness, availability and technical superiority of English manufactured goods.

Louis Napoléon confessed to being weary of imprisonment, but hesitated to flee, since then as now opportunities were thrown in his way so that the problem of his existence might be harmlessly solved by the usual "shot while attempting to escape," if possible in the back. Or so he pretended. Besides, being an honorable man, almost, indeed, in Lord Malmesbury's view, an *English* honorable man, he could not very well break his word, without some reasonable pretext. This, in 1845, his father was so good as to provide. The exiled ex-King of Holland had always been a connoisseur of the fine art of sinking, but now he recognized in his own case the advent of the real thing. He was sixty-eight and his doctors assured him the end could not be far off.

Louis Napoléon wrote to the Minister of the Interior, on December 25, 1845, asking permission to visit his dying father and giving his word to return to prison afterward.

On the 2d of January, 1846, the Council of Ministers rejected his request. On January 14 Louis Napoléon write to the King. Louis Philippe was agreeable, but his ministers were not.

Honor was now satisfied. Louis Napoléon, with the aid of Dr. Conneau, began to plot his escape. On the 24th of May he kept to his bed, and Conneau told inquirers that he was ill. On the 25th he walked out of the fortress disguised as a workman, in a blouse and loose trousers and with his moustache shaved off and his face corked. Over his shoulder he carried a shelf from his library, to hide his features. A carriage was waiting outside the fortress, and in it he changed and was driven to the station, where he took the first fast train to Brussels.

When the escape was discovered, Conneau was handcuffed and sent to prison for three months, but then released. His own sentence for his part in the Boulogne affair had long since expired, and he had stayed on at Ham only out of a sense of personal loyalty to the Prince.

Louis Napoléon went from Ostend to London, where his reception was enthusiastic. He had already used a British passport in order to reach Brussels. But he could not get passports to go on to Florence. The Austrians refused out of deference to the French government. (A passport in those days was not a book one carried but a pass one got.) A French route was impossible. He thought of a sea voyage, but the Grand Duke of Tuscany, which was of course Austrian, refused to allow him to land.

The ex-King of Holland had himself moved to a villa at Leghorn, just in case a sea voyage should prove possible. There, on the 25th of July, at ten in the morning, he died of cerebral hemorrhage. It was a pious death. He had become religious in his later years. For the time being the body was stored in the crypt of the Church of Santa Catarina at Leghorn.

He had made a new will on December 1, 1845. It left Louis Napoléon (referred to throughout as Napoléon Louis, which, as a matter of fact, was how Louis Napoléon sometimes signed himself after his elder brother's death) 1,200,000 francs in cash and the domain of Civitanova, which was worth another 642,000.

Unbeknownst to even the spies of Elizabeth Patterson Bonaparte, Louis of Holland had grown very rich, so now his son was at last far from poor. For of course there was more to the estate than that.

The Dutch property was left to the city of Amsterdam, its income to be set aside to relieve flood victims. He left 150,000 francs to his illegitimate child, a Sèvres vase to the Grand Duchess of Tuscany, and Canova's colossal bust of Napoléon to the Grand Duke. "I leave all my other goods, my palace at Florence, my large domain at Civitanova, and all my movables, real estate, bonds and held debts, all that which at my death constitutes my estate, without exception, to my sole heir, Napoléon Louis, the only son who remains to me, to whom I leave in particular my library, with all the decorations and souvenirs which it contains, and as a further testimony of affection, all those objects which had belonged to my brother, the Emperor, which are in a piece of furniture dedicated to that purpose."

It was his wish to be buried at St. Leu. The French government made no difficulties. The Prince de Condé, whose father had bought the estate of St. Leu in 1819, did. He had already had what Bonaparte bodies were in the chapel of the château moved down to the St. Charles church in the town. The ex-King of Holland would have to be interred down there. He was laid to rest on the 26th of September, at six in the evening, in the presence of a double row of gendarmes and National Guardsmen, Princess Mathilde, Prince Napoléon (Jérôme and his son had just been allowed to return to France), and Dr. Conneau, who had come to represent the future Napoléon III. The Marquis Boccagio represented the Beauharnais. So though he did not get back to St. Leu, at least the ex-King of Holland got as far as St. Leu-la-Forêt.

In 1851 Louis Napoléon had a new chapel built and a new mausoleum installed, surmounted by a heroic statue of the King of Holland in his Dutch court dress.

XXIX

Now Louis Napoléon had only to remain in England, conspire, spend money which at last he had in hand, and wait. But it was Jérôme who got back to France first.

There was no end to Jérôme's vanity. The weaker he grew, the stronger it became. If others had been sometimes disappointed in his merits, he had never been. Even in old age, and his old age was lecherous and hideous, he remained complacent before his glass. He regarded himself as the legitimate heir of the Emperor, and neither he nor his son were ever to look upon Louis Napoléon as anything but an upstart. This did not prevent their taking full advantage of him.

Jérôme now had three sources of income, his daughter Mathilde, who avoided him, his third wife, the Marchesa Bartolini-Badelli, who made him work for it, and if all else failed, his second son, Plon Plon, Prince Napoléon, who had a pension of 30,000 francs a year drawn against Württemberg. So he began to come into his own again. He must have had some charm, for he made many friends, though he seldom kept them. One of them was Victor Hugo, who often intervened on his behalf. It was known that both Jérôme and Plon Plon were hostile to Louis Napoléon, so in 1847 they were allowed to return to Paris, in Jérôme's case after an absence of thirty-two years. As it turned out, he was just in time for the Revolution of 1848, that uprising which, in the words of a contemporary politician, was "a revolt without a cause."

Guizot's governmental corruption finally received too public a publicity. Instead of justifying himself, Guizot ignored the scandals. He had far from ingratiating manners, and refused to allow of any change or to admit any members of the opposition to a part in the government. This naturally led those out of office to attempt to remove him, and they were assisted by a revolutionary upsurge which covered Europe. The Pope took advantage of it to improve his own position. "Italy had to dance the carmagnole, such is the fantasy of every people when they are set free," said the French politician X. Doudans, of that movement called the Risorgimento. Less wise than the Pope, Guizot refused to dance.

There were three financial scandals in a row, capped by a social one, when the Duc de Praslin murdered his wife during the course of an affair with the governess of his children. No sooner had Praslin taken arsenic than the Prince d'Eckmuhl stabbed his mistress with a knife and the Comte de Mortier tried to butcher his children. Not only was the bourgeois regime discredited, so was the peerage.

"After it has taken me seventeen years to restore authority in France, in a single day, in a single hour, you have overthrown it again," Louis Philippe told the President of the Court of Peers. "What a muddle. A machine which is always going wrong."

On the 22d of February, a spiteful, rainy day, though the downpour was incessant, crowds began to gather near the Madeleine and in the Place de la Concorde. They were dispersed, and though they had broken up and burned all the chairs and benches in the Champs Élysées, the matter was thought over.

But on the 23d, also a rainy day, the crowds came back again. The government foolishly called out the National Guard. Always an unreliable force, most of it now went over to the insurgents. Refusing to have troops fire on the National Guard, the King dismissed Guizot and his Ministers instead. "You are more fortunate than I am, all of you," he said.

Guizot resigned and went into hiding. That night crowds paraded the streets with torches, demanding Guizot's death, and also made an assault on the Ministry of Foreign Affairs. This was guarded by the 14th Line Regiment; there was a scrimmage, and the crowd had its martyrs. The bodies were piled on carts and hauled around Paris.

The King put Bugeaud, who had made a reputation for himself in Algeria, in charge of the troops, which began to move at six the next morning. Unfortunately Bugeaud, though an excellent soldier, was, in the words of the Comte de Morny, "a regular old washerwoman in politics," and gave the order not to fire.

On the Place de la Concorde, in front of the Tuileries, a mob gathered and tore the Municipal Guard, which was protecting the Palace, to pieces.

At eleven, Louis Philippe, in uniform and on horseback, reviewed his troops on the other side of the Tuileries, in the Court de la Carrousel. Some soldiers shouted, *"Vive la réforme,"* and Louis Philippe lost his nerve, went back to the Tuileries, and spent the next few hours doing nothing but sitting in a chair.

"You must not sign. You must not abdicate. We must die here," shouted the Queen. The mob had by now reached the Château d'Eau, which was only 200 yards from the guardhouse of the main block of the palace. The King abdicated in favor of his grandson, the Comte de Paris. He then took off his hat and his uniform coat and called for a round hat and an overcoat and his keys. When these were brought him, the King, the Queen, the Duc de Montpensier, and a few followers went through the deserted palace toward a gate leading to the Pont Tournant, where they had to wait for carriages (two broughams and a cabriolet) to be brought around. In these they fled to St. Cloud, and from there toward the Channel coast. On the way, Louis Philippe was heard to mutter, "Worse, worse than Charles X. A hundred times worse than Charles X." Which was true. Charles X had withdrawn in a slow and stately order, whereas immediately behind the fleeing royal family, the mob had entered the Tuileries and sacked it, breaking open the wine casks in the cellars so hastily that some of its members were drowned. Upstairs, the Republican Lagrange mounted the dais in the Throne Room and shouted, *"Vive la République."*

Thiers, who had hoped to ride back into power, was so stunned by the crowds that he could only repeat, "The flood is rising," and barricade himself in his house (the barricades were built by his servants).

The Duchesse d'Orléans, an Italian woman of some spunk who had been left behind, took her two sons to the Chamber of Deputies, hoping to be made regent. The mob rushed the chamber and she had to flee through the President's house towards Les Invalides, her children being handed on to her over the heads of those Deputies who had fled behind her.

Louis Philippe reached England on the British steamer the *Express*. He was to live in exile at Clermont until his death two years later. Guizot joined him.

In Paris, Lamartine proclaimed a republic but had no idea what to do with it. He announced it to be "pure, holy, immortal, popular, and peaceful," but there his knowledge ended. The professional politicians who soon had it in hand did no better.

All three of the male Bonapartes most intimately concerned fired off letters to the press.

"Gentlemen," Jérôme publicly informed the Provisional Government, "the nation has at length torn up the Treaties of 1815. The old soldier of Waterloo, the last surviving brother of Napoléon, returns at this moment to the bosom of the great family. For France the era of dynasties has passed. The law of proscription, which struck me down, has gone with the last of the Bourbons. I ask the Government of the Republic to decree that this proscription was injurious to France, and that it has disappeared with all else that the foreigner forced upon us. Pray be assured of my respect and devotion."

His elder son, Jérôme Napoléon, had died in 1847, but his younger son, Plon Plon, who was with him, wrote the King of Württemberg a republican letter for the press, signing it Citizen Bonaparte. All this accomplished was that the King of Württemberg cut off Plon Plon's yearly pension, saying he felt sure so sincere and ardent a republican would feel pained at receiving money from a King.

Louis Napoléon was in Paris by the 28th of February. "Gentlemen: The people of Paris having by their heroism destroyed the last vestiges of a foreign invasion, I hasten back from exile to place myself under the flag of the Republic which you have just proclaimed. Without any ambition but that of being of service to my country, I announce my arrival to the Provisional Government, and beg to assure them of my devotion to the cause which they represent, and of good will to themselves as individuals. Accept, gentlemen, this assurance of my sentiments."

The gentlemen were so alarmed at his sentiments, avowed and disavowed, that he was immediately requested to leave the country. He did so on the 29th, leaving behind him another letter. "I thought that after thirty-three years of exile and persecution, I had at length the right to find a home in my native country. You think my presence in Paris at this moment may prove embarrassing to you. I therefore withdraw for the present. You will see in this sacrifice a proof of the purity of my intentions and my patriotism."

It was an open letter, designed to put the government in the wrong. He went back to London, for he had learned much in the last few years, among other things the uses of cunning and patience. In the nineteenth century, when suffrage was cleverly limited, there was nothing the democratic politician feared so much as the power of the people, which is to say, of the man who did not have the vote.

So Louis Napoléon proposed to cow his political opposition by an appeal to the people. This meant suborning those who controlled the people, which meant directing an extensive propaganda. But propaganda was the one subject of which Louis Napoléon was master; he could afford it now, and in addition, there were suddenly many who would advance him money. He was the coming man, with only two drains upon his private purse, gambling (almost exclusively cards) and Miss Howard.

Miss Howard was one of the first of the proper tarts, a thoroughly respectable woman before and after the fall. Born Elizabeth Haryett, she was the daughter of a Brighton bootmaker and was an "actress." The first to ransom her from the stage was James Mason, who had a rich father, but no other claims upon her or the world's attention. She then moved on to Major Francis Martyn, also rich, who wished to marry her, but had an invalid wife living. He made her his hostess, set her up in a house in St. John's Wood, an unhealthy but then expensive part of London, and signed over to her houses and valuable land (prudently held by trustees, the interest to be hers for life). Thus, at the age of eighteen she became a woman of independent means and at nineteen a mother. The child was registered as her brother rather than as her son, for she was incurably delicate-minded about such matters. Martyn Constantin Haryett also had a large sum settled on him.

Martyn introduced her to Louis Napoléon, then thirty-eight. She confessed she had an illegitimate son. He replied he had two, the "fruits of captivity." She then told Martyn it was not him she loved, it was the Prince. Martyn seems to have taken the news with stolid British phlegm. It is even possible a stiffened upper lip curved into a slight smile. His attitude toward her had in any case become fatherly. It is difficult to understand how Louis Napoléon fascinated women, for in appearance he was slight and unhealthy looking, as though someone had taken a razor to the Cowardly Lion. But fascinate them he did. Miss Howard took a house separate from Martyn and spent part of her considerable income to pay the Prince's debts. What she was after was respectability. She took lessons in history from Kinglake (who attempted to seduce her, though without success), crossed the channel with the Prince in June of 1848, and undertook the education of his bastards by La Belle Sabotière. They were brought up with her own. She regarded herself as married to him, and gave him 200,000 francs to help finance his *coup d'état*.

In the end she proved somewhat difficult to get rid of, but at last accepted the title of Comtesse Beauregard, with reversion to Martyn's son, and in 1854 married Clarence Trelawny, who though a commoner frequented the house of her friend, Lord Normanby. He was a scoundrel, interested only in sport. So respectability evaded her. She died in 1865, at the age of forty-two. But she had given the children in her care a respectable education. Her own son and the Emperor's two bastards, learning on reaching their majority that they *were* bastards, were so deeply shocked in their moral sense that they cut her at once and blamed her for their condition ever after. So her later years had been somewhat lonely.

This, however, was in the future. For the present, Louis Napoléon took her everywhere, and was to do so for six years (until he married Eugénie). When people complained, for the concrete cant of the Victorian age was setting fast, he replied, "I detest this pedantic rigor." As indeed he did. "I think I may be forgiven an affection which injures no one, and which I do not parade." But he was not forgiven it, particularly not by his Empress, a thing he could not comprehend, for as he once said indignantly about Eugénie to the Princess Mathilde, "I was faithful to her for six months."

During 1848 France was inundated by Napoleonic propaganda. When the first elections for a Constituent Assembly were held on April 23, Louis Napoléon allowed three of his cousins to be nominated, Pierre Bonaparte, the son of Lucien, Napoléon Bonaparte (Plon Plon), and Lucien Murat. All three were elected. He himself held his hand, and waited for the government to hang itself. He did not have to wait long.

The regime was semisocialist, the economy was centralized in a few hands, and the most pressing problem was the large unemployed and in many ways unemployable proletariat. The government's solution was the setting up of the National Workshops. These were the pet notion of Louis Blanc, the liberal historian, a brilliant but arrested man—"with his smooth face, his clear piping voice and childlike appearance, [he] was so small that when he was over twenty people thought he was barely twelve or thirteen." He was totally innocent of any knowledge of the intricacy of economics, and oblivious to man's preference for being paid first and working later.

The National Workshops were a national disaster. The foremen did not dare to discipline the workers, and the workers had no desire to maintain production. A series of strikes brought all industry in Paris (and anywhere else the National Workshops were set up) to an expensive, bankrupt standstill. The socialist Deputies defied the government to close the shops, since the workers were now masters of the city.

By May Louis Napoléon judged it opportune to stand for election. The government, which now feared him, said it would enforce the law of exile if he was elected. The Prince was returned by the departments of the Seine, Yonne, and Charente-Inférieure. He prudently lurked in London, and resigned his seat, the better to prove that he was not attempting what he was busy at.

He thus missed the violence of the Red Revolt of June 1848, which broke out when the National Workshops were closed and the socialists took up arms. The insurrection was put down by Cavaignac, a military man, who then ruled as a military dictator. His rule did not last long.

For once, Louis Napoléon had a member of the family on his side. This was Mathilde, Princess Demidoff, separated from her husband, estranged from her father and her brother, and living in Paris on an allowance of 200,000 francs a year. She was an ambitious woman, had not forgotten that her cousin was a bachelor even if she was married, and supported his rise both with her influence and with her money.

By now it was possible for Louis Napoléon to pose successfully as the Savior Across the Water. In September he allowed his name to be put forward at supplementary elections in five departments. All five elected him. Mathilde poured in more money than ever. He crossed to Paris on the 26th of September, and took rooms at the Hôtel du Rhin, which had an excellent unimpeded view of the Vendôme column. He was now in truth Prince de la Colonne.

He took his seat, but was an ineffective orator. Some thought this ineptness a deliberate attempt to prove to the government it need not fear him. In particular he took no part in the drafting of a new constitution. It was ready by November 12, and stipulated that the President should be elected by universal suffrage, the vote to be taken December 10.

The result was a well-organized landslide, so well engineered that its results startled even him. Universal suffrage was a comparative term, as it must always be in politics. Out of a population of between

32,000,000 and 35,000,000, 6,982,822 voted for the two principal candidates. Louis Napoléon received 5,534,520 votes and his only significant opponent, the dictator Cavaignac, 1,448,302. He was now Prince President.

It had been predicted that the French *rentes* would fall if Louis Napoléon was elected. Instead, they rose. The English decided that he was, after all, "a man of considerable ability."

On the 19th of December "Citizen Louis Bonaparte" was formally announced to be President from that day until May of 1852. In his oath he said, "I swear to remain faithful to the democratic Republic and to defend the Constitution." He then moved into the Élysées Palace and began, though very privately, to plot the advent of the Second Empire. It had been from the Élysées that Napoléon I had dictated his second abdication.

Louis Napoléon, who had no desire ever to abdicate, went about making himself permanent with secrecy and caution. It took him over two years to succeed, and his plan was concocted in two stages, the first to lengthen his term of office.

He had first to placate his relatives. Mathilde was, at first, no problem. But Jérôme and Plon Plon were tireless against him. It was easy enough to remove Plon Plon, for the time being, as Ambassador to Madrid (at Bordeaux on the way he gave a public speech designed to undermine his cousin). Plon Plon made a public disgrace of both himself and France as an Ambassador, but at least for the moment he was out of the way.

That left Jérôme, who was meddlesome, sixty-five, and had already squandered the fortune of his third wife. He was made Governor of Les Invalides, with a suite of rooms there and an income of 45,000 francs. Louis Napoléon also provided a donative of 12,000 francs for immediate expenses. By way of gratitude, Jérôme kept in touch with the opposition leaders, and bade his son do the same.

Plon Plon, unable to undermine the French government, applied himself to undermining the Spanish. "He is a braggart and a coward, quarrelsome and dissolute, the embodiment of every evil quality. His father was a mischievous rascal, but he is even worse," said Vieil-Castel, the diarist. Queen Isabella demanded his recall. When the matter was put to Louis Napoléon, he made no difficulties. "I see what you are driving at. I know my cousin well. He is a monster." Plon Plon was recalled.

What Jérôme wished to do was to keep his position as Governor of Les Invalides, even if it meant turning out the nephew who had given it to him. So while he pretended to support the Prince President, Plon Plon was diverted to the filial and more congenial task of making friends with the opposition.

Mathilde acted as the Prince President's hostess, since he was not married. She moved herself and her lover, the Dutch sculptor Nieuwerkerke, a former page to Charles X, into the Élysées palace. This position, for so long as it lasted, adequately satisfied her considerable vanity. She was not to join the opposition until Louis Napoléon married Eugénie and so displaced her. Mathilde always referred to the Empress as *Elle*, sometimes in her presence. But for the time being she was cooperative enough.

XXX

W HEN France has a cold," said Metternich, at the time of the Revolution of 1830, "all Europe sneezes."

"My name," said Louis Napoléon, "is a complete program in itself."

These two quotations succinctly sum up the events of 1849 to 1852. The National Assembly was divisive and hard to control, but the constitution was so framed, by some liberal oversight, that the Prince President could, with some juggling, act as his own Prime Minister. This he showed himself willing and, in those days, able to do. Nor could the liberal left reduce him, because he had a clear popular majority.

"The government stands for order, authority, religion, the welfare of the people, and national dignity, particularly in the country districts," said the Prince President, who knew how to threaten the capital with the power of the provinces. For France is so centralized a state as to fear its own provinces as much as other men fear the unknown. The government deputies were therefore caught between the will of the people they claimed to represent, the Prince President who clearly represented them, and the well-to-do bourgeoisie, who would stomach no more civil disturbances.

"My true friends," said Louis Napoléon, "are in the cottages, not the palaces." This was the truth. To keep it so, he began to make extensive tours of the country districts, and went on making them during 1849, 1850, and 1851. He was applauded everywhere.

The bourgeoisie, who had been alarmed by Proudhon's doctrine that property was theft, or rather by the doctrine's popularity, were on the side of dictated order. The people were also on the side of dictated order. The stumbling block was the Constitution: the Presi-

dent could not succeed himself. When the Chamber refused to amend
the Constitution so he might stand a second time, Louis Napoléon
began to turn elsewhere, and he was not without allies, for after so
many revolutions there were those who felt that their only safety lay
in an intelligent well-informed absolutism.

A majority of the voting population was of the same opinion.
When Louis Napoléon toured the provinces, he was often greeted
with *"Vive L'Empéreur."* The Chamber refused to vote money to
pay for these tours. Louis Napoléon got it elsewhere. In 1850 the
Assembly countered by suspending universal suffrage, thus depriving him of some 3,000,000 working-class votes. The only effect of
this was to give the Prince President the support of the newly disen-
franchised.

In effect, neither the Assembly nor the President meant to wait for
or abide by the coming elections of 1852. Thiers said of the President, in November of 1851, "within a month we shall have him
locked up in Vincennes." "Take care he does not put you there,"
said his auditor. "The army is with us," said one of the republican
leaders. This turned out not to be true. Though Changarnier, who
commanded the army at Paris, was an Orléanist republican, his
troops were not.

It was time for a *coup d'état*. Louis Napoléon hesitated. He was
timid for a dictator, and shrank from bloodshed. He also had the
would-be dictator's overdeveloped sense of the judgment of history. The situation was saved by his half brother, the Comte de
Morny, who was made Duke for his pains. Morny was not squeamish. It was his idea to wait until all the Deputies were in Paris and
then to arrest them. "In troublous times to arrest a party man is to do
him a service. You cover his responsibility to his own party and you
keep him out of personal danger."

The coup was planned for December 2, 1851, the anniversary of
the battle of Austerlitz. It was a well-kept secret. Everyone felt that
something was about to happen, but nobody knew what. The undisturbed routine at the Élysées did much to lull suspicion. Everyone
played his role extremely well. Louis Napoléon gave a dinner party
the evening of the 1st, and before that, a long interview to the Hon.
Mrs. Norton, a tireless English scribbler, novelist, and perambulating
gossip column whom he had known in London. This was to disarm
British opinion. The dinner party seemed notably relaxed. Morny
left early and dropped in at the Opera. "It is said they are going to

sweep out the Assembly. What will you be doing?" he was asked. "I shall try to be on the same side as the broom," he answered.

After the dinner there was a reception. The Prince President was affable to everyone. Occasionally he excused himself to smoke a cigarette, thereby being able to consult with his secretary, who was preparing the orders for the *coup d'état* in an inner room.

The guests left shortly after ten. A council was at once convened in the President's study, at the table at which Lucien had written out the first Emperor's second abdication. It had a top inlaid with a Roman mosaic. The chief conspirators were Persigny, the publicist, Maupas, Prefect of Police, General St. Arnaud, Minister of War, and the Comte de Morny.

At eleven the President shook hands all around and went to bed. Morny went to the Jockey Club. Persigny sat up waiting, in case there should be a hitch, and Maupas and St. Arnaud marshaled the police and the army.

The Imprimérie Nationale was surrounded by police while proclamations were printed up. No one was allowed to enter or leave the building until they were ready for distribution. Shortly before dawn, fifty parties of police went through the city and arrested the leaders of the Assembly and Generals Changarnier, Lamoricière and Le Flo. Thiers, Crémieux, and about sixty other politicians, legitimists, Orléanists, moderate republicans, and socialists were taken at the same time. The publication of newspapers was halted, clubs and cafés were closed at dawn, and so that there should be no shortage of food and no disturbance among the workers there, the market carts at Les Halles were swiftly unloaded and dispersed. When the sun rose, the proclamations had already been posted. The police side of the *coup* had gone off smoothly.

St. Arnaud took care of the army. The Assembly was surrounded, and all railway stations, telegraph offices, open spaces, points of vantage, and ministerial offices occupied or guarded. The proclamations said Louis Napoléon appealed to a national plebiscite to elect him for ten years and to grant him total ministerial responsibility.

At seven-fifteen in the morning Morny entered the bedroom of the Minister of the Interior. "You are dismissed and I am your successor," he said.

"Auguste [de Morny] has been heroic," wrote Flahaut, his father, to his wife.

At seven Persigny, who had been out in the streets, came back to the Élysées to report that all seemed to be well. He had arranged that the Prince President should show himself to the public later in the day, surrounded by his staff. Messengers were sent through the city to summon his supporters. At eight they began to arrive.

Princess Mathilde of course lived at the Palace. She was much gratified. At Les Invalides they took the news less well. Jérôme had a conference with Plon Plon. They decided to do exactly what they had done before. The ex-King of Westphalia would put on his general's uniform and go to the Élysées. Plon Plon would strengthen his ties with the radical opposition. That way, one or the other, or perhaps the both of them, would survive.

Jérôme was depressed. At nine a cavalcade left the Élysées, the President (also in a general's uniform) first, then Jérôme, then General Exelmans, a Napoleonic leftover. They received an ovation (artillery had been drawn up around the Place de la Concorde, in case they should not receive one).

Nevertheless, 300 deputies met to declare Louis Napoléon an outlaw. "We have right on our side," said the President of the Assembly, "but then we are the weaker party." 200 of the Deputies were arrested. The High Court of Justice, which had met to proclaim the same thing, was dispersed by the Municipal Guard. The theaters remained open. So did the shops. Life went on much as usual. The Russian and English Ambassadors paid courtesy calls at the Élysées.

The Republican Committee of Resistance formed itself and scheduled risings for Wednesday the 3d. It was their hope that troops would refuse to fire on working men and that the provinces would rise. Neither happened. The army surrounded the insurgents with a *cordon sanitaire* and moved in on them on the 4th. Disturbances in the provinces took the form of sacking churches, attacking priests, and stoning landed proprietors, all of which merely made Louis Napoléon all the more acceptable to the middle classes. As the troops moved in on the insurgents at the capital, the Minister of War announced that those taken with arms in their hands would be shot without trial. Most threw down their weapons.

By the evening of the 5th it was all over. Official casualties were stated to be 215, much less than in 1848. 26,000 people had been arrested, most of them Republicans. They were tried by special courts, as rapidly as possible. 200 were exiled to Africa or Cayenne (Devil's Island). The sufferings of the others were not severe.

The plebiscite was held on December 20. It authorized the Presidential ten-year term by 7,439,216 votes to about 650. Though contrived, there was no evidence that the vote was in any way rigged.

"I left the limits of legality," said the Prince President, "in order to reestablish lawful right." He was greatly reassured. "When France is satisfied, the world is at ease."

"Will the Emperor keep the peace or start a war?" asked the German historian and politician Ranke, a year later. "I don't believe that a static government will in the long run satisfy restless France, but Europe will not tolerate French aggression."

For the moment he did neither.

He had made only one mistake. He ordered the Orléans family to sell off its landed property, which amounted to confiscation, and nullified Louis Philippe's donation of personal property to his sons. Though the money went to charity, four Ministers resigned in protest, one of them Morny, and Princess Mathilde was equally upset.

Jérôme was made President of the freshly nominated Senate, with the Luxembourg as his official residence, which added to his sizable income. He was not grateful.

It took Louis Napoléon a year to reestablish the Empire. During a progress through France he allowed himself to announce that he would yield "to the wish of France." A new plebiscite was held, and the result was never in doubt. Almost 8,000,000 voters approved the measure. Only 250 opposed it. On December 2, 1852 (Louis Napoléon had a passion for anniversaries and precedents, and went to St. Cloud, where the first Emperor had awaited a like gratification), the Prince President heard himself proclaimed "Napoléon III, Emperor of the French."

His first step was to move into the Tuileries, where he had been born. Almost as rapidly as she followed him there, Princess Mathilde, to her undying chagrin, had to move out, for his second step was to marry Mlle Eugénie de Montijo, whom he had met at Mathilde's in 1850. He married her for two reasons. No royal house in Europe would have him. And she had held out for marriage.

Though merely provincial counts of the second class, the Montijos had risen rapidly. Eugénie's grandfather, William Kirkpatrick, was a canny Scottish merchant who had assumed American citizenship, which did much to preserve his income, and become United

States Consul at Malaga, which had done nothing to diminish it. Her father had died in 1839, leaving his half-Scottish wife a wealthy woman, with a town house in Madrid, a country estate, and various investments. Mme de Montijo had already contrived to marry her elder daughter off to the Duke of Alba, as high a marriage as any nonroyal Spaniard could look to. Now she took the Emperor in hand.

Eugénie was a beauty, a prig, a religious bigot, a cold and vain woman, a romantic, and given to meddling in politics, which she did not understand. She was highly emotional and talked far too indiscreetly. But by January 15, 1852, she was Empress of France. The family hated her and the French people did not love her very much.

The family would have hated anybody, but for the opinion of France she was herself largely to blame.

"She sparkled, not exactly with intelligence, but with that Andalusian sprightliness which is one of her attractions," said the Austrian Ambassador.

In 1856, after several miscarriages, she finally produced an heir, the Prince Imperial, Lou Lou. Plon Plon pettishly refused to sign the birth certificate, which, as First Prince of the Blood, he was supposed to do. It took five hours to talk him around. "I have been here for twenty-seven hours," said Princess Mathilde, his sister, also in forcible attendance. "Are you going to keep us here longer? What is the point of refusing to sign? You will not prevent the attestation, and your ill humor will harm no one but yourself."

"He has heaps of brains, but he makes detestable use of them," said Eugénie. "But what can we do? We are not living in the Dark Ages, and the time is past when inconvenient cousins can be removed."

In other words, the Bonapartes were acting true to form. Indeed, one of Louis Napoléon's less welcome and more onerous task, as Emperor, was to deal with the various Bonaparte descendants, cousins, nephews, nieces, and byblows who soon enough managed to bring themselves to his attention. A swarm of locusts descended on the Empire, and he took care of them, not as his uncle had done, out of misplaced filial feeling, but because he was lonely and to increase the prestige of his regime.

XXXI

THE chief leech was, as always, Jérôme. The sole surviving member of the elder generation, he was reputed to have the same voice as the first Emperor, and he always wore the insignia of the crown of Westphalia in his buttonhole.

He had been in Paris since 1847, at first in modest quarters in the rue d'Alger, surrounded by some silver, a spurious Titian, an equally spurious Rembrandt, a bust of Napoléon I in bronze, and a table service engraved with the Westphalian arms. "In his manner he showed a little vanity," wrote Victor Hugo. "I would have preferred to see pride."

Sometimes he got mixed up. One day, on a walk through Paris, he turned into the Pavillon de Flore and was actually halfway up the stairs before a guard turned him back. In the old days the Pavillon de Flore had been his home.

By now he had reluctantly bedded most of the Marchesa Bartolini-Badelli's fortune out of her. His place at Les Invalides not only paid a good salary, but had perquisites which included a wing of the building as living quarters, many servants, and fifteen horses. With what Mathilde gave him, his income was large. The terms of her settlement with the Czar and Demidoff were that she should give him 40,000 francs a year until such time as he "attained to a position from which he could not be removed." In addition to the 40,000 francs from Mathilde, he had 45,000 francs as governor, 3,000 as a member of the Légion d'Honneur, and 12,000 as general of a division. It was not enough.

Plon Plon was now old enough to terrorize his father, whom he bullied endlessly. "I remember with what childish joy," wrote Baron du Casse, "[he acted] when his son could not come to dinner at Les

Invalides." Jérôme would then borrow money from his aides and send out for a reservation at a good restaurant and a box at the theater. He always allowed Petit, the commandant at Les Invalides, to cheat him at cards, because Petit was not well-to-do and had few other sources of additional income. This always made Plon Plon furious.

Jérôme's method of getting things out of Napoléon III was to shout at him. "You have nothing of a Bonaparte about you," he shrieked one day, referring to the ex-King of Holland's doubts about his third son's paternity.

"I have his family," said Napoléon III.

Jérôme demanded to be made Marshal of France (the rank carried a stipend of 30,000 francs a year). He got what he wished, but was outmaneuvered by his daughter Mathilde. Since one can be removed from the position of Marshal only by death, this was the permanent position stipulated in her separation settlement, so she promptly cut off his allowance of 40,000 francs. Since this meant that his net loss was 10,000 francs a year, he never forgave her, and at once ordered that any officer under his command who set foot in her house would lose his commission. While he was at it, and still angry, he denounced the Emperor for having granted the request which had resulted in the 10,000-franc loss of income.

By way of reply, the Emperor gave him the Palais Royal to live in and made him President of the Senate, an office he was too indifferent to politics to bother with.

It was not easy either to support or to put up with Jérôme. He had acquired his last mistress, a woman always referred to as Baronne de P . . . y, who completely dominated him. As usual, with Jérôme, her husband had to be somewhere in the offing. Both Plon Plon and Mathilde objected strongly to the Baronne de P . . . y. Seeing Jérôme and the woman at the Opera one night, Mathilde opened her fan.

"You feel warm, Princess?"

"No, but I do not like to see the old when they have just got out of bed."

Plon Plon had no such sensibilities, but was enraged at the amount of money Jérôme spent on the woman. Jérôme, who was sixty-eight to seventy-six during the liaison, now had to pay for his pleasures, instead of being paid for them. The only thing that reconciled Plon

Plon to the Baronne was the fear that the Marchesa Bartolini-Badelli, Jérôme's third wife, might have a child and so diminish the family inheritance.

He and the Baronne therefore put their heads together and denounced the Marchesa as being the lover of Jérôme David (himself the illegitimate son of Jérôme, though nominally the son of the painter David), who was often about the Palais Royal. This could not be proved, but was enough to drive the Marchesa back to Italy. She was not sorry to go. Jérôme had drained her dry. After Jérôme's death, the Emperor granted her a pension of 12,000 francs a year, from his personal funds.

People began to say, when Jérôme appeared on the street to ogle the girls, that he looked like an anachronistic gambler. And so he was. He was a machine to spend money. He had no other use.

In 1858 he had a fit of apoplexy. During his illness, Plon Plon and the Baronne de P . . . y had shouting matches across his bed, as to which should take care of him. Mathilde also sometimes looked in. Partially paralyzed, Jérôme could only lie there and follow the debate.

His deathbed was not edifying. He had a stroke while gambling with his aide, and died in 1860, at his country house at Villegenis, in Seine-et-Oise, on June 24. While he was dying, Plon Plon counted the silver, and after he was dead, Plon Plon refused to go to the state funeral. He said he could not conscientiously attend a *religious* ceremony. The Emperor decreed a state funeral. While it was going on, Plon Plon turned the Baronne out of the Palais Royal. The will turned out to be inconvenient for everyone. Mathilde was in it asked to deduct the (fictitious) 250,000 francs dowry she had received when she married Demidoff from her part of the estate. The battle between Plon Plon and Mathilde about this had to be settled by the Emperor, before it could come to court and shame them all. Mrs. Patterson Bonaparte emerged to bring suit for her legal share of the estate, for she was nowhere mentioned in the will. Needless to say, she lost.

The Emperor attempted to placate them all, supplementing Jérôme's pension to Mme Bartolini-Badelli, arranging for Betsy's grandson, Jérôme Bonaparte, Jr., to receive 30,000 francs a year, Plon Plon 1,000,000, and Mathilde 500,000.

• •

301

If Jérôme had been difficult to cope with, Plon Plon was much worse. A neglected child, he had grown up shifty and arrogant. He was incapable of cooperating with anyone and he had a loose tongue. He detested discipline and was surly with visitors. When he refused to take off his hat, Mathilde removed it for him. This was their way of greeting people, in youth.

"Look," said Jérôme one day, in Italy, "There is the Empress Marie Louise." They were driving through Parma.

"It is not the Empress. It is only Mme Neipperg," said the young Plon Plon. It was a touch he carried over into mature life.

Louis Napoléon had tried to tutor him in mathematics and Latin, at Arenenberg, when they were young. Hortense had left him 20,000 francs in her will. "You are the only member of my family whom I love as a brother," wrote Louis from Ham. But later matters changed. "At one moment [he] seems to sympathize with all that is great and generous; at another, he is empty, arid, and deceitful."

His conduct as Ambassador to Madrid has already been referred to. After the *coup d'état*, he said to Victor Hugo, "Louis is a disgrace to the family, if indeed he belongs to it, the dirty bastard." Then he tried to patch things up. "My dear Louis, all my feelings of brotherly friendship revive as keenly as ever." So he was made a Senator, and given a seat on the Council of State and a residence in the Palais Royal. After serving on the committee for the Great Exhibition of 1855, he was elected a member of the Académie des Beaux Arts. He wrote a book called *Napoléon et ses détracteurs,* in which he nowhere mentions himself. But then, it was about the earlier Napoléon.

He served as a general during the Crimean War, but not for long. This did not prevent his taking part in the victory celebrations in Paris afterward. "If he should ever come to the throne, which God forbid, France will be in for a bad time," wrote Vieil-Castel. It was necessary to remove him again. So he was sent on a mission to Berlin, and, in 1858, appointed Minister for Algeria and the Colonies. He was not sent to Algeria. He would probably have raised a revolt. It was better to have him in Paris, where an eye could be kept on his movements.

After his unfortunate verbal explosions, it was his habit to retire to Prangins, which he had inherited, to sulk. In 1861 the journal *Opinion Nationale* published a little sketch of him. "This is the man who

solicited the honor of leading the French to . . . the assault at Sevastopol, and returned to Paris shrugging his shoulders because of
the delays of a siege which seemed to him to be stupid. . . . This is
the man who, with vigorous arm, undertook the government of Algeria, and threw it up in disgust because he had not sufficient freedom of action. . . ." The *Opinion Nationale* was owned by the
Prince, but it is impossible not to suspect some irony.

At the same time that the Second Empire ran its course, the House
of Savoy was planning to take over a unified Italy. Napoléon III
intervened, and was given Savoy and Nice as his reward. Plon Plon
was married off to Princess Clotilde of Savoy, a child of sixteen. It
was likened at the time to the mating of an elephant and a gazelle.
Everyone felt sorry for her and she was received with sympathy.
She was big-lipped and clumsy, but her piety was reinforced by
gentle charm. Her first act on reaching the Palais Royal (her future
residence) was to fumigate her quarters with imported holy water.
Plon Plon complained that she wished to be beatified, and went back
to his mistresses, of whom he had a good many.

Plon Plon and his wife and sometimes Cora Pearl, the courtesan,
continued to live at the Palais Royal, where he received visitors in a
room decorated with Venus rising from the waves and a portrait of
Rachel a former mistress. His bedroom was hung with yellow silk
(as someone pointed out, the color of jealousy), Princess Clotilde's
with blue.

Plon Plon also had a Pompeiian house in the Champs Élysées, dedicated to Napoléon I, where he entertained prostitutes among the
family portraits. He never went to the Tuileries unless forced to, and
liked to make inflammatory speeches against the Emperor. At family
dinner parties, he pointedly refused to toast the Empress.

Napoléon III said one day, "You consort with all the enemies of
my government." Plon Plon replied that he never dropped his old
friends.

In 1869, Plon Plon wrote of the Emperor, "The old man is failing
rapidly, he is more weary than people realize. There is no controlling
hand. The Empress is a fool, incapable of government except among
dressmakers, and yet she aspires to reign. She awaits with impatience
the death of the Emperor, in order to become Regent. If he dies
there will be a revolution, and then my hour will come."

But his hour never came. He was too universally detested. After the fall of the Empire, he removed to Rome, where Victor Emmanuel made him Count of Moncalieri. He managed to get himself elected President of the Conseil General of Corsica, but his colleagues loathed him so much that they refused to attend any meeting at which he presided. So that was the end of his political career. In 1884 both his elder son and the Bonapartist party renounced him. He died in 1891, at the age of sixty-nine.

Though he had offered to join Napoléon III in exile, the offer was firmly refused. Plon Plon had two sons, Prince Victor Napoléon, from whom all male Bonapartes now living are descended, and Prince Louis Napoléon Bonaparte, a career officer in the Russian army.

Though no more endearing, for she was a highhanded woman, Princess Mathilde (1820-1904) was a less unsympathetic person than her brother. But the Emperor's marriage, since it displaced her at court, soured her disposition.

To the 200,000 francs Demidoff was forced to allow her, Napoléon III added an equal sum. She could live well, therefore, mostly with Nieuwerkerke, her lover, a sculptor of pedestrian talent. He gave her painting lessons. She, among other things, gave him quarters at the Louvre. The liaison continued until the Empire fell, and then, since it ceased to have advantages, Nieuwerkerke deserted her.

Her detestation of the Empress led her to avoid court. Like Elisa before her, since nothing else was available, and nobody wanted them, she quietly annexed the arts. She was *Notre Dame des Arts*, Marguerite of Navarre reborn as a Bonaparte, wrote the brothers Goncourt. She had both more dignity and more ability than Elisa. Only Victor Hugo and George Sand stayed away from her salon. One of her eccentricities was that nobody was ever announced at her house, on the proud theory that they were so well known as not to need it. And, indeed, she had both the Dumas, Sainte-Beuve, Gautier, Merimée, Flaubert, Labiche, the Goncourts, the director of the Comédie Française, Taine, Renan, Messonnier, Gavarni, Carpeaux, Viollet-le-Duc, Ingres, Gounod, Vernet, Auguste de Morny, and Nieuwerkerke to play with. Gautier, among other duties, was her librarian.

For a while, Sainte-Beuve was the odd flower of this bouquet. She had him made a Senator. But when he committed the imprudence of publishing articles in *Le Temps*, an opposition journal, she got into her carriage, marched into his house, shook her muff at him, and dismissed him. For Mathilde was an ardent Bonapartist, and refused admittance to anyone who criticized the first Emperor or the family.

Vieil-Castel, that androgynous spider from the Louvre, took an unkind view of her. Of course, such was his view of almost everyone. "All is to be forgotten except that great man whose acts are beyond dispute and in whose record it is treason to find a blot [Vieil-Castel lived only to find blots]. . . . She pretends to be liberal in her views . . . but she detests anyone who does not agree with her. She pretends to have some knowledge of pictures and of art generally, but she has not. . . . Her major-domo gives her guests most detestable dinners and poisons us with nasty wines." Curiously, he credited her with charm.

Princess Mathilde remained unruffled. "His little guillotine is always kept greased for action," she said, and had him sacked from his post at the Louvre (Nieuwerkerke was his immediate superior).

When the Empire fell, she remained unaffected, if not unmoved. "Is it fair that I should suffer so much? I have never been ambitious and only wanted to be loved for myself," she said. She had to promise not to meddle in politics, but was allowed to remain in Paris.

On the fall of the Empire Nieuwerkerke fled to Italy, without saying goodbye. His sinecure was gone. Demidoff died the same year. Instead of remarrying, she took another lover, this time a minor poet, Popelin. He did not love her either. She was sometimes depressed, but always gallant. She began to encourage the young, among them Maupassant, Coppée, Bourget, Anatole France, and even, in passing, Proust, who put her in *À la Recherche du temps perdu*, by way of reward. On the other hand, she cut Taine and Sardou, for criticizing the first Emperor. To criticize the second was, however, permissible.

She lived much too long, and felt it. In old age she got fat and developed dewlaps, and lived in a cavernous clutter of chinoiserie and Empire furniture, assisted by four dogs, Phil, Tom, Miss, and Lolotte, in going her wistful, arrogant, sequestered way. On her death, her considerable estate went to her nephew Louis, the one who had become a Russian general and distinguished himself in the Russo-Japanese War. Forced to flee by the Russian Revolution, he settled at Prangins, where he died in 1932.

Her husband, Demidoff, consoled himself with the acquisition of more Napoleoniana, on which he squandered his fortune. In 1851 he went to Elba and bought the villa of San Martino. He then traced down as much as he could of the dispersed Empire furnishings, and did not care what he had to pay. Sometimes, for a fee, Jérôme helped him to find this and that. After 1860 he stepped up the rate of his purchases, and excavating the hill in front of the villa, built in the hole a Napoleonic museum more grandiose than anything Napoléon had been able to construct on Elba, with a portico in the Tuscan order, architraves and metopes filled with Imperial N's and bees, marble floors, and not much in it. Demidoff spent so much on the building that when he died in 1870, his nephew, who was his heir, sold off the collections in order to have something to inherit. The sales took place at Florence in 1880, and brought in much less than the objects had cost. The villa was also sold. It became a municipal museum, however, and it was possible to buy back some of the dispersed Demidoff collections between 1900 and 1914.

Demidoff's ultimate gift to Elba was a copy, in shiny black, of Napoléon's coffin. The lid is removable, and a replica of the Emperor's death mask and hands in bronze lies on shelves inside. He also gave money for a yearly mass to be said for the Emperor on the day of his death, May 5.

It was the opinion of the day that the most accomplished of the Napoleonids, not excepting the Emperor, was Hortense's illegitimate son, Napoléon III's half brother, the Comte (his own idea) later the Duc (Napoléon III's creation) de Morny. "He had it in him, if he had been honest, to be a very great man," said the British Ambassador. But he was not honest. He was underhanded and shrewd.

Napoléon III was jealous of his abilities, and so never made proper use of him. On the other hand, neither did he interfere with Morny's incessant and shady speculative enterprises, though he complained that his corruption would disgrace the reign. The corruption came in only two forms, womanizing and finance. In appearance Morny resembled an affronted egg of excellent family.

Born in 1814, he first met his mother in 1829, and by 1831, according to his grandmother, a woman with high standards in the matter, was already profligate. He was accomplished at making the right friends in the worlds of business and diplomacy. His first mistress of any standing, the Comtesse Le Hon, wife of the Belgian Ambassador and daughter of a wealthy banker, conspicuously helped. She financed his investments in sugar. He lived next door to her, in a small house known as the Niche de Fidèle.

When Louis Napoléon became Prince President, he cultivated an acquaintance he had scarcely made before, and though neither man liked the other, they worked well together and saw each other at least once a day. Auguste de Morny took a guiding hand. "The Prince has scruples, but there will soon be great events," he said. He engineered the coup, drove the Prince President to attempt it when his nerve failed, and then resigned from office when the House of Orléans had its property confiscated. Morny was not without his allegiances and loyalties, and the Orléans family had been good to him in the past. There was a distinct cooling off between the two half brothers.

"It will become a government of nonentities," said Morny, and withdrew. He was not far wrong. Though later he became President of the Chamber, his political career was over.

Morny was known as the Comte Hortensia and made no bones about introducing the Comte de Flahaut publicly as his father. This in turn made the Emperor edgy.

Morny had extensive investments in Mexico and so was not without some guilt in urging the Maximilian fiasco on the government. To be exact, he had been promised a profit of twenty percent on a capital of 75,000,000 francs, advanced in the form of a loan by the financier Jecker to the government France was bent upon setting up in Mexico.

Sent on a mission to Russia, Morny married a maid of honor to the Czarina, Sophie Troubetzkoy. The dowry was 500,000 francs, and besides, he wanted to be settled. "Marriage seems to me a paradise compared to the life I lead; no hearth, no child. It is horrible."

Mme Le Hon, to whom he had broken the news of his marriage somewhat brutally, threatened to sue publicly for the money she had advanced him. She had said this amounted to 6,000,000 francs. She accepted 3,500,000 out of the Privy Purse (which was not large; the Emperor was not greedy and had accepted 25,000,000 francs annually only on Persigny's advice, having been willing to settle for a smaller sum).

"Such ingratitude," said Mme Le Hon about this hushed-up scandal. "I found him a sublieutenant, and left him an Ambassador."

Morny's wife frequently did not bother to come down to dinner in her own house, despised politicians, and devoted herself to her children, of which there were four. Morny took up with opera singers. But the couple got on well.

Morny launched Sarah Bernhardt, and, as M. de Saint-Rémy, wrote little comedies for the theater. *Monsieur Confleury restera chèz lui* is still sometimes performed. *Les Bons Conseils* is another. It can at least be said that they are thoroughly professional, unlike the earlier Bonaparte efforts in the theater. Halévy, a protégé and friend, helped him to touch them up. Offenbach sometimes wrote the music. Daudet was one of his secretaries. Morny knew all the best second-raters of his day. On the other hand, he was one of the first to collect the Impressionists. And he practically founded the casino at Deauville.

He tried from time to time to get the Emperor to grant more freedom to the opposition, on the grounds that if it was not granted it would be taken. His was prudent advice, but not heeded in time. He died in 1865, at the age of fifty-eight, of natural causes, though it had been his habit for years to perk himself up with doses of arsenic. After his death, there was no one left to advise the Emperor half so well.

Of Napoléon I's illegitimate children, Léon Denuelle and Comte Walewski, the only one to play any part in the government was Comte Walewski, a stolid, reliable, chivalrous, but not particularly competent man. He was old enough to remember his mother's farewell to the Emperor at Malmaison in 1815. On the death of her husband, who had recognized Alexandre as his own child, Marie Walewska had married General d'Ornano. When she died in 1817 Alexandre had been sent back to Poland to be educated. He had afterward rejoined his stepfather in Paris. Everybody knew who he was and nobody had anything against him. While serving under Talleyrand in the London Embassy, he had married a daughter of the Earl of Sandwich. This gave him his leg up in the world.

Napoléon I, in his will, had specified that Alexandre was to join the army. Not being able to join the French army, he had enrolled in the Foreign Legion instead, but not caring for it, had resigned and become a French subject. He bought a newspaper, which failed, and wrote a comedy, called *L'École du monde*, which was only a moderate success. But he had attracted the attention of the politician Thiers, and it was Thiers who had made a diplomat of him.

His English wife died, and he too, for a while, became the lover of Rachel. The liaison ended in 1846. Next he married a Poniatowska, who turned out to be an excellent diplomatic wife. When the Monarchy fell in 1848, he volunteered to serve as Minister to Tuscany. He played no part in Bonapartist politics, and was at first overlooked. Later Napoléon III had him transferred as Ambassador to Naples and made him a Commander of the Légion d'Honneur. He was then sent to London, where his instructions were, as much as possible, to reproduce Paris at his embassy, in order to give the British "a center of perfect taste, elegance, and *bon ton*, so that all your guests should repeat the flattering yet truthful phrase: Everyone has two countries, his own and France." In fact, it was Napoléon III who began this artful piece of propaganda, which is with us yet.

The London Embassy was a success. When the Emperor and Empress paid a state visit to Windsor and the Queen and Prince Consort went to Paris, Walewski superintended both visits. The latter visit produced the celebrated anecdote about the chairs, to the effect that whereas Queen Victoria never looked behind her when she sat down, because she knew the chair would be there, the Emperor and Empress always instinctively looked first to be sure. Like most cruel little stories of the sort, it had much truth in it.

There were equally cruel stories about Walewski. Vieil-Castel, as always reliable, called him "an old roué without ability." Greville, another grump, said he was "an adventurer, a ready speculator, without honor, conscience or truth, utterly unfit, both by character and capacity, for high office of any kind."

Though Walewski had inherited the Walewski and d'Ornano estates, and Napoléon had deposited a nest egg for him at Naples, the Count was not rich. But if he was an adventurer he was a remarkably conscientious one. He repeatedly tendered his resignation when he disapproved of the Emperor's policies (Napoléon III made him Minister for Foreign Affairs). Napoléon III as repeatedly refused to accept it. "I should like you to reread my *Idées Napoléoniennes*, which I wrote in 1837. My convictions have not changed."

His convictions had not, but the world had. Walewski finally managed to get out from under in 1859. On Morny's death he became President of the Chamber. He was not a successful President, for he did not know how to moderate among the unruly. He resigned in 1867 and died in 1868. Ollivier called him the wisest if not the cleverest of Napoléon III Ministers, Merimée a mediocrity; Vieil-Castel was as malicious as ever; and the Emperor, while saying he was not a statesman, admitted that, on the other hand, France had none.

Comte Walewski left four children by his marriages, and one by the actress Rachel. The latter he adopted, as Antoine Jean Colonna Walewski. Antoine entered the French consular service and did well. The legitimate children were also advantageously distributed.

As for Napoléon I's other illegitimate son, Charles Léon Denuelle de la Plaigne, he turned out much worse. In 1815 the first Emperor had created him a count and settled what amounted to 75,000 francs a year on him, drawn against a tariff on all wood sold by the state from the forests of the Moselle. This pension was swiftly abolished by the Bourbons. Léon's mother married three times; her last husband was the Minister of State for the Grand Duchy of Baden, which made her Countess of Laxburg. Napoléon III gave her a pension, and she did not die until 1868. She caused no one any bother. Léon was harder to deal with. He was a compulsive gambler. At the time of the establishment of the Second Empire he was forty-four and penniless. He also wished to be given the proceeds from the sale of the Moselle woods from the year 1815, plus interest, a sum which amounted to over 800,000 francs. Napoléon III refused to allow this, but paid his debts and cut him in on the profits to be made from the new railway lines (Morny also made a fortune speculating in these). Léon merely squandered the money, and tired of paying his debts at regular intervals, Napoléon III cut him down to an annual pension of 50,000 francs from the Privy Purse. Léon died in 1881, leaving three sons, all nonentities. The family then changed its name to de Léon. Among other virtues, Léon had been a bit of a ponce.

Napoléon III had a half brother on both sides of his family. His father's illegitimate son, François Louis Gaspard de Castelvecchio, was given a position in the Department of Foreign Affairs in 1856, in the Cabinet of the Ministry later in the same year, and afterward named Paymaster of the finances of Nice, then of Rennes, and finally of the Alpes-Maritimes as a whole. On November 7, 1860, he was made Count. But he was not given an allowance from the Privy Purse. He and the Emperor are said to have looked much alike. He died in 1869.

• •

In addition to these, Napoléon III had illegitimates of his own, two by La Belle Sabotière and one, very dubiously, unless she visited him at Ham, by his mistress, Miss Howard. There was also Miss Howard herself to be dealt with.

Miss Howard had been that rare thing, a generous mistress. But she proved expensively difficult to get rid of. It is true she had lent him large sums of money. It is also true that she had a lien against one of his Italian states, Civitanova, for 40,000 pounds. Both loan and lien were repaid. By 1855 she had managed to extract some 218,000 pounds out of him. She wanted more. If she was to be discarded, she meant to make him pay for it. She demanded 50,000 francs a month. Since she had been prudent to keep compromising documents in her possession, she got it.

She went into retirement, but emerged in the winter of 1864 and 1865, in order to display herself in her carriage before the Emperor and Empress as much as possible. She also liked to go to the Opera on state occasions, to focus her opera glasses pointedly on the Imperial box. She was given to ungovernable rages, and her death in 1865 was perhaps a mercy.

Her son, Martin Constantin, was in all probability Martyn's, not the Emperor's, but Napoléon III made him Comte de Bechevet. There was no pension, since he inherited what his mother had already extorted.

About the two sons by La Belle Sabotière there was never any doubt. Alexandre Louis Eugène was born February 25, 1843, Alexandre Louis Ernest in March of the following year. The first was made Count d'Orz, and the second Count de Labenne, though not until 1870.

There was a third child, by Marguerite Bellanger, the one of the Imperial mistresses everybody detested. It was said she was the daughter of Heindereich, the Paris hangman. This was untrue, but shows the esteem in which she was held. In 1864 she claimed to have borne the Emperor Charles Jules, on whom he settled the estate and château of Monchy. Later, Marguerite admitted the child was not his, and that she had perpetrated a hoax.

But the real plague was the Napoleonids. There were so many of them that in 1852 the Civil Family of the Emperor was established. This stipulated that the title Imperial Highness could not be used by the brother, nephews, and nieces of the Emperor, who were only to rank as Prince and Highness. The women, when they married, were to take their husbands' ranks and titles only. This decree was aimed primarily at the almost unbelievable number of children and grandchildren Lucien had managed to generate. In 1870 it was revised, so that Plon Plon and Mathilde might form exceptions to it.

The drain on the public purse was heavy. Among them, the Jérôme Bonapartes managed to extract more than 37,500,000 francs from the Imperial pocket; the five Murats got 500,000, and the Lucien Bonaparte descendants well over the same sum. In 1868, twenty-one of Lucien's descendants and offspring had pensions drawn against the Privy Purse. So had ten of the Murats. Jerome Patterson Bonaparte, Jr. got 30,000 a year, Princess Bacciochi 250,000 francs, and Jérôme's third wife also had her pension.

This, however, was only the beginning. Baron Jérôme David, Jérôme's illegitimate son (and godson), had his annuity, and rose to be Vice-President of the legislative body and Minister of Public Works. There were many more. The Murats came back from America. Prince Lucien was made a Senator, and the Princess was given 20,000 francs a year. Their daughter, Princess Anna, a favorite of the Empress Eugénie's, was married to the Duc de Mouchy, a virtual dwarf, and over the years absorbed some 2,250,000 francs from the Emperor's pocket. Lucien Murat hoped to be made King of Naples, an ambition smashed by Garibaldi. In old age he became gouty, and had to be carried in and out of the Folies Bergères, where he spent his evenings. He died in 1878. Thanks to Napoléon III, his sons all made good marriages. Prince Achille, being dead, was more independent, but his widow, too, was given a pension.

The worst plague was the sons of Lucien, Prince of Canino. He had had five. Charles Lucien, the eldest, who had gone to America, was an ornithologist of some note. His *American Ornithology* appeared in 1825, his *Mammals of Europe* in 1845. He married Joseph's daughter Zenaïde. He was no bother. Paul, though promising, shot himself, either intentionally or by accident, no one knows which, during the Greek Wars of Independence. Antoine, the one who had helped to murder one or two Papal guards, merely fizzled out, and bothered no one. The fourth, Louis Lucien, though made a Senator with emoluments during the Second Empire, spent most of his time in London, and, indeed, in 1884, accepted a civil list pension from the

British government. He was a philologist, specializing in Basque and English dialects, on which subject he published more than 200 books and pamphlets. He had no interest in politics, and died in 1891.

The problem was Pierre. Born in 1815, he grew up to become a stormy, boisterous adventurer. He went out to America to join Joseph, and then on to South America, where he fought under the insurgent Colombian general and would-be dictator Santander. As a soldier of fortune, he was to take part in wars in Albania and Turkey. After 1848, he came back to France and was elected Deputy from Corsica. His mode of conducting a debate was to beat up fellow deputies. Napoléon III found this embarrassing, and shipped him off to the Foreign Legion. He was so insubordinate in Algeria that he had to be cashiered. Returning to France, he was recognized as a Prince and given his 100,000 francs a year. He had some property at Corsica, but it brought in nothing.

In 1853 he contracted a common-law marriage with Justine Ruffin, a girl from the streets by whom he had two children, Prince Roland and a daughter. A civil ceremony was followed (in 1867) by a religious one. Justine was seventeen years younger than he was. After the fall of the Empire, he married her yet again, this time at the French legation in Brussels.

Prince Pierre was known as "the Corsican wild boar." In 1870 he helped to bring the Empire down by shooting a journalist, Victor Noir. Prince Pierre's aim was unfortunately all too accurate. It was difficult to get him off, and the publicity was ruinous.

After the fall of the Empire, Princess Justine kept Pierre and her children going by running a milliner's shop in London. It was quite a successful milliner's shop. But the Bonapartes were proscribed again, and the family cut him dead. A little later they thought better of this decision.

For in 1880, Prince Roland, their son, born in 1858 and intended for a military career, though he preferred scientific research, married Marie Felice Blanc, the daughter of the Baden Baden waiter who had founded the gambling casino at Monte Carlo. Mlle Blanc had a dowry of $5,000,000 and a palace on the Mediterranean. The Bonapartes experienced an overwhelming resurgence of family feeling, and were reconciled with the Prince Pierre branch of the family. In 1882 Princess Marie died four months after giving birth to a daughter, also Princess Marie, who later married Prince George of Greece, in 1907. Again, the dowry was probably large. Princess Marie Bonaparte is the anthropologist whose chief claim to attention is that, some forty years ago, she advanced the theory that people come to funerals because they are glad to have survived.

Another dubious figure of the period was Princess Bacciochi. (She dropped the name Camarata when she separated from her husband in 1830. She does not seem to have missed him. Neither did anyone else.) Elisa's daughter was as businesslike as her mother had been. She went to Paris in 1851, and before the Empire fell, milked it of 6,000,000 francs. In 1853, after a futile appeal to his mother and to Prince Jérôme, her only son committed suicide because he could not pay his debts. He had incurred them on the Bourse, by speculating upon the effects on the money market of the Emperor's marriage. His mistress, Elisa Le Tessier, followed him a few days later by locking herself into an airtight room with a pan of lighted charcoal.

The Princess Bacciochi retired to her estates in Brittany, where, like Faust, she devoted her later years to drainage projects, stomping about the bogs, a gruff and mannish creature. She died in 1869, leaving her property to the Prince Imperial.

In addition to these people, Napoléon III also had to find places for the Beauharnais and Tascher de la Pagerie cousins, which included the descendants of Stéphanie Beauharnais, who had married the Grand Duke of Baden. These had married into the Saxony, Portuguese, Rumanian, Baden, and Hohenzollern-Sigmaringen families, and included the Princes of Hohenzollern-Sigmaringen, and Monaco, and the Counts of Flanders. Count Tascher de la Pagerie was made Grand Master of the Emperor's household, and his son First Chamberlain. They received 40,000 and 30,000 francs a year, respectively. The former was also a Senator of the Empire (15,000 a year more). Since this particular branch of the Tascher de la Pagerie was Bavarian, it promptly put the Imperial Household into Wittelsbach blue livery. There was also a sister of the younger Tascher, Stéphanie. Canoness of an abbey in Bavaria, she held no office in the household, but gave amusing balls.

The American Bonapartes turned up again. By 1853 Bo's Americanism had cooled sufficiently for him to think it would be a good idea to get a military commission for his son from Napoléon III. The

Emperor was not averse. Bo visited Paris in June of 1854, and was given a document making him a French citizen. Jérôme at once objected that he could never consent to Bo's living in France. "I answered him," wrote the Emperor, "that if your residence in Paris was embarrassing, you alone were to be the judge of that. . . . You must, without irritating your father, continue to pursue the way you intended."

In August of 1855 the Emperor proposed to make him Duke of Sartène. The object of this was to induce him to give up the family name and his rights as eldest son. He refused the honor.

In 1856 the King of Württemberg came to Paris. Plon Plon made this an excuse to attack the rights of his half brother and to demand that the Family Council forbid Bo to use the Bonaparte name, "which does not legally belong to him." On July 4, 1856, it was decided that he was entitled to the name, but to nothing else.

Bo did not care for this. "As I was born legitimate, as I have always been recognized as such by my family, by the laws of every country and by the entire world, it would be the height of cowardice and dishonor to accept a brevet of bastardy. . . . If the Family Council has rendered an illegal and unjust decision, at least it has been stopped by the impossibility of depriving a man of the name which he has borne from his birth to the age of fifty years without its ever being contested. Being the victim of calumnies, intrigues, and lies, it only remains for me, Sire, to repeat the desire which I have made known to your Majesty in my letter of the 20th March—to go with my son into exile, and await the justice which I am convinced heaven will render to me sooner or later."

In 1861, the year after Jérôme died, the Pattersons brought suit before the Paris Court of First Instance, to have Elizabeth's marriage declared valid.

Since to do so would have given Bo prior claim to Plon Plon in the succession, the result was never in doubt, but difficult to arrive at. The court finally decided that the Imperial Family Council took precedence over the law. A letter was read in court, in which the ex-King of Westphalia protested the decrees issued by Napoléon III in favor of the Patterson Bonapartes, on the grounds that "they cast a doubt on the legitimacy of my children and prepare for them a scandalous lawsuit. . . . They constitute an attack upon my honor. . . ."—by annulling his second marriage, not to mention his third.

A compromise was arrived at. The Patterson Bonaparte grandson, then thirty-one, who had been given a commission in the French army, had served in the Crimea, and was a welcome and frequent guest at the Tuileries, was allowed to remain in France, to keep the Bonaparte name, and to receive his annual pension from the Emperor's purse of 30,000 francs, but the Patterson marriage was declared legally null and void in France.

It may be seen that even without the Empress, in herself a source of frequent annoyance, the Imperial family was a far from restful one, being far more numerous and just as rapacious, if less gaudy, than it had been under the First Empire.

N APOLÉON III had a mind controlled in everything by the precedent of his uncle. Partly this was a matter of propaganda,
but on a fatal level, it was a matter of compulsion. His year
was thus always cluttered with the observance of anniversaries, and
he attempted to pursue ancestral policies to disastrous results, further
impeded by the fact that he possessed none of his uncle's abilities
either as a commander or as a statesman, and not one jot of his military strength. In addition he seems to have misunderstood the nature
of the Napoleonic period, which was less a reign than an interregnum, during which an anachronistic military state filled the gap between two great world movements, the revolutions in the New and
Old World which overturned the old order, and the rise of the middle class as the rulers and the displaced proletariat as the suborners of
the pragmatic, nationalistic state.

A very small man of no special gifts, except personal charm and a
genius at juggling plebiscites, and with the misfortune to live during
a period when England was an imperial and economic colossus and
German affairs were directed by Bismarck, a political genius of the
first order, he simply sank. The Second Empire, though it began
well, was a glittering if ostentatiously vulgar social success and an
international political disaster. The only wonder is how he managed
to keep it afloat for eighteen years.

His habit of progressing by parallels began with the Empress, who
combined the worst features of Marie Louise and Joséphine, so he
never could tell exactly which of them she represented.

Her reputation was distinctly shabby, though for no good reason,
and her mother, the Dowager Countess de Montijo, was by way of
being an international joke, a bouncy, hearty woman with a loud
voice, frankly bent on selling her daughters to the highest bidder.

Eugénie, who was Countess of Teba in her own right, was the more beautiful of the two sisters, but also the more eccentric. It was the Victorian age, in Spain it always had been, at least for women, and she got herself a shopworn reputation by patronizing bull-fighters and riding bareback and alone through the public streets. It was a groundless reputation, for she was not only proper, she was virtually frigid. She was also as ambitious as her mother, and landed her fish by pleading chastity. "The Imperial Pamela [has] obtained her reward," said the London *Times*, when the marriage was announced. She was twenty-six. Louis Napoléon was a waterlogged forty-five.

It was the universal opinion of her age that she was a great beauty. We must take it on faith. Character survives the portrait painter, but fashionable beauty seldom does. But she had auburn hair, a graceful figure, an alabaster skin, a theatrical manner, and an expression of extreme vivacity.

Plon Plon, a rejected suitor, behaved with his customary spite, and during the ceremony of the Imperial Civil Marriage, held during the evening of January 29, 1853, was the only person present to wear black evening dress rather than a uniform. He was in mourning. The Emperor made him general of a division, so he could never be so again.

The religious ceremony took place at Notre Dame, to the music from Meyerbeer's *Le Prophète*. The Emperor wore a uniform too tight for him, and Eugénie, though otherwise irreproachable, was wearing one of Joséphine's diamond tiaras, which neither fitted nor suited her. "Perhaps there was a shade too much dignity and religious fervor," said Hübner, the Austrian Ambassador, "but these are little mistakes she will correct as she gets used to the footlights." She never did.

She was Spanish, which meant that though she could be frigidly and correctly formal, in privacy she wore shirtwaists, plain skirts, and bullfighter's jackets, and did everything but smoke a cigar. She also fancied herself as a reincarnation of Marie Antoinette. In fact, she was well endowed with the histrionic sense, and went so far as to take lessons in deportment from the tragedian Rachel, the universal Bonaparte mistress, though she did not know that, and even Plon Plon knew better than to say so.

There was never a coronation. Napoléon III thought that one

could not be held without the presence of the Pope, since Napoleon I had had that, and since the Pope refused to come, it could not be held.

Nonetheless, Eugénie had risen to a grandeur considerably greater than the dust and desuetude of Teba. The Imperial Privy Purse consisted of 25,000,000 francs, the same as Louis XVIII, Charles X, and Louis Philippe had had. The dotation of the crown was worth about 5,000,000 francs a year in rents, for it included the Tuileries, the Élysées, the Louvre, the Palais Royal, several private houses in Paris, and, outside the city, Versailles, Trianon, Marly, St. Cloud, Rambouillet, Meudon, St. Germain-en-Laye, Campiègne, Fontainebleau, Pau, and Strasbourg, Villeneuve l'Étang, La Mothe-Beubron, La Grillière, the Sèvres porcelain works, the tapestry factories of Gobelins and Beauvais, the state furniture stored in warehouses on the Île des Cygnes, and the woods of Vincennes, Sénart, Dourdan, and Laigue, all of which were timber-farmed. For a good many years, not inappropriately, the Paris Opera was administered by the Royal Household. It was managed, as were the official theaters, by Count Bacciochi, a relative by marriage of Elisa.

It was a period of pageants and harmless dancers. Count Walewski provided a *Quadrille des patineurs*, with Polish skaters. There was a pageant at the Ministry of the Marine, emblematical of all the countries of the world. Naturally France came first, carrying a tricolor and an olive branch. Europe was portrayed by Jérôme's third wife, the Marchesa Bartolini-Badelli, Mme Rimsky-Korsakov was Asia, attended by crocodiles and houris, Princess Jablonowska, announced by the overture to *L'Africaine*, came as Cleopatra, with a drugged lion cub, and Mme de Montaut was a Sudanese warrior on a dromedary. When "Yankee Doodle" was played, America was revealed in a hammock, surrounded by Peruvian Incas and California miners. At one such entertainment the Emperor's current mistress appeared as a Red Indian, dressed mostly in feathers.

At the Imperial Villa in Biarritz, the doors had to be widened and the rooms enlarged, because it was impossible to get a crinoline in, and at the Tuileries, the couturier Worth supervised the installation of a freight elevator, so the Empress might descend when ready without having to negotiate stairs in her enormous skirts or otherwise ruffle her appearance. It was considered a privilege to be able to share with the Empress her freight elevator.

As for Paris, it had been vastly improved by Baron Hausmann's avenues and alterations. Though the great boulevards were in part constructed to prevent mobs from taking refuge in narrow alleys during insurrections, they made the city handsome, as well they should have done, for by the time they were completed they had cost some 3,750,000,000 francs.

The Emperor, who had hemorrhoids, anemia, and kidney stones and suffered from hyperesthesia, presided over an age of increasingly desperate extravagance. If he had been allowed to arbitrate over his best of all possible worlds, he would have been a good ruler. His only personal vice was a little lechery. As far as public welfare went, he encouraged public works, established or reestablished the Crédits Foncier, Mobilier, and Lyonnais, patronized industry and science, saw to mass housing, built almshouses, and pushed the Cobden Commercial Treaty, which was advantageous to French agriculture (wines) if not to its industry. Sainte-Beuve hailed him as Saint-Simon (the economic philosopher, not the saint) on Horseback. Employment was high (so were prices).

But the motto of the regime, as under Guizot, was *Enrichessez-vous*, and many did. The Comte de Morny, since diplomatic baggage is immune from examination, when he went to Russia took along a large haul of salable jewelry, and when in Paris, juggled railroad stock. Others did even better.

"The country is a vast public and private gambling casino," said his father.

Unfortunately Napoléon III was a man of mediocre ability, internationally outclassed, and though he could be unprincipled, he was never unprincipled enough. Nor did he have at his disposal a body of first-rate administrators, and he tended to interfere with and hamper those he did have.

The Empire had ten good years, and eight very bad ones. Increasingly the Emperor withdrew from public sight, and with it, lost his one effective weapon, his charm and prestige. A lonely man, his isolation was in large measure his own fault. It was not so much that he himself could not bear to be contradicted as that he did not like to have his dreams interrupted.

Once, when they were driving through the Parisian streets, his companion asked him why he did not respond to the cheering.

"Because I know mankind," said Napoléon III.

He worked very hard, but found it difficult to make decisions.

And the work consisted more of reading the newspapers to check publicity, making grandiose schemes, and planning incessant public improvements, than of controlling international politics and domestic economics.

The Empress was not much help. She was overemotional, educated beyond her capacity, misinformed, and heavily under the influence of her Catholic clergy, which did not at all suit her efforts to rule a predominantly anticlerical country. That she was a priest-ridden prude did nothing to improve her relations with the Emperor, who was a randy agnostic. The only person she was really ever fond of was her sister. And she had enormous pretensions.

"I tremble not from fear of assassination, but from ranking in history below Blanche of Castile and Anne of Austria," she wrote to her sister shortly after her marriage. It was an odd assortment of idols. Blanche of Castile was all very well in her day, but Anne of Austria is not one of history's more respected meddlers, and nineteenth-century France had no Richelieu, let alone a Mazarin.

She had no wisdom. Indeed, for a time there was danger the Empire might be ruled by planchette.

"At the moment," wrote Baron Hübner, "she has thrown herself with all her Andalusian ardor into table-turning." He suggested reading and solid instruction as an alternative. His recommendations were not followed.

She had fallen into the hands of Daniel Dunglas Home, otherwise known (it was the poet Browning who called him so; Browning could not stand him) as Mr. Sludge the Medium.

Séances were held at court. The Empress held a bell, the Emperor an accordion. Spirits removed the bell and played "charming airs." The airs on the accordion were less charming. A footstool galloped toward Eugénie from the other end of the room. Invisible hands made their presence felt. "I must see Mr. Home again and then we shall see more," Eugénie wrote her sister. She saw more. Her dead sister appeared to her. "It is reality," she wrote Paca. "And I hope to convince you." Mr. Home's spirit controls began to offer political advice.

Mathilde protested and Comte Walewski threatened to resign unless Home was gotten rid of. In the end, but with some trouble, he was unmasked, imprisoned, and then expelled from France. The Empress was displeased.

"Never did a futile creature bring to inordinate ambition a meaner intelligence," said Maxime du Camp, adding that in his opinion she had never grown up. Disastrously, as Napoléon III grew weaker, she grew stronger. Though she claimed not to be under clerical influence, her judgment in international politics was wholly swayed by her belief in territorial independence for the Pope and in Catholic Supremacy. She insisted upon sitting in on the Emperor's councils, until finally expelled by the pressure of his Ministers. When France wished to intervene in Italy, it was necessary to send her on a trip to Scotland to get her out of the way. This visit to the home of her ancestors, the Kirkpatricks of Closeburn, only had the effect of returning her refreshed and more convinced than ever she was born to rule. It was she who had urged on the Emperor the disastrous attempt to make Maximilian Emperor of a Mexico under French influence. She had wished to compensate the Church for the loss of a large part of the Papal States with a wider sphere of influence elsewhere. Afterward she exonerated herself completely. "I am not ashamed of Mexico. I deplore it but I do not blush for it. I suggested it at Biarritz in 1861, when some conservative and clerical émigrés urged intervention by France, Spain, and Italy, who had nationals there. We were misled about the resistance."

She could not be removed from Councils of State until 1869. By then it was rather late. She was pro-Austrian and violently anti-German. When told the latter were the race of the future, she snapped, "We are not there yet."

Though it is not true that she called the Franco-Prussian war "*ma petite guerre*," she had done much to egg it on.

"She and she alone has been the cause of all France's misfortunes," wrote Princess Mathilde, who hated her. "This woman has ruined the best and most generous of men and with him our poor country." This was untrue. The best and most generous of men had ruined himself. But she had always been there to assist.

The trouble with a dictatorship, from the dictator's point of view, is that he is expected to do something in order to reinforce the national prestige and to keep the people from thinking. Napoléon III did not lack for ideas. He had ideas, said Palmerston, which chased around in his head "like rabbits." But they were not always very sound ideas. He commenced with the Crimean War.

That muddy, mismanaged conflict was a complex matter. Russia wished access to the Mediterranean and had to be contained. Such was the British view. France, having no other allies, and with Austria and Prussia against her, needed a British alliance. Austria, having Balkan territories, favored Russia to contain Turkey. The Emperor, though he sent his fleet, did not want to send his troops, and suggested that Russia's Polish recruits be encouraged to desert instead. Finally he was forced to send 90,000 men.

The war went badly and was unpopular in France. Eugénie and Napoléon III made a state visit to England, where they were very popular, less with the government than with Queen Victoria, who was completely won over. Napoléon III was made a Knight of the Garter, much to the distress of Prince Albert, who did not feel a parvenu should have it.

The visit was returned. Napoléon, who had come to Boulogne to receive the royal party, was very nearly killed when his horse shied and tried to bolt over a precipice. He had gone to much trouble to make a State Visit to France pleasurable, going so far as to have Victoria's favorite pet dog brought over, so she might seem more at home. It was four and a half centuries since a ruling English monarch had appeared in the French capital. A street was named after Queen Victoria. She went to the Exposition of 1855. Jérôme distinguished himself by refusing to conduct her around Napoléon I's tomb at Les Invalides. He said he had no fancy for crocodile tears such as these English royalties would shed. Someone else was found to show her around. She went with Prince Edward. "Kneel before the tomb of the Great Napoleon," said Victoria. Prince Edward knelt. "God Save the Queen" was then played. It made a good impression.

The visit had been a success. Queen Victoria, who compensated for a limited vocabulary by underscoring words one, two, three, or four times, depending upon the intensity of her feelings, described herself as "*delighted, enchanted, amused,* and *interested.*"

She was also *charmed* by Napoléon III, which was *unusual.* It was extremely difficult to charm Queen Victoria with anyone interesting. As a general rule, only her immediate relatives moved her. She returned to London, taking the Prince Consort with her. The Prince Consort found the Bonapartes vulgar. But the Queen never forgot the sedate, but to her quite frothy, enchantments of Paris, and kept the connection up.

Napoléon III had opened Versailles for the occasion, and there had been a ball in the Galérie des Glaces. The gardens were illuminated, and the fountains played in color. A firework setpiece showed Windsor Castle, and the legend God Save the Queen. All told this fête cost 500,000 francs, but it was money well spent. After the King of Prussia was proclaimed German Emperor in the Galérie des Glaces, fifteen years later, Victoria was to take Napoléon III and Eugénie under her personal protection in England.

When Sevastopol fell on the 8th of September, there was a Te Deum at Notre Dame (on the 13th). France remained unenthusiastic. Napoléon would have withdrawn his troops, but the English would not let him. In his turn, the Emperor grew unenthusiastic about the English. In January of 1856 Russia agreed to an armistice, to be followed by a Congress at Paris to arrange a peace treaty (also to adjust in France's favor a few clauses of the treaty made by the Congress of Vienna, forty-one years before). At the end of the congress, and after two previous miscarriages, the Empress Eugénie finally gave birth to a male heir, on Palm Sunday, March 16 (the regime seemed haunted by Sundays—its disasters came then, when the week's work was done). The relief was profound. The child consolidated the reign and made less likely the advent of Plon Plon.

"Louis will be dreadfully ugly; already he has a nose like a man's," said the Empress. She did not like children very much. It was another echo of Marie Louise, to whom she never thought of comparing herself.

Théophile Gautier wrote an ode:

> *C'est un Jésus, à tête blonde,*
> *Qui porte en sa petite main,*
> *Pour globe bleu, la paix du monde,*
> *Et le bonheur du gendre humain.*

The last line was, perhaps, going too far, but it was certainly an auspicious day. A political amnesty was declared, and the Imperial Couple said they would give a gift to every child born in France the same day. Unfortunately this turned out to be in the neighborhood of 3,000, but the gifts were duly provided. The same year, Pope Pius IX sent the Empress Eugénie the year's Golden Rose, on a lapis lazuli base. It was given for eminence and purity, and she was much pleased, until she learned that the year before it had gone to Isabella II of Spain, a woman not noted for her morality.

Napoléon III turned his attention to civil affairs, at which he was better than at politics. The railway lines rose from 3,600 kilometers at the opening of the reign to almost 30,000 by the end of it. The per capita wealth doubled. Imports and exports quadrupled. But he was not equal to his own ambitions.

The Second Empire was a house of cards, but the game was poker, and the stakes were power. Napoléon III, though everyone complained that it was impossible ever to tell what he was thinking, was not a good poker player. He could keep his face rigid, but he was a poor bluffer and did not know the mathematics of political odds. His next experiment in *Realpolitik* was in Italy. Here too he was outclassed by the statesman Cavour, whose purpose it was to liberate Italy only in order to put his master, Victor Emmanuel of Savoy, at the head of it. Cavour might be described as a diplomatic *sapeur*. Instead of trying directly to win over the Emperor, he first suborned his intimate advisers. Dr. Conneau, Count Arese and others were all won over first. Then he released a rabbit into the field. The rabbit in this case was the Countess Castiglione, a cousin of Cavour, a coldblooded raging narcissist, a libertine, and the most marmoreally insipid woman of the day. She was a titled *grande cocotte*. Her explicit instructions were that she was to seduce the Emperor, and from memoirs of the day, it seems that Victor Emmanuel himself had primed the pump.

Napoléon III was so rejuvenated by her attentions that one day, instead of using the door of his carriage, he jumped nimbly out the window. The liaison lasted perhaps a year, and became notorious. La Castiglione, to judge by her photographs, though of good family, looked like any expensive kept woman of the *demimonde*, but unhealthier. She was unbelievably stupid; in addition she was a clinical case for the alienist, for she lived not only for, but in her own mirror. Nonetheless she regarded herself as a heroine of the Risorgimento, and later tried to get large sums out of Victor Emmanuel on the strength of her seduction of the Emperor. The latter was so important to her that she gave instructions that she was to be buried in the gray (the most fashionable color for such things in those days) nightgown in which Napoléon III had first taken her to bed. But her only real use, since it was impossible to discuss anything with her but her own appearance, was that she made it possible for other Italians to have casual access to Napoléon III, at the house he had rented for her in Paris.

It took a long time to jockey Napoléon III into intervening in Italian affairs. He was slow to decision and shrank from violence, and he did not wish to use his army. Though he was personally courageous, bloodshed made him sick. And then, there was always during his reign the danger of a debacle.

On January 18, 1858, a muddleheaded Italian patriot, Orsini, with the assistance of three or perhaps four confederates, fearing la Castiglione to be inefficacious, tossed several bombs at the Imperial barouche, as it was delivering Napoléon III and the Empress Eugénie to the theater. It was a confused affair. "Remember that, till the cause of Italian freedom is gained, the peace of Europe and your own security will be but an empty dream," wrote Orsini to the Emperor. Apparently it was an effort to bomb him into intervention. The Emperor escaped unscathed, the Empress had a slight cut from broken glass, and 150 people were killed, none of them Italian. The Emperor, who had met Orsini socially, tried to have him exonerated, but someone who has slaughtered 150 people in peacetime cannot be whisked out of court, even by an Emperor. Orsini was executed. The argument ran that, a hero of the Risorgimento, he had been forced to attempt to kill the Emperor because so far the Emperor had not intervened.

Napoléon began to intrigue more closely with Cavour, and Plon Plon was married off to the Princess Clotilde. It was Napoléon's plan to dismember the Austro-Hungarian Empire, from which Hungary, Galicia, Lombardy, and Venetia were to be detached. Austria, to avoid this, offered to free Parma and Modena, and to guarantee the freedom of the Piedmont and to reform the Papal States.

The offer was not accepted. Cavour promised Napoléon III a sufficient territorial bribe, and so managed to maneuver him into position. "The die is thrown," he said. "Now we can eat our dinner."

The dinner was Austria's holdings in northern Italy. Napoléon III sailed for Genoa on the yacht *Queen Hortense*. He turned out to be a squeamish commander, but the French armies fought what was to be the only successful campaign of the Second Empire. The battle of Magenta was won, and he himself directed the storming of the heights at Solferino, and did so ably. But he was a man who had spent his life in the study, and after an unfortunate ride to the Milan railway station, through a field of corpses and the gangrenous dying, he decided not to pursue the war. Nonetheless, he had liberated

326

Lombardy. He retired in a state of well-advertised disinterest. The Prussians as a diversion had mobilized troops and sent them toward the Rhine.

When it was discovered what he had been paid for his disinterested intervention, the Prussian, Austrian, and English chanceries made so much noise that he shrank back into himself. His reward had been French Savoy and Nice. It must be said this did make him seem less altruistic than he would have liked to appear. "This man," said the Prince Consort, "is a walking lie." "The Emperor," added the Austrian Ambassador to Paris, Richard Metternich, who was a very good parlor pianist but not nearly so good a diplomat, "has the knack, *whatever he does*, and *whatever happens*, of seeming *innocent.*"

Politically it was the high point of the reign. The campaign had been quick, profitable, and inexpensive, it had been possible to disguise it as a righteous crusade, and the number of dead and wounded had not been large. There were parades. But the Pope objected, which meant that Eugénie objected, too. She had had no training for a dynastic marriage; she had, indeed, the outlook of a titled commoner, and having no liaisons herself, was already estranged from him because she regarded him as sexually impure. He tried to reason with her, but she had, when aroused, a shrill voice which penetrated even the walls of the Tuileries. In her view, sexuality was not unconnected with insanity, and even before the Emperor began physically to fail, about 1860, she had evolved the scheme of replacing him by a Regency directed by herself.

Napoléon had two virtues which amounted to vices. He was inordinately kind, and incredibly patient. He could not bear to sack an official, for fear of hurting his feelings, and seldom if ever did he put Eugénie in her place. At the most he would make some ironic remark, and she was beneath the reach of irony. She was emotionally jagged, and had only three techniques: she could storm like a virago, always in private, she could charm, always in public, and if she could not get what she wanted any other way, she cried. The third was the one he found most unbearable. Their apartments were one above the other at the Tuileries, connected by a winding stair. He paid her a visit every day, and must have been aware of her up there, sometimes, waiting.

In the beginning Napoléon III's relations with the Church, which in France had much secular power, had been excellent. It supported him, so he supported it. But the Pope was still in Italy a secular power, the administration of the Papal States was shocking and anarchic, and they barred the way to a unified Italy.

The Pope was Pius IX, elected in 1846 and a comparatively young man. He had been forced to flee Rome during the uprisings of 1848, and was maintained there now chiefly through the support of the French government, which had provided a French garrison. The French garrison stood between those who wished to unify Italy and the Papal lands. Even Napoléon III wished the extent of the temporal sovereignty diminished. Unfortunately, to a fondness for sapphires Pius IX added a fondness for temporal power. He was supported by Cardinal Antonelli, his chief minister. Somewhere Napoléon III had heard the proverb that he who eats the Pope will die of it. But that did not prevent nibbling.

In 1859 Napoléon caused to be printed a pamphlet, ostensibly by a journalist, La Guerronnière, actually mostly by himself, entitled *The Pope and the Congress*. In this he advocated reducing the Papal territories to a minimum. "The smaller the territory, the greater its sovereign. The Pope will be more powerful then in his weakness than in his strength." The Papacy could not bring itself to agree to this paradox until the Concordat of 1929. The Empress Eugénie could never bring herself to agree to it. And neither, of course, could the Gallican Church. Though Napoléon III kept his troops in Rome until the end of the regime, he was caught between the crossfire of liberal and Catholic opinion in France, and could protect himself from neither.

In 1864, Pius IX published an encyclical denouncing the chief liberal movements of his day as heretical. Since this struck at the political organization of France, the government prohibited the publication of the encyclical there. Thirty bishops protested, and so did Eugénie. The Emperor's relations with both were from then on additionally strained. By the end of the decade the Empire had begun to collapse. Napoléon III had managed to alienate Austria, infuriate the Pope, and displease England, and could not cope with the unification of Germany. Shortly he was to outrage the New World as well.

Thus, though on New Year's Eve 1859 the Emperor was induced to waltz the Empress at midnight into the new decade, on the first striking of the clock, no matter how charming the gesture, they had entered upon their fatal time. Prince Metternich, with his wife the only other guest, then played the Austrian national anthem on the pianoforte. It was not auspicious. The waltz had been Viennese, too. Bismarck and Austria were fighting for control of the Germanies. The Emperor, by a vacillating policy, succeeded in alienating both.

He had a map room in his private apartments. In fact, he had two, one to plan the reconstruction of Europe on ethnic lines, the other to reorder its political divisions. He was inordinately fond of maps. But no matter how often he changed the borders or moved blocks of wood about, or how sensible the abstract perfection of his schemes, they came to nothing, for he had no *Realpolitik*, and England, Germany, and Russia had. His attempts to settle the Polish question came to nothing. Russia was lost as an ally. Austria became hostile. His efforts to intervene in the Schleswig-Holstein question were a disaster. England finally got control of Egypt.

He turned, as he always did when defeated in any practical plan, to literature, and began work on his *Life of Julius Caesar*, late at night, with a corps of assistants, wearing a dressing gown over his pink silk underwear. Over the mantelpiece in his study hung a sketch of the First Dictator by Ingres. Earlier he had thought of writing a novel about a grocer, but on the whole, Caesar seemed the nobler project. Caesar was, of course, himself, and is presented as the very model of Bonapartism. Of Caesar's wife there is little mention. The work when published turned out to be an imposing monument to self-justification, and bored such of its readers as it did not embarrass, neither a large group.

The Emperor liked to go hunting in the costume of the age of Louis XIV, and once, during a game of hide and seek in the forest of Fontainebleau, was found hiding in a hole in a tree. In short he tried a variety of roles and postures, none of which worked, and the intellectual diversions of the court were on the pattycake level. When they were bored, they sent for the Metternichs. Prince Metternich played the piano a little. Princess Metternich introduced a variation upon bobbing for apples, which proved a boon at Compiègne, where the afternoons were apt to be dull and the conversation meager.

In the early 1860's came the ruinous intervention in Mexican affairs, ostensibly to protect French investments there. Maximilian and Carlotta were dispatched to a country they could not begin to understand, held for them by a French army that did not know how to hold it. Nor could Napoléon III afford to finance a long war, or to maintain a regime incapable of maintaining itself. A well-meaning man, Maximilian was at no time Emperor of much more than the immediate grounds of the palace at Chapultepec. Mexico was a vast country without roads. Benito Juárez had merely to retreat, to come back all the stronger. Nothing came of Mexico but a crippling blow to French prestige, death for Maximilian, madness for Carlotta, and a splendid painting by Manet which deliberately echoes Goya's no less splendid paintings of executions in Spain, prompted also by a Bonaparte.

Bismarck continued to make his German preparations. He took over Schleswig-Holstein, and managed to convince Napoléon III to remain neutral during the Prussian-Austrian war of 1866. A leader in the *Times* pointed out that "It is an old saying that an army of sheep commanded by a lion will beat an army of lions commanded by a sheep." Bismarck won. A further blow to French prestige was that France received no concessions from Prussia in exchange for her neutrality.

The only two triumphs remaining to the regime were both civil, the Exposition of 1867 and the opening of the Suez Canal (engineered by Eugénie's cousin, Ferdinand de Lesseps) in 1869.

The Emperor was failing physically, but the Paris Exposition of 1867 was an opulent display, a charade, for behind the scenes everyone knew how swiftly the Imperial power was slipping. Most of the crowned heads of Europe, and a few from northern Africa and Turkey, were in attendance. During one review news leaked out that the Emperor Maximilian had been shot at Puebla. Prince and Princess Metternich, the Austrian Ambassador and his wife, left the reviewing stand at once.

But the most distinguished visitor, the one everybody watched, was Bismarck, in his customary white uniform. Of a family much older than the Hohenzollerns whom he served, handsome, distinguished, not only the most powerful diplomat in Europe, but a man of stone poise, and forceful character, he was the immediate future of France. He got on well with Napoléon III. Indeed, he felt protective toward him and sorry for him. He got on well with everyone, except that he was a little frightening. For of course everyone knew that the age belonged to him.

It is seldom noticed, though often described, that the losing side takes up the fashions of the side that is to win, often long before the victory. During Napoleon I's rule, Empire fashions swept more of the world than he did. And now it was Bismarck's name which became the vogue. At the Paris salons and at the private showings of the couturier Worth, Bismark brown began to replace such popular hues as Magenta (named after the battle), Eugénie blue, Mathilde (a pearly white), and Nuance Teba (a powdery green, somewhat envious). In 1866, 1867, and 1868 Bismark brown swept Europe. It was a kind of Hagganah (or nigger) brown, not pretty to look at. The word was written Bismark, for of course it must be French. It became duller, and was known as *Bismark malade*, then lighter, as *Bismark content*, to be followed by *Bismark en colère* (very lively). There was also a *Bismark glacé*, and a *Bismark scintillant*. It was available, apart from dress material, in Bismark boots, Bismark gloves, Bismark parasols, and Bismark bonnets (made of Bismark straw trimmed with Bismark lace). These bonnets were worn on top of the Bismark chignon, which meant one had to dye one's hair a Bismark brown. In short, one could be Bismarked all over.

Men, too, though unobtrusively, were forced to wear it. Bismarck himself seems to have ignored it. His own white uniforms did for him.

In the other Imperial occasion, the Emperor played no part. The Empress Eugénie went out in November of 1869 to open the Suez Canal. The Khedive Ismaïl of Egypt, who had been educated in France, rebuilt Cairo for the event, but was so deeply in debt that he had to sell 20,000,000 pounds worth of shares in the canal to the British, who were thus able to gain control of a project essential to them and which they had vigorously opposed. Though Aïda was not ready in time, an opera house had been built in which to perform it. It was a glittering visit, beneath the pyramids, in the desert strip. It changed the political geography of the world. It was a triumph for France. But Britain had bought it up.

Nonetheless, profits on the remaining French shares were astronomical.

Eugénie was an inveterate traveler, which is to say, a restless woman. One thing that distressed her as Empress was that she could no longer go about from hotel to hotel, as she had in her maiden days, and live out of a suitcase. She was to see Egypt again. In 1905, when the tomb of Yuya and Tuya was opened, and almost every-

331

thing in it had been packed up, an old woman appeared and imperiously sat in the one remaining piece of tomb furniture, a royal chair. The chair was 3,300 years old, and Eugénie a frail sixty-nine. She was so gracious as to remark on the Empire style of the carved heads on the arms. Then she went away, long out of power, and more imperial than ever.

In 1869, she was not to return to France for long. Napoléon III's popular mandate shrank in twenty-two years from thirteen to one, to four to three for him in the country as a whole, and three to one against him in Paris and the larger provincial cities. His increasing habit of merely withdrawing from criticism, rather than squelching or circumventing it, helped no one. He was prematurely worn out and in agony from the stone. Despite the evidence, which they found highly annoying, of popular mandate, those whose career was based upon their representation of the people's will demanded reform. In 1869 Napoléon was forced to accept the resignations of Rouher and Baroche, two economic advisers and accomplished bureaucrats who had done much to keep the regime afloat, and in December, to ask Ollivier to form a new government. At the same time a liberal Empire was announced ("I have never believed and never shall believe that a Bonapartist regime can support liberty in any form," said Persigny). It was not a very liberal Empire. "As for order, I answer for that," Napoléon III informed the Chamber of Deputies. He wished to keep foreign affairs in his own hands, though those were shaking. "Who indeed can be opposed to the forward march of a dynasty founded by a great people in the midst of political disturbance, and fortified by liberty. More than ever, we should regard the future with fearless eyes." Ollivier, the new premier, announced, "In whatever direction one looks one can see no sign of any troublesome question, and never in history was the maintenance of peace in Europe so certainly assured." It was the eve of the Franco-Prussian war.

Ollivier was a silver-tongued orator—no other cliché will do—but like many members of an opposition, he had not the faintest idea of how to run a government, and was totally lacking in statecraft. He was also given to congratulating others upon their recognition of his own supreme virtue, which made him few friends. He was one of Plon Plon's protégés, and wished to make the latter Minister of the Marine. Napoléon III refused. Ollivier also had a maidenly squeamishness about sullying his reputation with the hazards of office, and had had to be wooed. "Sire," he wrote, "it needs a violent effort on my part to plunge into the conflict, and I do so only because I have faith in your Majesty."

Nor did foreigners take a favorable view of the man. "His task," wrote Lord Clarendon, "requires tact, experience, firmness, knowledge of men, and a few other qualities in which he seems singularly deficient, and I cannot think his Ministry will last." Lord Clarendon was right. It did not last. Later, in the fourteen volumes of his autobiography, Ollivier endeavored, without succeeding, to say why. Since he could not admit to his own faults, he found it difficult. But he was the leader of the opposition, and so he had had to be given his turn.

The new government was installed on January 1870, and promptly wasted four months drafting a new constitution. The result was a dyarchy, since Ollivier presided over the Council of State, and the Emperor over Ollivier.

What brought Ollivier, the government, the Emperor, and the country abruptly down, was the question of the Spanish marriage. Isabella II had been forced to flee Spain in 1868, and was living as a refugee in the Avenue de Roi de Rome. Her husband, to whom she never paid much attention, was lodged more modestly elsewhere in the city. Other sovereigns in residence were the blind King of Hanover (driven out by Bismarck), the King of the Two Sicilies, Francis II (driven out by Garibaldi), and the Duke of Brunswick, who had had to leave so hastily that he had sent his English valet, Shaw, back to steal his own diamonds from his own safe.

It was a matter of who was to marry the Infanta, and so control Spain. On Sunday the 3d of July, 1870, Prince Leopold of Prussia announced that he had accepted such a marriage. Neither France nor Britain could tolerate a Hohenzollern on the Spanish throne. There was a furor. On July 12 Prince Leopold withdrew his acceptance.

Without informing Ollivier, Napoléon III then demanded a further assurance from William of Prussia that he would veto any renewal of Leopold's candidature. It is impossible to understand why he asked such a thing. France had an unprepared army, an incompetent general staff, and no allies. Prussia had a strong army, a highly accomplished general staff, and the neutrality of Europe to count on. Moreover, Prussia, or rather Bismarck, was looking for an excuse to

333

crush France, in order to extend Germany's borders to their natural limit of the Rhine and to get back Alsace-Lorraine, whereas French demands in the matter of the Spanish marriage had already been satisfied.

King William courteously refused to reconsider the matter, which he regarded as settled and closed. The Prussian Ambassador reported this decision in a harmless dispatch to Berlin, the famous Ems telegram (King William was taking the waters there at the time). Like Metternich before him, Bismarck served a monarch who often needed prodding. Bismarck, who wished an incident, edited the quite harmless dispatch so that it read as an insult to French *amour propre* and published it, without either explanation or comment.

It made no sense whatever, but on July 15 the French cabinet voted for war, the Emperor clapped his hands and voted the same way, and at the Palais Bourbon, the government voted war credits by a margin of 245 to ten. "The Emperor did not want war," Ollivier told Maxime du Camp, "but he consented when he saw that I did."

"We had gone too far to retreat," said the Emperor. "That is the fault of one of my Ministers." It was his own fault. Ollivier was turned out of office, and his Ministry with him, on the night of August 9. Complaining of the ingratitude of France, when only he could save her, he fled to Italy, fearing assassination. He could never understand why he was never asked to come back. He took the line that France, spoiled by years of prosperity, needed this affliction. He spoke of God.

In Paris crowds marched up and down the avenues singing the "Marseillaise" and shouting, "À Berlin." The Empress became militant, the Emperor gloomy. He proposed to go to the front, though nobody knew where it was.

"You can't ride," said Princess Mathilde. "How will you manage on the day of battle?"

"You exaggerate."

"Look in the mirror," she said.

"You are right," he said. "I don't look frisky."

It was a swift war, a French farce that ended in a *Götterdämmerung*. All told, Napoléon III lasted a month.

ON the 29th of July Napoléon III took a private train from the station outside the park at St. Cloud, on his way to the front. The Prince Imperial, his son, who was fourteen, went with him, with a copy of the *Imitation of Christ* in his pocket, a gift from the Empress, designed as a corrective, for she knew that men when left among themselves were sometimes apt to be irregular. The Prince Imperial could not have had less freedom had he been sewn into his clothes. He was an odd, obliging, but deceptive child.

The train skirted Paris. Napoléon III could not bring himself to go through the mockery of an ovation there. The Empress was to be Regent in his absence.

The Emperor went to Metz. Here he found telegrams denouncing his own generals as incompetent, most of them unsigned, demands for men, horses, and provisions which could not be met, and the news that Bavaria had gone over to Prussia, and that Austria could not be brought into the conflict on the French side.

The state of the French army beggars description. To be exact, there was no French army, only a series of uncoordinated regiments, battalions, and hastily assembled conscripts, with no general or specific battle plan, to be aided by Algerian troops which did not arrive. Its matériel was either defective or nonexistent. A decade and a half of speculation in the quartermaster corps had seen to that. The few crack troops were for display only. There was not one competent general present, and the Emperor, who was Commander in Chief, could not be brought to give orders. Indeed, he did not know what to do. During the entire war, the French troops took only the tiny railway siding of Saarbrücken, which at least put them on German soil for a few hours. Apart from that, nobody knew what to do when the border was reached. So the fighting took place in France. The French literally did not know where they were, for so confident had the War Ministry been in the first days of mobilization that it had provided maps of Germany only and entirely forgotten to print up any for France. The Emperor was ill to the point of agony, of a condition which was inoperable, because he refused to allow a diagnosis, let alone an operation, to take place. It was difficult for him to stand. In the opinion of his doctors, he was probably dying. This seems to have been his own opinion, too.

The Germans rolled over the French armies at Weissenburg and invaded Alsace. Napoléon III's staff asked him to resign command of the armed forces. He did so, and fell back on the Verdun road. On the night of the 13th, by moonlight, he inspected the bodies on the battlefield. On the 14th he was in flight, through a bombardment, with the Prince Imperial, who was totally bewildered. Once a year, as a special favor, he was allowed to bivouac with the troops, but war was not like that. By the 18th the Germans had overrun Lorraine and were moving up on Metz, virtually unopposed.

In 1867, Frossard, the Prince Imperial's tutor, had devised an excellent plan for defending France in the event of Prussian attack. But it made no allowance for a French defeat. And now there were no French victories.

At Châlons the Emperor was joined by Magenta, MacMahon, and Trochu; all generals, and by Plon Plon, who was by no means displeased at the French reverses.

"The Emperor commands neither the army nor occupies the throne," said a general.

"I seem to have abdicated," said Napoléon III.

This is what Plon Plon wished. He suggested sending Trochu to Paris, as military governor, to check the Empress, who was acting as Regent, the Emperor to follow. Trochu was sent but the Emperor did not follow.

Plon Plon, to get him out of the way, was sent to Italy, to see if Victor Emmanuel would help. There he remained until after the end of the war. The Prince Imperial was hustled toward Belgium on the 26th, to save him from the Germans. He reached it safely, and then crossed over to England.

The Emperor went on alone, attended by a private surgeon to relieve his pain, which was done during the morning and again in the evening, by drugs and pressure. He had a pitiable time, ignored, sometimes unrecognized, fallen in, shunted back and forth on slow unscheduled trains, not knowing what had happened, and not much caring, totally discredited. It was a worse end than Louis Philippe or Charles X had made, a far worse one than that of Napoléon I. For at least Napoléon I had known how to fight, though he had finally lost.

He reached Sedan, where he was joined by MacMahon with what was left of his army. Sedan sits in a valley. The only way to defend it is to occupy the heights. MacMahon omitted to do this. So Moltke moved up in his stead.

Toward the end the Emperor rode up and down the lines, hoping that someone would shoot him. Nobody did. It was impossible to communicate with Paris. The end came on the first of September. The Germans bombarded Sedan, which was full of refugees and fugitive troops. By evening Napoléon surrendered with some 83,000 men. 3,000 had been killed by the bombardment, 14,000 wounded.

On the 2d, Napoléon III met Bismarck, who was courteous but firm. The terms were that both he and his army be taken to Germany as prisoners. There was nothing to do but agree. On the 3d Napoléon III was on his way to Wilhelmshöhe, where he had stayed as a boy, when Jérôme was King of Westphalia. In one room he found a portrait of his mother, Hortense.

Bismarck began the march on Paris. On the 4th the Empire fell.

On August 4 the Empress held her last reception at the Tuileries. It was theatrical. She wore black net and a jet diadem, in mourning for the defeats of France, and the ladies of the court likewise wore deep mourning, the footmen and other officials, black. Only the military men kept to their uniforms.

Ceremonial was maintained until the end. M. Maillard, who was more or less head housekeeper, and kept a record of such matters, entered in his register, somewhat later, "I have been unable to put things away in their proper places; they have not allowed me time to do so." Notices were placarded in the palace, saying, "Death to thieves."

Maillard had been distressed, in the last days of Ollivier's government, when a new sort of political visitor came in increasing numbers to the Tuileries, that the guests kept stealing the napkins (twenty-six on January 16, twenty-seven on February 13, twenty-eight on May

18, forty on June 10). Breakage also increased: the hands that held glasses and plates were becoming unsteady (as of April 1, 1870, 474 pieces of china and 183 pieces of glass had been smashed that year).

As always, collapse was preceded by disorder.

The Empress, who had tried to depose the Emperor before, in favor of the Prince Imperial and herself as head of the government, refused to have him back in Paris. On August 18 she virtually forbade it. "My mother gave birth to me in an earthquake, under a tent in the garden. What would the ancients have said of such a presage? They would have said I was born to convulse the world," she announced. But she did not know how. She stayed in the Tuileries. After the Ollivier government fell, and sustained by daily doses of chloral, she tried to rule herself. "The dynasty is lost," she said on August 6. "We must think only of France now." Unwisely, she summoned the Chamber. The deputies immediately voted a want of confidence in the government. Eugénie formed a new cabinet. It was made up of Imperialists and absolutists. When someone asked her what the Emperor might say of one of her suggestions, she snapped back, "*Nous suffisons ici.*" At the head of the War Department she placed General Palikao. He was an incompetent booby about whom nothing was of interest except the oddity of his name.

Trochu arrived from the front to take over the defenses of the city. He was an Orléanist and had a squint. Eugénie regarded the squint as first cousin to the evil eye. She refused to allow him to do anything, but blamed him for everything. She again forbade the Emperor to return to Paris without a victory. She had flung him over. As for her son, she cabled such messages to the front as: "For the Prince's safety, ignore orders from the Emperor, as he cannot judge." She could not judge either.

Mérimée, the friend of the family, and in particular of the Empress, whose love letters to the Emperor he had written himself, for she was not good at such things, thought she should not think of fleeing to England. "I should prefer the Far West, I think, or some forgotten corner of the Adriatic."

It was his advice that the Emperor should commit suicide, so he planned for Eugénie alone. The Emperor tried to be shot by German soldiers, while riding his lines, but he did not commit suicide. He was a professional gambler, and professional gamblers do not kill themselves.

Eugénie had other schemes. At one time she thought it would be a good idea to arouse the enthusiasm of the people (who hated her), by riding through the streets. This idea was given up because no one could find her a black riding habit, and she refused to wear any other kind. Next she thought of expiating the sins of France by becoming a hospital nurse. It was all fantasy. She was disturbed, and always got restless at sunset, out of fear that a revolution might break out during the night. She dreamed she was insane, and as she told Princess Metternich, always wept on waking up, to discover she was not.

Such was her mood when, on the 4th, she received the Emperor's telegram, announcing his surrender, brought to her at the Tuileries by the Minister of Internal Affairs.

The effect on her was literally indescribable, since Filon, one of the Prince Imperial's tutors, and Conti, an aide, though shattered by it, refused ever to repeat what it was she said. She appeared at the head of the winding stair down to the Emperor's apartments, and simply went off her head for five minutes. She left Napoléon III no virtue or physical quality intact. Then she swept down the stairs, and began to ransack the Imperial private papers, of which she took away with her a goodly number, though she ever afterward refused to allow them to be published.

Thiers and the government had received the news on the afternoon of August 3. There had been riots in the outlying districts of Paris, and now the disorder became worse. Crowds began to surge down Haussmann's admirable boulevards. People collected outside the Palais Bourbon, shouting "Dethronement. Dethronement." A police station was attacked. When beaten back, the mob then hurried to the Louvre, to protest against the brutality of the police.

Rouher, the Emperor's former Minister and adviser, said that the revolution would begin the following day. At the Tuileries it was decided to appeal to Trochu to restore order. But Palikao had already forbidden Trochu to do anything. Trochu, who had been roundly snubbed by Eugénie and her petticoat government, decided to obey.

On the 4th people began to tear down the Imperial eagles from shops and lampposts. Eugénie hesitated. "I had no fear of death," she explained later. "All I dreaded was falling into the hands of viragos, who would defile my last scene with something shameful or grotesque, who would try to dishonor me as they murdered me. I fancied them lifting up my skirts. I heard ferocious laughter, for, you know, the *tricoteuses* have not died out."

She would not even have remembered her jewels, had not her personal maid dumped them into Princess Metternich's skirt.

On the evening of September 3 and 4, the night session of the Chamber ended, and carriages and calèches began to roll across the Place de la Concorde. It was a clear night, which was a pity, for torrential rains might have dampened down the crowds enough to prevent a revolution. Some cavalry cleared them away so the carriages might pass into the city. Nobody was very easy.

The Empress had refused to sanction extreme measures (firing on the crowds). She held meetings and received such dignitaries of the Empire as still felt it safe to call at the Tuileries. On the 4th she rose at six, and paid a visit to an ambulance she had installed in the Tuileries playhouse. After that she heard mass and distributed money to the chaplain and officiants. More councils followed. Luncheon was served at eleven-thirty. It was eaten by twenty-eight people, mostly her immediate entourage, for it was a Sunday, and on Sundays there was only an honorary staff in attendance. The only outside guest was Ferdinand de Lesseps. Telegrams were delivered to the Empress at table.

In the midst of this agitation, improbably, a deputation of Orléanist deputies waited on the Empress, to request that the Comte de Paris, the Orléanist pretender, be crowned King of Greece, and that she abdicate. She refused to agree to either. Outside the crowds were shouting, *"Vive la République. À bas l'Espagnole."* Princess Clotilde came over from the Palais Royal, Prince and Princess Metternich paid their respects, and so did the Chevalier Nigra (the Sardinian Ambassador). Jérôme David, accompanied by a few daring ministers, came to say that the crowd had invaded the Palais Bourbon and proclaimed a Republic. They were themselves now on their way to the Hôtel de Ville to see the same thing done there.

The Empress said no one need stay. With a slight and embarrassed hesitation, everyone present left. She then went to her private apartments, hurrying along the emptying corridors accompanied by the Metternichs, Chevalier, Nigra, and her reader, Mme Lebreton.

As the Court Chamberlain was leaving, an usher showed him the day's audience book, in which were the names of all those who had called, and asked what should be done with it. The Chamberlain, M.

de Cosse Brissac, wisely tore out the relevant pages and put them in his pocket.

The last entry was made by M. Maillard, who noted "Sept. 4, 1870. Her Majesty the Empress left at half past one, by way of the Palace of the Louvre. All the personnel left about four o'clock in the afternoon, after the occupation of the Palace of the Tuileries by the National Guards."

There was a good deal of coming and going, none of it near the Imperial apartments. Accompanied by the Metternichs and Nigra, and providentially carrying a jewel box, into which her diamonds had been dumped, Eugénie prepared to flee. There had not been time to burn even personal papers, but some had been sent out ahead.

To flee, though safe and easy, was not so swift. Napoléon III did more to the Louvre and Tuileries than anyone else had done in over 400 years. He had joined both palaces by galleries on either side, thus making it the largest building in the world. It was well over a quarter of a mile long. The galleries and rooms of these connecting barrages of masonry had never been used or finished. Hurrying by jumbled furniture, shavings, dusty mirrors, and no less dusty windows, from which one could see and hear the crowds below, catching a glimpse of themselves from time to time in the glass, they fled through door after door and empty corridor after empty corridor, down rooms damp and never used. Behind them, far behind them, the mob began to break into the Tuileries. At last they reached the older parts of the Louvre, a cluttered museum, and descending, hailed a fiacre from a side door. Eugénie took refuge with her American dentist, who got her as far as Deauville.

She nearly went down crossing to England on the nearest available boat, an English yacht. The British Foreign Secretary, Granville, could only applaud her bravery. "Her misfortune is great, although it is much owing to herself: Mexico, Rome, war with Prussia."

At first the Empress and her son stayed at Hastings. "When I am free," wrote the Emperor, "it is in England I should like to settle, with you and Louis in a little cottage with bow windows and climbing plants." So his family decided to await his arrival in a large and inconvenient Georgian mansion at Chislehurst, Camden Place, belonging to a Mr. Strode, who, they discovered, proposed to live with them. It took some time to disabuse him of this idea.

Napoléon III's detention at Wilhelmshöhe was neither onerous nor long, for his German was fluent, and unlike his countrymen, he had no animosity against the Germans. He was charming, considerate, dignified, and tactful, and soon had everyone won over. In 1860 he had given the Jurist Migne a house in Paris, as a gift. Migne now wrote offering to sell the house and forward the proceeds. Napoléon III was touched. He also refused. Money had never mattered to him, and he had still those holdings his father had left him in Italy, and thought he could live on the income from those. His last (platonic) mistress arrived and played him Boccherini and Martini's *Plaisirs d'amour* on the spinet. Her name was Mercy-Argenteau. La Castiglione passed by. Plon Plon and the Countess of Montijo, his mother-in-law, offered to come but were tactfully refused. He gave Mme de Mercy-Argenteau some of Hortense's pearls when she left. Eugénie paid a visit. It was a cool and short one. The Prussians had refused to treat with her, over the capitulations. She left accompanied by Count Clary, another of the endless Bonapartist reminders of past time, and made a visit to Hanover and the Hague.

Napoléon III crossed to Dover on March 19, 1871, just a few days too late for the Prince Imperial's birthday. Both Lou Lou and Eugénie were on hand to meet him.

The abdication of the Emperor and the fall of the Empire did not mean the end of the Franco-Prussian war. It continued for six months, chiefly because the Prussians, and in particular Moltke, underestimated the power of the provinces to resist. This was organized by the politician Gambetta, known as Molasses Junior, who escaped from besieged Paris in a balloon and rallied the outlying forces.

At Paris, as soon as the Empire fell, the Republic formed a Government of National Defense. It foolishly concentrated all its forces in the capital, though there is no record of a besieged city ever having been able to lift its own siege, without outside help. Half a million troops were bottled up there.

Though the French troops in the countryside often fought well, they could not defeat the venality of their own government, which had so profiteered on war supplies that boots came apart, cartridges refused to explode, and muskets would not fire. It was a severe winter, and rather than quarter troops on potential voters, the politicians of the capital ordered them to sleep on the ground. The peasantry refused to sell foodstuffs for less than double the normal price, if at all. So the French were dying of semistarvation and exposure, whereas the Prussians, who had no voters to placate, commandeered the peasants' food supplies and billeted their troops in private houses. In addition the extreme centralization of France, which dated back to the days of Louis XIV, made it impossible to defend either the country or its capital.

The siege of Paris, which lasted from early September until January 28, 1871, is a celebrated horror, equaled only by the excesses of the Commune by which it was shortly to be followed. There was an ample supply of foodstuffs, but the government was afraid to ration it, with the result that it was soon used up. Within five weeks, after rationing had finally been imposed, the meat allowance shrank to three and then to one and one-sixth ounces a day, and people began to find out how to curry rat and fricassee elephants from the Jardin des Plantes. The same thing happened with flour. The Germans, who had their military quarters at Versailles, kept the city tightly invested.

Paris held out for almost five months. Worse than starvation were the deaths caused by bad sanitary precautions, which more than doubled.

When the city capitulated, an indemnity of 200 francs was extracted from it, and the Germans occupied strategic forts around the city until it was certain this would be paid. The indemnity for the whole country came to $5,000,000,000 and Alsace-Lorraine. The cost of maintaining the occupation troops amounted to about the same sum.

On the 1st of March the Germans entered Paris, while the citizens stood about and shouted, "*On ne passe pas.*"

This applied to the chain under the Arc de Triomphe. It was cut, and the Germans then marched through the arch and down the Champs Élysées. Most shops were closed. Women who spoke to the Germans were horsewhipped, beaten, and sometimes raped by their fellow French, who thus demonstrated their patriotism.

The German armies were efficient, well trained, well disciplined, and spruce, but their fantastically spiked and spread-eagled and death's-headed helmets were not to the French mode. The comment running in the crowds was, "*Formidable, mais tout cela manque de chic.*"

Chic, however, had not done much for the French army.

343

At night the Germans camped in the Bois, but in a few days with-drew. On the 18th occurred the uprising of the Commune. It was made possible because the government had been afraid to disarm the National Guard. The Germans did nothing to interfere. The result was civil war between Thiers and the Provisional Government at Versailles, and the Communards in the city. It lasted from March 18 until May 28, and was, on the part of the Communards, a vicious, bloody, and irrational melodrama. Its capacity to govern may be judged by the antics of one member of the Council of the Commune, Allix. He had invented a system of "sympathetic snails" which was to replace the telegraph as a rapid form of communica-tion. They were to wave their antennae at each other in serried rows, across the countryside, in mucous semaphore.

Order was reestablished by Thiers, himself to fall from office (as President of the Republic) two years later. He sent in troops and crushed the rebellion. 12,000 Communards were killed in the fight-ing, and 9,192 in the Courts.

Bismarck was not present. He had stayed at Versailles from Octo-ber 1870 to March 6, 1871. He had seen to it that King William was proclaimed Emperor of Germany in the Galérie des Glaces, at Ver-sailles, the subject of a justly celebrated painting by Menzel, that master of light. He had gotten everything he wanted. And so he had gone on to other things.

The Tuileries did not long survive the departure of the Bona-partes, or of Bismarck. After the rising of the Commune, on March 18, 1871, the palace was used for public concerts. The last of these occurred on Sunday, May 21. At that time the Provisional Govern-ment, at Versailles, under Thiers, ordered the troops to move in on Paris. The Tuileries was defended with barricades and artillery bat-teries.

On the 22d of May Marshal MacMahon's troops reached the Arc de Triomphe. The Champs Élysées then became a shooting range, down and up which the Tuileries and MacMahon's armaments fired at each other.

While this bombardment was going on, eleven vans were brought into the Tuileries, through the Place du Carrousel. They contained furniture, papers, and art works looted from Thiers's house. They were to serve as tinder. On the 23d several carts loaded with barrels of gunpowder came in through the Court of the Louvre. It seems relatively certain that General Bergeret had orders from the Committee of Public Safety, which ruled Paris, to fire the Tuileries, for it seems unlikely he would have done such a thing on his own initiative. The actual task of setting the powder trains was intrusted to Boudon, a drunken former hatter, and Benot, an ex-private. Boudon spread liquid tar and turpentine about the Pavillon de Marsan. With the aid of brooms, most of the rooms were daubed with petroleum or tar. A train was laid out as far as the courtyard, and this Benot fired. He then went to the Louvre barracks, for a leisurely supper. At about midnight, when coffee had been served around, Benot invited his fellow officers out to inspect his work. There was a loud explosion.

"It is nothing," said Bergeret, his commander. "It is only the palace blowing up." He then sent a message to the Hôtel de Ville. "The last vestiges of Royalty have just disappeared [as a matter of fact they were to burn for the next three days]. I wish that the same may befall all the public buildings of Paris."

It was, in fact, both a blow for Liberté, Egalité, Fraternité, and a form of architectural suicide, intermixed with sheer spite. Victor Benot, in the interests of literacy and freedom, had fired the library of the Louvre (the royal library of France), some forty thousand books, many of them incunabula or manuscripts, handsomely bound. For this service to the public welfare, he was later tried and transported for life to New Caledonia.

By ten in the morning of the 24th of May, the Ministry of Finance, the Palais Royal, the Hôtel de Ville, the Prefecture of Police, the Palais de la Justice, the Palais de la Légion d'Honneur, the Cour des Comptes, the Théâtre Lyrique, the Caisse de Dépôts et Consignations, and a careful selection of the better larger private houses of Paris were all aflame. At least the buildings had been chosen by someone of aesthetic taste. It was a final blow for liberty.

Fortunately Napoléon III's additions to the Louvre were so solidly built that the fires set in the Library, to the great vexation of the patriots of the Commune, did not spread to the picture and sculpture collections. But the Tuileries was a gutted shell, too expensive to restore, and was finally torn down completely, some years later. It had been a symbol of the Bonaparte regimes, though built originally by Catherine de' Medici. Now the site is gravel, balustrades, plane trees, and short grass. All that remains is the Pavillon de Flore and the Orangerie. All the connecting galleries were torn down, except the Pavillon de Rohan and some additions on the river side.

The Commune ended in a bizarre fashion, for the last place in Paris the Communards were to hold was the Père-Lachaise cemetery. So that when the time came to shoot them, getting them into the grave was an easy task.

To restore the column in the Place Vendôme, which Courbet the painter had toppled as a symbol of Bonapartist tyranny, took much longer.

U NLIKE the first Emperor, Napoléon III had never believed in
the immutable truth of his own gamble. He had lost, he accepted that he had lost, or seemed to have done so, and he
was utterly worn out. At the time of their various landings in England, the Prince Imperial was fourteen, the Empress forty-five, and
the Emperor sixty-three. Plon Plon was still against him, Mathilde
remained neutral in Paris, the immediate Imperial family was proscribed, and the Bonapartist party in France was headed by Prince
Achille Murat.

The British government took an anti-Bonapartist position, and so
did the British aristocracy. But Queen Victoria was attentive. She
even visited Camden Place. Her example was enough to secure the
Emperor, his wife and son an anomalous but tolerated social position
in England.

That mediocre but emphatic, imperious, and sentimental woman
had always taken a personal view of politics. Her manner toward
Napoléon III himself, though finely shaded and modified by the real-
ization that he was once more not only a commoner (almost) but out
of power, was cordial, and to Eugénie, warm. Eugénie, a melodra-
matic woman who kept her several selves in watertight compart-
ments, had managed to forget that she had estranged herself from
her husband, tried to get him to abdicate, and forbidden him to return to his own capital, not to mention that she had wished to oblit-
erate him. She had entirely forgotten that hectic five minutes on the
stairs. She now saw herself as the loving, loyal protector of a man
fallen through no fault of his own, though of course he *had* made
mistakes. She swathed him in a sickroom affection, and since he knew
he was dying, he did not altogether like it. Sometimes he took little

347

visits to Brighton and the Isle of Wight. But in his usual courteous way he did not complain. "Never a word of complaint or resignation," said Eugénie. Lord Malmesbury was equally impressed. "His quiet and calm dignity . . . were the grandest examples of moral courage that the severest stoic could have imagined. I confess I was never more moved." The Emperor was probably relieved. For the world had simply been too big for him. La Gorce, the historian of the Second Empire, felt him to be a combination of Don Quixote and Machiavelli. Alas, he had neither the spiritual grandeur of the former nor the ability of the latter. He had only been a politician and a paper demagogue.

The household at Camden Place was not in need. Napoléon III had 60,000 pounds in cash, and his properties in Italy and their income. The Empress Eugénie had sold the more impressive of her jewels for 150,000 pounds. They could live comfortably. Their ambitions now centered on Lou Lou, the Prince Imperial, who was hard-working and affectionate.

"The Prince Imperial," wrote Queen Victoria, "is a nice little boy, but rather short and stubby."

During the week the Prince studied with his tutor, Napoléon III read, as was his custom, the newspapers, and Eugénie denounced all those who had not supported her during the Regency, mostly Trochu.

"What time is it?" she asked one day.

"Madame, it's forty-five minutes past Trochu," said her lady-in-waiting.

It was a nerve-wracking bore. Sometimes, in the evening, there were séances. Sunday was better. On Sundays public entertainers and French émigrés came down on the three-o'clock train from Charing Cross. But then they went away again.

"This is the raft of the *Méduse;* every now and then we feel like eating each other," the Empress explained, for though histrionic, she was no fool.

Chislehurst is in Kent, which is one of the better parts of England, but none of the exiles could stand the climate, which was damp, rainy, and dreary and confined them to the upstairs front gallery of the house, when they wanted exercise. It was not a very large gallery. Everybody walked there, back and forth, fifty times a day, the ladies-in-waiting, the servants, the political hangers-on, Dr. Conneau, who had joined them, the Emperor himself, who gave several hours of perambulatory political instruction a day to the Prince Imperial there. The gallery was dominated by a bronze bust of Machiavelli. Mr. Strode, the owner of the house, came down once a week (usually Thursdays) to hobnob with royalty, his one pleasure. Everyone found Mr. Strode a trial.

During the summer of 1871 Eugénie went to Spain to visit her mother, arrange about her property there, and rest her nerves. This had the tonic effect of giving those at Camden Place a rest from them. Eugénie had always been extremely unpopular in Spain, and yet she always came back refreshed.

Acting on God knows whose advice, Napoléon III sent the Prince Imperial up to King's College, London, then a distinctly cockney institution, as a day boy. The other boys did not know how to consort with a Prince, so they ignored him. The courses were too advanced and technical for him to follow. He was miserable. All he learned was a little of England, by looking out the train window, on the trip up and down. After not quite a year he was transferred to the Royal Military Academy at Woolwich, where he was soon happy and did much better. Though not so stupid as his tutors thought him, the Prince was never more than inconspicuously bright. However, he turned out to have other and socially more acceptable virtues, and was both pathetically and diligently eager to qualify as what he wished to be, a military man. He was L'Aiglon without the address, or the radiant appearance. And had he been as intelligent as the King of Rome, it would only have been wasted. His father's good manners, which he had acquired, turned out to be more useful.

Conditions in France were chaotic, and at first it had seemed that there was no possibility of a restoration. But in the spring of 1872, the Bonapartist minister Rouher, who had set himself to organize (and head) a Bonapartist party, was elected to the National Assembly as a member for Ajaccio. Plots began all over again. Napoléon III turned to journalistic propaganda, most of it embarrassing. He wrote social notes for publication in the French press, describing the extreme cordiality and condescension of Queen Victoria's visits to Camden Place. The Prince Imperial's tutor was set to work to write an explanation of the debacle of 1870, under the Emperor's guidance. It was an ineffectual and inconclusive document, since Napoléon III could

349

never bring himself to blame anyone for anything, least of all himself.

In August came the annual Napoleonic birthday fête, this year held at Camden Place, with bushels of Imperial violets, speeches, and many visitors. The Emperor now projected a return to Paris in the Spring of 1873, and Eugénie began to plan a reduced, economical court to live at the Louvre, and in the spring and autumn go no more expensively away than Trianon.

"Yes," said the Emperor. "I know that I am the only solution. Only it is a pity I am so ill."

Indeed he was so severely ill that he finally submitted to examination, and after that to surgery. On the 9th of January, 1873, he died of complications attendant on a series of operations to crush his kidney stones.

The funeral was a national event. Not for the first time England took to its heart a Bonaparte. "An enormous name has passed out of the living world into history," said the *Times* leader. To Plon Plon's agitation, the writer meant not just Napoléon III, but the name Bonaparte itself.

It was a dreadful funeral. The upstairs gallery at Camden Place was turned into a mortuary chapel. Since it was the only communication corridor to the upstairs rooms, everybody had to go by the coffin twenty times a day. Embalming had turned Napoléon III's never attractive and always dead-looking face chrome yellow. The Imperial violets piled up around the bier had an all-pervasive, crushed, and overwhelming smell, like that of sweet rancid tea leaves. Eugénie's grief was harrowingly spectacular. There were too many mourners. The Prince of Wales and the Duke of Edinburgh came. So did every dignitary of the Empire who could get there. Plon Plon came, and so did Mathilde, but made the mistake of popping up to London to see the Crystal Palace, which did not please Eugénie, who, swathed in black, was making the most of it. Diplomatic representatives from just about every European country attended, and so did 4,000 miscellaneous Frenchmen. Chislehurst is a very small place, and the local Catholic chapel (one reason they had settled there—England has not too many rural Catholic chapels) could seat only 200. Somewhat awkwardly, the Prince Imperial was acclaimed as Napoléon IV outside the chapel. He disclaimed the honor. "I don't believe," said Filon, the Prince Imperial's tutor, "that grief, in any crowd of men, has ever reached such a paroxysm." The Emperor was temporarily laid to rest in the chapel vestry, because there was not much room.

Immediately afterward Plon Plon threw his customary scene. The cause was the Emperor's will. Drawn up in 1865, in expectation that the Prince Imperial would succeed to the throne and the civil list, it left him only a watch seal which had belonged to Hortense, and gave everything else to Eugénie, for it had been arranged that on the Emperor's death and the Prince Imperial's accession, she was to move, as dowager, into the Élysées, where she would need the money, and Lou Lou would not.

Napoléon III left an estate of 60,000 pounds, his Italian holdings, and Arenenberg, which, since his fall, he had refused to visit, on the grounds that it was too much like going back into the egg. The Empress was richer than that in her own right, not only from her jewels, but because she had holdings in Spain and a few investments. Lou Lou also had money in his own right, the bequest left him by Napoléone Camarata, Princess Bacciochi, Elisa's daughter, but it was tied up, and Eugénie did not mention it, for she had turned saving and miserly.

Nobody else was mentioned in the will.

Plon Plon shouted that there must be another will, in his favor, unless the Empress had torn it up. The Emperor's desk had been sealed on his death. Plon Plon raged into the study, broke the seals and went through everything. Then he claimed the papers had been previously ransacked.

Eugénie, unaware of what he had been doing, decided to be reconciled to him, sent for him, and tried to be gracious. "Let the past be forgotten," she said.

"Madam," said Plon Plon, "in a short time I will acquaint you with my intentions." And he did. He demanded absolute control of the Bonapartist party and complete and sole guardianship of the Prince Imperial, together with a public statement that she was unfit to bring up her own child.

The immediate storm this modest proposal raised completely ruined Plon Plon's political chances, which had never been great, and revived the Empress.

Queen Victoria rallied to the cause, by presenting the Prince Imperial with an autographed copy of *Leaves from the Journal of Our*

Life in the Highlands, and by becoming a Bonapartist on the spot. "The Queen does *not* think the Bonapartist cause will lose by the poor Emperor's death," she wrote. "On the contrary, *she* thinks the reverse. *For* the peace of Europe SHE thinks (though the Orléans Princes are her dear friends and connections and some relations, and she would not for the world have it *said* as coming from her) that it would be best if the Prince Imperial was *ultimately to succeed*."

Mathilde, who was fond of Lou Lou, went so far as to repeat herself, and told Plon Plon he was a fool.

So now the Prince Imperial was the Pretender.

Lou Lou was an odd child. It was said at the time that he had been born bored, and certainly it was so hard to hold his attention, that for many years it had been thought he was retarded mentally. He was also ugly, having Napoléon III's dead almond face, Eugénie's eyes, which were those of an ox in shape if not in color, and the stubby scuttling Bonaparte legs. He had been too much with the ladies as a child, except for the man who taught him riding, and had been brought up as a sort of toy, tricked out in "cute" military uniforms since the age of three, and kept up so late at night for social entertainments that his sturdy health had almost been wrecked. Eugénie alternated between being violently possessive and sternly shrill, and neglecting him completely, though in public she could be a charming parent. It is unlikely he would have survived childhood, had it not been for Miss Shaw, the English nanny sent over by Queen Victoria. Apart from her peculiar notion that all ills, emotional and physical, could be cured with a fresh fried strip of bacon, Miss Shaw was the only sensible ally the boy's excellent but hamstrung French doctor had, and since she was a domineering and clamorous woman, as close to a real mother as Lou Lou was to know, she pulled him through.

But the Prince Imperial was a deceptive child. He had not, it turned out in his teens, been born stupid. On the contrary he had watched and observed, but he had been waiting. He was one of those indestructible children whose only defense is silence. He was a splendid horseman, and had a slight aptitude for mathematics. He had military ambitions, and unlike his father, was not distressed by carnage or by blood, though unlike his great-uncle, he could not regard such matters with indifference. It developed he had never studied because he had not seen the point in it. He was clever with his pencil, and drew well. Now that he was at Woolwich College, where he was happy and did see some point to it, he studied his head off. He did not mind roughing it. He had all his father's good qualities—charm, tact, grace, genuine kindliness, personal address—and only a few, but those dangerous, of his mother's bad ones. He possessed enough character to stand up to her, when necessary.

After Napoléon III's death, life at Camden Place went better. Eugénie was a born gadabout. Now she packed up, and decided everyone should go to Arenenberg for the summers.

It was sixty years later, but Arenenberg, despite a few hideous Second Empire additions, was basically unchanged. It was still Hortense's house and Hortense's Napoleonic shrine. It was easier for the Bonapartists to come here than to England. And the Prince Imperial liked it very much. So did Eugénie. "The pearl-gray English sky is like a dish cooked without salt, you must be very hungry to feel an appetite for it."

Bonapartism, however, did not go well. The Occupation of Paris had been followed by the Commune, the Commune by civil war, and the civil war by the Thiers government brought in from Versailles. In 1873 it fell in its turn, and was succeeded by the MacMahon septennate. It did not last seven years, and was a planned interregnum, many thought, to bring back either a Bonaparte, an Orléanist, or a Bourbon. MacMahon was an absolutist, but conservative and ineffectual. The Constitution of 1875 gave him the powers of an absolute ruler, but he would not exercise them. Finally he became so disgusted that he resigned at the end of six years rather than endure a seventh, for the Chambers he had to work with were predominantly liberal, radical, and impractical.

A movement to restore the Comte de Chambord (Henri V, the Bourbon pretender) came to nothing. He was childless, and the Comte de Paris (the Orléans heir) was his successor. The Comte de Chambord was a brainless reactionary who sank himself by demanding that the white Bourbon flag be restored.

Rouher advised the Prince Imperial to back a plebiscite. But it was impossible to hold a plebiscite.

On Lou Lou's eighteenth birthday, and coming of age, March 16, 1874, it was decided to hold a demonstration at Camden Place. It turned out to be a gala success. The French government forbade its nationals to attend, and the British railways ran special trains from London to Chislehurst, decked with tricolor banners and boldly lettered: "Majority of the Prince Imperial." Plon Plon refused to come, and announced his disapproval to the British press, in letters signed, "A Republican." Nobody paid any attention. The Channel boats were heavily crowded. In London, the theaters made a point of playing Queen Hortense's air, "Partant pour Syrie," that unofficial hymn of the Second Empire whose tune the Empress Eugénie had never been able to carry. There was even a new song:

> Dans son exil, au tombeau de son Père,
> Il a puisé de grands enseignements.
> De ce tombeau jaillira la lumière,
> Napoléon vient d'avoir dix-huit ans.

Thousands of people descended on Chislehurst, including the Prince's old wet nurse, who made a favorable impression. She was a representative of the loyal people. 3,000 were fed in one tent on the grounds of Camden Place, and the audience for the speech was too large to be contained in the other, whose flaps were tied back, so everyone could see and hear. The weather, for once, was balmy. The clock on the façade of Camden Place chimed half-past one. Its motto was "Better Death than Desertion." The Prince Imperial appeared from the house, gave a good speech, and charmed everyone. The burden of the speech was that a plebiscite, France's eighth, would be sure to restore him.

It went off, and down, extremely well. The sunset of that day was meteorologically remarkable. It had an extraordinary afterglow, which made the world flare pink. During it the Prince Imperial appeared once more before the people.

Next day, everyone at Camden Place locked himself up with the newspapers. They were favorable. The whole thing had gone off splendidly. It was only that nothing came of it. The French government's revenge was to suspend the Duc de Padoue, one of the speakers, from his office as mayor of his village. This made the French government look ridiculous. He was a doddery, senile, harmless old man, a Bonaparte relative.

The Prince Imperial went back to finish his studies at Woolwich, was made much of by the Czar during a visit, gave a few speeches on behalf of and to his graduating class, and did well. "The Academy will, I am sure, always feel proud that he distinguished himself in their school, and that he should have acquitted himself so honorably, and above all, *behaved* so well!" wrote Queen Victoria.

But he was isolated, powerless, and impotent, at a loss for an occupation; and Eugénie refused to allow him enough to maintain himself as an English gentleman, let alone as a French Prince. Outwardly he was reckless, animated, and charming. Inwardly he was humorless and gloomy. He was ambitious, and there seemed no way. Under his mother's influence, he became an absolutist and an imperialist, which is to say, in this case, an advocate of something perilously close to the divine right of kings. It became difficult to explain the differences between Frohsdorf (where the Comte de Chambord was) and Camden Place. Worse, he became devout, which would not serve to make him popular in a country violently anticlerical. "You know, I believe Napoléon I was, at bottom, a very religious man," he said to his tutor one day.

Eugénie was worried. "He is not *ambitious*, and that chord would be mute, but he has above all a sense of *Duty* and he is *daring*." Her epistolary style was beginning to resemble the dear Queen's.

He applied to be conscripted in France, was turned down, and went off to Aldershot instead, for British military maneuvers. He was hampered by the incessant presence of Eugénie. "I never ask her anything, because I do not admit that anyone can refuse me," he is claimed once to have said, about something so trivial as the acceptance of an invitation to dinner from some of the Murats.

Eugénie was much obsessed by death, and had become more difficult than ever. Her pressures were small inexorable maternal ones, in addition to which she sometimes cut off supplies. They became so minute after the death of her niece, that it was necessary to send her off to travel. In Paris, Plon Plon was busy explaining that Lou Lou was mentally deficient. "My friends! Nothing has been respected! The Emperor's son has spoken for the first time—and against me." This was an effort to divide the vote in Corsica, the one French department the Bonapartists could always count on.

The Prince Imperial could not control the Bonapartists. They had discovered it was pleasanter to be a Bonapartist without a Bonaparte, and would not obey him. France was rich, bourgeois, and content, and wished no political disturbance. The Prince Imperial resigned himself to wait another ten years.

Eugénie made another trip to Spain. It did her good. But Clary, her financial adviser, as the Clary family had been to Napoléon I, died, the family physician and friend, Dr. Conneau, died, and Eugénie had another fit of nerves. So in 1878 the Prince Imperial escaped on his own for a trip to Scandinavia. When he came back, he went into British society, where he was a success.

"Aren't you afraid of the Queen?" asked Eugénie.

"Not in the least, the Queen is very fond of me."

It was thought he would marry the Princess Beatrice. He joined clubs. But then, since he was still kept on a short financial leash, he began to cancel invitations. Society can be expensive.

Eugénie, who, like her mother, was a matchmaker, took alarm and arranged for him to be given half his father's estate and all of Princess Bacciochi's legacy, now the larger for seven years' compound interest. It made him independent. He could take a house of his own in London, if he wished. "But if he learns to be dull he will have learned something that Frenchmen hardly ever know and which will be very useful to him."

Tired of this futile existence, he applied to the government for permission to go out to Africa, as an observer of the Zulu war. The government disapproved to the point of panic, but Queen Victoria arranged for him to go. Plon Plon, when he heard of the scheme, said it was because the Empress Eugénie had taken every cent of the Prince's money, so he had to serve as a trooper. Princess Mathilde, who was a violent Anglophobe, was so furious to see him join a British troop that she refused so much as to wish him well, though she had been most fond of him.

"*Eh bien, bon voyage,*" sneered Plon Plon. Mathilde did not go so far as that. She merely left letters unanswered.

Eugénie, needless to say, was prostrate at the plan. On the 26th of February, the Prince Imperial went up to London, and on to Windsor, to take his leave of the Queen. He returned to Camden Place the same night. At midnight the servants lined up in the long gallery to be thanked and said goodbye to. There was a high storm outside. The Prince made his will. It mentioned only three Bonapartes, his mother, Prince J. N. Murat, and Prince L. L. Bonaparte, and, apart from souvenirs to personal friends, left his estate entirely to his mother. It said nothing about the future of Bonapartism, which as far as he was concerned would die with him, asked that if and when possible he should be reburied in France, and omitted Plon Plon entirely.

Next morning he left. Eugénie's conduct after his departure was not graceful. She refused to see any of her French friends, on the grounds that she had not the strength for explanations. To be blunt, she dropped them. She even quarreled with her mother, though true, she had some provocation. Mme de Montijo had a habit of sending crisp little telegrams, of which "Rumor of the Prince's death, is it true?" is a sufficient sample. Speaking only to the British, Eugénie held herself in readiness to go out to the Cape, a maternal Florence Nightingale, with just a dash of Rachel in *Phèdre*, to give the mixture zest.

The Prince Imperial, once he reached Africa, for the voyage was terrible, began to enjoy himself. He was ravished by camp life, very glad to be away from a household of women, and even liked the Zulus, who were, indeed, an admirable people, and an opponent well worth the fighting against. He got on well with the officers and men. A military life suited him. The only drawback was that he did not want to be an observer, he wanted to participate. He found the African landscape stunning. For the first time in his life, he was joyously happy.

On June 1, 1879, he set out with a small raiding party under one Lieutenant Carey. Carey was pillow-headed, a career man, a gusher, and a coward. Encountering some Zulus in the boskage, he panicked, and without giving orders to his men, spurred his horse and fled. There were six men and one Zulu in his party. Five of the other men followed him.

The group had begun to unsaddle. The Prince Imperial managed to cinch his girth, but as he tried to vault up, the pommel came away in his hand. The suppliers had been profiteering, and under a too thin tissue of leather, the saddle was merely paper. Though he put up a stiff fight, he had been deserted, and the Zulus cut him down at about four in the afternoon. Later his horse came into the British camp, with its saddle torn. The horse's name, oddly enough, was Fate.

Though the Prince was clearly missing, Carey, for it was the dinner hour, refused to go look for him until the next day. Except for the importance of the Prince, this was reasonable enough, for the night was dark, and the Zulus were artists at ambush. But the truth of it was that Carey had panicked. He sat in his tent until late, writing to his wife.

"My own one: I am a ruined man, I fear, though from my letter which will be in the papers you will see I could do nothing else. . . . Still, the loss of a Prince is a fearful thing. . . . My horse was nearly done, but carried me beautifully. . . . My own darling, I prayed as I rode away that I should not be hit and my prayer was heard. . . . Poor boy! I liked him so very much. He was always so warm-hearted and good-natured. Still I have been surprised. . . . Oh Annie! How near I have been to death. . . . I have been a very very wicked man, and may God forgive me! I frequently have to go out without saying my prayers and have had to be out on duty every Sunday. . . . Both my poor despised horses have now been under fire. The one I rode today could scarcely carry me, but did very well coming back."

This high Victorian gurgle, when it came out, made a very bad impression. Next day the Prince's body was found, stripped, but not mutilated, except for a small nick, a Zulu precaution against vengeful ghosts. He was covered with wounds, none of them in the back, and it was clear from the scuffled earth that he had put up a stiff fight, and been brought down only with difficulty. Carey was cashiered.

The Empress Eugénie learned of the death by cable, on the 15th of June, and collapsed. In France there was an outbreak of Anglophobia. At Camden Place, the Bonapartes and Murats began to arrive. Eugénie would speak only to Anna Murat, the American daughter of Prince Achille and a favorite of hers, to whom she gave a brooch as a talisman. Only Queen Victoria was welcome, and came often.

It took three weeks for the Prince's body to reach England. During that time his posthumous letters kept arriving, ebullient, cheerful, and content. He had enjoyed himself so very much. He had only been twenty-three. There were also surprises. It was discovered that he had kept concealed in the hilt of a truncheon he always carried with him a collection of scurillous accounts of himself and his relatives, clipped from the French press, and some nasty articles about the proneness of the family to die of cancer. A note was found on his body, proving conclusively that Carey had been in command and had deserted his men. And there was a codicil to his will, explicitly cutting Plon Plon out of the succession, in favor of Plon Plon's elder son, Prince Victor, then a schoolboy. Not knowing of this, Plon Plon appeared at the funeral as chief mourner.

Prince Murat received the body, and Rouher and Pietri, as executors of the will, insisted that the coffin be opened, so that the Prince might be identified. He had been so badly embalmed that the skin of his face had to be pulled into shape and held there in order for it to be certain that it was his. The coffin was then shut again and forwarded to Camden Place, where once more the long gallery was draped in black and purple and smothered in violets.

It was a harrowing funeral. Queen Victoria ordered the Cabinet to attend, and stormed in such a passion, that the Ministers for War and the Colonies actually went, in full dress. The French government refused to allow Napoléon III's chief officers, including MacMahon, to come. Queen Victoria arrived, which was unprecedented, and so did Princess Beatrice, Princess Alice, and Alexandra, Princess of Wales. It was a military funeral, with full honors. At the mass in the chapel, Cardinal Manning preached the sermon. Once more there were special trains, and the crowds were huge. Princess Mathilde, who had come over, told Queen Victoria that Lou Lou had been too impetuous and must have had *l'esprit malade.*

Eugénie offered to be reconciled to both Mathilde and Plon Plon. Plon Plon, who had just heard of the codicil, called a carriage and drove off at once. Mathilde came.

A little while later, an official military tribunal, to the fury of the military, exonerated Lieutenant Carey and restored him to his rank. Eugénie had intervened for him. By way of reward, Carey began to bombard her with explanations of his conduct. He was transferred to Bombay, where he died six years later.

Of the Prince Imperial, nothing remains but the horrible tomb house Eugénie caused to be built at Farnborough Abbey, a statue erected by Queen Victoria in St. George's Chapel at Windsor, since he was refused burial in Westminster Abbey, and hundreds and hundreds of drawings of French soldiers of the time of Napoléon I and Napoléon III, well drawn, but not drawn well enough; for the Prince Imperial, though a born draftsman, had not been allowed to take the necessary lessons, which might have diverted him from his proper calling. There are also a few pieces of crude sculpture, executed under the encouragement of Carpeaux, one of his riding master, very good; one of his tutor, not too bad; and one of Napoléon III.

It was the end of Bonapartism, for the French would have nothing to do with Plon Plon, and Prince Victor, who had inherited his father's towering self-esteem, had only social ambitions, which he was content to fulfill exclusively as a hanger-on at the Italian court.

Queen Victoria had taken Eugénie off to Balmoral, which did her infinite good. After that she indulged her mania for incessant traveling, to Scotland, to Egypt, to Arenenberg, to Spain, to the Mediterranean, even to Paris, where she stayed at a hotel opposite the gutted shell of the Tuileries. When asked if this did not disturb her, she said no, for "The Empress died in 1870."

Nevertheless, complaining that she herself could not die, she outlived everyone by forty years, dying only in 1920, at the age of ninety-four. The Prince Imperial's body was never returned to France. So Napoléon III, Eugénie, and Lou Lou lie in marble effigy in the mausoleum she had built at Farnborough, in the middle of a thick wood. It is unvisited except by priests, when masses are said for them, for the chapel is permanently endowed, on their anniversaries and on the anniversary of the first Emperor's death. There is a caretaker.

THE American Bonapartes outlived the Imperial branch by sixty-six years.

      Betsy Patterson Bonaparte did not visit Europe again. Instead, she became the eccentric and in some ways the Hetty Green of Baltimore. She, too, was fantastically long-lived. "Once I had everything but money," she said, "now I have nothing but money." She was worth perhaps $1,500,000, most of it in highly profitable Maryland and Baltimore real estate. Her income was about $100,000 a year, of which she spent about $2,000, plowing the rest back into her capital and living in a boarding house. She had at no time had less than $10,000 a year, almost always much more, but she claimed her life had been ruined by poverty.

Her definitive remark about her marriage was: "Had I waited, with my beauty and wit, I would have married an English Duke, instead of which I married a Corsican blackguard." She had often, in the old days, obtained additional money from the French by threatening to marry an Englishman, titled if possible. On one occasion, when she had claimed, inaccurately, Mr. Oakley, a secretary at the British Legation, as a suitor, Napoléon I had offered her a credit of $25,000 not to. But those days were long in the past.

Her eccentricities were of the cheese-paring variety. When she had her bedroom carpeted, she refused to allow the areas under the wardrobe and bed to be counted in the measurements, since they did not show. When she went out to dinner, she always shoveled the bread and rolls into her purse at table, for as she said she sometimes got hungry at night. She refused to pay a laundress, and always did her own underclothes, whether in Europe or America, at home or in a hotel.

Bo predeceased her, in 1870, leaving his country estate, Bella Vista (some 300 acres, a house, and extensive farm buildings) to his elder son, Jerome Napoleon. Judging that the younger, Charles Joseph, would amount to more, Mme Bonaparte bought the elder out and gave the estate to Charles Joseph. Otherwise she restricted her benevolence to the giving of one hundred dollars each, at Christmas, to not more than three relatives.

She continued vain of her beauty, and once asked an acquaintance back from Europe if she had not heard of her beauty on the Continent. She was given to admiring her portrait by Stuart, and was touchy about her age. If anyone asked what it was, she said she was "nine hundred and ninety years, ninety-nine days and nine minutes," and cut him or her dead thereafter. And indeed she kept her entire beauty well into her sixties. Though she brought her son up as a Catholic, and his sons were also Catholic, because it was the Bonaparte faith, she never gave up her own Protestantism, because, as she said, "it was the footstool her ancestors had sat on." Her descendants were Catholic "because that was a religion of Kings, a royal religion."

It was her habit to carry her valuables around in a carpet bag. Sometimes she would give the carpet bag to someone else to carry, but if so, always held on to his arm. Formerly she had used a small trunk for the same purpose. She was a hoarder, and her rooms were cluttered with such things as her husband's wedding coat and a dress given her by Pauline Borghese. Her opinions of America did not alter. Her view of local government was dim. "Baboons were in the Senate and Monkeys in the House, which was carrying republican principles out to their legitimate ends."

At the age of ninety-two her digestive tract failed, and she had to live on brandy and milk, quite a lot of brandy and very little milk. It was her first illness and also her last. She died on the 4th of April, 1879, during her ninety-fourth year, and was buried in an isolated plot at Greenmount Cemetery, since *she wished to be by herself*.

Her estate was divided evenly between her grandsons, Jerome Napoleon and Charles Joseph. Charles Joseph, though the younger, was the one she had preferred. So he got "the portraits of King Jérôme, his grandfather, and that of myself—the three heads on one piece of canvas painted by Stuart; a cabinet portrait of myself painted at Geneva by Massot, and also the portrait made of me by Kinson," as well as "all histories of my life written by myself, my diaries, dialogues of the dead [it would be interesting to know about those, but they seem to have disappeared], letters received by me from various correspondents, and all manuscripts whatever belonging to me." Also the family jewels, some of them dating from the days of Jérôme, King of Westphalia. Also, said Charles Joseph, "a great deal more of the Madeira of my grandfather than I shall in all probability ever be able to drink myself." Never a womanly woman, Betsy had preferred brandy.

Bo, who had died of cancer of the throat—so there was little doubt of his being a true Bonaparte—though he qualified for the bar, had never done anything in particular. It would be kindest to call him a gentleman farmer, and let it go at that.

His elder son, Jerome Napoleon, born November 5, 1830, did not amount to much either, though in his youth he had served on the Texas border with the Third Cavalry. As has been said, he went to France, where he accepted a commission as a second lieutenant in the Seventh Dragoons, under Napoléon III, and served in the Crimean War, and also in Algeria during 1856 and 1857. In 1857 he was transferred (as captain) to the First African Chasseurs, in time to take part in the campaigns of Montebello and Solferino. He was on the Emperor's staff, where he proved adept at gathering in medals— the Crimean, the Légion d'Honneur, the Medjidie (Turkish), the Médaille d'Italie, and others. In August of 1870 he became a member of the Empress Eugénie's Dragoons, remained for the fall of the Empire, the siege of Paris, and the Commune, and returned to America only in 1871. He then married a granddaughter of Daniel Webster and became a stockholder in the Newport Canal. He was always ready to entertain important French visitors, otherwise lived a sociable life, and being tall and thin, looked like a scrubbed-up Edgar Allan Poe. He moved to Washington, and interested himself in politics and diplomacy. He died of cancer of the stomach in 1893.

He had two children, Jerome Napoleon Charles, born in Paris in 1878, and the last male American Bonaparte to survive; and Louise Eugénie, born at Baltimore in February of 1873, who married Adam, Count Moltke-Huitfeldt, a Danish diplomat, in December of 1896. Of this marriage there are many descendants, and it was to this branch, and to the Catholic Church, that the American properties of the Bonapartes finally in part reverted.

His brother, Charles Joseph (born 1851, died 1921), was the last Bonaparte anywhere to play any part in public affairs. He married, on September 1, 1875, Ellen Channing Day of Connecticut. There were no children of this marriage. Charles Joseph was a corporation lawyer (chiefly he managed the Bonaparte investments) known alternately as "Souphouse Charlie" and "The Peacock," both of which epithets he did much to earn. He was a colorful if irritating man.

The epithet "Souphouse Charlie" arose from a speech in which he said, "There is absolutely no difference in principle between a public souphouse and a public free school." The term "The Peacock" arose both from his shape and waddle and from his habits, which were methodically outrageous. For instance, every morning he took a lunchpail into the office with him, from Bella Vista to Baltimore, a distance of fourteen miles. This would seem endearing, except that he drove in in state, behind a Negro groom in livery, and the lunchpail was solid silver. The lunch, prepared in his own kitchens by his own staff, contained, sometimes, an apple.

He was hardboiled, perpetually smiling (but it wasn't a very nice smile), witty, cautious, arch-conservative, philanthropic, and distinctly chilly. Among other social reforms, he was in favor of lynching, which he felt to be a much misjudged custom. "I believe that very few innocent men are lynched, and, of those who have not committed the past offense for which they suffer, a still smaller proportion are decent members of society. It is, of course, an evil that the law should be occasionally enforced by lawless means, but it is, in my opinion, a great evil that it should be habitually duped and evaded by means formally lawful." This bland but irrefutably bloodcurdling cold common sense did little to enlarge the circle of his adherents.

His philanthropies issued from the same principles. "Children take much more kindly to kisses than discipline, and paupers to soup than a job." He was Vice-President of the Society for the Suppression of Vice (though several of the properties he owned in Baltimore were sporting houses, and nobody ever dared to close them down).

Some of his other *obiter dicta* are equally direct. "Inability to bear the spectacle, or even the thought of pain endured by any human being, however criminal or degraded, is regarded, more or less consciously, by many persons as a mark of what they call 'refinement' or 'culture.' Morbid shrinking from the use of physical force against evildoers . . . is a moral malady of the age. . . . 'Need anybody cry' if an officer's revolver does now and then save our Courts the trouble of trying a burglar, and cut off his chance of 'burgling' again when released or escaped from prison?"

All in all, he was more respected than loved, and had always to be appointed to national office, for there was no chance of his being elected by popular mandate. It is perhaps not surprising that when Theodore Roosevelt, a crony of his, became President, he sensibly and tactfully relegated Charles Joseph to the Board of Indian Commissioners. "This had," says Eric F. Goldman, the official family biographer, "its appropriateness."

Transferred to the Post Office Investigation, he pushed his examination of the fraud involved so vigorously that he almost netted James D. Cameron, a friend of Roosevelt's who had been eager to see an office machine of his own invention installed in all national post offices, the better to serve the public weal. So Charles Joseph was sent out to Indian territory again. He did not want to go, but Roosevelt *pressed* him.

He did not go down well in a political milieu. For one thing, as an Overseer of Harvard University, he had, in 1901, refused to allow an honorary degree to be given to President McKinley, on the grounds that it would cheapen the distinction. Charles Joseph, by now known as "Charlie the Crook Chaser," resigned all his posts by November 1, 1904, first endorsing an injudicious statement by a naval official, to the effect that "the Service [Indian Affairs] would never be worth a damn until the well-meaning people in it had been hanged."

When Roosevelt was reelected, Charles Joseph was made Secretary of the Navy, which surprised even him (he was having lunch at the White House when the announcement was made). It was a stopgap measure until the Attorney General, Moody, could be induced to resign, at which time (July 1, 1906) Charles Joseph would be transferred to that slot.

A cigar company at once asked to name a cigar after him. "No man is great unless a new cigar is named after him," said the accompanying letter. Charles Joseph refused, so it is not possible after all to be able to smoke a Bonaparte. Next, when the Joint Encampment of the Knights of Temperance named their meeting place Camp Bonaparte, Charles Joseph had a bottle of grandfather's Madeira brought up from the cellar to celebrate. The Navy Department was less happy to have him, picturing him, said the Baltimore *Evening Herald*, as "A creature not unlike the 'Hound of the Baskervilles,' with flaming eyes and hanging tongue and wolfish teeth and never so happy as when turning things topsy turvy." Bonaparte's little speech upon taking over his office was not reassuring. "I hope we will all get along well together," he said, "but if we don't, since you can't discharge me, I suppose I will have to discharge you."

There was a certain amount of interoffice alarm. "Bonaparte is too new I am afraid to be put so suddenly in contact with the Senate," wrote an official.

As it turned out he was not allowed to play much part in the making of policy, because Theodore Roosevelt wished to run the Navy himself, and did so. Charles Joseph's only positive act was to advocate the breaking up of *Old Ironsides*, on the grounds that it was so rebuilt nothing was left of it anyhow, and that it was an expense. This opinion raised such a storm of national protest that the notion had to be abandoned, though Charles Joseph helpfully suggested that if it could not be broken up, it could be used for target practice. $100,000 was appropriated by Congress to restore the ship.

He presented one budget, a good one, and after a year and a half was removed and made Attorney General.

"How do you feel about moving over to the Department of Justice?" he was asked.

"I feel that scratching names off [office doors] so frequently may hurt the glass."

He remained as Attorney General of the United States until Roosevelt finished his second term. He was a trust buster with the best of them. His specialty was big business. "One of his infirmities," said a friend, "was his hostility to certain forms of economic progress." He himself saw it as an attack on "our big, strong, greedy, overprosperous . . . animals of the pig order."

In private life, Bonaparte believed in restraint, and he entertained on a large scale only once while in Washington. That was a dinner for the President, given aboard the *Mayflower*. For the only time in her life, his wife wore the Patterson Bonaparte jewels. She was a pale woman of a reserved and bleached distinction. Charles Joseph did not like the origins of his house referred to. He didn't much like Washington either, and usually commuted from his house outside

Baltimore. Even the water in Washington always seemed to him to look "like a stronger coffee than you generally get at the average hostelry." Mostly he preferred to stay at home and read Dickens to his wife, an occasion at which the wearing of the Patterson Bonaparte jewels would have been inappropriate.

In short, he was a crusty but extremely quotable old crank. Though his later years were devoted to Catholic charity work and the family estate, he could always be relied upon for a stinging epithet on almost any subject.

After his death in 1921, his elder brother, Jerome Napoleon, became the last surviving American Bonaparte, for Jerome Napoleon, who had married a middle-aged widow, had no children of his own either, though she had by her previous marriage. Jerome Napoleon was an international socialite of no great moment, fame, or accomplishment. In old age he sometimes posed for the Gentlemen of Distinction advertisements designed to make Calvert Whiskey popular. In 1945, he died of injuries sustained when he tripped over the leash of his wife's dog, in Central Park. He was sixty-seven.

With his death, all branches of the Bonaparte family became extinct in the male line, except for that of Jérôme, Plon Plon, Prince Victor. But these people lived in Italy and played no part in public affairs. So that the whole enormous clan has shrunk, in the 150 years since 1815, to one semianonymous, little-known, and in no way ambitious male heir.

Though the Bonapartes as a living force have long ceased to be of any importance, the same cannot be said of their dead bodies, which were to be of political use to a disconcerting assortment of people. The reputation of Napoléon III and of the Second Empire was so shabby that those at Farnborough were left to rot there. But such was not the case with Napoléon I, his descendants, and those of Jérôme.

Louis Philippe had begun this form of nationalized body snatching by bringing the first Emperor's body back from St. Helena, in 1840, which was a great success, of the sort that does neither good nor harm but makes everybody feel better. There were 1,000,000 spectators, and balcony seats on the Champs Élysées sold at 3,000 francs each. 100,000 people sat on six tribunes erected outside Les Invalides.

Napoléon III also moved dead relatives about and built large monuments. In 1851, as Prince President, he had ordered Mme Mère and Fesch removed from Italy to Corsica, and a large bronze was put up in Ajaccio to Napoléon I and his four brothers.

He also tried to get L'Aiglon's body back from Vienna, but in this he did not succeed. When the Nazis occupied Paris during the Second World War, and during Marshal Pétain's regime, as a sop to French pride, they had L'Aiglon's coffin returned. It arrived in Paris on the night of December 14/15, 1940, where it was delivered at Les Invalides at one in the morning, during a snowstorm, accompanied by a motorcycle escort. But the French were less interested in L'Aiglon than the Germans were.

The most recent person to pay any attention to the Bonaparte legend has been, as one might expect, General de Gaulle. In 1942, the only surviving male Bonaparte, Prince Napoléon, having been captured by the Germans and then set free, joined the Resistance movement. Though wounded during the Normandy landings (the seventh Prince Murat was killed in the same campaign), he asked de Gaulle for permission to join the French army (the Bonapartes, of course, were still proscribed in France). "Prince Napoléon has himself abrogated the law of exile," said de Gaulle, but refused to allow a person of such historic interest further to expose himself to mortality. The law of exile was officially and legally abrogated in 1950. Prince Napoléon has since had a son and a daughter, the first Bonapartes to be born on French soil in ninety-four years.

In 1951, somewhat tardily, Napoléon I's father, Carlo, who though consistently overlooked had fathered them all, was dug up and taken back to Ajaccio from St. Leu, where he had formerly been deposited (his first grave had been at Montpellier). There, after a ceremony complete with bunting and Imperial bees, he was laid to rest beside Mme Mère, in the chapel Napoléon III had caused to be built as a family mausoleum. It is not surprising he had been overlooked. He was only a fop who died young. Of the family, it was Jérôme who had resembled him most. And again, of the family, it was only Jérôme's line which survived.

The Bonaparte arms show two stars, separated by diagonal bands, dexter. The American Bonapartes bore the arms reversed, to create a bar sinister, which seems unfair. As for the unusual name Napoléon, with which the Emperor saddled all future Bonapartes, it was the name either of Neapolus, martyred under Diocletian in the fourth century, or else of an imaginary saint. His name day, and therefore that of the Bonapartes, is August 15.

Denver
1964–1965

371

Cavour, Camillo, 325, 326
Cayla, Mme de, 236
Chambaudoin, Mme de, 157
Chambord, Comte de, 354
Champ d'Asile, 211
Changarnier, Nicolas, 294
Charlemagne (poem), 39
Charles X, King of France, 95, 126,
　132, 135, 144
　as king, 236, 238, 239, 240, 262
Charles Francis, *see* King of Rome
Charles Jules, 311
Charles Louis Napoléon (son of
　Louis), 90
Charlotte (daughter of Joseph), 210,
　222-23, 225, 242
　death of, 270
Charlotte of Bavaria, Empress of
　Austria, 233
Chateaubriand, Viscount François
　René de, 130, 133
Chase, Samuel, 28
Chaumont, Comte de, 209
Chaumont, Treaty of, 46
Christine, *see* Boyer, Catherine
Christine Egypta (daughter of
　Lucien), 247
Civil Family of the Emperor, 311-12
Civitanova, 311
Clam-Martinic, Graf von, 98
Clarendon, Lord, 333
Clarke, Henri Jacques, 60, 66, 76
Clary, Count, 342
Clary, Julie, Queen of Spain, 21-23,
　26, 46, 52, 67, 134, 209, 276
Clary, Nicolas, 22, 47
Clay, Henry, 208
Clotilda, St., 42
Clotilde of Savoy, Princess, 303, 326
Clovis the Frank, 42
Cochelet, Louise, 168
Collège Henri IV, 132
Comic Shipwreck, The (operetta),
　35
Commerce (ship), 208
Commune, 344-46

Compiégne (château), 38
Condé, Prince de, 95, 283
Conneau, Dr., 271, 273, 275, 278, 282
*Consideration of Swiss Politics and
　Military Affairs, A,* 252
Constant, Benjamin, 138, 143
Conti (aide), 339
Cooke, Edward, 125
Corinne, 188
Cosse Brissac, M. de (Chamberlain),
　340-41
Courier, Paul Louis, 185
Crimean War, 322-23

Dallas, Mrs., 224
Dalmatia, Duke of, *see* Soult, Nicolas
David, Jacques Louis, 10, 93, 129,
　301
Davout, Louis Nicolas, 36, 145-48
Day, Ellen Channing, 365
Decazes, Duc Élie, 165
De Gaulle, Charles, 369-70
Demidoff, Prince Anatole, 207, 306,
　307
　marriage of, 219, 260-61
Denon, Baron Dominique Virant, 62
Denuelle, Léon (son of Napoléon),
　146, 197, 310
Derniers moments de Napoléon, 201
Dietrichstein, Count Maurice
　Proskau-Leslie-, 231, 234, 235,
　237, 241, 248-49, 251
Dino, Duchess of, 245
Disraeli, Benjamin, 272
Doudans, X., 285
Dronot, Count Antoine, 122, 124
Duchand (Pauline's lover), 99-100
Dupont de l'Étang, Count Pierre,
　105
Duras, Duchesse de, 132

East India Company, 191
Eckmuhl, Prince d', 285
Edinburgh Castle (excursion
　steamer), 273-74

374

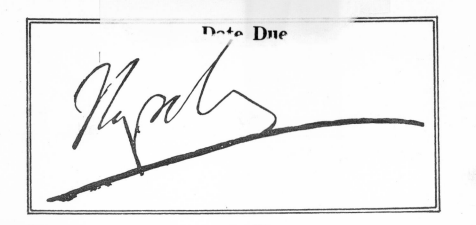